Praise for

You Can See More From Up Here

...In this novel, Guerin beautifully captures the powerful contradictions of the relationship between father and son, which combines elements of friendship and antagonism. The author gradually discloses Walker's epiphanies about his dad, which not only transform the protagonist's personal opinion of him, but also the future arc of his own life. The prose is confident and confessional throughout, and Guerin draws the reader into the compelling story by having Walker unflinchingly reveal his sense of disappointment in himself. Like the journalist he is, Walker clamors for the truth, whether it's consoling or not. A poignantly told story of ruminative remembrance.

— Kirkus Reviews

In Mark Guerin's *You Can See More From Up Here*, a nineteen-year-old and his father face up to a conflict of generational ideologies when a workplace incident sends reverberations through their small town. ...Alternating between a summer [in 1974] and the winter thirty years later as Walker sits at his dying father's bedside, the book examines the dichotomy of a strict father and his conscientious son, both products of their respective times. Its mood is retrospective at first, as Walker reconciles his dying father with the disciplinarian he knew. Sections from the past soon envelope the book, though, and are meticulous and absorbing in their details.

The characters and settings shape each other, and tension among characters results in the suspense that propels the story. Foreshadowing connects one chapter to the next. By working toward doing the noble thing and making amends, Walker helps his father confront his own internal dilemmas. The book's end is cathartic, bringing all of the emotional subplots to a head. Racial issues are handled with honesty.

Mark Guerin's debut maneuvers through heartbreak with grace, navigating family expectations, a community's pervasive racism, and how peoples' actions shape others' opinions.

— Forward Reviews

You Can See More From Up Here does what all great novels do, smartly evoking a forgotten time and place, tugging at the heart strings of our seemingly innocent desires and relationships, and forcing us to confront our culpabilities as a protagonist confronts his own. On the surface, this is a book that explores a troubled relationship between father and son, but it is also a book about power, about race, privilege and the failings we inherit. Guerin achieves all this with great tenderness and an impressive command of story and time. What we see at novel's end are the far-reaching consequences of what originally seems a simple but regrettable act.

— Michelle Hoover, author of *The Quickening* and *Bottomland*

The structure of short, present-tense chapters mixed with longer past-tense ones worked beautifully, tickling my anticipation and constantly luring me forward, maintaining suspense as Guerin divulged each new discovery. The author skillfully navigates the twist of familial bonds as a father and son confront distrust, lies, and unspoken expectations. Racial clashes and economic disparity compound their struggles, making for an intense and satisfying novel.

— E.B. Moore, author of *An Unseemly Wife* and *Stones in the Road*

You Can See More From Up Here is an achingly real and thought-provoking novel about a son's quest to understand his troubled father and the long-ago summer that changed both of their lives. Alternating between 1974 and 2005, this novel vividly evokes the toxic behavior that keeps fathers from making genuine emotional connections with their sons, and the violence and bigotry lurking beneath the surface of a seemingly normal family in a bygone era (that is sadly not all that different from our own). Its unforgettable characters will leave you reflecting on your own family and the power of the past to shape the present, long after you've finished turning the pages.

— Emily Ross, author of *Half in Love with Death*

A powerful father's looming presence fills every page of *You Can See More From Up Here*, Mark Guerin's stirring debut novel about the past's ineluctable presence in the present. With a steady hand, Guerin excavates the snarled roots of a dysfunctional family, the corrosive effects of class conflict, and the deeply buried lies that only a novelist of great scope and insight can bring into the revivifying light of day.

— Michael Antman, book and theater critic, novelist, and author of *Everything Solid Has a Shadow* and *Cherry Whip*

Toggling between 1974 and 2005, this heartfelt, haunting, and beautifully told coming-of-age story explores the complexities and long-lasting residues of an unresolved father-son relationship, while also exploring class and race differences that resonate in today's America. *You Can See More From Up Here* will stay with you, prodding you to consider how your own path has been shaped by your perceptions of reality and how complicated the truth can be, even from a good vantage point.

— Belle Brett, author of *Gina in the Floating World*

You Can See More From Up Here

by

Mark Guerin

Golden Antelope Press
715 E. McPherson
Kirksville, Missouri 63501
2019

Cover Design by Jason Anscomb

ISBN: 978-1-936135-71-4 (1-936135-71-X)

Library of Congress Control Number: 2019944011

Published by:
Golden Antelope Press
715 E. McPherson
Kirksville, Missouri 63501

Available at:
Golden Antelope Press
715 E. McPherson
Kirksville, Missouri, 63501
Phone: (660) 665-0273
http://www.goldenantelope.com
Email: ndelmoni@gmail.com

For my father

One

I sat half-naked on an exam table in my dad's infirmary at American Motors. One hand gripped my arm. The other pressed a stethoscope to my chest. It burned. My shoulders jiggled involuntarily, goosebumps frosting across me in a wave. Breakfast curdled in my gut, rearranging.

"You okay?"

His breath made me gag. A dead animal inside him. He'd lost all his teeth in the war—malaria or malnutrition—and his ceramic dentures didn't make up for the putrid smell, nor did the incisive blue eyes or the meticulous grooming of his white mustache and hair.

"Uh-huh."

A beige ceiling fan wheeled and wobbled dizzily above us. It was early June, and I was sweating. And chilled.

"Sit up straight, Walker." Like I was still a little boy and not a college student. At that moment, maybe, I was.

* * *

I'm on a plane accelerating up a runway at Washington National when that tableau of my dad poised over a bare-chested, teenaged me flames up yet again, an ember in a thirty-year-old fire that won't go out.

When Piper called my cell earlier this morning and told me Dad had been in an accident and I needed to come home, that triggered it, brought it all back. 1974. That exam room. That summer job. The meat hook. The Camarasas. Their disappearance. The girl I loved, gone.

For years, I've meant to make him tell me his side of the story. *Hell, if I've been wrong all this time, set me straight.* But here I am at forty-nine, a few years younger than he was then, and my sister is telling me he's in a coma, and I might never talk to him again.

I can't get it out of my head. The details have banged around inside there so long, I'm sure they've dulled, stones rounded by years of repeated bashings against a beach. But back then, as I sat on that exam table? It was razor-edged.

* * *

I shivered as he moved the stethoscope, here and there, around my chest, each touch a circular freeze burn. With both hands, he felt on either side of my neck, under my ears. That breath right in my face. Another gag.

"Come on." He cocked his head. "You can't get sick on your first day."

"I'm fine," I said, struggling to keep my breakfast down.

With a grimace, he lifted my eyelids, one at a time, shining a light, blinding me. Something came to me from years before. *Mouse hole. Cozy Couch. Tiny TV. Mouse hole. Cozy Couch. Tiny TV.* A mantra from when I was a kid and he chased me around the house, cat and mouse, like in the cartoon, *Tom & Jerry.* If only I could find a way back to my mouse hole behind the mop board, watch my tiny TV on my little couch, warm and cozy, while Tom fell into one of my traps. Exploding. Electrocuted. Burnt to a crisp, dissolving into a smoldering pile of black ash.

Finally, my father backed away, jotted something on his clipboard. I could breathe again, mouse hole dismissed. I straightened.

"Go weigh yourself." He nodded toward the corner. I climbed down off the table and stepped up onto the scale, its plate shifting around. "One twenty seven?" He had his chin up, white eyebrows raised, awaiting confirmation.

"Five," I said when the needle settled.

"Even skinnier than I was. Back here." He waved me over. "Arms at your side. But taller, right? Five ten?"

"Yes. You know all this stuff." I stood in front of him. "Why do you need to examine me?"

"Some defects hide," he said. His precise words. Then he grabbed my hand and stopped what it was doing, an old habit of mine, clenching, unclenching, like gasping for air. He gave me a pointed nod and scribbled something on his clipboard.

"You're putting that down?" Stupid hand.

"Relax." A chuckle as he wrote. "You remember that pitcher who had tendonitis before the Cubs signed him, that reliever—" Something like that as he ticked little boxes, precise blue check marks. "Didn't make it through spring training, and they were stuck with his contract? Same deal here."

"It's not like you have a roomful of Mickey Mantles with bum wings out there." I'd never seen a scruffier bunch than the other new hires waiting their turn with me in the outer room.

"A hernia, here. Heart problem, there. Adds up," Dad said. "Can't make a good car with broken parts."

I saw myself reflected in a cracked windshield, a dented chrome bumper. So sensitive, my dad.

I'd never been in such a place, let alone worked, so they did look like broken parts. That mutton-chopped guy in torn army fatigues at the water cooler. That black kid with the comb sticking out of his off-kilter Afro. That grizzled old broad, gray hair hacked short, wearing elastic-band jeans, flipping through a *Life* magazine, Richard Nixon on the cover. Will he resign or won't he?

But then, no one in that room had a name as pretentious as Walker or Frazier or Piper. No good Catholic gave his children names like that. No, these folks had first names for first names—and real calluses, not little bumps on their middle fingers from taking notes in auditorium seminars.

That old woman smirked at me, shaking her head. I got it. My Chicago Cubs t-shirt was too clean, my blue jeans too blue, my new steel-toed work boots too shiny. I wasn't fooling anyone. This scrawny bookworm, china in a shop full of bulls.

* * *

The engines roar and I'm thrust into my seat. The plane lifts, tilting me back. We bank, and I'm canted toward the window. We circle D.C. like a kite tethered to the bright spike of the Washington Monument at high noon. With heavy snow cancelling so many westbound flights, I wasn't sure this flight would ever get off the ground. But here we are, climbing, leveling out. Could I still get there in time? If so, for what? I don't know. A final, desperate appeal? It's bound to get bumpy, especially that landing at O'Hare—if they don't divert us first.

Maybe the memory always starts in that exam room because, in the four years we'd lived in Belford, I'd never been there before, seen him in his new role, wearing that name badge:

Dr. Michael Maguire
Plant Physician

What a shock it was! What a comedown from the days when he had a nickel-plated eagle on his chest instead of a plastic rectangle. Colonel Maguire, Hospital Commander at Chanute Air Force Base. That factory office was a demotion, too. One big room with two examination areas enclosed by curtains, no air conditioning, his papers spread out over a drawer-less table in the corner. So much for the hand-crafted oak desk he'd had in Chanute, the family portrait enveloped in the warm light of the brass lamp, the Persian rug, the wood paneling, the two leather sitting chairs around a cherry coffee table—furnishings that might have come right out of our comfortable home on Senior Officers Row.

Here, it was white walls and linoleum, harsh overhead lighting, beige-painted metal chairs and file cabinets. That wobbly ceiling fan, liable to unscrew itself and behead someone. Not a stick of nice furniture or a family photo in sight. Maybe he didn't like being there any more than I did.

* * *

As he ticked off another box, Dad said, "Okay, so, pull down your underwear."

"What?" I froze.

"It's required, Walker." He finally looked up, but not at me. Around me. The wall behind, the ceiling. "I have to check for hernias. Company policy."

Not even the mouse hole could help with this. I stood, trembling, and peeled down my jeans in little jerks and shimmies. Then my briefs.

"For Christ's sake, Walker. It's a summer job, not a death sentence." As if all this pitiful quivering was about the job.

Shaking his head, he moved into me, almost a hug as his chin hovered over my shoulder. Warm, calloused fingers poked into my pelvis, above my pubes. My eyes watered as I held my breath, my heart hammering. Then he prodded up into my crotch, under my balls.

"Enough!" I said, shoving him away. "Just write something down." I pointed at the form.

He exhaled, as if about to speak, then grabbed the pen, shaking his head. He wrote.

I'd pushed him away! Take that, Cat! More and more, I'd done that. I was eye to eye with him now, the same height. Sure, he still had thirty pounds on me, but maybe I could finally take him. If not for how that noxious breath withered me, that is, those twists of disapproval in his voice minimizing, making me fifteen again, eight, four, cowering in cold sweats. "It's my job," he whispered, an apology of sorts. "You can get dressed now."

Shakily, I zipped up my jeans as he continued writing. I pulled on my shirt.

At the end of the room a set of double doors awaited.

Plant personnel only
No visitors past this point

I stood there, my arms folded at this new challenge, my fist, hidden, clenching, unclenching. I'd planned on spending my summer out in the sun with my best friend, Kurt Swanson, washing cars at his father's car lot, not building them inside that goddamn sweatshop.

Dad stopped writing and looked up, regarding me, a re-examination.

"Look, Walker. I know you don't want to be here." The words came out quietly. "But it might actually do you some good. Places like this—" He waved at the door. Though this administration wing was the size of the White House, it was nothing compared to the assembly plant outside that door, waiting to swallow me up, an endless corrugated-steel edifice as big as the National Mall. "This is the kind of life people have who don't make it through college."

"You ended up here."

"You know what I mean. You'll work with your hands. Your body, your mind going to waste. Your co-workers a bunch of—" He searched for words, shaking his head, then seemed to think better of it. "You've been given so many opportunities. A chance for the best education, a successful career. Is that the kind of person you want to be? Like your brother?"

"He doesn't work in a factory." At that time, Frazier lived in Chicago, cooking at a diner.

"Just as bad. Maybe worse. No stability, no prospects." As if my dad had nothing to do with Frazier's situation. Like someone else had disowned him and cut him off. "And the way you've screwed around at school? I thought you hit bottom when you got arrested last summer, but now I don't know. Do you want me to think you're a bum? Is that it? That you're wasting your life? Is that what you want?"

I shook my head. Always with that arrest, like the judge hadn't let me off. But no, the good Maguire name had been tainted in the newspaper's police log, a minor in possession. Boone's Farm Wild Grape and a six of Bud. Scandalous!

He grabbed my arms. "I'm serious! Is this how you want to end up?"

"No!" I cringed, leaning back, shoulders squeezing together.

"Then prove it." He shoved me away. "Show me you can do something for once. Apply yourself. Pay attention. You screw around here, people get hurt. So you have to do what they tell you, follow the rules. You think you can do that?"

"Yes, I can do that!" I straightened. I could yell, too!

"Okay, then. And maybe, if you see what this life is like, you'll think twice about where you're headed."

Dad bent over my paperwork.

Where I'm headed! Years of medical school. Poking at people. Really great career, Dad.

It wasn't as if I didn't like college. I loved the courses and the professors, too. Just not *my* courses. I'd sneak into lectures on the British Monarchy, Charles Darwin's *Voyages on the Beagle*, Chinese Philosophers, 20th Century Classical Symphonies, The Geography of Rivers, The History of Indigenous America. I was a wedding crasher, dancing with all the exotic women. I'd sample the ethnic music and strange gourmet dishes before they tossed me out, uninvited, unworthy. Back to the tunnel-vision world of Pre-Med. Biology. Chemistry. Microscopes and slides. Germs and atoms, always reminding me how small I was, how insignificant. That's what he wanted for me. Play the game his way or, like Frazier, not at all.

"Walker," my brother had said when I'd called him the day before, "tell Dad to go fuck himself and come live with me in Chicago." Yeah, right. And sleep on the floor of his tiny, roach infested studio. And how was I supposed to pay for college?

"College is bullshit. You don't need it."

"I'm not dropping out. That's your bag, not mine."

"Then you'll figure it out," he said, "as soon as you get back on your feet."

For four years now, ever since he'd decided there were more important things to do with his life than finish college, Frazier had been getting 'back on his feet,' making latkes and Reuben sandwiches at a Jewish deli. He didn't care if he had to scrape by, as long as he could run his theater company at night, hang out with all those starving actors Dad would never approve of. Not to mention the plays they did, industrialists turning bombs into gold, soldiers bayoneting babies. If getting 'back on my feet' meant walking in Frazier's shoes, why let myself get tripped up to begin with? It was a goddamned summer job. I could handle it, couldn't I?

"Before I forget," Dad said. "I ran into your girlfriend's father in the plant last week. What's his name?"

"Norm. Norm Ditweiler." Ex-girlfriend's father, but Dad didn't know that yet.

"Yeah, that's him."

"How come we haven't seen her? What with school out, I'm surprised she hasn't been over to the house." So Norm didn't tell him? Or maybe, Norm didn't know about the 'Dear Jane' letter I'd sent her.

"She's been busy," I lied. "Working in her Mom's hair salon. They're open evening hours now."

"I get a kick out of her, a new hairdo every time we see her. You never know what she'll come up with next."

"Yeah, right."

"Well, anyway. When I told Norm they were sending you to the loading dock, he offered to take you under his wing."

Fuck me. I didn't like Norm to begin with, even if he was sweet to Gayle. Always with a can of beer in his hand, throwing his arm around my shoulder. "Walker Maguire!" That big, drunken grin and boozy breath, like I was some kind of prize. The doctor's son going out with his little girl. Now, the jerk who dumped her? Perfect.

"Okay," I mumbled.

"'Okay'? I thought you'd be happy to have someone keeping an eye out for you."

"Sure, Dad. That's great. Thanks."

"Well, then—" He signed his name at the bottom of the form. "You get a 1-A, fit for fighting." He nodded at the double doors. "You ready?"

Two

My plane lands safely at O'Hare, and against the advice of the rental car agent, I pull out into the storm for the eighty-mile slog up I-90 to Belford. It's rush hour, and I expect the highways to be gridlocked, but it's only the surging snow slowing traffic to a crawl. Most drivers must have heeded warnings to stay home. Fortunately, I catch up with a phalanx of plows headed west, their yellow, gyrating lights beacons I can follow through the thrumming bursts of snow and gathering darkness. As they push forward, the trucks make huge waves of the mounting drifts and reveal black ice on the road. The salt they spray helps, but it's slow going. Instead of a two-hour ride, it's four and a half hours of fogged windows and white knuckles. I correct again and again for the wind buffeting me towards the shoulder, glad I rented a four-wheel-drive. I'm so adrenalized there's no chance I'll fall asleep.

At long last, the sign for the Belford exit rears up out of a squall, and I pull off. The car creeps along silent, snow-packed streets, dimly lit by snow-veiled lights, everyone inside by now, having supper. I'd stop somewhere to eat, but I don't want to risk losing the few moments I might have with him searching for a place.

A mile down Main Street, I recognize the squat, white one-story building that houses the *Belford Daily Telegram*, and I remember the email Kurt sent me weeks ago saying the editor would be retiring this coming June, 2005. I still can't believe he thought I'd be interested in the job. Here, in Belford. With a shake of my head, I cast aside the absurd notion and take a left.

Several blocks later, I spy St. Francis Church. Of the four times I've returned to Belford in the past thirty years, this building was the focal point of two of them—Piper's wedding and Mom's funeral, both of which happened in winter, '82 and '94, respectively. Rather than a warm, green welcome, I always seem to return in leafless late fall or, like now, to cold and snow. Watching the snow-clad church slide by, I'm reminded how on those frosty occasions I wore dark suits and stuck to the script as best man and mourning son. I'd faded into the background, and my family seemed barely to notice that they hadn't seen me in years. My only other visits were two Thanksgivings, the 'Strawberry Thanksgiving' almost twenty-five years ago, and the one fourteen months ago, the last time I was here. Each of these visits I left feeling heartsick and defeated.

A block further on, I spot the familiar white statue of St. Francis in front of the hospital. I pull around back, the deep snow creaking under the wheels. I grab my backpack and crunch through the knee-high drifts to the entrance. After I shake off the white stuff, I make my way to an eerily quiet ICU, thinking there must be fewer medical emergencies when everyone's snowbound. I tell the desk nurse I'm here, half-expecting her to say I'm too late. I'm not. She tells me where to go.

There's Piper rising from the chair by his bedside, a motion that gives me an excuse not to look at the bed. Her curly, shoulder-length hair—too red, not her normal red—is poofed up on one side, as if she's slept on it. She's in a pair of old blue jeans and an ancient NIU sweatshirt she normally wouldn't wear to pick the paper up off the porch. Her face is so pale and colorless, her eyes without their usual clarity. Then, it occurs to me—she's not wearing her mandatory blush, lipstick and eye-liner. It's scary, this unprecedented indifference to appearance.

She hugs me, and for the longest time, won't let go. She whispers in a croaking voice, words garbled by hiccups and snuffles, so glad I'm here, Frazier's stuck at LaGuardia, then breaks off. She pushes me away, heading out the door, all too much for her, or did she say something about tracking down the doctor? Once she's gone, my mind goes blank, as if the printer of her words had no ink. What did she say?

I take a second to hang up my coat, lodge my pack in a corner, before finally edging toward his side.

Actually, he doesn't look so bad. That is, for a ninety-year-old who'd totaled his prized purple Cadillac. Sure, there's a bruise on his forehead, greenish blue, but he seems composed, somehow. He could be sleeping. Hadn't Piper said something about him hitting the gas when he meant to hit the brakes? That would be just like him. Always going when he should be slowing down. Only, this time, he turned a hydrant into a geyser.

An IV drip hangs off his arm, but at least he's breathing on his own, his breaths small waves breaking on a beach, their slow withdrawals followed by toppling exhalations.

On one machine, his heart rate etches erratically in green lines, painting a picture much scarier than I get looking at him. I focus on him instead, his impossible-seeming serenity.

Piper returns with a tall, young doctor in a white lab coat. She's got him by the sleeve, telling him to tell me everything.

"Tell Walker about the MRI results," Piper says, going so far as to pat the man's chest. When he's not specific enough, she adds, "Tell him about those lesions you found," and "Tell him what you told me, why surgery is not advisable." As if she's testing him, daring him to repeat his pessimistic findings to my face, like they are an insult, an accusation. The man calmly explains that there's no real swelling, nothing that would require surgery. And besides, at my dad's age, surgery would likely lead to life-threatening complications. As if matters could get any worse.

But Piper is relentless. She makes him go over all the tests they performed, medications administered, possible causes of the coma, including stroke, metabolic imbalance and hypoxia—terms I don't understand and quickly lose track of. She's been up two days straight, sure, but she isn't simply loopy from lack of sleep, and she isn't defaulting into little sister mode, appealing to me for older brotherly guidance. She's desperate, as if I can offer a second opinion, tell the doctor he's got it all wrong, that it can't possibly be as bad as all that.

"As I've been saying—" The doctor edges toward the door. "All we can do at this point is wait." But Piper's expression begs for more. "And, maybe talk to him," the man adds, hopefully. "A familiar voice might bring him round. It does happen."

It's a bit patronizing, but Piper seizes on it anyway, working up a hopeful grin, willing to grab onto anything. She turns to me once he's gone.

"What do you think?"

Wouldn't you know, the one time she actually wants my opinion, and I've got nothing. The doctor's tired, patient expression as he listened to her concerns and answered her questions said it all. He was attending to my sister's needs, not my father's. He didn't even look at my dad. Not once.

"I think you should get some rest. Go home. Take a nap. I'll keep an eye on him, call you if anything changes."

"And you'll talk to him?"

"Sure. Absolutely."

She nods, grabbing her coat and purse. She gives me another hug, a kiss on the cheek.

"It's good to have you back," she whispers, then leaves.

I sit down at his bedside. *Talk to him*, she says. If only I could.

Three

When I stepped through those double doors and onto the American Motors plant floor, it was if I'd been thrown into Dorothy's tornado as she twirled from Kansas to Oz. From the black and white of suits and ties, I entered a whirlwind of color: fenders in metallic greens, blues and silvers hung on moving hooks. A man on a giant red tricycle. A miniature train in yellow with no driver. Of actual automobiles, I spotted only bits and pieces—tires and bumpers, hoods and headlights in carts and bins and boxes. They shot past me on hooks dragged from wires or bounced along belts that floated above the floor. Everything rattled by amidst a maze of shelving racks, metal pipes and electrical cables. And the smells—gasoline, paint, unfamiliar stenches of spine-straightening toxicity. And the noise—grinding, screaming, punching, whirring, squealing everywhere, sparks flying and curses, too. Winds of sound, smell and movement rocked me this way and that.

"Takes a few minutes to get your sea legs," Mr. Kelly shouted into my ear. The foreman was a balding, middle-aged guy with black, horned-rimmed glasses and a rounded brown mustache that, unlike my father's, curled over most of his mouth. If he hadn't been wearing that necktie, a woven green thing thick as a cotton sweater, you'd never know he was management, what with the faded, button-down, short-sleeve shirt and khaki pants, stained, the cuffs frayed, scuffed-up boots. Amidst the din, his drawl was difficult to decipher, even when he shouted. My job, I deduced, was to sub for guys out on vacation.

"Your dad ever give you the tour?"

"No," I shouted back, recalling Dad's office—not a place he'd ever want to show off.

"Well, this here's Main Street, the trim line." Kelly explained how all the other lines converged on this line, which began with finished chassis, on top of which auto bodies were fastened. Then, from the sides, lines dropped in doors and car seats, and from above, angling down, dashboards, windshields, hoods and trunk lids.

Kelly grabbed my arm and yanked me aside. Another of those driverless trains, the size of a carnival ride for toddlers, motored on through, barely missing us. A little red light spun around on the roof of a yellow engine that pulled three empty wagons. I stared after it, baffled.

"Magnetic tape," Kelly said. He pointed to a stripe of silver along the floor. "These tuggers are supposed to stop on their own if someone's standing in the way, but I don't trust the little fuckers." He nodded down the aisle. "This way." We followed the tape and passed through an ever-shifting maze of rumbling assembly lines and hustling workers, each chassis like a honeycomb swarmed by bees—being built up, sprouting mirrors and seats, stick shifts and tires.

The infirmary had been hot, but it was balmy compared to the plant. I hadn't walked a hundred feet before sweat prickled down my back, under my arms. My heavy boots warmed into little ovens, my feet swelling like loaves. Fans blustered in every direction: big as wagon wheels in the aisles, little ones clamped to workstations. But the hot air simply circulated, a roiling stew.

Kelly leaned close and reminded me I'd be working with Norm Ditweiler, one of his loading dock crew. I nodded.

"I hear you're dating his daughter," he added. "Sweet girl, that Gayle."

"You know her?" Clearly, not well enough to know we'd broken up.

"I had a barbecue on Memorial Day that Norm brought her to." Funny, nobody wondered why 'my girlfriend' was spending her holiday with her dad and not with me. "Gotta say," Kelly nudged my ribs with his elbow. "Best looking girl there." He gave me a thumbs up. It made me want to punch him, ogling Gayle, even if she and I had broken up.

"Company picnic, that is." Kelly added. "Don't want you to get the wrong idea."

"Wrong idea?"

"Norm and I, we palled around when we were teens. But now that

I'm foreman—Well, you get it, being the doc's son and all. Management, right?"

"Sure," I said. "I guess."

After a good hike, we climbed into a golf cart and drove for ten minutes, merging onto a sort of miniature super highway down the spine of the plant, humming with golf carts, bicycles and those weird trains—tuggers, he'd called them. Finally, we reached one end of the massive building. Here, Kelly stopped me and pointed.

"Parts come in here, the east side. Cars go out the west." He might as well have said, 'The sun rises in the east and sets in the west,' the place was so big. "This is where you'll be working."

The receiving area stretched at least a city block wide and several more long—so vast I couldn't tell where it began or ended—like a giant wharf inside a building, a door for every dock. Instead of unloading ships, workers emptied dozens of semi-trailers and boxcars, all of which seemed wheel-less and half-buried in the floor the way guys walked straight into them. Their berths were recessed into the concrete. Some guys unloaded using forklifts, but most did their work by hand, carting parts out and over to the empty wagons the tuggers pulled. These men made it seem so easy, hauling around these big old mufflers, fuel tanks and radiators, one or two at a time, tossing them up onto those wagons like they were nothing.

Kelly kept talking but all I could hear were the *beep, beep, beep* of the forklifts backing up or slamming pallets down or dragging them screeching across the floor, sounds that echoed off the metal ceiling, three or four stories up. Completely deaf to it all, Kelly chatted away as he led me in. We threaded our way between Parthenon-sized columns made up of metal bins, big as bathtubs, stacked like Legos. I was a kid in the big city for the first time. I couldn't stop staring at all the skyscrapers. A tug on my sleeve. The foreman pointed out Norm Ditweiler, laughing with another guy over an oil drum. I hadn't seen Gayle's father since March when I came home for a day to tell her I was headed to Florida for spring break and not spending it with her—one of several sore spots that led to our breakup.

Norm caught sight of us, nodded, smiled and started over, flapping a pair of leather gloves against his thigh. A tall guy, maybe six two, he had always lumbered, but today he had more hitch in his step than I remembered, one leg swinging faster than the other. Usually when I saw him, he was sprawled and immobilized on his living room couch. The lime-colored overalls he wore on top of a dingy white t-shirt reminded me of Mr. Green Jeans on the kids' show, *Captain Kangaroo*. What little hair he had—a birds-nest mess at home—he'd combed and gelled to his scalp in long, dark streaks. As always, his beard was stubbly; his nose, the lumpy pink of a wad of bubble gum. With a sweaty hand, he shook mine.

"Walker Maguire. How you doing, buddy?" He slapped me on the back, then grabbed me around the shoulder, drawing me to him like we were old pals. Same old Norm. He turned me, presenting me to Kelly, his voice loud. "Didn't I tell you Gayle and Walker would make a handsome couple? Practically part of the family, aren't you?" Another hug, squeezing.

The foreman nodded.

Norm wished. During the two years Gayle and I had dated, he'd brought up numerous 'opportunities' he wanted to 'cut me in on.' A food cart, selling hot dogs outside the AMC parking lot. A landscaping company to mow lawns and trim trees. I knew why. Unneeded bundles of cash must be stashed about a doctor's house, right? Forgotten Easter eggs that might help fund one of his crazy schemes if only I'd dig it up. Complaining to Gayle did no good. She'd say not to knock it if it gave him something to think about beyond that soul-sucking assembly line.

"So," Kelly began, "can you get Walker a pair of gloves and put him on seat frames? Like we talked about?"

"Oh, yeah," Norm nodded, giving a little smile. "That new training method."

"That's right. Lester Nelson," the foreman turned to me—"He's the guy you're replacing—I had him stockpile a few extra wagon loads before he left on Friday. That'll give you time to get up to speed before the lines run low. I'll check in with you in a while to see how you're doing. You good with that, Norm?"

"Whatever you say, Mr. Foreman, sir." He made a formal bow, his tone, slave-like.

"All right," Kelly said, closing his eyes—he was clearly tired of Norm's act.

"Just joshing." Norm bumped his elbow against mine. "In high school, little Billy Kelly used to tag along after my guys, always trying to hang with the big boys. Finally, it was either beat the shit out of him or let him join, so that's what we did. Hard to imagine him being the big boss sometimes." He wiggled his fingers at the man.

"Old times," Kelly remarked, forcing a grin. "Oh, and before I forget, make sure you give Walker the usual talk about the buttons."

"The button talk. Will do."

Buttons?

"By the way, Billy—" Norm grabbed the man by the elbow. The foreman eyed the hand, and Norm let go. I liked how the boss handled him.

"Mr. Kelly, sir!" he corrected himself, patting the man's sleeve, as if to clean it off.

"What do you want?"

"I don't want to keep you, but I was curious about that forklift job. You hear anything yet?"

"Sorry, no news yet. Maybe tomorrow."

"Oh," Norm nodded, then as the man turned to leave, he caught him again. "But you did put in a word for me, right?"

"I did what I could, Norm."

"I mean, old times and all—" He rubbed his hip. Kelly's expression didn't change. "New times, too. Gayle's boyfriend, here. The doctor's son?" Me? Who was I? "Hell, Billy," Norm said with a light-hearted chuckle, "we talked about this whole thing at the picnic."

"I said, I'll do what I can, and I will."

"Okay. That's all I wanted to hear." Norm backed off, hands up in surrender. "All I wanted to hear." Kelly started to walk away.

"Oh, and one more thing, Billy—"

The foreman stopped in his tracks. His head dropped, chin on his chest. He turned around, heavy-footed.

"What?"

"I only wanted to say, thanks for the picnic. We had a great time, the family and me."

"All the guys did, don't you think?"

"Well, sure, but I mean—" Norm flapped his hand back and forth between them, trying to forge some connection. "It *was* like old times, wasn't it?"

Kelly regarded him a long second.

"Smoking cigarettes behind the garage so the wives wouldn't see?" Norm nodded at the man, adding, "and you took more than a sip from that pint of JB I brought. Admit it, you did."

"Yes, I did." A regret, not a fond memory.

"Damned right, you did," Norm said with a big nod and a bigger grin. "*Just* like old times."

"Now, do you think we can we get back to work?"

"Absolutely, back to work we go, heigh-ho, heigh-ho." He raised his thumb. Kelly turned again, stuck his hand in the air and gave us a little backwards wave.

"Fucking guy," Norm whispered as we moved away. "Gets a little promotion and thinks he's king of the world."

I followed him deeper into the dock, shuffling along to keep pace.

"You all right?" I asked. "I've never seen you limp so bad."

He frowned, slapping his side. "This hip of mine. Hurts like a bastard on humid days like this."

"And you can work like that?"

"Hah!" Norm chuckled. "That's why I need that forklift job. Get me off my feet, stop all this lifting." He stopped and turned to me. "You saw him. You think he'll give it to me? Kelly?"

I raised my hands into a shrug.

"Can't read that guy." Norm shook his head. "He can see I need this job, don't you think?"

"Sure," I said. Anything to get him moving.

"Damned well better." He moved off again, limping over to a supply station against a steel beam, a stack of metal drawers, fire-engine red. He mumbled as he searched through a drawer. "Don't know how much more of this bullshit I can take."

He pulled out a pair of yellow, leather gloves and slapped them against my chest. I worked the stiff things onto my hands.

"So anyway, how you doing, Walker?" I couldn't help but admire his attitude, how quickly he could write off his limp. "You excited about your first day of work?"

"I guess." Being here when I could have been working outdoors at Pops Swanson Motors with his son, hosing down whenever I wanted to cool off, ogling the girls that cruised past on Main Street. But no, that Fernando guy Kurt worked with got to keep the job Pops had promised me, and all I got was a free car wash for my Datsun on Saturday when I stopped by to tell Kurt's dad that I couldn't work for him. Yeah, I was thrilled to be here.

"Hah!" Norm guffawed, slapping me on the back. "You know, when your Dad told me you were taking a summer job here, I was a little surprised. Not lifeguarding at the pool or caddying at your dad's golf club—"

"My dad doesn't play golf."

"You know what I'm saying. I'm proud of you." He nodded at me. "Takes a special kid to tackle a shit job like this when you don't even need to be working at all, am I right?"

It always surprised people to see me holding down a job. I never got much of an allowance, far less than Kurt got. As a kid, I'd delivered newspapers and mowed lawns, and for the last two years, I'd stocked shelves at the IGA. But when classmates saw me working, they were always like, "You slumming, Maguire? Seeing how the other half lives?"

"So, seat frames?" I said, antsy to get going.

"Oh, come on," he said, slapping my back again. "It's not that bad. You'll survive. Probably. Look at me. I'm still here. Barely." He punched himself in the chest a couple of times, proving how sturdy he was.

"Okay, then. Seat frames!" Norm slapped me on the back yet again. I'd have slugged him if he'd done that one more time. "No more fucking around."

He pointed the way to a rust-colored, Northern Pacific boxcar in the last slot against the wall.

"Nice shirt, by the way." Norm poked the Cubs logo and chuckled. Maybe, he was complimenting me. I said thanks.

Then he pulled up short and grabbed my elbow, stopping me. "So, um, I won't bullshit you, but Gayle's been pretty unhappy since she got that letter from you."

He *did* know. So what was this crap about me being part of the family? "She was really hurt. Sweet kid like that. Stood by you through thick and thin for three long years. We thought you two were going great guns, even with that arrest last year, the age difference and you being off at school and all. Then, 'bam,' to get it in a letter like that? Wow. Knocked her for a loop. Me and Barb, too."

As if I'd beat her up or something, Christ.

"It wasn't working out, me downstate at college, her in Belford."

"But a letter?" He shook his head. "Not cool, Walker. Not cool."

He waited for a response. I shrugged, conceding the point.

"Now look, you still like her, don't you?" As if that's all that mattered.

"Sure, I still like her, it's only that—"

"Well, that's what counts, son." He grabbed my shoulder, pinching that neck muscle, massaging it. "You can't let life get in the way of love. Some things you have to work around, know what I mean?" He slapped his bad hip.

I didn't know what he expected me to say.

"What you two need is to have a talk, juggle some of the details, that's all. You can do that much, can't you?"

I shrugged, as much to make him let go of me as anything else.

"I'll take that as a yes." Then, without missing a beat, he said, "Now, what say we get you to work before Billy blows a gasket."

While Norm puzzled at the dark wall of black tangled inside the boxcar door, I fumed. As if it was that easy to solve a problem it had taken me two type-written pages to explain to Gayle. Life *was* getting in the way of love, but I couldn't see any way around it.

I shook off the thought and tried to fathom what was packed into the boxcar in front of me—glints of black wire, like a million sprung and spread Slinky toys jammed in together. Then I detected the crackling sound of a baseball announcer.

"Mays is O for his last six." It came from a big transistor radio on top of a pile of wooden pallets between my boxcar and the next. "Full count. Wilson needs to throw strikes now."

It dawned on me. All through that deafening trip from the admin building to the loading dock, like a singer drowned out by the big, brass band accompanying her, this same game had been playing on different radios along the various lines.

But Mays was on the White Sox. White Sox territory! Sox fans hated Cubs fans. And here I was sporting a Cubs shirt. Norm hadn't admired my shirt; he'd made fun of it. I crossed my arms over the big blue "C."

"What are these again?" I asked, trying to forget my stupid shirt.

"Seat frames. You'll unload them from this boxcar and put them on that train so they can be carted to the seat line."

"The seat line?"

"It's where they cover them with foam and upholster them before they're hauled over to the trim line. Then, they're bolted into brand, spanking new AMC Ramblers, the ugliest goddamned cars in America."

I tried to imagine this whole process.

"You sit on them, doofus!" Norm pulled on his leather gloves with a grunt. He reached into the mess of wire, this nasty cave. "Never unloaded one of these puppies myself, but my guess is you just yank'em out." He seemed to be grabbing any old random curl, favoring that hip. Nothing gave. Norm's feet slid forward as he leaned back, butt pushed out, pulling, trying to dislodge something.

"That's the new training method?"

"Yeah, right." He laughed, then tried again and failed. "Maybe pull harder, huh?"

"You want help?" I offered.

"I can do it."

He grunted, yanking hard. The ten-foot, floor-to-ceiling wall of seat frames shivered forward, tilting, wobbling back and forth. He flung out both arms and hugged it. "Hold on baby, hold on!"

"Are you sure nobody else can help us with this?"

"I may not have a college degree, but I think I can figure this out."

"I'm only saying—" I put up my hands.

He peered back into the car.

"Lester Nelson's the only guy who ever unloads these babies, and he's off sitting in a canoe on the Eagle River, sucking down brewskis and casting for trout, the lucky bastard."

I backed away as he steadied the wall, putting a hand here and there, calming a nervous horse.

"Phew, that was close!" he said, grimacing. Drawn across his yellow gloves were lines of black grease. Some kind of anti-rust coating from the seat frames. So that's why I was sniffing, my eyes watering. The things were slick with it. As he considered our predicament, the guy working the next boxcar nodded at me, flashing something bright. I did a double-take. A big metal hook curled from the end of his arm.

"Who's that?" I asked, keeping my voice down. A pink, cotton-tailed, big-eyed bunny stared out from the guy's red t-shirt, its long, floppy ears folded over, its cartoony grin broad, and bucktoothed—something a kid should wear, not a grown man.

"Oh, that son-of-a-bitch?" said Norm. "That's 'Meat Hook' Manny Camarasa."

"He has a hook for a hand?"

"No, no, no," Norm laughed. "He uses that thing to haul those fuel tanks around."

"Oh," I said. Of course. *Meat* Hook, not *Captain* Hook. "And did you say Manny?"

"That's right."

Fernando had told me about this guy. When I'd said I'd be working here instead of the car wash, he mentioned a neighbor by that name, a good friend who unloaded boxcars here and lived across the street from him on the river. A little envy was unmistakable in the way Fernando talked about him, like Manny had it made, a job like that. So this was him. Mexican, and like Fernando, dark complected with shiny black hair, a head shorter than me, but broad in the torso. A presence that came from width rather than height. A block of a man.

"Hardly says a word." Norm yelled: "Do you, Manny?" The man searched for the source of the summons, but couldn't locate us.

Unlike Fernando's, Manny's face was weathered and lined with wrinkles, as if he'd spent years working in the sun. Reminded me of the Seminoles I met over spring break in central Florida, but without the war paint, leather and feathers they wore for their shows. If wrinkles were like tree rings, this guy would have been ancient, except for his energy, the way he inserted that hook through the little hole in the tank's lip and hefted the thing over his shoulder and onto his back like a giant marshmallow. When he caught me watching, he threw me this huge smile, unnerving the way it carried up into his dark eyes, as if he was always about to laugh, or maybe, to cackle.

Confiding again, Norm said, "Barely speaks English, the fuckin' wetback."

I cringed.

"You speaka *Inglésa*??" he yelled. Manny nodded and disappeared inside his boxcar.

Wetback. Hadn't heard that term since leaving for college, but people here talked that way, especially about the migrant workers Green Giant bussed up here every summer to work the corn and pea fields. But Manny didn't live in one of those camps. In fact, it turned out that he lived right across the river from my house.

"AMC wouldn't hire illegals, would they?"

"Oh, come on, Walker. You think these wily coyotes can't outfox those pencil pushers up in Administration?"

I gave Manny another glance. He gave a quick wave, hustled up to the tower from which the radio blared and turned it down.

"*Tirelos para abajo todos juntos!*" he yelled out.

"What did he say?"

"Beats me," Norm said. "Speak English, you little fucker!"

He elbowed me as if I was an accomplice. Asshole. He disappeared inside our boxcar. Manny started to talk again but another of those tuggers rumbled by, and I didn't catch anything he said. We traded shrugs.

"There we go," Norm yelled, stumbling out of the boxcar with this wiry thing, a giant metal spider, all coiled legs and pinchers. But then he doubled over, dropping the thing. "Fuck me!" He squinted, rubbing his hip, bent over.

"Jesus, Norm. You all right?"

"Yeah, yeah, yeah." He waved me away. "I'm fine. Fuck." His face was a swirling pool of pain.

"Maybe I should get Kelly."

"Don't even think about it!" He grabbed my arm, squeezing.

"But Norm—"

"I'm fine, goddammit."

"Okay."

He straightened, scanning the area, as if worried someone might see. Before us, the frame had sprung open like a bear trap, unfurling into a black skeleton of a four-foot wide, bench-style car seat. He grabbed it, limped it over to the train and tossed the thing clattering into the first of the three wagons, then leaned back against the yellow engine. He exhaled, catching his breath, and after a second, motioned me over.

"Now," he began, rubbing his hip, breathing hard, "The button talk."

"The button talk? You sure you don't want me to find Kelly."

"I said, 'No.' Look—" He peeked around to see if anyone was watching. "If you tell Kelly, he sends me home and the paychecks stop coming. I come down with the flu or bump my head on a boxcar, they pay me sick leave, but if this hip acts up? 'Fuck you, Norm.'"

"Why's that?"

"I had it when they hired me and couldn't get my doctor's permission to work, okay?"

"But you are working." I said, confused.

"Only because they made it a, whatdoyoucallit, a 'pre-existing condition' they don't have to pay for, no thanks to your dad."

I stood up straight, not sure if I was being insulted.

"He's only doing his job, I know, but it sucks. I'm a cripple, not a fucking criminal." He sighed.

"You been dealing with this all this time?"

"No." He waved it away. "Wasn't a problem until they put me on this fucking loading dock, lifting all day. Christ." He shook his head. "Anyway, the button talk."

"The button talk. Okay."

"Now, did you see those big red buttons as you were walking in?"

I nodded, picturing the buttons here and there along the line, like giant red mushrooms.

"Well, imagine this place is the city of New York, and pushing that button causes a complete blackout. Or it's the Titanic, and that button shoves an iceberg in its path. You see where I'm going?"

I tried to swallow but couldn't.

"You push that button and it stops the line. No money comes in when these butt-ugly Ramblers aren't moving out. Thousands of people end up standing around, thumbs up their asses, getting paid to do squat. And for those suits up in Admin, that's a fucking disaster. So," and now Norm slapped the little engine again, "once you get a train filled, you press this button, here." He pointed. A smaller, green mushroom on top of the train engine. "And this little tugger takes off down the line to be unloaded. Empty trains come every, what, I don't know. Every fifteen minutes for my mufflers. But if an empty comes up *before* you fill the first train, it means you're falling behind. And what do you think happens if you fall too far behind and the seat line runs out of frames?"

I blinked at him, my gut sinking, breakfast going from bad to worse.

"It stops, so no seats are going to the trim line. And what happens when the trim line runs out of seats?"

I studied him. Quotas. Time limits. Buttons. *Suck-ass summer job.*

"That's right. The red button. If you can't push the green button, they push the red one. And you'll know. You'll think it's a goddamned fire alarm, tornado warning, air raid siren. Like the world's coming to an end. But guess what...." He slapped a hand on my shoulder. "It's really the sound of you, my friend, becoming Mr. Totally Fucked. You understand?"

With a shiver, I nodded, considering the little train and its big brother boxcar. How in hell would I survive this? Kids always picked me last in gym class, yet Kelly expected me to come 'up to speed' in a couple of hours. At least, baseball players got spring training. I didn't get shit. My spine went cold and tingly.

"Now, I don't know how big this stockpile is Lester built for you. Could last an hour, maybe two. But that line's a hungry bastard. You don't keep it fed, it'll eat you up. So you best get to work."

He slapped me on the back one more time, then deserted me, limping back toward his boxcar of mufflers, two berths over. As he passed in front of Manny, Norm feigned a punch at the smaller man, pulling up short, just teasing. Manny faked a counter-punch, losing the smile a second, then smiling again, a not-so-friendly game the two of them played.

Manny's gaze fell on me, and his smile widened even further. I gave him a weak grin back, not sure what to make of him. Or any of this.

It took a full minute to free my first frame, holding tight on the greasy curls so as not to lose my grip. I worked it, side to side. When it pulled out, the wall shivered and buckled, ready to topple over. I soothed it back into place as Norm had. Reminded me of that game where you build a tower of wooden blocks and pull them out one by one, trying to keep the whole thing from falling down. What was it called? *Jenga*? I was already out of breath. I wiggled another frame out, then ran the two of them to the train.

Again and again, as I nursed the frames out, the wall threatened to fall, and I'd have to gentle it back down, my gloves black with eye-watering lubricant. Finally, the wall shrank enough I could pull frames off the top, but after one wall was done, another was right behind it and I was back to playing *Jenga*, again, easing out frames, one by one. After sending several trains on their way, I tired, unable to keep up the same hectic pace. As I started on the third of three wagons, an empty train pulled up. Panicked, I rushed to the wiry wall and held it up with one hand, prying the coils apart with the other. My fingers slipped, getting tweaked and pinched.

My heart jackhammered away inside my chest, and I got that light-headed hypoxia Dad told me came from my bad lungs not having anywhere to put the oxygen. (Did he write down I was a preemie on that stupid form of his?) Slowing down, however, was not an option. By the time I got that train filled and sent off, Kelly was twenty feet away, sleeves rolled up, those thick arms of his folded on his chest. He stood, chewing his mustache, a corner of his mouth raised. It was a smirk. He was smirking. Norm and Manny were working their boxcars, lifting and pulling their parts out with ease. Everyone on down the line—gas tanks, mufflers, bumpers, radiators, doing a slow, heavily-laden dance with effortless grace. They'd glance over, then at each other, their heads shaking, but mouths widening. More smirks. A private joke. Were they all in on it, this job they'd given me? Clearly, the shittiest job on the dock. But why me? They didn't even know me.

Norm had the biggest smile—Norm and his pre-existing condition. Maybe he'd put Kelly up to this, a way to get back at my dad. Or it could have been Kelly's idea, this 'new training method.' Maybe they all had something against my father, and they were taking it out on me.

I couldn't stop to think about it. Another empty might show up any second. That hungry bastard of a line, salivating. The lights of New York flickering; the Titanic, tanking. I was stuck with these nasty seat frames for two more weeks and then, no thanks to my father, some other god-awful job for another two, and then another and another, the whole blamed summer. I couldn't stop or I'd be fucked. Mr. Totally Fucked.

Four

I sit there, staring at him for the longest time. I want to empty my story into him, pour it in and fill him up. Make him see what he did, how people felt about him, about me. As if that might open his eyes, bring him back.

At long last, I reach over to his hand. Before I can touch him, there's a shock. I yank my hand back. Did that happen? Perhaps I only imagined it, a kind of psychic static charge. Maybe it draws energy from the neurological trenches his hands carved in my psyche. One therapist told me these memories are so painful that no subsequent memory has been profound enough to pave them over, and these flashes can seem real, like they're happening right now.

"It's all in your head," people say. Women, mostly. The impatient ones, when I've tried to explain my moods, my mistrust, the distancing and drinking I do. If only a machine like that ECG could etch in green lines the peaks of terror, the valleys of depression and self-loathing. If only the damage disfigured in a way you could see. "It is in my head," I'd say and point inside and show them the scars, real as a slashed cheek.

It's unsettling to see him so quiet. Apparently he's mellowed since Mom passed and he quit drinking. The Thanksgiving before last was the last time I saw him. He seemed happy, carefree. It was infuriating to hear him telling tales of his youth, his days as a stableboy at the Armory, wiping down the polo ponies. His election to junior commodore of the Chicago Yacht Club. Why couldn't he have been so affable when I was growing up here? Why couldn't my childhood have been so carefree?

I scan the length of him, his chest rising ever so often, then falling. I'm supposed to talk to him, but I don't know what to say. Nothing about that summer, of course. Not when he's so defenseless. But maybe current events. I ask him what he thinks about the recent Tsunami in Indonesia, all those people killed. He was there during the war, after all, but even so, he doesn't bat an eye.

I imagine his mind as a kind of kite set adrift in that windy old head of his, buffeted here and there by dreams and aimless gusts of thought, while my voice, what little I can manage above a croaking whisper, jumps for the string, trying to catch it and reel him back to earth.

But I know my father. If he could hear me, my liberal bent tinting every word royal blue, and him, unable to respond, to argue—he'd think I was torturing him. So I shut up, find my pack and take out my laptop. I open a blank document. I still make those fists, a fish gasping, but it only amplifies my anxiety. As it has all my life, writing reins in those feelings, corrals and channels them.

So I'm letting these keystrokes do my talking. The thing is, I *need* to talk to him, *really* talk to him, hear his version of those events, and now I don't know if I'll ever have the chance.

I want to love him. I do. The last time we talked was on his birthday in November. I'd called him and, before I hung up, I told him I loved him. Now, I'm so glad I did, while he was still able to hear me. And I wasn't simply mouthing those words, though I have to admit, it's a qualified love.

You see, that place of loving him is a secluded sanctuary I've been building alone, by myself, for years. As a kid, I considered such places a Shangri-La, fantasy worlds other boys lived in with their fathers. Not me. Not us. Even though we've lived apart, I've worked on it, sought help, found professionals with whom I could talk about him.

I grew to appreciate how his own tough childhood—weak father and tough mother—might have shaped his own bad behavior, how his many years in the Air Force may have twisted his notions of parenting. I'm what happens when you raise a kid the same way you command a soldier. I've learned I can't get over my Dad because my anger and exile are the only power I have over him, and by not coming home or when I have come home, by not addressing my issues, I've resisted giving up that power, holding onto my anger instead.

Aided by this growing self-awareness, I've tried completing my island castle, making peace with him, at least, in my own mind, even making progress toward actual *rapprochement* by coming home for that Thanksgiving after so many years away.

Not that I got very far. Though I intended to sit my father down and talk things through, I barely skimmed the surface those four days, never diving into those deeper waters I needed to explore.

I remember being in the den with him, Frazier and Piper when we finally got around to discussing what I'd been doing all these years since Mom's funeral. We started with where I lived, New York City, at that time, same as Frazier. Dad fairly bristled, saying one didn't live in cities so much these days as fester in them, swimming in a stew of rats, garbage and homeless people. Frazier just rolled his eyes and gave me a telling smile. He'd been hearing those comments for years now, coming home Thanksgivings as he did, or Christmases, one or the other, leaving me to fend for myself for the holiday he wasn't around. He was used to it. Dad being Dad.

Piper steered the conversation away, talking about how Belford had changed since the last time I was home, less a farming and factory town now than a bedroom community, all the people moving there to commute to tech jobs in Chicago's western suburbs. And then Dad asked what kinds of stories I was working on. As soon as I told him I was covering John Kerry's campaign for the presidency, that come January, I'd be following him from state to state during the primaries, the conversation ended. As if we could talk about Kerry's support for gay rights, the pro-choice movement, or his immigration stance. Dad just nodded, no follow-ups, at which point Piper noted that the football game was about to come on. Steering away, again.

Dad may have been loose and easy talking about his own life, the good old days, but about mine, not so much. Frazier had warned me. Dad never asked about his life either. The theater world of 'fairies' and 'fruits' my brother inhabited. His partners, post-divorce. It shouldn't have come as a surprise that Dad never asked who either of us might be seeing, as if we travelled in the same circles, and didn't have relationships one could discuss in polite company.

Still, it made me angry how little he seemed to care, all those years I'd been gone. And the thing was, we hadn't even talked about the stuff that really burned in my gut. When I say I wanted to dive into deeper waters, I mean those bottom-feeding emotions that stir up and eddy in me every time I think of that summer of 1974.

But I didn't give up that Thanksgiving. I tried. I really did. At one point, I got Dad alone in the kitchen while Piper was doing his laundry and unable to carjack the conversation. I had to make myself a drink before I could dive in, swim down. And then, while he made the gravy, sifting flour into the turkey pan, I tried to work up to it. But we only bantered. Foolish stuff about the Cubs' iffy off-season acquisitions, incredible bargains Dad had unearthed at the Belford flea market. Meaningless chatter. As this went on, I drank, and then, semi-soused, went quiet, watching him cook. The things I'd meant to bring up—about that summer I worked at AMC, about Manny Camarasa—they spun like an old apple I was bobbing for in my beer, unable to get my teeth into. Similar scenes were repeated several times over those four days, failed attempts to talk drowned by alcohol. I left feeling as if that edifice of love I'd been so carefully trying to construct had fallen apart, the scaffolds splintered, the towers razed.

I've never been able to finish building this thing because my love for him has always lacked something crucial—a keystone of sorts. Ancient cathedrals and castles are full of stone arches the two sides of which are held together simply by the weight of one giant keystone—a trapezoidal-shaped stone mounted on top. It's as if, all these years, I've propped up those two sides by an act of will and imagination, waiting for him to fill in that gap, so I can back away and see if my creation stands on its own. Because if he can't bridge that divide, well—maybe that's why people, from time to time, have told me, "Walker, you're barely holding it together."

Here's what's missing: I need to know what happened to the Camarasa family. Why'd they disappear? Was he or was he not responsible? Back then, he told me he 'took care' of them, kept using that phrase—they were 'taken care of.' I'll always remember that, the way he said it, its meaning winking at me the way he put it, like what he really did was send them away, sent away the girl I loved, that's how he took care of them.

Strangely enough, when I called him on his birthday two months ago, we almost stumbled over that topic. The fact was, I wasn't calling to give him my good wishes. I was just looking for a peaceable pretext to tell him I wasn't coming again for Thanksgiving. As I was leaving the previous one, Piper had made me promise to come again this year, but I just couldn't. Not after how I'd felt for weeks following that visit, so dark and down. No way I was going to repeat that.

He'd been in such a lousy mood on the phone. First, he'd insisted

I was still living in New York instead of D.C., but I let that pass. Then, I asked him how he was doing with winter coming—just making conversation. He boiled over, burbling out a list of his projects, how he'd installed all the storm windows himself, attached the snowblower to the John Deere, cooked his meals; washed, dried and folded his laundry, paid his bills. His outburst baffled me.

"Isn't Piper helping you with—"

"I'm not leaving this house!"

Then I got it. In an email to Frazier and me, my sister had floated the trial balloon of assisted living, which Mr. Oblivious, here, took for a passing concern about Dad being alone in that drafty old house. I had no idea negotiations had neared critical mass—or that his ability to care for himself might, at long last, be deteriorating.

"Sure, Dad." I didn't want to get into the middle of their argument. "No problem. Uh, how are your Bears doing?" I said, lamely changing the subject, leaving Piper to be the bad guy.

Dad grumbled out brief answers, the conversation fizzling, nowhere else left to go but the purpose of my call, so I told him I'd decided not to come home for Thanksgiving, saying I had to cover the House's debate on a big bill President Bush had proposed.

"Yeah? What bill is that?" It stung me how unphased he was by my decision not to come, like the bill was the important thing. It took a second to recover and answer his question.

"It's an immigration bill. A temporary amnesty for illegal workers, so they can come and go from the country." That should have put an end to the conversation—a topic he'd never want to discuss with me of all people.

"I read about that," Dad said.

"Oh yeah?" I stopped breathing, how close we'd suddenly come to the heart of our problems.

"How if they want to become citizens, they'll have to go to the back of the line. No special treatment."

"And what do you think about that?" I ventured.

"It's only fair, isn't it?"

"Right," I said, feeling burned, that old anger in my gut. Put them in their place. *Just like you did with the Camarasas,* I wanted to say. Back of the line, folks. Where you belong. Instead I said I had work to do, I'd talk to him soon. I wished him a happy birthday and closed with a perfunctory, "Love you, Dad," as if I said it all the time.

"Me, too," he said. Just a thing you say to your son.

Afterwards, I told myself he's such a healthy old goat, I'd still have a chance to talk to him someday. Someday, we'd have that talk. And now, here I am, alone with him, facing my last chance, my last someday, and I don't even know if he can hear me.

Because of what happened to the Camarasas, Dad's house stopped being my home. Yes, I've returned. But never to live, never in the warmth of June or July. I can't come without being obliged, can't drop in without calling, walk in without knocking, when the corn is high, the lawn green. Why, Dad? Why is it always so cold when I come home?

Yes, I'm to blame for holding so tight to my precious anger, for not insisting my dad tell me what happened to that family sooner. Now I have to figure this out myself—and before he's lost forever.

In my head, the story of that summer always starts in that exam room that first day, but I'm convinced, none of it would have happened if we hadn't moved to Belford to begin with.

Five

In my family, we all assumed Dad would be an Air Force lifer. Wherever they sent him, no matter what they asked him to do, he'd be true until the very end. And why not? They promoted him, moving him up the chain of command, from captain to full colonel, from general surgeon to head of surgery to hospital commander. Every move—from air bases in Pennsylvania to Hawaii to Mississippi to Wyoming, where I was born, then the Philippines, and finally Illinois—came with larger houses, greater responsibility, bigger staffs to manage. Then, in 1969, seemingly without warning or explanation, the top brass gave him his walking papers, ten years before he was ready.

"That's how the military works sometimes," he sighed, so matter of fact, you'd think it was a minor inconvenience, a tree limb in the road we'd have to skirt around.

"Half his life he's given them and bam, he's out. Just like that?" I whispered to Frazier that day. "He doesn't seem very upset about it."

"Get upset with his precious Air Force?" my older brother smirked. "The day he leaves, he'll probably march out the door, saluting all the way."

That day was still a few months off, the Air Force having given him six months notice. But the fact remained, he was only fifty-five, with three kids—one, about to start college—and a wife to support. As it turned out, finding a job took every moment of those six months. He called hospitals and wrote to medical practices, scoured the back pages of journals with long names, made trip after to trip to Chicago and its suburbs to attend interviews, doctors conventions, surgical conferences, and administrator symposiums. It wore on him, we could tell, from the way he raised his voice behind closed doors with our mother. How easily he snapped at me for a dirty dish in the sink, at Frazier for hair too long, a shirt untucked. (But not at Piper—never at Piper.)

I thought he was being picky, waiting for the perfect position in the choicest town. He could get a job anywhere, couldn't he? A doctor? Colonel? Hospital commander?

Mom certainly wasn't worried. In fact, the longer it took Dad to decide, the greater Mom's anticipation. In the *Chicago Tribune* real estate section, she pointed out ads for homes in fancy suburbs—Wilmette, Evanston and Lake Forest—magnificent places along Lake Michigan. Castle-like Victorians, brick Tudors, steel and glass Contemporaries, historic Colonials—all on lovely, winding, tree-lined streets with nearby private schools. This property had a heated pool, that one a lakeside dock, this one a gazebo, that one a tennis court.

So, it was with a mix of confusion and excitement that my siblings and I sat down with Mom and Dad at the dinner table one night to hear Dad's choice. He'd already told Mom, and she'd been weird, reassuring us with forced smiles about the 'interesting' place we were headed, the 'fascinating' town with its 'unusual' opportunity.

"You'd think we were colonizing Mars," Frazier smirked, always the wise ass.

But no. Dad announced that we were moving to Belford, a factory town in northern Illinois surrounded by corn fields.

"So, that's another Chicago suburb?" Piper asked.

"Well, no," Dad said. "But it's home to an automobile assembly plant run by the American Motors Company. They make the Rambler and the Gremlin. You've seen the ads on TV. I'll be their company doctor."

"Oh." Piper said, nodding her head "So, is the company sick or something?"

"No, sweetie. But five thousand people work there building cars. It can be dangerous. People get hurt. It'll be my job to take care of them."

"But what about Lake Michigan?" I asked.

"Yeah, what about the *swimming pool*," Frazier emphasized, "the *dock* on the *lake*," his voice oily with sarcasm.

"Well," Mom said, "we won't have a pool, but we will have a river that runs behind a big back yard, and we'll have a dock on the river where you can swim and fish, and we'll have a big house. I'm sure it will be beautiful."

"You haven't seen it yet?" I asked.

"Trust me," Dad said. "It's the best place in Belford."

"So…an automobile factory?" Frazier said, his mouth twisting. "You couldn't find a job at a hospital or a clinic?"

"I looked at medical practices and hospitals, yes, but you know what? This will be a challenge, like being back on the front lines again, handling emergencies. Only not off in some god-forsaken jungle somewhere. Right here, in America."

"You know what?" Frazier confided in me later that day. "Dad couldn't get a better job. All those years in the Air Force, all those medals and promotions, and what does he have to show for it? A shit job in a shit town."

I didn't believe my brother. He just wanted to see the colonel, the hospital commander, brought down a few pegs and put in his place. To me, it was noble what Dad was doing. He wasn't in it for the money, the prestige. He had enough of both, didn't he? He was shooting for something honorable, putting his war-time skills to best use. Besides, he could work anywhere, do anything, couldn't he? I was proud of him and looking forward to our new home.

Six

Life in Belford wasn't like the Air Force, of course. It was unlike any place we had ever lived, as was our house, that "mansion on the river," my new classmates liked to rib me about, as if my address told them all they needed to know about me.

Some mansion. Sure, it sat on a hill that swept down to a river, the Piscasaw, but right across the water sat the Ironworks Foundry, a rusty bucket of a building that clanked and hissed all the time, smoke from its stacks darkening the air. And if ours wasn't the best house in town, as my father promised, it was the biggest, a stately, brick box built before the Civil War by the owner of a clawfoot tub factory torn down eons ago. The house had sat empty and neglected for years, and Dad got it cheap. And I could see why. Nobody else would be crazy enough take it on, re-shingle the massive roof and re-paper those moldy walls, tackle the rust that turned the copper plumbing green and caused the Edison-era wiring to short out, making us blunder around in the dark until our father fixed it.

He could have done better if he wanted to, I was certain. Something new and modern, but he'd always loved fixing things and, like the job, the house presented new challenges for him to work on. It was all part of his new outlook on life, his grand plan. And as his kids, we had to adjust our expectations to get with the plan, and that included those about schools.

At Chanute Air Force Base, Frazier, Piper and I had attended a K-thru-12 base school with a buttoned-up dress code where the teachers were as strict with us as Dad was with his men. But now a fresh start awaited all the Maguire kids. Frazier was just starting college. At fourteen, I was just entering Belford High, and at nine, Piper was a fourth-grader at Lincoln Elementary.

While Piper and I were more than prepared academically, neither of us was ready for Belford kids. I know I wasn't. The girls' skimpy skirts, the boys' dirty blue jeans and t-shirts, the way everyone swore and bullied each other, fooled around in class, gossiped and laughed so freely in the hallways, smoked in the parking lot after the last bell—and not just cigarettes.

It was a challenge, but I found it refreshing. Whatever it was like for Piper in grade school, though, she wasn't adjusting, and she wouldn't hold her tongue.

She had been tops in her class in Chanute, "a natural born leader," according to her report cards, "respected by all her classmates." Dad had made a point of reading these accolades out loud while he glowered at me, a boy who was none of those things.

But life changed for Piper in Belford. She was starting all over, and she thought the starting line was way behind her, as were most of the kids in her class. She wasn't about to wait for them to catch up. I could only imagine what she was like in school, her raised hand waving tirelessly, the teacher praying for someone else to call on who wasn't always right. She liked to boast to me how she scolded her classmates, telling them they "shouldn't swear," or "my Daddy is a doctor and he says cigarettes will kill you," or "bullies are no better than *hooligans*," one of my father's favorite words.

When Piper told these stories at dinner, Dad would say, "that's my girl," even after she explained how her classmates laughed at her, called her "stuck up" and a "smart ass." Dad scoffed to hear such comments, such coarse language, as if no one could blame Piper for her classmates' behavior.

"Did you tell your teachers?" Mom would ask.

"Of course, I did."

"No!" I jumped in. "That only makes it worse."

"She has to tell someone!" Dad would say. "She's the only child there with a shred of civility."

Our Base school teachers may have taught us to tattle, but it was a colossal mistake in Belford, as was the way Piper blindly followed my parents' advice to "stand up for herself" and "set a good example." Within weeks, nobody would talk to Piper at all.

I took a different tack, listening at the edges of conversations. Kids bragged about seeing REO Speedwagon or Ted Nugent at the Belford Auditorium, about how they snuck into slasher movies full of topless women at the Drive-In. This is what I needed to know. What people liked here. How they spent their time. How to score bags of weed from a guy called Reefer Richie in the park. How you could get a drunk named Wild Bill to buy you a forty-ounce bottle of Colt 45 if you gave him money to buy his own. Crucial information for surviving in Belford, but of little use if you had no way to apply it, no one to use it with. And I didn't.

I wasn't interesting. Oh, kids perked up when I mentioned living in the exotic South Pacific, until they heard how boring life was being a virtual prisoner on a small air base where every house was identical to the next, every father wore the same blue uniform and flat-top haircut. I was so square, never swearing or speaking up unless spoken to.

At least I did well in class, or so I thought, getting good grades on all my tests and quizzes. Like my sister, I couldn't help raising my hand, making and unmaking my fist, knowing that here I had all the answers for once—until some jock raised his hand.

"Oh, I don't know the answer," the kid said to the teacher. "I was just wondering, if doing this with my hand will make me as smart as Maguire. Guess not!" At which everyone laughed.

Much as I tried, I did no better than Piper. The only thing I had learned was how not to make friends. That left Piper with me and me with Piper. And both of us with our parents.

For the hour of TV Dad allowed us each night, we watched Walter Cronkite do play-by-plays on blurry missions to the moon that took hours to land, or *Special Reports* on war crimes, grainy bombing campaigns, or troop buildups in Vietnam, all accompanied by campus protests that got so out of hand the National Guard had to be called up.

"Sneaky little bastards, those VC," my father would grumble. He knew. Clark Air Base, where we had lived in the Philippines, was only a B52 bombing run away from Vietnam. He often flew over there on secret missions he couldn't tell us about.

"Why don't they mow them down?" Dad barked at the television after one too many drinks. "That's how we handled the Japs. Mow them the hell down!"

And then he'd launch into one of his many war stories: the day he killed a Japanese soldier, the day they landed on the beach in New Guinea and it was his job to set up a portable hospital. Blah-blah-bah.

Seeing Piper and I had nothing better to do, Dad drafted us to help with his projects. We'd peel old paper off bedroom walls, then sand, the dust turning our hair as white as his, then roll on that gloppy paint with its new car smell, only inside a house.

When we weren't doing chores or pitching in with the house, we'd sit at the dinner table and play board games, something we hadn't done since the days of *Candyland* and *Operation* when we were little. *Sorry, Monopoly, Parcheesi, Clue, Checkers*—they passed the time, but I wearied of Piper nattering away about how mean the kids were in her school—pulling at her long skirts, making fun of the old Oz books she carried around. Unlike her, I'd learned to shut up, so at least kids stopped bothering me.

Leaving the military wasn't all bad. It loosened Dad up, for one thing. After a few months, he stopped timing our TV hours or inspecting our clothes before school. He slept in on Saturdays unless the lawn needed mowing or the leaves raking or the weeds weeding. If there was work to be done, he'd be up first thing, dragging me out with him to take up arms and rakes and hedge-trimmers. He even let his hair grow a little. Instead of the usual pink scalp through buzz-cut stubble, we could see just how white his hair had become.

"It makes you look so much more distinguished," Mom said to him one day, getting on her tiptoes to kiss him on his way out the door, her finger sliding down his white temple.

"Older, you mean. That's because I am," he said, kissing her palm before leaving for work.

Dad drank more, too. Rum and Cokes that Piper, using Dad's hourglass-shaped aluminum jigger, enjoyed mixing for him—a shot of Rum in a frosted highball of Coke and Ice. Two, three, four every night, and then he'd curse and bang around the house as he put up new shutters or painted a ceiling. He often cut himself or hit his thumb with a hammer, spouting "Dammit!" like it was the only swear he knew. He also got very tight whenever Mom mentioned money or asked him how his day went. "Fine," he'd say, and that was that.

My mother loved the new house, the hours she could spend reading Pearl S. Buck and James Michener on her bedroom's chaise lounge, the way the large yard and the river reminded her of her father's horse farm with the stream outside its kitchen where she'd caught tadpoles as a kid, the fields of hay she once wandered. It wasn't the town or the house she had trouble adjusting to.

But she was hesitant when I asked for a pair of high-tops like the other kids sported in Belford. The penny loafers I wore to the base school were completely uncool here.

"Did you see how your father acted when I mentioned replacing those drafty windows, getting that new roof he promised? So, we have to watch our spending," she said. This, from the woman who'd dreamt of heated swimming pools behind big houses on the shores of Lake Michigan. Her loyalty was like the tiny smudge of lipstick that always appeared on this off-kilter incisor she had. She could wipe it clean, only for it to re-materialize seconds later.

But needing money? I wasn't buying it. Dad was a doctor, after all. Doctors were well paid. Maybe he was frugal, responsible, careful. But, poor? Not my dad.

Seven

For months, I ate alone in the cafeteria, until one day this skinny, blond kid plunked down his tray across the table from me. The one in my Geometry class who cracked jokes nobody laughed at. Christ. If I wasn't a loser before, associating with him was bound to make me one. I eyed him. He eyed me. Hell, I had nothing to lose, so I mumbled a "Hey."

"Hey," he nodded back. "You're that kid who lives in the mansion, right?"

"It's not a mansion," I mumbled.

"At least, they don't call your place a fucking *hacienda.*"

Oh, yeah. This was the guy kids called *Pablo*, or the *Burrito Bandito*, or the *Taco Fucker.* Weird names for a kid with blond hair, blue eyes, pasty white skin.

"I'm Kurt, by the way." He reached over to shake my hand. "Kurt Swanson. My father's Pops Swanson?" Definitely not Mexican.

"Okay…?" I drawled.

"Don't you ever watch TV? Pops Swanson Chevrolet?"

"Oh, right." That guy in the double-breasted suits who drawled '*Come on down and bring the family*!' reading it off a card as he waved the camera closer.

"That's my dad," he nodded, smiling, as if that told me all I needed to know about him. "So where you from?" He asked the first of a series of questions I, surprisingly, warmed to, starved as I was for company.

Doing the dishes with my mom and sister that night, I told them about my conversation with Kurt.

"He thinks his dad is this big shot car salesman—" I snickered, wiggling my fingers in the air. "He just got his learner's permit, asked if I wanted to see that new *M*A*S*H* movie at the Drive-In."

"Your father wouldn't want you seeing that. And with an older boy, too?"

"Just a few months," I said, as if his age needed defending, too.

When the *M*A*S*H* preview first aired, Dad almost chucked his drink at the TV. It made such a mockery of what he did during the war, moving and manning mobile hospitals, the most deadly serious four years of his life.

"I'm not sure I want to go. He's kind of weird."

"Well, I'll go then," Piper said, as if I was turning down a pardon from a prison she was desperate to flee.

"It's not a movie for young girls," Mom said.

My sister crossed her arms in a huff.

Faced with another weekend of her whining, I accepted Kurt's invitation. It was a Drive-In, after all. Nobody'd see who I was with—or so I figured. Then, Kurt drove up in a dazzling, pale blue Impala you couldn't keep your eyes off of. *Must be nice to get your pick of the car lot,* I thought, ducking down in the seat. Once we paid, parked and hooked the speaker to the driver's side window, Kurt produced a joint.

"You're smoking that here?" I asked, peeking around. I'd never been around anyone smoking marijuana before.

"Everyone does it here," he laughed, lighting up, pointing at the smoke-filled cars around us.

That didn't make the night any more relaxing. Maybe it was the pot, making me choke and cough, the dizzying smoke with its pungent, musky-earthy scent, or maybe the way he watched the show with its silly surgeons pranking each other like school kids, but Kurt commanded as much of my focus as did the movie, the way he hooted and hollered at every joke, repeating lines. I kept wondering—*who is this guy?*—especially when, on that big screen, a tent flap was flipped up, revealing the white flanks of a naked Nurse Hoolihan, showering. Arranged in seats in front of the shower tent, the surgeons toasted her with martinis, wolf-whistling the mortified woman while she shrieked and struggled to cover up. Kurt loved it. Okay, I found it titillating, too, but still, it wasn't exactly funny. None of it was. And not just the way the doctors chased after the nurses. The movie ignored the soldiers being operated on, never showing their faces or giving them names or stories. Maybe because I was high for the first time I was being a prig, but everything was a joke, and not in a good way, more like laughing out loud at a funeral, pretending nobody was dead. Unless, that was the point and I didn't get it.

Still I didn't complain. To Kurt Swanson, I was worthy. He asked what show we should see next and if I'd like to shoot pool sometime, already making plans to get together again, giving me more opportunities to get out of the house.

So, the following week, Kurt took me to Rambler Lanes. We didn't play on the nine-foot tables in the Billiards Room the factory workers used, but on this beat-up, coin-operated table in the lobby. I admitted I didn't know how to play, and I expected him to kick my ass. Instead, he taught me how to hold the stick and visualize shots, gave me time to practice. For an excitable guy with little patience for anyone else, he was great with me. We played Eight-ball for a buck a game, pretending our singles were twenties and hundreds, big bucks like the factory workers played for in the other room. He even let me win enough games to break even.

So, we hung out. Sometimes I even slept over at Kurt's house, the two of us taking over the basement. We'd watch *Combat!* and take hits from a bottle of malt liquor he bartered from Wild Bill. One night, I worked up the nerve to ask the question that had been bugging me.

"What's with those names people call you? Taco bender? Pablo? Where'd that come from?"

"Oh, that crap. It's all my dad's fault, trying to save the world." As he sipped from the bottle, he explained how a few years back, his father had accompanied a customer on a test drive that took them into the country past the camp at Green Giant where their migrant workers lived.

"That canning factory on the river, upstream from our house," I said.

"That's the place. They bring up busloads of Mexicans to detassel corn and pick peas every summer."

Kurt explained how his dad saw some bare-chested migrant kids playing a pickup baseball game that day. They used a plastic bat and a tennis ball, and ran bases made from t-shirts and cardboard in a rutted field. Pops had recently donated lights to the little league so Belford boys could play night games, and here these poor kids couldn't play organized ball at all.

"So he got this idea. He talked to Green Giant who talked to their workers, and they agreed to let these migrants' kids—the Camaros, he named them—challenge my Little League team, the Red Sox. If it worked out, Dad hoped to start a regular team with these kids and let them play in our League. And he wanted me to help out. At first, I said, 'No way. Those kids?' You know what I mean, the crap people say about them. Dirty, uneducated, good for nothing but picking peas. Plus, I'd have had to miss some crucial Red Sox games, and I was their best hitter.

"But then Dad said, 'just come and check it out.' So I gave in. These kids were so pumped to get real gloves, bats and balls, even if they were donated hand-me-downs. And the uniforms? We only had these Swanson Chevy t-shirts and caps he keeps for customer giveaways, but the kids acted like they'd gotten Yankee pinstripes. My dad's Spanish isn't great, so it was difficult explaining rules and stuff, but these kids tried so hard, even if it was a Chinese fire drill, kids running every which way. It was their big chance, you know?"

"So, you helped out."

"That's right. We practiced a few times. Then the day of the game came. The stands were packed with parents from town and the camp. It was supposed to be relaxed—let the rules slide, slow pitch—but it didn't turn out that way. People were mean, yelling out shit like 'Taco Bender' and 'Burrito Bandito.'

"What they call you."

"Right. 'Cause they didn't want no Mexicans playing in their little league, no sir. And the Red Sox, they rolled with the crowd. They'd lost those games I'd missed, so I got the worst of it. 'Spic-lover,' they called me. 'Traitor.' 'Judas.' They had to beat us, throwing hard, tackling guys on the baselines, arguing calls. The Camaro pitcher accidentally beaned a Red Sox hitter, and a huge fight broke out. Half the stands emptied onto the field, ready to string the kid up, so my dad stopped the game, and that was that. No more dream team. But it didn't keep people from giving me shit."

"But that was, what, three, four years ago, and they still treat you that way?"

"I quit the Red Sox. My Dad was like, 'Don't. You have to live with these people.' But I didn't care if they got bounced out of the playoffs. The way they treated him and the Camaros? What assholes!

Those migrant kids, they only wanted to play ball, you know? So, I say, go ahead. Call me a taco bender." He looked over at me. "You don't have a problem with that, do you?"

"No. Not at all." Unlike kids in mostly white Belford, those I grew up with in the Air Force came from all over.

"Good, because anyone who gives me any shit about it can go fuck themselves."

After that, I didn't slouch down in Kurt's Impala. I sat up straight. And if kids gave us shit, I told them to fuck off, too.

On those evenings I had plans with Kurt, Piper got mad that I left her alone with nothing to do. Like her having no friends was my fault.

The nights I hung around, she and I still played board games or watched TV, but she wore me out with her constant complaints about her 'stupid' fourth-grade classmates, how she tried to organize a game of kickball during recess and they ignored her, how they never did their homework and didn't care when the teachers got mad at them, how they didn't know half the stuff she'd learned in third or even second grade.

"When we read out loud in class," she said one night during dinner, "I have to wait forever while Mrs. Anderson tells them to 'sound it out, sound it out.'" Piper would mimic the teacher's high-toned patience. "Sometimes, I can't help myself. 'It's *fragrant*,' I'll say. 'Not *fag-rent*, not *far-gent. Fra-grant.*' Sheesh."

Dad chuckled at these stories, which she took as encouragement, only making things worse. Once we were alone, I'd tell her she'd never make friends acting so superior all the time, but she'd get mad, saying, "You're just jealous because Daddy thinks I'm smarter than you."

It was completely besides the point, but its truth stung.

I remember Dad sitting Piper down at the dinner table, the *Belford Daily Telegram* spread wide before her. He had her circle all the spelling and syntax errors she could find, as if I couldn't find them, too, if I looked long enough. Then he circled a few of his own, cut out the articles and wrote the editor a note, which he read aloud, emphasizing the line about how even a nine-year-old could see how deplorable the newspaper's grammar was. Then he mailed it off. She was so proud of that.

God forbid I should ever argue with her, even if I only wanted to point out that correcting everyone was no way to make friends. Piper was my father's baby girl, and crossing her made him go nuts. The thing was, the more nights I went over to Kurt's, the more annoying she became when I stayed home. She'd sneak out of the kitchen before the dishes were done. Roll paint on my shoe while we were helping Dad. Let the swinging door hit me as we exited the basement. So-called 'accidents' I couldn't let go without a push and or shove in response. Piper would wail my father's name, her "Daddy!" alarm, and he'd come running, shaking me, barking at me to "Grow up!" and "Stop being such a bully!" I was the bad guy, the instigator, the "little bastard." Why he refused to see how she cooked up these charges hurt me more than all his slaps, shoves and kicks combined.

Eight

The nurse said I should daub my dad's parched lips with a wet sponge every so often. He sucks at it like a newborn drawn to a nipple. It's so strange to see him helpless in a hospital bed when he spent his life helping people out of them.

Piper still hasn't returned, and I guess Frazier is still stuck in New York, waiting out the storm. The nurse told me that, before I got here, Piper never left my dad's side for two days. It's not surprising, considering she spent the last three decades with him since Frazier and I left town. I have to hand it to her. All these years keeping tabs, sneaking out of work on her lunch breaks, dragging her two boys away from their video games to mow Dad's lawn or shovel his walk. I can imagine her, coaxing the three of them to watch the Cubbies on TV, the boys keeping Dad busy so she could smuggle groceries into the fridge, tidy up, monitor his meds and peek into his checkbook to ensure his bills were paid, forging his signature on his checks when they weren't.

Her boys just started their winter terms, or they'd be here, I'm sure. Georgia? Florida State? Somewhere south. I should know these things.

She's taken such good care of Dad, it makes me wonder why he was driving that damned Caddy, especially because she's so protective of him. At least, where I'm concerned. Telling me what I can and cannot say. Like when I emailed her to say I wasn't coming for Thanksgiving, that I planned to tell him by calling him on his birthday, something I seldom if ever did. She'd wanted to be on the call, like I couldn't handle it alone. When I said 'no,' she said, "No religion, Walker. And no politics. And if Dad wants to rub Bush's re-election in your face, you should leave it alone." It occured to me she'd given me a warning just like that the last time I was home, always steering me away from Maguire family potholes.

Of course, our arguments about politics were nothing like the ones he and Frazier used to have.

Like that first time Frazier came to Belford after starting college. He hadn't seen the new house before, and he didn't come until Christmas, having spent Thanksgiving with friends in Chicago. It had been months since we'd seen him, and his hair was so long that Dad threatened to cut it off himself, he was so mad. It wasn't just Frazier's hair, though. Those paisley shirts and striped bell-bottoms, the leather boots with zippers and the vests with tassels. And his attitude, too. Brazen, with this weird sense of entitlement, of authority, like he'd come into possession of *facts*, deputized by some knowledge he'd gained while away at school, wielding the truth like a gun he didn't know how to shoot.

One night during dinner, the two of them got into it over the war in Vietnam. Before leaving for college, Frazier had turned eighteen, registered for the draft and received his student deferment. Now he was wondering if Dad knew what those unlucky boys who couldn't get such deferments were doing over there. Did he know they were 'pacifying' the very people they were sent there to defend, winning their 'hearts and minds' by dragging them from their homes into so-called 'security hamlets' a step above concentration camps.

Dad seemed taken aback, as if he'd been blindsided by details he couldn't confirm or deny, and yet he blundered ahead, saying those hamlets were probably there to protect people from communists trying to take over the south. He gained confidence when he brought up something called the "Domino Theory," claiming nothing else mattered if we didn't stop the communist advance in Vietnam before it spread to surrounding countries, toppling them one by one.

Being just fourteen, all I could grasp was an image of the game, their arguments like black tiles being slapped down, back and forth, as they tried to one-up each other. Dad would say if Frazier thought people's lives in Vietnam were hard now, just wait until the Communists took over. And Frazier would ask Dad if he'd ever treated civilians for Napalm burns or Agent Orange poisoning during his war—or had he watched Americans massacring women and children—to which Dad would point out the horrendous tortures Americans endured in North Vietnamese POW camps, the freedoms people all over the world lost under communist rule.

I'd grown up on daily military routines—the flag coming down at retreat every night at 5 pm, uniformed airmen marching down Senior Officers Row in formation every afternoon, helicopters and jets soaring off hour after hour outside our living room windows, everything like clockwork, comforting in its consistency and certitude. Hearing Frazier hammer away at my father was scary—the gears and pulleys of Dad's arguments flying off every which way.

Knowing no one in Belford, Frazier announced that the day after Christmas he was leaving to spend the rest of his school vacation in Chicago. Dad wasn't happy. Certain unknown persons had invited Frazier to a mysterious New Year's party about which he remained adamantly vague.

I needed to know who I should root for, him or Dad, but Frazier didn't have much time for me. His head was going a million miles an hour. He was making long, secretive phone calls to his Chicago friends, filling up on books like *Why Are We In Vietnam?* listening to *Hair* and songs like "Alice's Restaurant Massacree" and "I Feel Like I'm Fixing to Die."

When I got him alone and asked why he had to leave so early, he said, "Don't you see? There's a revolution going on!"

But I didn't see. I didn't see it at all.

Nine

On New Year's Day, 1970, a leaky pipe and a tin kazoo turned the steady drip of my troubles with Piper and my dad into a full-blown flood.

Piper and I were watching the Cotton Bowl—Texas against Notre Dame, Dad's favorite team. Mom was reading in her room, and Dad was up in the bathroom on his back, under the sink. He was missing the big game, trying to fix a leak, with little success, I knew, from the furious clank of tools against pipes, the curses that echoed down the stairwell.

Several times, Dad pounded down the stairs to mix himself a drink. He'd peek at the game, groan at all the scores he'd missed, then take the highball upstairs to launch another attack on the pipes.

I wanted to be helpful, so I yelled out updates. "Notre Dame scored, Dad! We're only down a touchdown!" He'd swear and his tools would clatter, dumped or flung.

At first, Piper seemed happy the holiday kept me home. She asked about the game, why a tackle got penalized for tackling someone, how instead of being four times as important as a quarterback, a fullback was less important. I'd say it had nothing to do with math, and she'd nod, less interested in the answer than in having someone to talk to.

At halftime, she started tooting that tin kazoo Mom had stuffed in her Christmas stocking. All sugared up on candy canes, she high-stepped around, imitating the marching band, humming the school's fight song through the kazoo, a nine-year old acting half her age. I didn't care until the game came back on and she blocked the TV. "Keep it down," I kept saying, nodding up the stairs. I pulled up a chair right in front of the TV screen.

"Did you see, Walker? Did you see my feet that time? I spelled your name!"

The Fighting Irish had mounted a drive to tie the game, deep in opposition territory, but it was hard to follow with Piper toot-tooting. The teams lined up for a crucial third down, and though I was wary of Piper's "Daddy!" alarm, I yelled at her, "Shut up!" Miffed, she leaned over me and blew that kazoo right in my ear. Without a glance, I flipped up my hand to swat it away, a buzzing bee. She shrieked, way too loud for such a fleeting gesture. I turned to look. Her mouth was all bloody, her top lip split open, the kazoo gone.

"Daddy!" she yelled, her cry shrill and long, tears brimming. It was my fault, all that blood, accident or not. I'd hurt her.

"I'm sorry. I didn't mean it!" I said, reaching over, so tempted to cover her mouth, stop her screams.

"No you aren't. You hate me, you big bully! Daddy!"

As he thundered down the stairs, I sprang from the chair and rushed into the back hall. Outside offered no escape. It was freezing and dark, the back stairs slick with black ice.

"Jesus Christ!" He bellowed as she sobbed, hiccuping. "What happened?"

"Walker did it!"

I stood frozen in the hallway. He filled the doorway, eyes blazing, shoulders raised.

I backed away, tried to say it was an accident, but he didn't buy it.

"How could you do that to her? She's a little girl!"

He leapt after me, swiping, and just missed. I peeled off along the hall past the living room, a dead end, the Christmas tree dark, and into the dining room. He chased me around the big oval table twice before he yanked out a chair, toppling it to block my way, detouring me into the kitchen.

I tried squeezing under the kitchen table, that mouse seeking its hole, his cozy couch, his tiny TV. Small for fourteen, a late-bloomer like all Maguires, I was barely over five feet and a hundred pounds. He yanked me up and out by the arm. One slap, two, three, foul breath in my face, while he held me with the other hand.

"I didn't mean it!" My eyes stung with tears as I blubbered and pushed at him.

"Don't you lie to me. You've tormented that girl ever since we moved here."

The words scraped at me, ragged wounds, flecked with gravelly little truths. As I scuffled to hold him off, my palm stiff-armed his shoulder, a fingernail scraping his cheek. His eyes flared, and he took his hand down and back, a throwing motion, underhanded, a wild uppercut to my gut. Jolted up onto my toes, I sucked in nothing, air gone, a vacuum. As I slumped to the floor, gasping, he pointed down at me.

"Don't you ever touch her again!"

The room faded to black.

I came to on the kitchen floor, flat on my back, alone, gulping air. My head burned, a big bump rising, raw and pulpy to the touch. My middle hurt, but oddly. Like it had been dented, knocked out of kilter. The overhead light twirled in circles. I closed my eyes and flopped over, pushing up onto my hands and knees. The turn made my gorge rise, and I puked, splattering the linoleum, then stayed there, panting. I hadn't meant to hit her, but I didn't see how close she was, how easily I could hurt her. So intent on the game, on my own little world.

Grasping the table leg, then the top, I hauled myself up but couldn't straighten. My hand fell on a dishtowel which I grabbed. Bent halfway, hands on knees, I wiped my mouth, then dropped the towel on the mess. *What if he sees that? What if he comes back?* A staggered trill of adrenaline drove me up off my knees. Holding my stomach, I wobbled out into the dining room. Thankfully, empty.

"It'll be okay, sweetie." In the other room, my father was back to being Daddy again, pleading at Piper. She'd cry a few seconds, stop to hiccup, then wail again. I'd done that. I'd made her cry.

Shuffling up the back stairs to my room, I crawled into bed, curling into a ball. I pulled the blanket over my head, covered everything, playing dead; but I couldn't hide my shaking, an uncontrollable chill. The game leaked up from the room below. All I'd cared about, that goddamned game.

Muffled talk. Dad, Dad again, imploring. Piper whimpering.

Mom came in and sat on the bed, moaning when she noticed my head.

"Walker, honey, what did you do?"

"It wasn't on purpose," I said, crying now.

"Okay, okay," she said, her hand on my cheek. "I know." But did she? Or was she only doing her job, being a mom, dispensing comfort.

She never showed up until afterwards. But who could blame her? She was a tiny woman, not quite five feet, and my father towered over her.

"I threw up in the kitchen. If he sees it—"

"It's all right. I'll take care of it. You just settle down, and I'll get a bandage for that bump." She raised her eyes from mine, examining my head. It was wet up there. Blood on my fingers. She disappeared for a minute, then came back with gauze and a wrap. Her hands warmed my forehead as she wiped the blood, then applied the gauze and wound the wrap. A musky intimacy made me take a deep breath, trying to capture all of it. She tucked in the end and kissed the top of my head, then left the room. Her warmth, her scent, and any chance that she believed me left with her.

The next morning, I stayed in my room until Dad backed his Ambassador out of the driveway. The bathroom leak was fixed. The dining room chairs, straightened. My head throbbed as I surveyed the scene—or the lack of it. Like nothing had happened. Mom drifted behind me with the laundry basket. She put it down and adjusted the bandage on my head, letting her hand alight on my shoulder, a nervous sparrow, hopping twice before flying off. Then she picked up the basket and hurried downstairs to start a wash.

In the kitchen, the only smell was a whiff of ammonia. Piper sat, eating cereal at the table, taking no notice of me until I sat down across from her with my own bowl of cereal. When she looked up at me, her eyes went wide, her hand to her mouth, but not to cover the three black stitches in her fat lip.

"Did Daddy do that?" She put her hand to her forehead, like it was her own injury.

"Yes," I said, a little too loud.

"But you'll be okay, right?"

I filled my spoon with cornflakes and glared back at her. She hardened, her eyes narrowing.

"Well, I *won't* be okay. Daddy says I'll have a scar!"

A *scar*? "I'm sorry, Piper. I didn't mean to hurt you."

"Now, *everybody* will laugh, and it's *all your fault*!"

The sparks in her accusation stood the hair up on my arms, as if her "Daddy!" alarm had gone off, again. I rose, weak-kneed, my vision tunneling, and left the room.

When I ran into Kurt at our lockers at school, he said, "Now that's one way to get a girl's attention," pointing to the bandage. "Oh, my Walker snookums, did the poor, wittle boy get himself an ouchy?" He baby talked, patting my head.

I mumbled something about falling off a ladder helping my father paint.

"Good thing he was there to fix you up."

I smiled. All day, I kept seeing those three black stitches, Piper's fat lip, the scar it would become. Nobody would see mine. Nobody ever saw mine.

Of course, kids did tease Piper. After our first winter in Belford turned to spring, after the stitches were removed, the scar resolved into the blister it would remain for the rest of her life, like a kernel of white rice stuck to her lip. Teachers called out Piper's tormentors for their snickering comments in class, "Big Mouth" and "Fatty Lips," promising punishment; but kids still found ways to haunt her. They'd stick anonymous notes in her locker. Groups would follow and taunt her after school so that she often ran all the way home. Piper tearfully reported these tortures to my father who in turn glared at me. But it didn't stop there. It got so if I did anything she didn't like, anything at all, it set off her "Daddy!" alarm.

If my radio was too loud.

"Daddy!" And he'd rip the thing out of the wall, a right hook that connected with my pride if not with my chin.

If I hogged the couch.

"Daddy!" And he'd drag me up and shove me down into a tiny corner of the couch, a berth deep in the steerage of that vessel, causing me to abandon ship altogether and retreat upstairs.

If I took the last piece of cake.

"Daddy!" and it was another cat-and-mouse chase around the house, chairs tipped over, punches thrown, another night I had to crawl up the backstairs and hide under the covers. His words, "selfish little bastard," echoed, while I tried to tell myself I was safe now, it was over.

That's the way it was for the next year and a half: *Mouse hole. Cozy couch. Tiny TV.*

After any one of these incidents, my mother might steal up to my room, sit next to me on the bed while I hid my tears. She'd put her arms around me, shushing me, whisper she was so sorry, he'd gone too far, he was having a hard time at work, he didn't mean to take it out on me.

"Why do you let him?" I'd say, one way or another.

Then, she'd cry, her whispered words lengthening into keening wails. "Because he won't listen to me." My arms ended up around her, me shushing her so he wouldn't come in.

Her visits did nothing to stop his attacks on Piper's behalf or to make me feel any less guilty for them, the bellowing force of Dad's oaths overwriting Mom's meek rebuttals and making me wonder: Was the kazoo no accident? Was some hate-filled cancer eroding my soul?

Ten

Over the course of those years, I talked Kurt into inviting me over to his house whenever possible, hoping to find escape from this cycle, but whenever I was there, it was something else I found.

Like that day we'd had a warm spell, snow melting enough that, after we shoveled off his driveway, we could shoot hoops without freezing. Pops Swanson drove up in his Chevy Camaro and rather than slog into the house like my father might have after a long day at the plant, Pops took off his suit coat, loosened his tie and asked for the ball. We played two-on-one, us against him. It astonished me, how father and son battled and bumped, Pops snatching at balls, fouling flagrantly and flinging the ball at the hoop. But Kurt didn't get mad. He laughed, backing into his dad repeatedly until he sent him sprawling onto the damp pavement.

"You're going to regret that," Pops said as he got up, wagging his finger playfully at Kurt. He sprang into action, snatching the ball back. After his dad scored, Kurt passed the ball into me, but it bounced off my chest and out of bounds. A fascinated spectator, I had forgotten I was even in the game, and from the way Pops grabbed the ball and faced off against his son again, it was clear I wasn't.

Despite this glaring difference in our home lives, Kurt and I were kindred spirits in at least one respect—our isolation, though Kurt's was more narrowly defined. He wanted a girl.

"If I had a girl," he often said, "I wouldn't care about all the other crap I get."

When our junior year began, he finally found one.

"Our problem," he said the first week of school as we dug into our lockers, "is we keep mooning over girls our own age." He nodded across the hall at two pretty freshmen eyeing us from their lockers.

"Aren't they kind of young?"

"They don't think so," Kurt said. The girls did seem to advertise their availability with the thigh-high skirts and tight tops they always wore.

After last bell, Kurt sauntered from our lockers over to theirs, leaning against them, arms crossed.

"You two always ride that stinky old bus that takes forever to get you home. Why don't you ride with us instead? I got a car."

They giggled at one another, whispering as they looked us over, then nodded their assent. They introduced themselves as Gayle and Patty, and a few minutes later the four of us piled into Kurt's Impala, Patty in front with Kurt, Gayle in back with me. That's all it seemed to take, getting them into the car, letting them run their hands along the leather seats, the chrome detailing on the door panels. Before I could stop him, Kurt had lit up a joint, but rather than being put off by this, the girls shivered with excitement and perhaps a flicker of fear, as if they'd hoped high school might be like this, but now they weren't so sure.

They coughed and gagged as they took turns. Kurt coached them to hold it in as they waved the smoke away, laughing at the ordeal, such pain for what pleasure, they clearly weren't sure. It made them silly and chatty, and we soon learned Gayle's mom ran a hair salon and Patty's dad handled the books for the Woolworth's on Main Street. They asked a lot of questions, which seemed like a good sign. The less they'd heard about us from others, the better.

"Your dad is Pops Swanson?" Patty marveled when Kurt started in—always leading with his 'famous' father. "The guy in the car commercials?" The girls went on and on about Swanson Motors, how big it was, how many cars he had, how they loved the red Stingray you could see spinning in circles through the showroom window.

"And where does your Dad work?" Gayle asked, expectantly, as if I could top Kurt. I mumbled something about AMC.

"Oh," Gayle said, sitting back. "Yeah, my dad works there, too. In the paint department."

"No, no, no," Kurt put in, chuckling, shaking his head. "Walker's father is a doctor. He takes care of all those workers, every one of them."

"Oh. Really?" Gayle sat up.

"They live in that big house on the river, the brick one."

"You live *there*?" Patty said, turned around in her seat, jaw dropped.

"That place is huge!" Gayle added. "It must be gorgeous inside."

I opened my mouth to speak, the light on me now, my chance to shine, but I could only exhale and glare at the back of Kurt's head. What could I say?

"Walker doesn't like to boast." Kurt gave me this furrow-browed look through the rear-view mirror like I was totally blowing it.

"Hey," Kurt said. "You guys like to bowl?"

"Bowling?" Patty frowned. So square.

"Or would your parents let you come out with us if you told them we were going bowling?" Kurt twiddled the joint, suggestively.

They guffawed at this, and after another whispered conference over the seat back, Gayle said, "Bowling is probably the only thing they might let us do with boys like you." She and Patty laughed.

Gayle and Patty seemed to like us, sure—for all the wrong reasons. But it was a start, and I reasoned, once Gayle got to know me better, maybe it could turn into something real. I had to admit, it felt good to walk with her between classes, to be seen with a pretty girl at my elbow—maybe not as pretty as Patty, with her button nose, but Gayle was so shapely, it was easy to forget she was only fourteen. Everyone remarked about her hair, which her mom had styled to look like Sandra Dee's in all those old beach party movies. And so I went along with Kurt's plan, which quickly became the blueprint for all our dates.

Patty insisted we stop at Rambler Lanes where she grabbed a Coke at the snack counter. That way she could still tell her mom she had fun at the bowling alley. Patty didn't like to lie. Then we drove out into the country, seeking a rumored country lane we'd never been to. After a few miles, we turned off on a dirt road and found amidst a copse of willows a half-dozen cars parked and filled with couples, beer bottles in the ditch along with empty condoms and rolling papers. We took our cues from the surrounding cars, heads pressed together, disappearing downward below seat backs. Awkward first kisses, tentative touches—all amidst giggling and a haze of pot smoke.

"Are you new at this?" Gayle asked, running the tip of her index finger down my lips. I nodded.

"Me, too." She whispered, eyes dazzlingly conspiratorial.

"Me, three." Patty, from somewhere in the front seat.

"Kurt, too?" Gayle asked.

Silence.

"Come on, Kurt," I said.

"It's okay," Patty said. "He doesn't have to say it out loud."

The next time out, we stopped for pompoms, popcorn or soft drinks at the Belford High football game, as promised to parents, then left at halftime to take part for the very first time in Belford's most popular teen activity—cruising down Main Street. Sure, we'd driven the strip before, but not at half speed, the windows open, greeting everyone driving the same way. That was cruising, but you didn't do it without girls in your car. Only losers did that. So to do it, at long last, with two girls like Patty and Gayle, the way they waved out the windows and people waved back, was like riding in a parade with beauty queens. After that first time out, Kurt was hooked, and cruising became the highlight of every double date. Until it wasn't.

The third or fourth time out, midway through the football season, the girls stopped waving because people stopped waving in return, the novelty of who we were and who we were with having worn off.

"We gotta do something," Kurt said, driving me to school the next day. He seemed genuinely worried.

"About what?"

"They're losing interest."

"The girls? They love being out with us."

"Not just the girls. Everyone."

I told him to forget about it. Like there was any way to make yourselves new again, especially with people who weren't friendly toward you to begin with.

Kurt found a way. The following Friday night, another 'bowling' date, I waited on the front porch for Kurt to pick me up when this Monster truck pulled into my driveway. A modified Ford pick-up, the truck's body, splashed with fiery flame decals, stood a good two feet off the ground. Its tires were half-again normal size, its engine rumbling hungrily, the muffler removed.

Kurt jumped down out of the truck and slapped the hood.

"What do you think?"

"Where'd you get that?"

"From my dad's lot. He said I could borrow it. It even has a back seat."

"Christ, Kurt." I had to marvel at his ambition.

"My friend," he said, "we are about to become the cruising kings of Belford, Illinois!"

And we did. Not only because that Monster truck attracted so much attention that night, turning Gayle and Patty back into waving beauty queens, but because every time we went cruising after that, Kurt borrowed a different vehicle from his dad's lot.

"As long as they come back in the same shape," Pops had made him promise. It was worth the hassle, no pot smoking inside, cleaning up after every date, a massive Chevy Suburban one night, a funereal black Buick the next. Convertibles were best—if Kurt could get his hands on one—the better to display our girls' delight to all our fellow cruisers, to be admired not only for our cars but our cleverness, too. After a while, cruisers sought us out no matter what we drove on those Friday and Saturday nights. We were a game to be won, a question to be answered: What will they be driving tonight? A hearse? A Jeep? A Volkswagen Bug? Spotting us, they'd pull U-turns, motor up alongside and dock with us like rockets synchronized and soaring above the earth, all to pay homage, to reiterate their admiration with a thumbs up, a Budweiser toast, a Doobie salute: The Cruising Kings had done it again!

While nights at home with my dad and Piper got better, only because I hid out in my room most of the time, those girls and Kurt's quirky cars turned the tide for the two of us all through my senior year, rewarding us with high fives in the high school's hallways, squashing the Mexicano insults. For a while, we were actually *cool*—at least, until the summer before college started, when disaster struck and Kurt and I lost our driving privileges.

It happened the weekend after graduation, when Kurt and I told our parents we were going camping. It wasn't exactly a lie. We just didn't point out that, instead of driving west to Galena where they assumed we were going, we were headed north to Wisconsin where it was legal for eighteen-year-olds to drink and where Belford graduates were converging for a celebration. Our destination was the Wisconsin

Dells, a tourist trap known for its gorge and its paddle-boat rides up the Wisconsin River, but favored by Illinois teens in particular for its many drinking establishments.

We had a great time, bumping in to our new Belford cruising buddies, bowling, shooting pool, flirting with girls from Chicago, bellying up to bars and ordering whole pitchers like real men, all grown up. About the best time Kurt and I ever had together, palling around, slapping each other's backs, getting sloshed and not caring who saw us, no parents to worry about. Totally free. A joyous preview of life once we turned twenty-one.

But that all changed when, the following day, we crossed the magical state line on the way back home. We were under-aged again, and us with a bottle of cheap wine, a six pack in the back seat. The thing is, I knew they were there, those bottles and cans, daring the world to stop us. I knew and I didn't care. The freedom the day before had emboldened me, the flirtation with adulthood giving me foolish courage. What I didn't know about was the broken tail light that gave the state trooper a reason to pull us over. What I couldn't stop was the sweep of his flashlight around the Impala's interior, glinting off a can.

Calling home from the police station, I was certain my father would go nuts again, and he was angry, especially about my omitting certain details of our trip.

"You lied to me," he said during the car ride home. "And I thought you'd grown out of that nonsense." Those old arguments with Piper, him always believing her word over mine.

But he didn't hit me. Maybe it was because that particular night he was sober. Or that I'd had a growth spurt of eight inches and was nearly as tall as him. Or because I was a complete wreck, unwilling to get out of the car, flinching in terror when he reached in for my arm, so afraid of what he'd do, what he'd say, all his assertions now proven true—what a loser I was, what a bum.

He didn't say a thing other than to glower at me uncertainly, unable to fathom what I'd become, how to deal with me any more.

That was the night I realized he hadn't hit me in a while and, what was worse, that he didn't need to anymore. That steely look alone was enough to freeze me solid, my gut clenched, my breath barely squeezing out, I was so tight. The damage had been done.

As punishment, our fathers took away our cars, banished us from our mobile kingdom. For the girls, it was kinda cool having 'bad boys' for boyfriends, and it wasn't like we were wanton criminals. But the Cruising Kings had been dethroned. We couldn't drive anywhere, let alone up and down Main Street. Not out to that country lane hangout amidst the willows, or to the movies at the Belford Drive-In or to the A&W carport—to any of the places we used to smoke and drink, getting loose, silly and sexy. All that summer, our double dates convened at Kurt's house or mine under our parents' watchful eyes, or when we were desperate to get away from home, at McDonald's or at the park.

Sitting with our girls at those picnic or restaurant tables, we took each other in, unimpaired by intoxicants and without the privacy we were so used to. As I listened unlubricated to Gayle and Patty giggle over the latest gossip from the hair salon, or to the dirty jokes Kurt had heard at the car lot, something cooled in me. I turned quiet and shy again, reduced to the kid I was when we first moved to Belford, listening at the edges. But I realized that no one ever laughed at Kurt's jokes because—unless you were drunk or stoned—he wasn't all that funny.

Then I went away to college and discovered I didn't have to fit in to fit in. It made coming home the following summer that much harder—and starting that summer job, harder still.

Eleven

The nurse sticks her head in the door. Piper is on the reception desk phone, she tells me. I put the laptop aside and trail her down the hall. A clanging makes her rush on ahead of me, pointing to a handset off the hook on the counter before she dashes into another room, the commotion in there, alarms chiming. My reporter's instinct is to follow, but I don't. The clock above the desk catches my eye. Is it really 1:30 in the morning?

I pick up the phone, my eye on that room.

"What's going on? What's all that noise?" Piper frantic.

"Nothing. Another patient down the hall. I'm at the reception desk." Staff run in and out of that room, voices raised, instructions given, equipment beeping, someone else's tragedy.

"Oh, thank god!" Piper exhales. "About gave me a heart attack." She catches her breath. "So how is he?"

"The same."

"No change?"

"Nope. The same. He's still, you know—" She wants more, but after what I've been writing, particularly about her, I'm not feeling very chatty.

"I know."

The noisy room has gone quiet. My nurse stands outside it, her hand over her mouth as she looks into the room, watching. Chilled, I turn around and face the other way.

"You okay?" Piper asks. "Did I wake you up? You sound funny."

"I'm fine. I'm—" I search for the right word. "I've been writing."

"Working?" She bristles. "While he's lying there—"

"Not working." How much should I say? "I'm writing about him."

"Oh," she says. "Not one of those—" She falters. "I mean. I don't care what the doctor says. It's too early to be thinking about—"

"Not one of those."

"Well, then what?"

"If you must know, I'm writing about what happened between him and me. Things we never discussed."

"Hmm," she says. "Well, good luck with that. I'm going back to bed."

Good luck with that. Just like her.

"Things you and I never talk about, either."

I switch the phone from one ear to the other. She sighs, her exhalation scraping through the mouth piece.

"Now is not the time, Walker."

"Now may be the only time. I may never have this chance again."

"Well, I don't want to hear about it. It's between you and him."

"Is it? Then why does it always seem like you are between me and him."

"He's dying, Walker."

That word, the first time anyone has broached the possibility, shakes me. She inhales so deeply, a quavering. Something melts in me. This isn't that nasty little girl. She's taken care of him all these years.

"Look, I'm sorry," I say, slumping against the counter, chastened. "I didn't mean to take this out on you."

"It's okay. Everyone's on edge. So—you're sure he's the same?"

"Still…whatever. The same."

"You'll call if anything changes?"

"Absolutely. I'll call."

"Okay, then. I'll see you in a few hours."

"Good night."

Twelve

Home from my first day of that summer job on the AMC loading dock, I took a long shower, the hot water massaging my aching back. I changed into cut-offs, a clean t-shirt and sandals, and climbed down the back stairway to set the table. It was weird, picking silver spoons, forks and knives from their shaped slots in the velvet-lined mahogany chest, my tortured fingers fumbling to work. Placemat first, folded napkin, salad and dinner fork to the left, knife and spoon to the right—assembly line steps to be repeated, mercifully, only four times.

In the basement beneath me, Piper played the piano. She had started lessons two years before and wasn't bad but preferred to make her own music, which meant she frequently stumbled, experimenting, stopping, starting, working the same riff over and over. It took forever to sound like real music, and tonight it was almost as painful as those goddamned seat frames. One phrase would sound out easy, but the next would snicker "Fuck you, kid. Just try getting me out." And Piper would hit this chord or that, sharp then flat, unable to figure it out. Was this whole day designed to drive me crazy?

Mom appeared, carrying a pitcher of lemonade she'd mixed up in the kitchen. In the late afternoon sun, her outline materialized through the sheer fabric of her blue *muumuu*, one of those colorful bag-like shifts she bought when we were in the Philippines.

I was about to tell her how hard my job was when Dad came thunking down the stairs in his usual summer attire, white linen pants and a Hawaiian shirt—big yellow flowers and Toucans—clothes he'd also picked up in the Philippines. God forbid Mom and Dad dress like normal parents. He made a beeline for the basement door through which my sister's piano playing continued to hammer, blasting when he opened it.

"Piper, sweetie—" A long-suffering, pleading tone. The piano stopped. "Do you have to do that right now? Dinner's almost ready. Why don't you come up?"

"Okay," she sang up the stairs. "In a minute."

As soon as the door swung shut, the piano started up again.

"Kid's going to drive me nuts with that thing," he mumbled, appearing in the doorway. "Why does she have to practice at this time of night?"

"You bought it for her," Mom said, filling glasses.

He squinted at the table, shading his eyes against the light that reflected up from the river and through the bay window. It hit the crystal chandelier and danced silver coins all around the room.

"Headache's bad enough without that racket." He headed to the front porch where it was his habit after work to gather up the evening paper, scan the headlines and, no doubt tonight, escape his daughter's noise. Of course, if I'd turned up my stereo after he'd told me to turn it down, he'd have been all over me.

"Piper's not even supposed to be here tonight," Mom murmured as she filled the glass in front of me. Her fine hair circled back into a bun, like a small, yellow onion.

"Why not?"

"Monday night is swim team practice at the Y. But something happened last week in the locker room she won't tell me about. She hasn't been out of the house since. Skipped her Girl Scout meeting last Thursday, and she won't listen to me." She watched me fold a napkin at the last place setting. "Do you think maybe you could talk to her?"

"Me?"

Not that things between us were as bad as before. In fact a couple of years back, when graduating to Belford Junior High produced no more friends for her than Lincoln Elementary, Piper had softened towards me somehow, as if her desperation for company had silenced her "Daddy" alarm—muted, but still in good working order, I was certain.

"What do you want me to say?"

"I don't know, Walker. Don't girls tell their brothers things they won't tell their mothers?"

I sighed. "I'll go get her."

"Thanks," Mom said, her hand on my elbow.

I tromped downstairs, the door swinging shut behind me. The piano stopped.

"I'm coming, I'm coming." Piper appeared at the bottom of the stairs. "Oh, it's only you."

"Yeah, um, but wait up." I lean against the stairwell wall, feet on two different steps. "Mom says you're supposed to be at the Y tonight? What gives?"

She shrugged.

"Don't you like swimming anymore?"

"I do." She kicked the wall with her sneaker. "I just didn't feel like it."

She'd probably said something, pissed someone off again. After two awful years in Belford, Dad had convinced her to join the swim team and then the girl scouts, explaining how many friends he'd made joining polo teams and sailing crews. Piper went, collected swimming trophies and covered her green scouting sash with achievement badges, shoulder to waist. Unfortunately, they didn't offer one for making friends.

"Piper." I raised an eyebrow at her.

"What do you care? You're never here anymore."

"I've been at school. So what happened at the Y?"

She shrugged. "It's none of your beeswax."

"Fine," I said. "I was only trying to help."

"Well then, get out of the way so I can go eat."

When we came into the dining room, Dad stood at the head of the table, carving. Piper and I sat down and watched him work. I was still seeing assembly lines: chicken from the platter in front, dumplings from the dish on his left; broccoli, from his right.

Across the table, my sister fidgeted. She hated dinner time. But clearly something else was wrong. I regarded her carefully.

She had changed, even since spring break. Grown. Slimmed down. Baby fat had disappeared, replaced by real cheekbones. Her nose had streamlined and straightened. When she caught me looking at her, she returned it with a bulgy-eyed ferocity. I turned away, that old electric chill tasering me.

Dad handed her a plate, which she put down, going into her usual routine. She'd take up her fork and knife and delicately dab at the food, rearranging it, her pretense at eating.

What was under that t-shirt? Was that a bra?

My face went hot. She'd never worn a bra. Was that why they had teased her? I peeked again. Not much need for it, yet.

Piper wrinkled her brows at me, probably wondering why I'd gone red.

Of course, you didn't need breasts to have boys gawking at you. Look at Kurt's girlfriend, Patty. She was pretty flat, but boys liked her—that perfect nose, those dimples, that smooth complexion, those blue eyes. But they weren't in the same league, were they?

I kept my eyes off Piper now, certain she'd figure out what I was thinking.

"Mrs. Wolf called this afternoon," Mom said.

"Yeah?" Dad stabbed a chicken breast with his silver serving fork. "About what?"

"Some of her heirloom tomatoes went missing last night."

"Goddamn wetbacks!" Dad barked.

We all froze. He'd never used that word, not with us, anyway. The day before, Mom had mentioned that someone had been stealing from people's backyard gardens up and down along the river, someone with a boat, but I hadn't given it much thought.

"Well, that's what they are!" He glared.

"They have work visas."

"To pick peas and corn. To stay in their camps. Not to move into town, overrun our neighborhoods, take jobs you kids could be doing, bussing tables and bagging groceries. Not to steal from our gardens."

"Now, Michael," Mom began. "No one knows who did it."

"Scavengers, is what they are."

"You're exaggerating."

"Am I? All those bleeding heart liberals keep saying those people are trying to make a living like everyone else, but do they pay taxes? Do they pay for the roads they drive on? The army that protects us? The schools that educate their children? Emergency room visits? No! I pay for that. And you pay for that!" He pointed at me. "It's snatched right out of your paycheck. And they? They contribute nothing because they get paid cash under the table."

"Doing jobs nobody else wants." Mom's little comments surprised me, how they slipped out, a leak in her fear of Dad she couldn't plug.

Meanwhile, Piper watched the debate, her head ping ponging back and forth, mouth open, eyes widening. It was clear who she rooted for.

"They're parasites. And if I catch one of them out there, I'll have them arrested! Mark my words."

Piper's eyes dazzled.

"How can you begrudge people a few fruits and vegetables when they're simply trying to survive," Mom said. "Make homes for themselves."

"You call those shacks across the river homes?" He waited for her to answer.

"As much as this house is to us."

She kept on eating while he stared at her, a challenge I couldn't quite decipher. Somehow, my Mom had taken a stance, daring him despite herself.

"And what's that supposed to mean?" Dad asked, his voice tight and pinching. "You have a problem with this house?"

"Of course not." She flicked at her broccoli with her fork. "I love this house." That off-kilter incisor of hers was red with lipstick again. "You've done beautiful things with it. And I love this yard, the orchard and the river. It's lovely. I couldn't ask for more."

"Sure you do," he grunted. "All the money we've poured down this hole. That stinking foundry. The slum upstream. Thieves in our gardens. It's idyllic. A goddamned paradise."

He sat and attacked his chicken, fork and knife digging at the porcelain plate as he cut, nails on a blackboard. If he hated the place so much, why the hell were we here?

"Aren't you in a mood tonight," Mom said. "Something happen at work?"

"Not at the table," he grumbled.

Not at the table. How often had I heard that one.

For a long while only the silverware clinked, the crystal water glasses pinged.

"Speaking of work—" Dad focused on me now. "How'd it go today?"

Christ. I fumbled for words. "Um—"

Piper raised her eyebrows at me, joining the inquisition.

"It was—hard," I managed, stabbing a chunk of chicken.

"No one ever said factory work was fun. But someone has to do it. *People trying to make a living.*" He dragged it out, drawing Mom's attention, then he turned back to me. "Anyway, they start new guys on the loading dock for a reason. Doesn't require much training, and it helps to weed out the workers from the shirkers before they can join the union and get locked in."

The workers from the shirkers? Some management mantra bullshit.

"But you survived," he continued. "And now, you see my point, right? Lucky for you, it's only a summer job."

"What I mean is, I don't think I'm built for that kind of work, you know, physically."

"You'd be surprised how many new guys come to the infirmary on their first day, complaining. Some don't make it through a shift. But you did."

Was that a smile? Nodding approval?

For one second, an absurd warmth welled up in me, a tiny glow of pride, but it was such a little turd. Big deal. I'd survived a day in an auto plant.

"And how was whatshisname? Your girl's father?"

"Norm?" I sneaked a peek at Piper. She mouthed 'your girl?' at me, eyes raised in puzzlement. I had told her we'd broken up, but not that I hadn't told Dad. I shook my head at her.

"Right," Dad said, cutting food. "What's he got you doing? Is he helping you out?"

"I'm unloading railroad cars. Seat frames. Even Norm had a tough time with it. That bad hip of his."

"Yeah, well. Norm made a deal with the devil, taking that job against doctor's orders. Not much we can do if that hip bothers him."

"He's applied for this forklift job so he doesn't have to lift and stand anymore."

"Hm." He nodded, digging at his plate. Was he avoiding my glance?

"Any chance you can say anything to help him get it?"

He sawed at his chicken.

"I can say something, but they usually don't consult me on those matters." He leaned toward Piper and inspected her plate.

"Try a little of the chicken, sweetie. Your mother makes a mean chicken and dumplings." He smiled at Mom, who smiled back.

"You know I don't like chicken, Daddy," Piper whispered, that little girl's voice. She stopped reorganizing her food and stared at it, no point to her pretense now.

Dad grinned at her, holding his knife and fork still, stalemated. When I was little, he used to make me sit at the table all evening until I ate my peas, but he couldn't push Piper to take a single bite of anything.

"You're not eating enough, kiddo. Don't want you getting sick now, do we?"

A shrug. "I eat." After dinner, she would cook herself up a bowl of rice like she did every night these days.

We ate in silence. After awhile, Mom rose and said, "I've got a surprise for Walker. His favorite dessert to celebrate his first day of work." She took our plates and a minute later returned from the kitchen with a massive strawberry shortcake, piled high with whipped cream and the fat red berries that could only come from our garden. I thanked her as she pecked me on the cheek and placed the confection in front of Dad to dole out.

Dessert was great, but what I kept chewing on was those seat frames. I couldn't let it go.

"The thing is," I tried again, "those seat frames they got me doing?" I caught my father's eye. "They come all tangled up. They may be light, but they're hard to get out. Seems like the toughest job on the dock." And then I pushed further. "Like maybe they gave it to me on purpose."

"What do you mean, on purpose?" Dad said, stabbing a fat berry.

"Well, maybe because of who I am." I peeked at him.

"Who you are." He straightened, lowering his fists to the table, fork and knife enclosed. "You mean, because you're my son?"

"Maybe," I said, a shrug. I dug through my dessert.

"Because of something I did?" He bristled. I should have known he'd react that way. But wasn't this exactly the kind of pitiless bluster that pissed people off, explained why Norm or Kelly or all of them would take it out on me?

"The game starts in a few minutes," Mom said. "Shouldn't we finish up?"

"I'm only wondering—" I ignored her, "if maybe you could talk to someone?"

"You know," he said, twiddling his fork at me. "You're starting to take after Frazier, always looking for the easy way out."

"Michael—" Mom started.

"I'm serious," he said, thrusting his head forward to shut her up. Then he turned his entire body in his seat to face me. "Is that your approach to life? Run away every time the going gets tough?"

"Dad—" Frazier was not a coward, but I could still feel my face going hot at the comparison, like there might be some truth in his words.

"You want to know what I was doing at your age?"

Christ. Here it comes.

"I'd just finished med school, wasn't much older than you, when they dumped me on a bloody beach on a tropical island in the middle of the Pacific Ocean—"

Not this story again. Seven men assigned to help him set up a treatment tent, but only five made it through the bullets and bombs across the sand to the trees. Blah, blah, blah. I knew it by heart. So did Piper, the way she cocked her chin at me, blaming me for setting him off. Even Mom darted her eyes at me, accusing.

"I only made it because a man died shielding me as we ran. Okay, five men. Still possible to get the job done. Unless, as we're working, we're being picked off by snipers in the trees, one by one, dismembered, killed—"

"Michael!" Mom glared at him from across the table. "That's hardly the same thing."

"You didn't see me running away, I can tell you. Lives depended on me. Lives, Walker." He sat forward again and stabbed a strawberry. "And you want me to *talk* to somebody—"

Piper gave me a sad grimace, shaking her head. Much as I loved those berries, I couldn't eat anymore, my hunger gone, replaced by that old tension, that old dread. Even breathing was hard, as if I was in a vacuum, squeezing my body up tight, clenched, braced for the blow that might come if I said one more word.

Thirteen

Always looking for the easy way out. Maybe Dad was right. Maybe I do that. At work, I'm the last to jump into the fray of a breaking news story—riots, revolution, war stories, preferring to be in the background.

Those few months I was stationed in Baghdad helped me understand. Yes, Dad, I've got a few war stories of my own. Mostly, I filed pieces from the relative safety of the Green Zone, but once when a field reporter about to go out on a combat patrol got sick, the bureau asked me to take his place.

Sitting in our armored vehicle, I spent hours getting roasted and tossed around, a cherry tomato in a stew of brown cammies, what the infantry called their camouflage uniforms. Our caravan of three Humvees banged around narrow, dusty winding streets going at a snail's pace. It was a parade that every person we passed—people we were there to protect, what little I could see of them—regarded with fear and hostility. How I sweated in that bullet-proof vest, that oversized helmet rattling my skull, and not only because of the heat.

Then, something exploded under our Humvee on an exposed bridge over the Tigris. I was sure I was a dead man, but once the guys got out, rifles raised and looking for targets, one of them announced it was only a blown tire. No sooner had I relaxed than a car pulled over, and a bearded man stepped out in an ankle-length white *thawb*, the black cord of an *agal* keeping the hoodlike *keffiyeh* in place on his head. My guys waved their guns at him, screaming at him to "get the fuck back" in his car, firing a warning shot to frighten him away. He could have been anybody, concealing anything beneath those robes. It was the longest thirty minutes of my life while they jacked up the truck and replaced the tire. And yet, nothing really happened. It was that atmosphere, so rife with suspicion, the bursting potential for danger gassing us into paranoia.

On the way back to base, my companions said the man had offered to help and was probably harmless. But each of them had a story about a soldier who'd stopped to help a crying child or a mother with a broken baby carriage or a grandpa whose wheelchair got stuck in a pothole—soldiers blown to bits for having heart.

Therapists have told me it's difficult for some veterans to leave these hard-hearted lessons behind and not incorporate them into their child-rearing reasoning, a 'tough love' ethos that cripples children as much as war cripples their fathers.

"What do they say about war?" one doctor asked me. "Interminable boredom punctuated by moments of terror? Your childhood in a nutshell."

It's so easy to blame Dad for everything. Some of the blame for what happened that summer, that very week, has to land squarely on my shoulders, doesn't it?

A glance at my father in his bed ratchets up the volume on those issues, the same way it always does whenever I think about him—the tension headaches I get, the gurgling in my gut.

I felt the same way after dinner that night, unwilling to let it go, especially watching the Cubs game a few minutes later. The Cubs, not the White Sox.

Fourteen

The Cubbies were up two-zip in the top of the ninth, Reuschel was throwing a two-hitter, and Dad was stoked, one hand gripping the leather armrest of his Barcalounger, while the other swirled a rum and Coke. On the couch, Mom and Piper had their heads together, working on a crossword puzzle.

"How can a man that big pitch that well?" Dad asked. "Must be 275, 300 and what, six-five?"

He may have forgotten our little set-to at the dinner table, but I hadn't. His temper could brew up like a storm out of nowhere, a crackling downpour that blew out in minutes, or it could rain and thunder all day. It was hard to predict.

Earlier, when Piper, Mom and I were doing the dishes, Mom had apologized for his outburst, explaining that he'd been having a difficult time at work. It was his job to decide who the company paid to go out on sick leave, and due to a wave of inexplicable injuries, everyone was complaining. Management hassled him every time he approved a claim, and workers protested every time he rejected one. Nobody was happy, she said, least of all him.

Now that I'd struggled through one day there myself, I was inclined to sympathize with Norm and the other workers, even if they were taking out their frustrations on me. Rather than soothe me, Mom's excuses only made me resent Dad's eruption at the table even more, especially his comparison of me to Frazier.

My brother was no coward. He had principles. Maybe he could have found a better way to explain them than by making a surprise visit home, the first we'd heard from him since Christmas break, when he and dad had argued so much. When he came to pick up some winter clothes, he appeared shockingly emaciated as well as drunk or stoned, according to Piper. I don't know. I was over at Kurt's. When asked what was going on and why he was so skinny, he had drunkenly proclaimed that college was establishment brainwashing bullshit, that he hadn't been there in months, and that he was living with friends in Chicago now. As for his appearance, he'd said he'd had a worm, but it was okay because he'd lost his student deferment and received a draft notice, and dropping all those pounds made him fail his induction exam. He'd gotten a 4-F for being underweight.

Good luck fooling Doctor Dad with that bullshit story. Had Frazier forgotten how Dad and his men had starved for months in the jungles of New Guinea when the Japanese cut off their supply routes? His men had wasted away to nothing, skeletons covered with flesh. As if Dad couldn't recognize the true effects of a worm when he saw it.

"That's a black eye to every man who had to go hungry to fight for his country," Dad had said.

So Frazier confessed, saying he'd lost the weight on purpose in order to fail the physical because this war was illegal and immoral, and he wouldn't fight a war he didn't support.

Okay, so maybe he wasn't a conscientious objector, strictly speaking, but he took a stand, and what does my father do? Disowns him on the spot. Maybe not in so many words. Like I say, I wasn't there. Mom told me later how my father went into this "No son of mine" tirade and made Frazier leave, told him he was cutting him off, or tried to. Having dropped out of school, Frazier said, he had a job working at a deli and Dad could spend his tainted military pension elsewhere. After that, Dad wouldn't speak of him, or let us discuss Frazier in his presence.

"Damn!" Dad barked. Lou Brock had blooped a single just beyond Kessinger's outstretched glove.

"It's only a single," I said.

"Until he steals second. You *know* Lou Brock will steal second."

"Where's he going to take it?" Piper asked, as if she didn't know. So gullible about some things, Dad didn't see she was teasing him, and proceeded to explain base running, oblivious to her feigned interest.

At work earlier, shouts had flared up all over the loading dock when the White Sox won their day game. A question occurred to me. One I knew the answer to but wanted to ask anyway, just to see him try to answer it.

"Why don't you watch the Sox?"

"What?" You'd think I had asked why he didn't prefer road kill to sirloin.

"Because the White Sox are bad," Piper said, peering over Mom's shoulder. A day earlier, I might have said the same thing.

"They're no worse than the Cubs," I said.

"Unicorn!" Piper shouted, pointing at the crossword. "A horse with a horn?"

"You grew up on the south side," I continued. "Martin Luther King Drive?"

"Grand Avenue!" Dad snapped.

"That was its name when your father lived there," Mom said.

"It's nothing like the street I grew up on," he added. Like I didn't know what he was really saying.

"But didn't you live near Sox park?" I asked. "What's it called?"

"Comiskey," Mom said, scribbling down a word.

Dad grunted, turning back to the television.

"Growing up," she said, "your father was only interested in horses and boats."

Polo ponies and yachts, she meant. My parents always tried to make light of it, how well-off their families had been.

"How can you walk that guy?" Dad yelled at the TV, flailing his arm. "Load the bases for Reggie Smith. That's just great."

"Your father had no time for baseball," Mom said. "He was always sailing or at that armory down the street."

"Working," he said. "I was a stable boy, grooming horses after games." So he *was* listening.

He'd once told me that after World War One, the military suffered a huge brain drain. With officers leaving in droves, polo became a carrot to attract officer-grade material, especially after a U.S. Army team beat the British in a world championship.

"Polo was as big as baseball in those days," he used to say. Right, Dad.

The game went to commercial while the Cubbies brought in a relief pitcher.

"But you played polo, too, didn't you?" I asked.

"Once in a while. They'd let me borrow a horse, sub in for a chukker."

"A Chukker?" Piper giggled.

"Like an inning. Lasted seven minutes."

"That's how we met, you know," Mom said.

"I love that story. It's like a fairy tale," Piper said, bouncing on her cushion, getting on her knees. "Tell it again."

It was an oft-told tale, but it offered an opening, perhaps a crack in Dad's military armor.

"Yeah," I said. "What happened again?"

"Well," Mom began, "your father joined the National Guard after he got out of medical school."

The National Guard. A chance to immerse yourself in the lifestyle of the rich and polo-playing without a full-time commitment to the regular army.

"They were cavalry," Dad once said, trying to downplay the wealthy class of enlistees the sport attracted. "Like in the movies."

Cavalry? They were there to play polo, Dad. Not Cowboys and Indians.

"And he wangled an assignment as the doctor on duty at the polo games," Mom said. "This was just before the war. And my father played."

Grampa Caspar was unabashedly wealthy. He owned a string of gas stations and was one of the early Henry Fords of motorcycle manufacturing. He bought a horse farm outside Chicago in the late 1920s and was savvy enough not to lose it in the Great Depression.

"My father loved polo, and he often scrimmaged with the 124th Field Artillery team. One day, he got hit by a mallet, gashed him right below the eye." She showed us, drawing a line across her cheek. "Michael patched him up, but Dad's eye swelled, and he couldn't see to drive, so your father drove him home. I was in the parlor, practicing this Brahms piece on the piano, when the front door opened and this young man entered in his service uniform, tall and slender, holding his cap to his chest. You remember, Michael?"

Dad shrugged, chin tilted at the game, a lefty in for the starter, Smith entering the batter's box, grinding his cleats to get a foothold.

"Anyway, I certainly remember," she pronounced.

"Why don't you ever play anymore?" Piper asked her. "The piano?"

My mom pointed at my dad, sticking her tongue out at him like a bratty kid making faces behind someone's back. Then she grinned and shook it off.

"Anyway, your father told my Dad he'd stick around to make sure the wound didn't get infected, but he really stayed so he could talk to me," she said with a nod. "We chatted all evening on the front porch. And the rest is history."

"That's so romantic," Piper said.

"If the farm hadn't been sold after my dad died, we might even have ended up there. Kept a couple of horses."

"Our own horses?" Piper said, pulling on her mother's arm. "I would have loved that. Why didn't we?"

Dad resisted the TV long enough to give Piper a smile.

"That's what your father *thinks* I want," Mom added, waiting for a response. He'd refocused on the television, shifting in the chair. "But I never even liked to ride, being so petite. Those big animals. The fact is, I'm perfectly happy here."

"That makes one of us," Piper grumbled, eyeing Dad, then me.

"Well, I am!" Mom said. "I love it. This house, too. Foundry and all."

My father was cold stone. A TV-watching statue.

"Are you listening?"

"I heard you," he mumbled.

Mom rolled her eyes, shook her head, picked up her crossword book and, with a frustrated flourish, bent the page back, studying it again. Piper joined her, sighing. But she'd made my point.

"You know, Dad," I said, "everyone in the plant listens to the White Sox."

"I'm not surprised," he said, taking a sip from his rum and Coke.

Mom lifted her head, and dropped her hands in her lap, giving him a disapproving frown as he swirled ice for a second. Piper pulled the crossword from her, writing in a word.

"Why?" I asked. My mother turned to frown at me now. I went ahead, anyway. "Why aren't you surprised?"

"Walker—" Mom tilted me a warning look.

Dad sipped his rum, half ice water by now.

"Because they're factory workers and not polo players?"

"Walker, stop." Mom sat up, alert. Piper took notice. Dad hadn't moved.

"You don't like working there very much, do you?" I added. That ember of anger from dinner refused to go out, and I'd hit on some truth. I was certain of it.

Mom didn't take her eyes off me. Piper lowered the crossword and stared at us.

"I mean—" And I shouldn't have said this. "If you hate the plant so much, why do you work there?"

He turned in his chair to regard me.

"Daddy doesn't hate—"

"No, no." Dad raised his hand, warding off Piper. "He's right. It wasn't my first choice. And I might prefer to work elsewhere. But sometimes, you don't get the choices you want, which makes what you do with the choices you have all the more important."

"You didn't have a choice? All those interviews you went on, all those conferences and symposiums, and this was your only choice?"

I wasn't arguing. He'd led us to believe he had plenty of choices,but that he'd chosen the job for the challenge.

He eyed me, gritting his teeth.

"It's getting a little late, isn't it, dear?" Mom stood. He looked at her, then me, then Piper, and at the television, thinking.

"Game's over, anyway," he said. He pushed himself up out of the lounger.

"Is that another thing I'm supposed to learn this summer? How it feels not to have a choice?"

Mom deflated, her disapproval of me clear; but Dad had turned to the TV, ignoring me, discussion over. Mom came and patted him on the arm, taking his hand. She nudged him out of the room. My heart thudded in my chest. I'd pushed back, stood my ground. And I was a little disappointed.

I'd expected push-back, an argument. Sure, he'd had other choices. He must have. Doctors were in demand. He could work anywhere. Couldn't he? I'd never considered it before—*him* before. Him being someone other than the guy who exploded, the guy always in command of everything. But maybe he wasn't. Maybe there were things he couldn't control.

"That sounded plain mean," Piper said, standing up and stretching. "You're just mad about that stupid job."

She headed past me, the basement door creaking. Now that Dad was upstairs and out of earshot, she'd attack the piano to her heart's content.

Maybe I was just mad, but I'd spoken up, talked back to him, learned something I didn't know. Such a meager victory, not worth pointing out. Like winning a foot race with no other runners. Only me, cheering for myself. Pathetic.

Fifteen

A new nurse comes into Dad's hospital room around 3 a.m., a cheerful Asian woman with long black hair in a ponytail. I close my laptop. She offers the occasional, sympathetic smile as she works, a busy, sturdy woman in blue scrubs. She glances at Dad's monitors, tilts his bed up and checks his airways. This woman is so delicate with the electrodes on his chest. Ever so lightly, she tugs on them to ensure the adhesive is holding but without pulling his skin or chest hair. She switches out his IV and feeding bags with great care, as if the slightest bump could awaken him. You'd think Dad was only asleep, that Piper and that doctor were wrong about his chances, that I could give him a poke, and his eyes would pop open, he'd look up, surprised, and sitting bolt upright, say, "Walker? What the hell are you doing here?"

Maybe that's why I'm writing, summoning the past, preferring to grapple with the feisty, energetic guy he *was* rather than with what's to become of him. Of me.

The nurse finishes up, giving the sheet over my dad's chest one final tug, and I'm curious.

"Did anyone tell you my dad's a doctor?"

"I heard," she says, turning to me. "Worked at the automobile factory, too. What an unusual place to be a doctor. That must have been very interesting."

"Yes, it was." *You don't know the half of it.*

After early years filled with polo ponies and yacht clubs, a thirty-year career as a battle-hardened military surgeon, a colonel in the Air Force and a hospital commander, I can see how that barren office, that old house in this factory town, might have explained his menacing moods at home, what he became when he drank. None of those factory workers gave a damn about who he was before AMC, how high he'd risen, how disappointed he was with where he'd ended up. I can see all that now. I couldn't see it then.

I was too young, too angry, still far too bitter about how he used to treat me to have any sympathy for his situation. And I had my own problems. I'd just broken up with my girlfriend. I had a job I hated, the prospect of a long, torturous summer away from a school I was just now learning to love, but only if I could enroll in classes my dad didn't want me to take. After that first day, I was dead tired and ready for bed.

But for others, apparently, the night was still young.

Sixteen

I was about to flick the TV off when, predictably, Reggie Smith banged out his fifteenth of the year, giving the Cards the lead. As he rounded the bases, a scratching came from the side door. I turned to see a face mashed against the glass, eyelids dragged up by fingers, eyeballs rolled up so only the whites shown. I jumped. Kurt Swanson, of course. He guffawed, bobbing, slapping his hand on the frame. He poked his head in, chuckling.

"Got you, didn't I?"

"You're hilarious," I said.

"Parents gone beddy bye?" He checked out the room, quick snaps of his head, blond hair flying. Being weird. Being Kurt.

"Yes, and I'm going to bed, too. I'm beat."

"Nah," he said, stepping inside. "You can't do that. You gotta have a nightcap with me first."

"I have to get up early," I said, though his appearance did perk me up. I'd seen him at the car lot on Saturday, the day after I got back from school. While Fernando did all the work, we'd shot the shit, bitching about my dad handing me a raw deal, making me take that job at the plant.

Kurt grabbed the remote from my hand and switched channels.

"Carson's monologue," he mumbled. "Never miss it."

Kurt sat down on the edge of the couch. Over a button-down shirt and white chinos, he had on that stupid gray flannel suit vest he only wore to impress his girlfriend.

"You see Patty tonight?" I asked.

His eyes were glued to Carson. "She's out in the car."

"Out in the car?"

"I had to scout out the sit-shur-ation first," he intoned, flapping a hand at me to keep quiet.

Carson joked about the New York Cosmos soccer team signing Pelé for $4.7 million, making him the world's highest paid athlete for a sport nobody liked and a team nobody watched. The audience roared, and Kurt let out a guffaw.

"Keep it down," I said. "You going to leave her out there?"

He waved me down again and laughed at another joke. Finally, Carson cut to "a word from our sponsors," and Kurt got up, ready to switch off the TV, but then stopped. Pops Swanson filled the screen, double-breasted suit and all.

"Isn't that last year's Fourth of July commercial?" I asked.

"Last year's?" Kurt chuckled. "That one's like three years old. Pops says it costs too much to make a new one every year. Had me and Fernando out in the lot this morning slapping up the same fraying flags and banners he's used for years. Cheap bastard. So anyway," he switched off the TV, "I'll just grab some brewskies from the car and meet you downstairs?"

"One," I said, but he'd already tossed me the remote and skipped outside.

Down the back hall, I opened the basement door, twanging the long spring. Piper's piano playing boomed. The door snapped shut behind me with a bang. I froze. The piano stopped.

"Walker?" Piper whispered from down below.

"Shhh. I'm listening."

Nothing. No sounds of movement from above. Thank God for that noisy air conditioner in their bedroom.

When I got to the bottom step, Kurt was rapping on the back door.

"Who's that?" Piper asked.

"Kurt."

"Really?" She swiveled around on her piano bench, eyes brightening.

"He's with Patty," I pointed out. Piper slumped. "Go upstairs."

"I'm not going anywhere." She turned back to the piano. "If I don't get this down, I'll forget it by morning."

"Piper!"

She started playing again, softly though, background music.

Kurt came in, hoisting a six of Budweiser right where Piper could see it.

"What are you doing?" I hissed at him, nodding at my sister's back.

"Oh, she won't tell," he said, then edged close so he could whisper. "Just so you know, this wasn't my idea."

What the hell did that mean? Then came pretty Patty, long, blond hair splayed out on the shoulders of her white blouse.

"Hi, stranger," she whispered. *The nightcap was her idea*? Or maybe she was here to give me a hard time for dumping her best friend.

She gave me a quick hug, holding my gaze. It baffled me until she turned to the back door, and I understood. Standing in the shadows outside the spill of the backdoor light was someone else, a girl with bare and shapely but familiar legs: Gayle. She edged into the cone of light. She smiled, her lips quivering, then she teetered, thrusting out a hand for balance. It was her shoes. Platforms. That wasn't like her. Nor was the weird, wavy hairdo or that short, black leather skirt, that sheer, pink spaghetti strap top baring her pale, white shoulders.

"I look silly, don't I?" she said.

"I didn't say that."

"It was a dumb idea." She grabbed the door jamb, bent and unstrapped one platform, then the other. Without those two-inch wedges of wood, she shrank back to normal size, just a high school girl playing dress-up.

"Do you want me to go?"

"No, of course not. Might as well join the crowd."

"Thanks."

As she passed, I winced at her perfume. Like my mom's.

Once she pulled off those shoes, it was as if she'd accepted defeat before she'd begun. I was tempted to grab her, give her a hug, all this for me; but in the brighter light of the rec room, her hair, brown last March, was blond now and shone like lacquered pine, swirling, controlled, every strand in place. Her lips shone so dark, a ruby red, her eyes so deep into some unnatural shadow, her make-up so strategically applied—maybe she hadn't given up after all and might still be battling.

Patty took one look at Gayle holding her shoes and let out an exasperated, "Gayle!"

"I told you it wouldn't—" Gayle stopped, clamming up when she caught my eye, but smiling, not frowning.

A can of beer was popped open.

"Kurt!" Patty glared at him. "Not with Piper here."

"It's okay," Piper said. "I'll be in high school this fall."

Kurt did a double-take, looking her up and down. "Wow, Pipes. You certainly *will* be in high school this fall."

"Honors English and Math. I get to be a Hall Monitor, too. Nobody's skipping class on my watch, you can bet on that." Bound to make her more popular than ever.

"I really missed you guys," Piper said, beaming. She gave Patty a token glance and returned her gaze to Kurt, blushing. In the past, whenever Kurt came over, she'd hang around until I shooed her away, but I'd never seen her crush on him this much. "It's been months," Piper added, twisting a little side to side, a bashful child.

"Hey, Pipes," Gayle said.

"Hey, Gayle. Wow, you look great!" Piper's jaw dropped.

"Thanks," Gayle whispered, crimson with embarrassment—or was it pride? I couldn't tell.

"I love that hair. And that outfit. It's so cool."

Gayle gave Piper a long hug, their cheeks touching. "But look at you," Gayle said, backing away. "You're a proper young lady now."

"I don't know about that." Piper blushed.

"You must have grown two inches since I saw you last."

"Finally," Piper said. "I thought I'd end up tiny as my mom."

Everyone regarded her as if fascinated by her growth spurt.

"Okay, okay," I said. "It's time for you to go upstairs."

"While you're having a secret party? Not on your life. And I'll tell Dad you were drinking if you try and make me."

"Piper—"

"Let her stay, man." Kurt pulled another can from its plastic collar. "It's better Pipes learns how to party from us than some jerk-wad high schoolers who only want you-know-what from her." Kurt started to hand Piper a beer.

"No way," I said, intercepting it. "I'm not giving beer to my fourteen-year-old sister."

"Oh!" Piper dropped her shoulders, pushing out her bottom lip, pouting.

"Can't say I didn't try." Kurt shrugged at Piper, who sighed in return.

"Now go to bed," I repeated.

"No," she said. "And you can't make me." She did everything but stamp her foot.

The others were all giving me this 'let her stay' shrug of impatience. I turned to Piper. I could never make her do anything. So I shook my head and popped open my beer. "Okay, but no drinking, you understand. You're too young."

Her eyes brightened, jazzed to be finally included, no doubt.

As usual, Kurt's next move was to turn and pick a hat from my father's collection on the back wall. With a finger, he flipped at a conical grass coolie hat and a giant gourd hat, both worn by peasants who worked rice paddies, then settled on my dad's Pith Helmet. It still bore the sweat stains my father put there while trooping through the jungles of New Guinea. Kurt popped it on.

He attempted a deep, British accent. "'Doctor Livingstone, I presume?'"

"Take that off." I snatched it back. "My dad'll kill me if this gets wrecked."

As Kurt and I settled into the two easy chairs against the hat wall, sipping from our beers, the three girls, Gayle in the middle, sank into the couch under the windows, their six knees in a row, peas in a pod. Piper and Patty admired how Gayle's red nail polish matched her lip gloss.

Patty looped glances between Gayle and me, expectant, raising her eyebrows, willing me to speak. Clearly, it was her idea to insert Gayle into the Trojan horse of Kurt's nightcap visit. What did she expect me to say? And now Gayle eyed me shyly. The room went quiet.

"You do look nice," I said. "The hair, especially."

"Thanks. My mom did it for me. It's a flapper style from the twenties."

"Daddy'd love that," Piper said. "He's always going on about your hairstyles." She nodded at me. I stared her down.

"He was probably our age when women wore their hair like this," Gayle said. "I was sort of hoping to see what he'd think of it." She craned her neck toward the stairs.

"He's in bed," I nodded at her.

"Oh, well." She leaned back. "Some other time maybe."

We smiled at each other, not sure how to proceed beyond pleasantries, an awkward silence building. I started to feel a buzz, the beer telling me I could handle this, with a little help. I took a few more swallows.

Patty jumped in. "Kurt says you're working at AMC this summer."

"Not that I want to."

"But you have to? On account of your dad. You can't quit and work with Kurt?"

"Well, he can quit if he wants," Kurt said, taking a swig. "But Pops isn't hiring now. In fact, he was relieved Walker got work at the auto plant because that meant he didn't have to let his good buddy Fer-nan-do go, the wetback."

"Hate that word," Patty snapped.

Surprised me too, coming from him.

She added, "And what makes you think he's illegal?"

"He pays him in cash, Patty. The rest of us get paychecks."

"Well, so what. I thought you liked Fernando."

"I did," he shrugged. "Until Pops started crowing about the excellent fucking job he does, excuse my French. Everything spic and span, while all my work's for shit."

"Maybe if you paid a little more attention—" Patty added.

"Don't you start on me, too!" he barked.

"Stupid word," Patty mumbled. "'Wetback.'"

"It's getting pretty popular," I said. "My dad used it tonight. And Gayle's dad, at work today."

"My dad?" Gayle said.

"This guy on the loading dock. Fernando lives across from him." I give Kurt a glance. "Manny Camarasa, I think his name is. Norm's convinced he's an illegal, too."

"Birds of a feather," Kurt said.

"A big company like AMC doesn't pay in cash," I said.

"Maybe he's got them convinced he's legal," Kurt said.

"You know, it's not illegal to hire illegal immigrants," Patty said. "Learned that in Civics this spring," she added. "It's all very confusing, if you ask me."

More silence as we pondered this. Did Norm know this?

"Well, I started a summer job today," Patty jumped in again, keeping things rolling. "Didn't I, Gayle?"

"Working with me and my mom," Gayle added.

"Cutting hair?" Kurt laughed.

"Nooo. I couldn't cut hair to save my life. Gayle's old job running the cash register, now that she's a learning to be a hairdresser. It's amazing what she can do with a curling iron and a can of hair spray," Patty said, leaning back, presenting Gayle, the grand prize winner. Apparently, Gayle hadn't told Patty what I thought of her plan to work full-time in Barb's hair salon as soon she graduated high school. "Some day she'll be a hairdresser to the stars. Probably win an academy award."

Gayle rolled her eyes at her friend's overkill, but Patty might have been right. Earlier that spring, Gayle had mailed me a Polaroid of a boy in the high school play she had transformed into a male Marilyn Monroe, right down to the red lipstick and mole. She'd been so proud of her work, standing behind him, hands on his shoulders—a little too cozy, I'd thought.

Patty nudged her friend, then leaning in, whispered, "Go on," nodding at me.

"I don't want to." Gayle shrugged.

"Gayle—" Patty elbowed her again.

My ex sighed and stood up, smoothing her little leather skirt. She took a step towards my chair. "Can we have a talk, maybe? Outside?" She held a hand out.

I stalled, scratching my head. Kurt snaked across the room and took Gayle's place between Patty and Piper on the couch. He draped his arms around their shoulders, causing Piper to brighten, Patty to dim, rolling her eyes at him.

Sighing, I finished my beer and grabbed another before I let Gayle pull me up.

"Have a nice talk," Kurt said, grinning.

"Thanks, jerkwad."

"Good luck, you guys." Patty smiled, as Gayle pulled me toward the door. Patty thrust both hands up in the air, her fingers crossed.

Seventeen

From atop the grassy plateau behind my house, you could see how the lawn sloped down through a modest orchard to meet the Piscasaw River. The orchard, if you could call it that, consisted of two cherry trees, three apples, two pears, and a garden patch slowly populating with those giant strawberries, a special variety my father had planted, big as a toddler's fist. Between the orchard and the river was a grassy area where we used to play football. The river's edge was lined with willow trees, their branches hanging like thick, unkempt hair.

A few months after we moved to Belford, Dad planted the willows, the fastest growing tree he could find. He'd had enough of the eye-sore across the river, the Ironworks Foundry. The willows still had a long way to go. At this late hour, the rusting, corrugated steel buildings, six stories high and showered by floodlights, stood out against the night sky. White smoke huffed from the foundry's smokestacks, two of them as big around as an ocean liner's. Every few minutes some large, newly poured shape chunked out of its mold. Different things, depending on the molds that customers sent them. Giant gears, flanges. You never knew. Statues, maybe. Wrecking balls. But they always came out with the same chunk, followed by the same hiss, as if the place had exhaled after taking a hugely satisfying dump.

To the left of the Foundry, I noticed some new willows Dad must have planted that spring, tall thin, scraggly-looking trees tied to stakes by twine. I couldn't help chuckling.

"What are you laughing about?" Gayle said, coming up to my side.

"Those guys we were talking about, Manny Camarasa and the guy Kurt works with? Fernando?"

"Yeah?"

"They live right there." I pointed at the fishing cottages the willows were years away from being tall enough to hide. "Right across the river."

"Huh."

"My dad said one of the reasons he bought this place was because you could see more from up here than any other place in town. And what does he do?"

"What?"

"Covers it all up. Tries to, anyway, those willows." I pointed. "The Foundry, I can understand, but those cottages? They were there long before Manny and Fernando moved in, and they don't look any different now than when we first moved here."

"Huh."

"Like they make them look any worse."

"Right," she nodded, as if she really cared. "So, anyway," she began, "I wanted you to know, this was Patty's idea, my coming over. She won't let anything go."

"Always trying to save the world," I said, opening the second beer, drinking.

Gayle sat down in one of the two wooden Adirondacks that looked out over the river and rested her head on its high, fan-shaped back.

"Patty can't stand the idea of the four of us not hanging out anymore. I'm sorry I went along with it. I mean, you made it crystal clear in your letter you didn't want to see me." She folded her arms against a cool breeze.

I sat in the other chair.

"Sorry about the letter. I thought I could explain myself better that way. And I didn't say we couldn't be friends." I offered her the can.

"Friends." She scoffed, shaking off my offer. "Like that ever works."

In a rectangle of light thrown out from the basement windows, she kicked at a dandelion puff in front of the chair, the white seeds exploding upward, then floating, suspended.

"Why you couldn't call me to talk about it…"

"You're right." I got up and walked to the lip of the hill, over its gentle curve and started down. This was why I wrote the letter. This conversation I wanted to avoid. Gayle was fast on my heels, of course. I stopped near the closest cherry tree, drank, put down my can and reached into the low hanging branches to pick. I held up a cluster of plump, red and yellow fruits for her to choose from. She found a ripe one.

"I must have read that thing a dozen times, but I'm missing something." She popped the cherry in her mouth, then pulled a slipped spaghetti strap back onto her shoulder. "Like this might have to do with a certain girl?"

Kurt. That guy never kept his mouth shut.

"Well, it's not like you weren't palling around with that boy in the school play."

"Jeremy? I told you. He's gay," Gayle said.

I huffed at her.

"You think a straight guy would let me doll up his hair like that?"

I sucked in a cherry, imagining again her hands in his silky hair, warm on his shoulders.

"What do you want from me, Gayle?"

"I want to know, was it this girl or what?"

"No, it wasn't." It went way beyond the girl. I grabbed the beer out of the grass and drank, thinking. "Do you remember, when I went away to school last fall, how we planned to see each other, trading off. You'd come to school one weekend, I'd come back to Belford the next?"

"We've been over this. My mom needs me at the salon on Saturdays."

"But you *never* came down. It's only an hour away, Gayle. You could have found time. Sundays. "

"I'm in high school, and your college friends are two years older than me."

"I'm two years older than you."

"That's different. I know you. You're from home."

"That's my point. You refuse to even meet my friends, see where and how I live at school, let alone talk about going to college."

"I don't need college!" Gayle said. "I want to be a hairdresser. By the time you finish school, I'll be all trained and ready to go wherever you want."

"So, it's that easy."

"Why not?" She slipped her hand under my arm. "Why make it so complicated?"

I rubbed her hand, miserably sensing its welcome warmth. I drained the rest of the beer and tossed the can up onto the plateau.

"Her name is Capricia," I said, feeling a pleasant stab at her Marilyn Monroe boy.

"This girl?" Gayle pulled away.

"Yes. She's a poet. I met her at this reading she gave. She introduced me to her friends. A bunch of liberal arts majors. People you'd never imagine in Belford."

"Because they're liberals?"

"No, that means they had majors like English, Philosophy, Theater. And that was when I heard about that spring break trip."

"To help the Seminoles, yeah, you told me. But you didn't say anything about this Capricia going."

"Nothing happened," I said. "We roofed houses during the day, and at night we talked, not only her and me but everybody. About all these books I'd never read. Ideas bouncing and building, the topic changing on a dime. I could barely keep up."

"Sounds *really* fascinating," Gayle said.

"But that's the thing. It was. The way their minds worked, skipping from politics to movies to art. People. Places. Did you know that on Friday nights in Chicago, all the art galleries open and give away free wine. People wander in and out, looking at paintings and getting drunk."

"Hmm."

"And there are these tiny theater companies that put on plays in warehouses. Hospitals. Old mansions. You go room to room, watching different scenes, even becoming part of the play."

She nodded slowly, then shrugged. I wasn't getting through. I pulled away, vaguely scanning the tree for ripe fruit, for how to make my point. I turned to her.

"The final day of our trip, when I nailed that last shingle on a roof, it was like I'd actually done something. It got me thinking. What am I doing? Why am I even in college?"

"But what's this got to do with me?"

"They're different, these people. They didn't mean to, but they made me feel—uncomfortable. What could I talk about? Cruising in Belford? Necking at the drive-in? Getting sloshed in my basement?" *My hairdresser girlfriend.* "I'm only saying. There'd come a time when you'd feel uncomfortable with me, in the same way."

"If I don't go to your fancy-pants college, you mean? If I don't talk about artsy bullshit? Why don't you start a roofing company here and give away your services? I know a certain house that could use a new roof."

"Maybe you're right. I could do that. But I can't live here anymore. My dad's right about one thing. I need to find out what'll happen if I fall off this track he's got me on."

"You mean, find a girl who's not a hairdresser."

"Find nobody for now. Not when I can't figure out how to live my own life."

I was ready for another beer, but she grabbed my hand and pulled me down the hill. The first few steps I stumbled along, resisting, but then I followed.

As we headed down the slope through the fruit trees, the lights of the Foundry flaked off the river's surface. At the river's edge, she sat on the stone bench between the willows, pulling me down next to her.

"So," Gayle said, holding my hand, "my dad told me he trained you today."

"Yeah," I said. "I noticed he was hurting pretty bad."

"I know. It's been tough since they moved him to the loading dock. I think I told you. He took out a second mortgage on the house so my mom could start her salon, and then when that wasn't enough to cover the lease on the building and the equipment, they took out a bank loan, too."

I knew this. Somehow, these facts always got worked into conversations with Gayle, cold winds that could not be kept out of a drafty house.

"So we need his job. But he's drinking more than ever. Taking pain killers. Can't do much around the house."

"What about that forklift job?"

"What forklift job?"

"Some job he applied for. He was talking about it today with the foreman. You met him. Kelly?"

"Oh yeah, at the picnic," she nodded, a certain embarrassment in her brow. He *had* ogled her. "But Daddy didn't mention a forklift job."

"Maybe because he hasn't gotten it? I don't know."

"Hm. You think he has a chance?"

"I don't know. He sure wants it bad." The pleading in his voice—it couldn't have helped his case. "But they were friends once, right?"

"Once," she murmured. "Invites us to this picnic. Daddy gets all excited, first time they've gotten together in ages, like it'll be the good old days, and it turns out to be this company thing Kelly wanted to throw because he'd been promoted to foreman. The entire loading dock. Kind of a bummer, really, watching Daddy trail around after him. But then, I was kind of bummed out to begin with." She glanced up at me.

"Yeah, right." My fault, of course.

"You remember last Memorial Day?" She grabbed my arm, squeezing. "All that suntan lotion?"

I did. On this river, the four of us. Patty and Gayle in bikinis; Kurt and I in trunks. We steered the runabout upstream to our favorite swimming hole, a big picnic packed in the stern. We spent hours in the hot sun, swinging off the bank on that old rope, dropping into the warm water. Gayle and I dragged a blanket deep into the elephant grass and flattened our own little spot while Kurt and Patty sunned on the bank. We discarded our suits, were sweating and so gooped up with suntan lotion that when we weren't holding tight, sliding into each other, we slid right off, howling with laughter.

She bumped against me, trying to lighten me up.

But we were here, now. The river lapping against the shore. At the end of our dock, the hull of our little motor boat knocked against the piling. The Foundry let go another big clunk followed by a hiss. The river's smell, something earthy and green, was wiped out by a gust from across the water, metallic, like Ozone or acid, blowing off the work going on there.

"In the fall, I'll come down and meet your friends," Gayle said. "Every other weekend, I promise. My mom will have to find someone else to work Saturdays."

"It's the day you love the most, though, isn't it? Your busiest, when you really get to work?"

"I *love* you."

"So you say."

"What do I have to do to convince you?"

"It doesn't matter."

"It doesn't—? Look, we have all summer, Walker. We can keep talking about it, can't we?" She put her hand on my leg, rubbing my thigh. And now, sitting under the willows, it *was* like last summer, as if nothing had changed. She'd been the only person in the world I could talk to until I met my roommate Ed Granger, Capricia, and her friends. The thing was, I could return to school, take the coolest courses in the catalog, but still flunk out and end up back here. And Gayle would be here for me if I let her. I couldn't disregard that, could I?

She kept rubbing my thigh, a warmth that spread towards my crotch, inviting and unwelcome. "It's so lovely down here tonight, don't you think?"

I stood.

"I think we should go back up."

"Oh." She gazed at the river, avoiding my eyes. "I see."

"I just—" I searched for words. "I have to get up early."

"Oh, right. Me, too," she said, jumping up, grabbing my hand. She smiled, shifting gears, as if I hadn't stopped her but rather steered her in a new direction. "If I'm not bright and chipper for the old ladies when we open, Mom complains I didn't get my beauty sleep." She pulled me toward the hill, grinning. "Beauty sleep? Get it?"

I nodded, forcing a smile, and let her drag me along, as if she was the one late for bed, not me.

Sure, I could have given in to her, to my own desires. But it wasn't just Gayle I was afraid of being seduced by. Every day in Belford was built the same, predictable way, with the same simple, solid parts, the same dependable people, the same comfortable life. It would have been so easy to get wrapped up in the assembly line of work and basement parties, drinking and sex, day after day, as if it was okay not to have a say in its design or construction. After all, this life worked well enough for so many. Why not me, too? The thing is, I wanted a say. Only, I didn't know what I'd say or how.

Eighteen

It's been a while since the nurse came in to give Dad a sponge bath and change his sheets. She sent me packing, and now I'm in the hospital cafeteria, where a few staffers trickle in for breakfast, converging on round tables. Nowadays, nurses don't wear those white uniforms and winged caps like they used to, and more of them are male, but you can still tell doctors by their white lab coats. Having eaten nothing that resembles real food since flying out of D.C., I down some coffee and a tasteless, packaged pastry. What I'd really like is a drink, so it's just as well hospitals don't have bars or I'd never be able to think through that summer.

My laptop's running low on juice. I've fired off countless stories from airports, sitting on the floor against a wall, plugged in while awaiting a flight. Okay for O'Hare, but a bit unseemly for St. Francis Hospital.

A bank of windows faces east, and outside, dawn lifts darkness off the horizon. The snow has stopped for the moment, but it's blowing and drifting, un-defining the world into vague shapes, adding long white shadows to everything. A plow beeps and scrapes its way through those drifts, a yellow light twirling on top, much like the red lights on those old tugger trains. I'm sure Kurt has his blade installed on his pickup and is doing the same right now, plowing his driveway. When he's done, he'll drop off Piper, head uptown and start on his car lots. Outside of car repair, there isn't a job at either his Chevy or Honda lots, no matter how menial, that he can't do better than any of his employees, thanks to Pops' training. No doubt his boys will take the same path and begin by washing cars.

I'm reminded again of Kurt's email still sitting in my Inbox, his offer of the editor's job. Kurt has become a regular Rupert Murdoch, infusing the *Belford Daily Telegram* with capital when, like so many other newspapers, it was on the verge of folding, another victim of the Internet. I couldn't help chuckling from afar as he basked in Belford's gratitude, a civic savior following in his father's charitable footsteps, heralded on the *BDT*'s chintzy web page. As if his parade of shiny cars didn't have something to do with it, a worry that sales might grind to a halt without the paper's colorful four-page ad inserts every Saturday. Being a majority stakeholder now (and probable beneficiary of deeply discounted ad rates), he assured me the job was mine if I wanted it. In fact, his co-owners agreed it would be quite a coup to hire someone with my national experience. My stories had been carried, in one form or another, by most of the papers in America, and he'd convinced the others I could elevate the *BDT*'s reputation and journalistic standards. And I'd only have to take a thirty percent pay cut for doing twice the work.

I'm still waiting for yet another shoe to drop, his stipulation that I print the occasional editorial explaining how certain corporate tax breaks and relaxed zoning restrictions are good for Belford, while incidentally helping him to expand his auto empire. He'll probably offer to write those himself. Good luck with that, Kurt.

What's wanting in Belford is a sales tax to fund a mass transit system that finally reduces this city's infuriating traffic and the need for people to buy cars. And bi-lingual schools, public housing, homeless shelters. One week of my editorials and he'd have my head—if our readers didn't lynch me first.

Unless I could adapt, soften, compromise. I am getting a little old for gallivanting around the globe, and I can easily imagine sinking into a comfy editor's chair, being the voice of a publication, even if its editions are smaller than the Comics sections of some Sunday papers. But maybe I could change that, too, change a lot of things around here. If not a subway, then a few new bus routes. If not bilingual classrooms, then maybe a few ESL teachers. Convince Kurt business can expand without burdening the general public.

I've sampled much that life has to offer, landed in countless places, many of them wonderful, full of art, culture and history, but I feel like I've never really *lived* anywhere else but here. Maybe it's because of all the moving around, living out of suitcases in hotels or, at best, renting furnished apartments month-by-month. Or because I never settled down, never found anybody who could anchor me in place.

Everywhere a way station between where I was and where I'm going, everyone just along for the ride.

No matter where I am, my heart's compass always points back here. To first friends. First loves. Therapists have said my fixation on Belford is understandable, the scene of all my unresolved conflicts waiting to be addressed. The scene of the crime, maybe. I'm not sure. The trouble is, home is still so cold and forbidding, it might as well be the North Pole. It's not Belford's fault. It's mine. My past I need to come to terms with, and only I can fix it.

Maybe all this snow is to blame, piling up whenever I come back. It makes me wonder if I shouldn't do a little plowing of my own, clearing a path to who I was, to who Gayle was, and Kurt, and Piper and especially my dad. These things happened, so I can't build snowmen, stage a winter pageant. I'm determined to find the scorching heat of those June days. Now that I'm on to day two of my summer job, the day of the big fight, my words need to drop like salt, melt through the years, and burn open those old wounds.

Nineteen

Before shift started, Kelly gave a shrill whistle, two fingers in his mouth. It hurt, making me regret that third beer before bed. He waved his crew over to what passed for an office—the aluminum camper-like building that sat in the middle of the dock. His sleeves rolled up, a pencil behind his ear, and his safety glasses hanging on a chain around his neck, he flipped through papers on a clipboard as guys straggled over.

Manny Camarasa perched on top of a fifty-gallon drum, boots lightly banging its curved belly, meat hook in hand. He smiled away, his pink bunny shirt weird as ever.

An arm encircled my shoulders—Norm Ditweiler. "Walker Maguire!" He patted my back. "Gayle told me you talked last night." He gave my shoulder three quick punches, breath like last night's booze, or maybe this morning's.

"Uh, yeah, but, you know, nothing's settled."

"But you're talking. That's the important thing." He did that jabbering thing with his fingers. "Communication. Am I right?"

"Sure."

"Glad to hear it. Now," he said, hugging me to his side, "Today's the day. I can feel it." I tried to pull away but he hugged me closer.

Kelly cleared his throat and spoke up, reading off a list.

"Number one. Bathroom stalls—"

Fighting sleep after my late night, I zoned out as the foreman berated guys for the perverted crap they kept carving on stall walls, requiring yet another paint job. Everyone snickered, elbowing each other, and Kelly moved on to an incident in Detroit, a kid who got hurt climbing on top of a boxcar.

I perked up at the mingled suggestion of boxcars and danger.

"Anybody need reminding what happened here last year?" he asked, scanning the group.

I did, but heads shook. Kelly pulled a sheet off the clipboard and held it up.

"Can I skip the speech? The warnings? The two weeks' suspension if you're caught being that stupid?"

Guys nodded.

"Thank you." He shoved the paper to the bottom of a thin stack. He started the next item with an exasperated exhalation.

"Number three. Broken parts. Again." Kelly took off his glasses and tapped them on his clipboard. "Too many lines are getting damaged goods from us." His gaze settled on me.

I'd been there one fucking day! My heart beat double-time.

Norm piped up. "Not surprising, considering the cheap-ass suppliers around Belford they come from. Am I right?" He elbowed me in the side with a wink. Guys grumbled agreements, as if Norm was entitled to spout crap to the foreman nobody else could.

"It's not the suppliers," Kelly said. "It's us. How we unload and deliver those parts. Breakage happens," going on, singsongy, as if he'd given this speech a million times, "but there are limits. Each man has a limit." His glare accused Norm, then me, then Norm. "Past that limit, it can't be considered accidental—or acceptable."

I couldn't help going crimson. What did he expect with those seat frames, the way they were jammed in?

Kelly dropped his arms to his side and spread them. "Look, guys, you're on the fucking loading dock, for Christ sakes. You're at the bottom of the food chain. There's nowhere else the company can put you."

"Unless it's in the seat of a nice, comfy forklift," Norm said, nodding at the guys around us. A few of them chuckled, shaking their heads.

"Right," Kelly said, taking a big breath. "About that. So, last item." The foreman flipped up all the sheets and, in a quick breath, read the bottom one. "Next Monday, Manny Camarasa will take over Moore's forklift job."

A stunned silence followed. Guys shared looks, eyebrows raised.

"Tough break, bud," Liam said. Norm stood there, his mouth open.

"Sorry," Kelly said to Norm before turning.

Manny slipped off his barrel, standing tall.

"Hold on," he said. "You're giving *me* this promotion?" Norm had led me to believe he didn't speak English, but he spoke it well, his voice surprisingly high, with little accent, and ripe with skepticism.

"Wait a minute," Norm said, letting go of me and pushing past Manny. "That job was mine, Billy."

Kelly stopped and turned. "I never said that job was yours."

"You're not fucking with me?" Manny said. "Like you do the new guys?" He flipped a finger at me, dismissively. "Playing one of your practical jokes?"

New guys? Practical jokes?

"You wanted it, right?"

"Hell, yes! Been passed up three times already."

"For good reason, you goddamned spic!" Norm spat out, going nose to nose with Manny.

"Come on," Kelly pushed between them, shoving them apart. He turned to Norm. Liam and a few of the others stopped to watch. "Look, I can't promise jobs. I can only make recommendations based on seniority and performance. That's all. Camarasa's been in the department four years—"

"Damned right, I have!" Manny nodded.

"But I got the numbers, man." Norm's arm shot out. "You know I do. And I'm fucking dying on those mufflers."

"Can we take this into my office?"

"No!" Norm backed off a step. "I deserve this job, and he doesn't. Right, Liam?"

The mutton-chopped man seemed unwilling to meet his eyes. Norm continued searching the crowd for support, settling his gaze on me. My jaw worked, but nothing came out. What could I say?

"That's sad, man," Manny said. "And practically part of the family, too."

"Fuck you!" Norm spun around, back at Kelly, barking. "You said you'd talk to them. You said you'd back me up."

"You *don't* have the numbers. Not when you include breakage. Sure, you're fast, but you're careless. And management, well, they liked the way Camarasa's meat hook idea—"

"You almost canned him over that stupid meat hook!"

"It improved his numbers. That's how you get ahead around here, not by—" He waved his hand around, searching.

"By what? Gimping around like a fucking cripple? Is that what you were going to say?"

"No. Flapping your mouth. Spouting off all the time."

"You're so full of shit." Norm pushed up to Kelly's chest, whispering fiercely. "I'm talking to the union. They'll back me on this."

"Be my guest."

Kelly turned and marched back to his trailer, slamming the door. Manny strolled past me toward his boxcar, smiling.

"It's not fair," Norm grumbled. "He's taking this fucking—this—" He flipped his fingers toward Manny, like he was nothing. "This *guy* over me. This *guy*?"

Nobody said anything.

"Where's the steward? I gotta find the steward—" Norm mumbled to himself, heading off into the plant.

After our meeting with Kelly, a new Northern Pacific boxcar awaited me, loaded floor to ceiling with seat frames, the air rich with eye-watering lubricant vapor. A tugger with three empty wagons sat behind, so I put on my gloves. The previous scene had been so remarkable, I couldn't help but keep it in mind as I worked. Norm had brown-nosed himself right out of that job—a promotion which Manny, on the other hand, couldn't believe was his, certain they were fucking with him. The wrangling preoccupied me until a second tugger train showed up when I had only halfway filled the first. *What the fuck!?* I checked my watch. *Only twenty minutes had gone by!* Was this the practical joke? I'd had thirty minutes per train the day before. *Holy shit!* I was fucked. Completely fucked.

I worked faster than ever, left hand pushing on the wall, holding it up, right hand yanking at frames, jerking them out. Then it happened. The entire wall leaned outward, ten feet tall of wire and coils, tilting. A couple fell from the top, spinging and spanging off the boxcar floor, ricocheting. I pushed with both hands, but it was too late. The whole thing began avalanching.

Turning, I put up my hands and arms to cover my head while frames kicked off me, hammering me down. Everything settled, and the clattering ceased with one final sproing. Quiet again. I felt around, checking myself for damage. My white t-shirt was imprinted with oily curls, but I only found a small cut on my forehead, a sore rib or two.

Around me, work had stopped. Everyone was turned my way. Kelly stood in the door of his office, hands on his hips, shaking his head. That fuck, speeding up my trains so I'd rush and ruin everything.

Two boxcars away, a muffler crashed into a tugger cart. Norm continued working. He'd ignored the whole calamity, like he didn't give a shit. 'Meat Hook' Manny poked a thumbs up with his free hand, smiling like crazy. *Good Job, kid!*

Seat frames lay all around me in a tangled mess. I needed to salvage this. I picked up one and then another, turning them over and around. The fact was, I couldn't tell an intact seat frame from a busted one. At least, the things unfolded on their own. Manny held his thumb up again.

Jesus! Stop fucking with me!

I didn't know what else to do, so I tossed the frames into the tugger wagon, trying not to imagine how many were broken.

Within five minutes, two at a time, I finished loading the first train, slapped its green button with my oily palm and sent the tugger chugging off down the line. The next one sniffed along the metallic tape and into place. I carted over all the remaining frames, one wagon load, then climbed back into the stinky boxcar. Another wall. One seat frame stuck out, so I tugged on it. The whole wall wiggled. I pushed that frame back in and pulled at a different one, higher up, playing *Jenga*, again. This time, the wall tilted forward. Shoved that one back. I'd never keep up working this way. Manny gave me yet another thumbs up. *Christ, Manny!*

The hell with it. I reached in and pulled. The wall strained and after a wobble, toppled. This time, I jumped out of the way as the ten-foot wall crashed down, a huge ruckus, spatters of black lubricant dotting my boots, far from new anymore. Mr. Meat Hook had disappeared inside his car, hiding out. Liam, three boxcars over, smiled, shook his head. Norm stared at me, inscrutably, and Kelly stood in his doorway, rubbing his chin. Was he savoring this, rehearsing how he'd fire me?

I finished with the second train, pushed the green button and sent it on its merry way before the next empty appeared. I was caught up. Sure, I was caught up—most of my frames probably busted to shit.

Finally, Kelly headed over, frowning. He must have gotten word from the line that all those seat frames in the first train were ruined. Between that and how pissed off he was at Norm, he was sure to put a stop to my stupidity before I wrecked the place.

How else could I keep up with the fucking tuggers, dammit?

I let out a huge sigh, tapped the floor with one toe, and waited for the ax to fall. Around the dock, others watched now, smiling, like Manny. Liam leaned over, hands on his knees, laughing. They all wanted me gone. The spoiled college kid; the soft, rich boy. The son of the doctor who fucked people over, like Norm with his bum hip. They'd sabotaged me, created an unfair situation bound to get me fired, to get back at the doctor, to make sure the job went to someone more deserving. Some practical joke.

Norm was the only one not smiling, probably still too pissed at Kelly to celebrate the revenge they were about to take on the doctor by getting me canned.

"Well, Walker, now that you've made a mess of these things," Kelly said, slapping the boxcar, "it's about time we stopped babying you with these pussy thirty, twenty minute trains and send them at a normal fifteen minute rate, don't you think?"

He reached out a hand, and smiled, expecting me to shake. I realized, I'd been making those fists, as baffling a behavior to him, I was sure, as was his offered hand to me. I shook my hand to stop it, but he was still smiling and seemed not to notice.

"You must have set a record yesterday—going a whole shift without those seat frames falling once. I was afraid if I didn't speed up the trains today you'd kill yourself working that fool way." He jiggled his hand, waiting for me.

"I don't understand."

"It's okay, kid," he said with a chuckle. "Training's over. You finally figured it out."

Still confused, I reached for his hand.

"Glove?" he said, pulling his hand back.

I took off the filthy glove and shook hands. Manny and all the other guys laughed, too. Everyone but Norm.

Twenty

At Northern Illinois University, when a guy pledged a fraternity, he knew when he was being hazed. Not with these assholes. Nobody told me seat frames were like giant cockroaches, impervious to harm, that making landslides of them was the preferred technique and not a fuck-up they'd fire you for.

But maybe the joke was on Norm, too—unless this was the 'new training' method Kelly had asked him to use. And yet, Norm didn't join in the laughter. Of course, he'd just lost that promotion.

The other men greeted me with smiles whenever I passed them that morning—genuine, welcome-to-the-club type smiles. They must have been cool to me before so as not to give away the joke. Which meant that maybe this hazing had nothing to do with my dad. Maybe he had been right all along, and I wanted an easy way out, someone else to blame.

At mid-morning break, Manny came over, squeezing his meat hook under his arm.

"I tried to tell you, man, but I'd have caught so much shit if I spoiled their fun."

I nodded at him. Thanks for nothing.

"Don't take it personal," he said. "Everyone fucks around here. That promotion? I'll believe it when I'm sitting in that seat Monday morning, raising that fork."

He turned to leave, but stopped.

"What's a kid like you doing here, anyway? It doesn't seem like your kind of job."

This wasn't meant as an insult, like Norm's dig had been. This guy seemed genuinely curious.

"It's not, but my father. He—" But I couldn't explain.

"Ah, the doctor. Yes. We've met. He reminds me of *my* father. Doesn't take shit from anyone. His son, especially, right?"

"Right."

"Well, hell." He nodded at me. "Maybe you'll learn something."

"That's what he said."

"Who knows? Maybe he's right."

For the first time, I thought maybe he was right. Maybe I was learning something.

The more I practiced that avalanche technique, the more refinements I made. If I grabbed the wall two feet up, I could pull down three columns of frames at a time. Tuggers came every fifteen minutes now, but I could load all three wagons in ten, leaving five to catch my breath outside the toxic stink of the boxcar. The red button concerned me, yes, but at least it wasn't a constant, hurricane-force worry. As the morning wore on, I developed a rhythm—create an avalanche, load a train, push the button; avalanche, train, button; avalanche, train, button. Eventually, the red button worry disappeared, replaced by something almost as bad. Boredom. Boredom and lethargy and body aches. My back was so sore, pain shooting between my shoulder blades, searing up my sides. Every few minutes, I straightened and reached for the sky, stretching my back, flexing and unflexing my aching fingers. God, I wished I'd gone to bed earlier.

A shrieking, honking noise blared out from somewhere, breaking my reverie, making me drop the frames I was holding. The *honk, honk, honk* continued. What was it? A fire alarm? A tornado warning, static-peppered? But, wait—was that the red button?

Manny pointed at me, his eyebrows twined together in accusation.

"Fuck!" I barked. It couldn't be me. I'd just sent a full tugger on its way down the line. But other guys pointed at me, too. *What did I do*!? A cackle made me turn. Manny bent over, slapped both hands on his thighs and shook his head.

"We're fucking with you," he yelled. "It wasn't you." Now, others laughed, too.

"Great." I said, nodding at them, relief filling me up like a balloon. Was everybody in this place an asshole?

I took a big breath and went back to work.

I focused on the sports talk blaring from Manny's radio. By now, I knew more about the Sox than I ever had the Cubs—how Carlos May's contract was up and management was deciding whether to pay him the big bucks or let him become a free agent; how the Sox closer, Goose Gossage, had burned out his arm, and how their knuckleballer, Wilbur Wood, saved their bacon by pitching an ungodly number of innings.

When the lunch horn sounded, I decided to follow the other dock workers instead of eating in my toxic boxcar. As I headed out between two stacks of bins, one of Manny's booted feet almost hit me in the face. He lay on top of a basketball-hoop-high tower of pallets he had climbed. Our new forklift driver, as of next Monday, could sleep anywhere, it seemed. Every break, he was on his back. As if he never slept at home.

I trailed after the others, zombie-like, leaning over and limping along. We converged on a corner of the building that could have passed for an indoor highway rest stop, an area surrounded by aluminum roadside guardrails enclosing six redwood picnic tables and two vending machines. I found the farthest table from the aisle and sat, facing the line, my first chance to see how it worked. The morning's labors had made me so ravenous, even the mayo I'd told my mom not to put on my sandwich tasted good.

The rest area was located right at the start of the trim line where half-finished metal undercarriages angled in from a side line, like planes swinging onto a runway for final takeoff. These automobile skeletons came with their nether parts installed elsewhere in the plant—gas tanks, transmissions, mufflers and drive trains. Now, workers brought in parts that required installation before car bodies could be attached—seats, carpets, dashboards, steering wheels, and shifting consoles. Some parts came from bins; others from ground-level or overhead conveyors, moving belts, baskets or hooks, that met the trim line at different points. Further down the line, descending like ski-lift gondolas from the paint shop one floor above, came the car bodies, freshly painted in baked-on metallic olive, navy and burgundy. Guys in heavy masks and gloves welded the bodies onto the chassis, blue sparks shooting in all directions. Past this assembly, other lines converged—doors, windshields, bumpers and hoods—but it was too distant to make out the details.

I was struck by the unhurried assurance of the workers, every step measured and choreographed as they walked alongside the slow-moving line. They'd position and bolt together parts big and small with air-guns on coiled red or yellow hoses. After they finished a tiny installation in one car, they wandered languidly back to the next, grabbing handfuls of bolts, screws or clips from bins along the way; then they'd start all over again. They perfectly repeated the same movements every cycle, graceful robots from the neck down, still vaguely human from the neck up, the way they talked as they worked, shouting and laughing at the next guy—or sometimes, gal—up or down the line. What were they discussing? Anything but this. The White Sox. Gossip about co-workers. Plans for after work. Their wives and girlfriends. Their kids. Dinner. Upcoming vacations.

At the table next to me sat two big guys playing cards, oblivious to the noise and commotion. Between them, a staticky transistor radio broadcast the preview show for the game this afternoon.

"Got you again, you worthless piece of shit!" one player declared. He flipped out a card with a back-hand flourish. The other one shook his head as if he always lost. They shuffled and dealt with the quick, sure movements of guys who play cards every day.

I didn't notice Norm limping up until he banged his big black lunchbox down on my table.

"Thanks for backing me up, Walker." He flapped open his box, so it fell over backwards, spilling out his sandwich, a thermos, a prescription bottle of white pills. "You're a great help."

"Sorry, Norm. I didn't know what to say."

"You could have told the truth. That job should be mine." He glared at me and peeled the cellophane off his sandwich. "That fucking Kelly. I even used that 'new training method' for him, and how does he repay me? Fucking jerk."

He *was* in on it.

One of the card players, the dark-haired one, piped up. "You could use a cup of joe before you go back to the dock." Then I got a whiff of it, the liquor on Norm's breath, hard and noxious. But not rum, like my Dad drank. Something even harder, like whiskey or gin.

"What the fuck do you know?"

"Hey, Norm," I whispered, putting a flattened hand on the table in front of him. "Maybe you should cool it."

"Don't tell me what to do!" he snapped. "This kid here?" Norm lifted his hand over his head and pointed down at me with his index finger. "This kid thinks he knows, 'cause this kid goes to college."

The players lifted their heads at me. I half-smiled back, hoping not to show how I was cringing inside.

Norm leaned forward, gut up against the table's edge. "*You* know Kelly's fucking me over, don't you? Even if the union steward's dumb as a radiator cap, you see—" He nodded at me, trying to draw out a response. I shrugged, a bit lost. What was I supposed to know after only one day? But maybe I did know something—that someone in the right didn't behave like this, drunk and raging, even if it was driven by pain and pills.

Norm slumped, waving me down. "Ah, what do you care? In two months, you'll be back in school, studying to be—what, like your dad up there in his air-conditioned office? A doctor? Filling out your little forms and fucking up our lives?"

My cheeks burned now, the spotlight on me.

"Come on, college boy!" He threw his arms out wide. "What are you gonna be when you grow up?"

Fuck, Norm, I didn't give away your goddamn promotion, and I'm not my father. Other guys watched us now, not just the two playing cards.

"I haven't decided."

"How about you, Norm?" The blond card player asked. "What do you want to be when you grow up?"

The other guy chuckled at this, and I smiled, too, relieved the spotlight had been turned back on Norm. He sniffed, ready to play along.

"Oh, hell. I wanna unload boxcars until my dying days. And let's have all the fuckin' wetbacks get the good jobs cause management's got a hard-on for some trick they've learned with a goddamned meat hook."

He leaned over the table towards me, his tone a sneer, "I bet that guy's not even named 'Manny Camarasa.' His real name is probably Diego or some crap, from some tin-roofed shanty town in Meh-he-co." He shook his head and spit off to the side. "'Cause a spic like that, who wears those faggoty bunny shirts, and smiles like such a queer fucker, every meal in a tortilla—there's no fuckin' way this prick is legal, I'm sorry."

People around me shook their heads or chuckled.

"Leave it alone, for Christ sakes," the dark-haired guy said.

"Fuck you, Mort," Norm said, unwrapping a thin, white bread sandwich.

Mort leaned toward me. "Don't mind him," he said. "He's still pissed he's back on the loading dock."

The other man, flipping out a queen of spades, said, "Pissed is right. Norm's got a weak bladder, don't you know. He used to have a sweet job on the chassis line, but the foreman got tired of sending in the relief man every twenty minutes so Norm there could drain his lizard without them having to stop the line, don't you know. Got so the only man the reliever had time to relieve was Norm."

"Fuck you, Bruce!"

"Fuck you," Bruce imitated Norm's nasal tone.

Norm grabbed his stuff and shoved it back in his lunchbox.

"Fuck all you guys." He got up and stomped off, wincing, his limp Egor-like now.

Mort and Bruce shook their heads.

"He's hurting, but that don't give him the right to be an asshole," Mort said.

"That's for damned sure," Bruce said.

I liked these two.

"Which line you guys work?" I asked, scooting closer to their table.

"Trim," said Mort, nodding up at the cars descending above us. "We do mirrors."

"Side-view—" Bruce pointed to himself and then to his friend. "And rear-view. 'Course, Mort and I aren't usually here at the same time."

"Bruce—" Mort warned. Bruce ignored him.

"We normally double-up, but when they hit the red button this morning, I had to call him in."

Double-up? Call him in? "Why did they hit the red button?" I asked.

"You didn't hear?" Bruce asked. "Someone tried to send out a Rambler with an automatic tranny and a clutch pedal, too."

Mort burst out with a guffaw and pounded the table. "Kills me every time I picture it," he sniffed.

It sure would be bizarre—part automatic transmission, part standard, a weird hermaphroditic hybrid out of an automotive freak show. No wonder they hit the red button.

"Can you imagine the poor fuck who tried to drive that off the line," Bruce said. "'What the hell do I do?'" His hands raised, he did a pretend a double-take between an imaginary automatic stick shift and a clutch pedal.

Mort and I both chuckled.

As the laughter faded, I asked. "What do you mean, you double-up?"

"Double up? Cover for each other?" Mort said. When I shrugged my ignorance, he elaborated. "It's when two guys working next to each other learn each other's jobs. So Bruce will do all the mirrors one day and I'll do them all the next."

"And when one of you is doing all the mirrors, what's the other one doing?"

"Doing?! I'm home sleeping, or out fishing, or watching the kids so my wife can go shopping, like I was this morning when this asshole called." He gave his partner in crime an accusing glare.

"Really?" I asked. "You can take off?"

"Well, it's not exactly approved. But we get away with it, at least until a disaster like that fuckin' mutant car happens. Management crawls out of the woodwork, snooping around, and we both have to come in so they see us working normal-like."

"You're paranoid," Mort said. "You see any extra management today?"

"Maybe not, but better safe than sorry."

"Anyway," Mort added, taking a sip from his thermos, "this mutant car can't compare to what happened on top of that boxcar last fall. You'd have thought the world was ending with all the ambulances and sirens and flashing lights. Couldn't double up for a week after that."

"Kelly said something about an accident," I said. "What happened?"

"Oh, some stupid kid on the dock climbed up on a boxcar and fell asleep," Mort said. "They backed the thing out of its berth with him still up there. The doorframe scraped him off and onto the tracks."

"Huh." I said. "Something like that just happened in Detroit."

"We heard. But here the guy got killed."

"Killed?"

"They think he must have got knocked out during the fall," Bruce said. "But that's not what killed him."

"No one saw him laying on the tracks before they wheeled in the new boxcar." Mort put an index finger up to his neck and drew it across his throat. Suddenly, my sandwich didn't taste so good.

"Anyway," Mort continued, "something bad as that happens, out comes management. Today, though, looks like they've already crawled back into their holes and we can get back to doubling up tomorrow."

"You got it, Baby!" Bruce said. "That guy fly-fishing at Riverside park in the morning? That'll be me!" He raised his hand so Mort could give him a high-five. Mort did so, reluctantly, it seemed, his day off spoiled by the mutant car. They went back to their cards, chatting with one another, but I was elsewhere, my mind bright red with a man sprawled on a railroad track, his body on one side of a rail, his head on the other.

Twenty-One

When the end-of-lunch horn sounded, I left Mort and Bruce and returned to my seat frames, steering clear of Norm. He was still pissed, talking to himself and slamming mufflers into his tugger wagons. By mid-afternoon, I had unloaded half my boxcar, working deep inside where the dark hooded me. The noxious lubricant tickled my nose and throat, and made my eyes water, so I opened the door on the opposite side of the boxcar to bring in more air, revealing the cinder block wall of the loading dock. Curious, I poked my head out. The metal rungs of a ladder, like giant staples, protruded from the side of the boxcar. So that's how you got to the top. And got yourself killed. I shuddered and retreated inside. The ballgame helped pass the time, but a rain delay stopped it in the third inning, and Manny switched off the radio.

Being able to fill a tugger in ten minutes left five with nothing to do. I stood in a shadow and watched Manny and Norm. On down the line, the men worked deliberately. Sure, they were older than me, but that wasn't it. They paced themselves. Not too fast. Not too slow.

I couldn't do that. Even though my hazing had ended, the red button was still a bear, chasing me. I had to get as far from it as possible. The following go round, I spent the extra time preparing, pulling down frames, unfolding and stacking them. That only made the next tugger fill up even faster. Jesus! If Kelly saw me standing around seven out of every fifteen minutes, he was sure to speed up my trains, goosing that bear, have it nipping at my heels. Hiding in the car wasn't an option. The heat and smell made me too dizzy. I needed to slow down, pace myself as the other guys did.

After I loaded two more tugger trains, sleepy, draggy boredom set in, weighing me down. With nowhere else to go, I began to see why someone might want to climb up top.

I must have had a death wish, contemplating that. Yes, I hated that fucking job, stuck back in Belford all summer, halfway to hell already. But it wasn't only that. It was the lunacy of the idea, ascending out of this rigid system, my every movement directed by time, by the company, by the future laid out for me. I was drawn to it the same way I was, earlier that spring, to a lecture on James Joyce's *Ulysses* when I was supposed to be attending Chemistry class. It was as stupid as driving around, underaged, knowing there was booze in the backseat, and daring the world to stop me. As stupid—and as tempting.

That guy who died must have emptied his boxcar before going up there. Why else would they have moved it? Anyone could see mine wasn't empty yet. He must not have heard the locomotive coming, felt it jamming its tongue into the coupling. Probably stoned. Or drunk. No way I'd do that without having my wits about me.

If my father got wind—and he would—two weeks suspension would be a luxury vacation compared to what he would do. How he would think of me. What a bum I'd be. What a loser.

But it would be such a kick to so royally piss him off. And it might be cool up there. A good place to lay low for two seconds. In the last berth, up against the wall, it was dark enough. Lying down, I couldn't be seen.

Maybe I could check it out for a second or two, see what the fuss was.

For the next train, I avalanched and stacked ahead of time again, but when the empty came, I hauled four frames at a time, jogging between boxcar and tugger wagons. When I finished, I bopped the tugger's green button, sent it sniffing down that trail of metallic tape, a robotic bloodhound. I checked the clock. Done in five minutes flat. That left me ten to play with. I was jazzed, my adrenaline spiking. An adventure awaited.

First, I made sure no one was watching. Then, pulling off my grease- covered gloves and leaving them on the boxcar floor, I slipped out its far door. With the wall behind me, I slid one foot and then a hand over to the staple ladder. I climbed three of the five rungs until my head poked up over the top of the car. My heart raced. Pushing atop the car, I slithered along, chest hugging the metal roof, up to the ridge. I peeked over. The dark calmed me a bit. If I couldn't see my own hand, nobody else could see me, either. Or could they?

This was so stupid. So bad. So bad it felt good.

The sun seeping in from outside described a big, white "n" around the boxcar. The doorway's lintel hovered inches above the boxcar's roof. A body could easily get scraped off, but you'd have to be completely out of it not to hear the train chugging, sense its massive weight as it hooked in and yanked backwards.

I wiggled forward over the ridge, keeping low. You could see everything from up here. Amidst all the scurrying workers, Kelly's RV-like office sat with its lone window. Inside, he flipped through papers, his head tilted down. He sipped from a cup, chewed on his mustache, twiddled a pen. Beyond his office, all thirty-two bays were visible. Up and down the line, forklifts beeped, banged and scraped, going in and out of boxcars and semi-trailers. Then there were the guys like me, carrying big, oddly shaped metal and plastic parts by hand. How most of these puzzle pieces fit in an automobile I couldn't quite imagine.

The towers of bins and pallets in front of my car mostly blocked my view of Manny, but every so often, he passed between them, a flash, a fuel tank on his back, its metal lip impaled on his meat hook. The next berth over, Norm rested on a muffler he had stood up on its end like a pregnant shepherd's crook. He caught his breath and wiped his brow, too tired or sore to act as pissed as he was earlier. After a few seconds, he limped over to the tugger and carelessly heaved the muffler onto a wagon, wincing as he did so. The thing clattered around until it settled. What a mess. No wonder they didn't give Norm the promotion. Tough to watch him, dragging that leg back inside his boxcar.

I pushed back and lay face down. Peeking at the big clock on Kelly's trailer, I counted down the minutes—six until the next tugger arrived. It wasn't exactly comfortable, but I slowly relaxed, muscles letting go of the tension they'd clung to all day. My eyelids drooped, then sprang up, setting off alarms all through me. I slid back over to the ladder and climbed down. Couldn't do that after every tugger train, but maybe now and then. Just had to be careful.

When the horn announced afternoon break, I climbed atop the boxcar again. I don't know why I found this so exciting. My little way of bucking the system. Like Mort and Bruce with their doubling up.

Less than a minute passed before something caught my eye. That eight-foot tall tower of pallets next to my boxcar shook, wobbling. A hand appeared on the top pallet, reaching and grasping a wooden slat. Next to it, a hook swung up. I ducked down. Manny dragged himself up on the stack, as big on top as a picnic table. After a while, I lifted my head again. I'd forgotten he liked to rest up there. He sat on his butt, tilting to the side. A fart? No, he pulled a thick wallet out of his hip pocket. Must have been uncomfortable. He put it aside, slid back and lay down. The taller tower of metal bins obscured his legs, so only his torso was visible. He jack-knifed one knee up to his chest, then the other. After a stretch or two, he relaxed, laying down, legs disappearing from view. He closed his eyes and lay one arm across his bunny-shirted chest.

I squinted at the clock. Ten minutes until break ended. I tried to rest, but having Manny right below unnerved me. I pushed up on my elbows and stared down at him. His mouth hung slightly open. Snoring, maybe.

Sure, he worked harder and smarter than Norm, but it was obvious Norm was dying on his feet. He needed the forklift job, even if Manny had earned it—if they were actually giving it to him.

Manny raised his head, tilted it in my direction, opened his eyes and gazed right at me. I froze.

Shit!

Nothing I could do. Two weeks suspension. My dad would kill me.

But he didn't move. Then, he started to smile. He chuckled, shaking his head at me, being so silly. He closed his eyes again and let his head drop back, as if it was none of his business. As if Kelly's warning meant nothing, an over-protective mom. Or maybe Manny was banking information to use against me later in case I crossed him. No one trusted anyone around this place.

Relax, I thought. *He won't tell.* If he didn't tell Kelly now, he wouldn't have any proof after I got down.

After a while, a curious movement froze me: fingertips on the far edge of Manny's pallet, feeling up and down. Four of them, a disembodied crab-like creature, scuttling along, quietly searching. The guy they belonged to had to be stretched on his tiptoes to reach that high. I was tempted to yell out, wake Manny up, but others might hear, see me there. So I hunkered down, said nothing. Probably, just another loading dock prank. Nothing to worry about. Not my business.

The crab fingers landed on Manny's wallet and stopped. *Manny didn't sense that?* Then the hand pushed up over the edge, the thumb joining in, fingers, sliding under the wallet, trying to get a grip, then grabbing.

An explosion of motion blurred by so fast I couldn't take it in at first. Manny's right arm flew up and over and down, flinging something, a glint of shining metal accompanied by a paint-peeling scream and a thread-like jet of blood. Manny went flying, pulled off the pallet by the thief. A loud double thump followed, the two bodies hitting the ground, leaving the tower of pallets to wobble. From somewhere below came cries and moans.

As quickly and quietly as I could, I clambered down the ladder. I side-stepped back inside the far boxcar door and came out the near one as if I had been resting in the boxcar and happened to be attracted by the commotion.

Manny and Norm Ditweiler both writhed on the ground. Norm's right arm was so surreal, the crab of his hand having evolved into a long skinny fish out of water, flopping around, Manny's meat hook, buried in it.

"Motherfucker!" Norm cursed with a drunken slur. He flipped the arm this way and that. The hook had entered the back of his wrist, gone through to the other side, and exited right above the palm. Syrupy blood ran off toward his shoulder, soaking his white sleeve dark red. When he dropped the arm to the ground, the flow changed direction, rolling in several long red streaks down his wrist, over the backs of his fingers and off their nails, dripping, a red puddle on the cement floor.

Workers gathered around, mumbling in disbelief. Moments later, Kelly ran up, skidding to a halt, eyes wide, chest heaving at the sight. After a second, he snapped out of it, pulled a walkie-talkie out of a belt holster and spoke into it, calling for help.

Norm's injury so fascinated me, seconds passed before Manny's groans made me turn. He arched upwards, one hand pressed into the small of his back, the other holding the top of his head, face twisting, animating a picture of pain that his silent suffering couldn't.

"You see what that motherfucker did?" Norm cried out. "That goddamned meat hook. Look at this arm. Look at it. Mother. Fucker!"

Kelly squatted by Norm's side.

"Simmer down, Norm." He patted his shoulder. "It'll be okay."

A golf cart raced around a corner and screeched to a halt. Then a second one arrived. My dad, of course, the company doctor in his white lab coat. He jumped out, hauling his black bag.

"Get out of the way," he barked at the gathered dock workers. "Come on, move, goddammit!"

I ducked behind one of the larger men, hiding. His manner, the brusque way he pushed guys around, chilled me. On their own, my feet slid backwards, forcing me to the rear of the crowd.

Two security guards in gray uniforms climbed out of the second cart, but their job was to hold the other guys at bay. Dr. Maguire was in charge. Everyone parted before him, Moses and the Red Sea. He inspected the scene, the two men on the ground, sizing up the situation. He crouched down.

"What happened here?"

"What happened?" Norm shouted, whipping his head around in a big circle. "That fuckin' wetback taco fucker tried to kill me. That's what happened!" With his other hand, he jabbed Manny's way, stabbing the air. "I'm gonna have you arrested, bub. Charged with 'sault and battery, 'tempted murder!"

He *was* drunk!

He pointed at Manny with the impaled arm, the meat hook bobbling around like an absurd piece of modern art. "Your ass is grass, amigo!"

Dad grabbed him by the elbow, holding him steady.

"Look at this arm," Norm cried, as if it just occurred to him. This was *his* arm, *his* pain, calling out but until this moment unable to reach him owing to some boozy busybody tying up the line.

"Oh, my Gawd!" He yelled, the pain finally getting through. "Oh, my Gawd!"

Meanwhile, Manny continued to writhe in slow-motion agony, his unfocused eyes circling their sockets. Everyone ignored him except me. I pushed through the crowd, weaving up to his side.

"All right, all right," Dad said, settling Norm's injured arm down. He opened his black bag and retrieved a package of gauze, unwrapped it and pressed it around the wound, turning it red.

"We can't take this thing out here," my father said. "But an ambulance is on the way. Hold this." He took Norm's other hand and pushed it onto the gauze, then opened another package and applied the cotton square underneath where the sharp end of the hook protruded and blood dripped in dollops.

In his bag, he found a length of yellow rubber medical hose, like the kind used in stethoscopes, and tied it around Norm's arm—a tourniquet, I realized, to slow the flow of blood.

Satisfied, Dad looked around. "What about him?" Dad stepped over to Manny and squatted down, putting a hand on his shoulder, trying to settle him while, with the other hand, he turned his head this way and that, examining. "Where are you hurt?"

"My back," Manny croaked, still writhing.

"Did anybody see what happened?" Kelly asked. Both men searched faces for answers.

I was nearby, so my father looked up and asked me. "Did you see it?"

In a second, I pictured everything: Those two columns, the metal bins, the wooden pallets. I could only have seen the fight from above them, atop the boxcar where I was forbidden to be. They'd suspend me; and my dad? He'd kill me. He stood up, towering. My mouth moved, but nothing came out.

"Did you!?" He stood, leveling his gaze at me.

Do you think you can do that? Pay attention? Follow the rules?

The world darkened.

"Quit that and tell me!" He grabbed my hand, stopped that thing I did, making a fist, unmaking it. His touch stung, a shock, and I couldn't help yanking away. Everyone gawked at me, waiting. "Did you see anything?"

Do you want me to think you're a bum. Is that what you want?

"No!" I said, pulling away, putting my hand in my armpit. My heart galloped and my vision blurred, narrowing. Fifteen again, being chased, seeking escape, that mouse hole.

"Then say so, for Christ sakes. I haven't got time for this." He scanned other faces. "How about the rest of you? Anybody else see it?" Men shook their heads.

He had dismissed me, just like that. I'd wasted his time. I shrank back into the crowd, slipping behind one and then another man. I took a huge breath. How long had I'd been holding it?

"Why is he hurt, then?" Dad asked, pointing at Manny, whose eyes continued to blink as he lolled around, back twisting. One hand went to his head, his face wandering to a world of pain far from here. He was too out of it to defend himself.

My father searched the men's faces, angry at their ignorance, skipping past mine. Ridiculous, that out of all these men here, nobody had seen anything. All of us, worthless fools. Beneath contempt. Oh, I knew that look.

The one with the mutton chops, Liam, went down on a knee, patting Norm's shoulder. But nobody helped Manny. Nobody patted him on the back. In fact, they glared at him, hands on hips, squinting. They were angry—angry at him!

"Wait," I said, pushing forward. People were jumping to conclusions. *Wait a second.* There was another story, that little white crab. The wallet. A couple of guys turned, annoyed, as if I was cutting in line. They didn't budge. Like I'd had my chance.

It was crystal clear now, the new story. It was Manny's fault. Manny the Mexican tried to kill Norm Ditweiler. But it wasn't true.

Or was it? I stood still, unsure whether to push forward or fall back. Maybe Manny had lain in wait, hoping Norm would do something, anything, to justify striking out at him for all his racist jabs and put-downs. Surely, everyone could see it, and wasn't it possible?

Dad leaned over Manny and spoke into his ear.

"Hey, I'm the one bleeding here," Norm shouted, each word drawn out long and gooey as taffy. Dad turned back to him, the gauze on his arm having slipped away. Blood dripped, a small but continuous trickle. Dad returned to Norm's side, crouched over him, holding the pad in position.

Sirens sounded in the distance, growing louder, closer. Blue lights flashed off the walls of the loading dock, repeatedly wrapping faces in light. An ambulance backed into an empty berth, and two EMT's pulled stretchers out of the cabin. *I could still say something.* My father and the EMT's shifted Norm onto a stretcher, telescoping it up. Dad held Norm's arm steady as the others wheeled the thing along and into the back of the ambulance. I only had to move, to yell out. But then they put Manny on a second stretcher and shoved him in next to Norm.

Someone tapped my shoulder. Mr. Kelly. He said something about having called Norm's emergency contact, getting Gayle at the salon. She'd asked him if I could give her a ride to the hospital since her mother was out.

"I'll have one of the relief men take over for you," Kelly concluded. "Walker? You listening?"

"Sure," I mumbled, watching an EMT swing the cabin door shut, then climb in front with my Dad. "I'll leave now."

The ambulance pulled out, sirens winding up, crying out, blue lights flashing round and round, then fading as the vehicle drove away. It left the bay empty, me empty, my chance to do something gone, wailing off into the distance.

"Back to work," Kelly bellowed around to the others. "All of you." He turned to me as the crowd dispersed. "Go on, then. Get your stuff. I'll clock you out."

I still couldn't move, my boots riveted to the loading dock floor. Should have said something. Set everyone straight. Now, it was too late.

"Walker!"

"I'm going!" Wrenching myself away, regret burning in my bones, I stumbled back to my boxcar to collect my lunchbox. On the way out, I cut behind Manny's sleeping tower and stepped on something thick and squishy. A wallet. Manny's wallet, right? I picked it up and took a step toward Kelly's office, but stopped.

I examined the wallet. Like I'd never seen one, black and curled, soft and butt-shaped. Manny might have had a bunch of cash in there. Or personal stuff. After what he'd done—or people *thought* he'd done—they might have felt justified in taking his money, ripping the thing apart. I sidestepped to peek inside Kelly's door. He wasn't there, anyway.

The hell with it.

I pocketed the wallet and headed for the gate. I'd give it back at the hospital.

Twenty-Two

In the cafeteria, I'm on a roll, but my laptop warns me it's dying. Crap. Not now. I gather up my things and wander out, looking for a place to sit, an outlet, a way back into my story. I cruise up long, wide hallways full of gurneys, carts loaded with equipment, orderlies, nurses, bright lights, shiny linoleum. I peek into waiting rooms. Too many people in this one. No outlets in that one. I climb stairs to another floor. Through a wide door I spot a row of empty seats. Inside, I spy an outlet behind one chair. I plop down, plug in. Flip open my laptop, drum fingers, await the screen. Where am I? Cardiac Care? Obstetrics? Unless, yes, those are babies crying. Maternity. Okay. Fine. The screen lights up. Now, where was I? That's right. Picking up Gayle. Going to the hospital. This hospital!

"Are you waiting to see someone?"

I lift my head, ready to rear up at this wrench thrown into my writing. But then I stop. That little mole over the nurse's left eye.

"You." The girl of my dreams. Here. In Belford.

"Me?" She smiles, dazzling me. It's been so long. And she's actually here. *Connie!* The eyebrow below the mole curls, disabling the smile. She's trying to place me, but can't. Thank god. My added weight, my wrinkles, my hair, prematurely white. Her gears turn, her eyes search my face. But they don't change to anger. To hatred. Good. "You're waiting for me?" she adds.

For the last thirty years! I'd know her anywhere. The shape of her face. Those eyes. Kind, as always. The sound of her voice. Wise. Tough. And her badge confirms it. Connie. Even if her last name is Wheeler now instead of Camarasa, it is still Connie. Here. How can that be? She's supposed to be in Mexico—or California or Florida—anyplace but here!

"That is—" I search for words, looking down at my laptop. My story! She's entered before her cue. I'm tempted to point at the screen and tell her that. Instead, something reasonable. Sane. Sociable. "I was waiting for someone to rouse me from this thing. I need a break."

With a slight turn of the head, her mouth open, she emits another flicker of recognition, about to ask the question. But then she straightens, thinking better of it, maybe. She speaks, a scripted question, her job.

"Are you family or friends with a patient on the ward?" Or is it really *Do I know you?*

"No. My father's in intensive care."

She folds her hands in front of her. No wedding ring.

"I'm so sorry to hear that." The flicker flames out. Just as well. After what I did to her.

How often I used to dream of her. Still do, even to this day, some teenaged version of her. I'd wake to her fading presence at the tiller of her little boat as she bites into a giant strawberry, then dives into the water, just out of reach, disappearing under the waves.

She preferred Connie to Consuelo, proving she belonged, but I have always liked her given name, the way it flows and sings. *Consuelo.* Must be forty-eight or so, and those shapeless blue scrubs don't hide a gain in weight, but I've put on the pounds, too. Her face is more detailed, intricate, wizened. A little gray in the temples. The same changes I see in my mirror. Time working at both of us.

"Yes, well, I needed a place to plug in, so I ended up here. Is that okay?"

"You're fine in the ICU, but this time of day, this waiting room is only for these mothers' families. Besides, don't you want to be by your father's side?"

First, Piper. Now, Connie, giving me a hard time. But Connie always gave me a hard time. What I liked about her.

"Yes, I do. It's just—he can't talk. He's in a coma, and it's difficult to sit there, you know, watching—"

"I understand, but if he wakes up, I'm sure you'll want to be there."

The fact is, I'm not sure.

"Of course," I say, a bit too loud. "I'm going. Thanks."

She nods a practiced smile, returns to her desk, glancing at me as I pack up, a raised eyebrow, another flicker. No doubt she's wondering why I can't keep my eyes off her. Not enough tinder for recognition to catch.

I never once considered she might be here. In this town. In this hospital. The very place I first saw her. But it has been thirty years, after all. Anything could have happened.

The Consuelo I always dream about hasn't aged a day. That girl was and remains a teen, and when I consider the woman, the real Connie, here, my dream Consuelo seems like such a silly fantasy, twinkling into my bed in the depths of sleep, turning it into a boat, rocking on the waves of a river.

A middle-aged nurse. I shouldn't be surprised. Working. Giving of herself. Nurturing and maternal. That's who she was. Consistent and loyal. Nothing like my dream sprite. It doesn't matter. Seeing her again is all the glass slipper I need.

I'm back in Dad's room now. His breathing is shallower, uneven. I put the wet sponge to his lips, but he doesn't suck. Paler than last night. At least, his hair is combed now. They shaved him.

I bend down next to him, get a whiff of that old Dad smell, the rot in his breath, making me gag. Some things never change. I lean down and whisper into his ear.

"Guess what, you old bastard. She's here. Right here, in this hospital. You thought you got rid of her, and she's right here under the same fucking roof! What do you think of that!?"

Of course, he ignores me as he always did, sleeping through my entire life. Never calling. Never visiting. I make a fist, so tempted. *Listen to me!*

I plunk back into the chair, dazed.

Back in Belford. But maybe it hasn't been long. Maybe it took her years and years to work her way back, clawing through the system. But, of course, she's an American citizen. Always was. She wasn't the one who had to leave. Then why did she? Where did she go?

And Wheeler, not Camarasa. Married. Or was. No ring, after all. Unless she doesn't wear it to work for fear of knocking the stone from its setting. Probably has six kids. Gets dropped off by a burly husband with a pickup. He owns a plumbing business and coaches basketball in the winter, and Little League, or more likely, soccer in the summer.

I'm not surprised she didn't recognize me. Unless, she didn't want to admit to it and have to deal with the usual embarrassment. "Aren't you—?" "How are you? How have you been?" All that false excitement. And then for the memories to come flooding back, all that bad blood. I was no prince to her. Our encounters were awkward, at best. Stilted conversations. Bumbled attempts to win her over. Except that one time, before that ice cream job took her away from me. That time down by the river, our faces so close together in the dark, conspiring. Maybe that never rooted in her the way it did in me. From that moment on, I knew the girl I wanted her to be, though maybe not the one she was. This one.

If I can keep in mind who she's become, that she's back here in Belford, maybe there's a chance I'll find out if my dad is any more the man of my nightmares than she is the girl of my dreams.

Twenty-Three

As we sat in the surgical waiting room, Gayle asked questions. How the fight happened. Why Manny did it. I kept saying, "I don't know," until finally I told her the whole story, but as if I *hadn't* seen it: I heard screaming, found the two men on the floor, Norm was drunk with a meat hook through his arm. But explained that way, it sure sounded as if Manny started it.

"Daddy can be a handful," she said, "but I can't imagine why anyone would attack him, especially the way he's been hobbling lately."

From the chair next to her, I patted her back.

"Poor guy can't seem to catch a break," she said, twisting her purse strap between her fingers.

Gayle's mom burst in, out-of-breath, double doors flying open. "How is he? Is he okay?" A wide-bodied version of her daughter, she had the same blue eyes and chevron-shaped eyebrows, but unlike chameleon Gayle, with all her hairstyle experiments, Barb had always worn her hair short, plain and bobbed, ensuring her customers' cuts out-shone her own.

"He's still in surgery," Gayle said. "They have to take something out of his arm." She eyed her mother cautiously.

"Something?" her mother asked.

"A meat hook."

"A meat hook?" Her jaw dropped. "Don't tell me Norm got mixed up with that 'Meat Hook' Manny guy he's always complaining about."

"Afraid so."

Barb glanced my way, and I nodded in confirmation.

She sighed, gazing off, out the window. That bright, June day would be one of the longest of the year, and not because the sun was nowhere near setting.

"I guess I shouldn't be surprised, the way Norm talks about that man." She turned. "So spill it. What happened?"

"Well," I said, trying to keep my story straight. "We're not sure. Nobody saw it. But we know Norm was drinking. It was on his breath, the crazy way he talked afterwards."

"So, Norman provoked him, said something to make him angry?"

"I don't know."

She pointed up the hall, anger twitching her finger. "My husband's in surgery getting a meat hook taken out of his arm and nobody knows why?"

Unnerved by her rebuke, I could only say, "I'm sorry, but there were no witnesses."

She slumped, all the energy sapped from her.

"Sit down, Mom," Gayle said. We made room for Barb on the couch between us. Her weight on the cushions made us lean involuntarily towards her.

"Manny got that promotion Norm wanted," I said.

"The forklift thing you were telling me about?" Barb nods at her daughter who nods back.

"That's what started it," I added.

"Figures," she said with a sigh. "Ever since Norm had to train under that man, he's had it in for him. My *husband*," she said, "couldn't abide a Mexican man telling him what to do."

"He never said that." Gayle shook her head.

"Maybe not in front of you, but he did to me." She set herself. "So why'd they give it to this Manny character and not Norm? Anyone could see he needs to get off his feet."

"The foreman said something about Manny's seniority, about how many mufflers Norm has broken."

Barb took a big breath. "Ever since Norman got thrown off the paint line for stealing paint chips, it's been one thing after another."

"That was a misunderstanding," Gayle said.

"Paint chips?" This baffled me. "I don't understand."

"It builds up on the walls and equipment—" Barb explained, then trailed off, distracted. She strained to see down the hall.

"More like globs than chips," Gayle jumped in. "Daddy brought one home, once. Golf-ball sized thing. He broke it open, and there were these colorful layers of paint. He showed it to a woman we know who makes cheap jewelry. She loved it, said she could make gorgeous beads from it, said she'd buy the stuff if he got more, so he chipped off a bunch of chunks and tried to take them out of the plant in his lunch box. Security stopped him. They were doing spot searches, looking for people who steal tools and such. He says he didn't know AMC collects and sells the paint chips."

"Oh, he knew all right," Barb said.

"Wait a second." I held up a hand. "The company *sells* paint chips?"

"Anything to make a buck, right?" she said. "Somehow, Norman convinced them he didn't know."

"Because he didn't," Gayle whispered.

"Your father has a way of twisting things."

"So they let it go?" I asked.

"They moved him from the paint line to the trim line," Gayle said.

"And he didn't last long there, either," her mother said.

"Because of Norm's—" Mort had mentioned this. "His bladder problems, right?"

"Bladder problems? Hah!" Barb chuckled. "That's when his hip began acting up, and the drinking started again."

"You don't know that for sure, Mom."

"Don't I? He *said* they couldn't stop the line for a guy who had to use the restroom all the time, but I can tell you what that man does when he goes to the restroom, and it's not number one or number two. I'm not sure they ever caught him, but they did send him to the loading dock, which he didn't fuss over much. He was happy they didn't fire him, at least, until they put him in that muffler car. Like they hope he'll cripple himself out of a job."

She stood, hands on hips, searching the floor for answers. She leveled her eyes at me again. "I don't get it. Manny's the one who got the promotion. He should be happy. Why would he attack Norman?"

"I know." I nodded. "But that's Norm's story."

She let out a grunt. "His *story?* You don't believe him?"

I shrugged. "I can't really say."

She mulled this over, then dropped her hands, put one to her forehead. "I guess it's just as well no one saw."

"What do you mean?" Gayle seemed puzzled.

"Because knowing Norman, and his dislike for that man, he probably—" she stopped. *Started it? Um, yeah!* She waved the thought away. “Oh, what’s the use?” She sat back down, the cushions jumping.

Gayle reached over and put her hand on her mother’s arm, patting. Barb permitted herself a sad smile that quickly disappeared even as she placed her own hand on top of Gayle’s.

“Here we go again, little girl. Time for another carnival ride with your father.”

They smiled grimly at each other.

Minutes later, my dad headed towards us in a blue surgical gown and cap. He pulled off the cap as he approached.

“Hello, Mrs. Ditweiler,” he said, reaching for her hand with both of his.

“Barb, please,” she corrected him.

“Barb.” He turned. “Gayle. Good to see you again.” He squeezed her hand.

“You, too.”

“Nice hair.” He nodded, appreciatively.

“Thanks.” She blushed, despite the situation.

“Did *you* do the—” Barb asked, turning toward the operating rooms, a bit confused.

“No, no, no.” Dad motioned us to sit. “I’m only here as an observer. The company likes me to monitor these situations.”

“Is he all right?” Gayle asked, wringing her hands.

Dad pulled up a chair and sat, leaning forward, elbows on knees.

“He’s fine, better than fine, actually. His arm anyway. Hip’s bothering him. But as far as that arm goes, he’s extremely lucky. Turns out the hook went directly between the radius and ulna bones. Here—” With his index finger, he pressed the weathered skin in a depression on the back of his own forearm.

“Missed both bones, slid past the median nerve, between the two principle flexor muscles, the Radialis and the Brachioradialis—that’s the meaty one here.” He touched muscle. “Bypassed everything except the radial artery which it nicked. That’s why there was so much blood.”

I couldn’t help admiring Dad’s easy, medical acumen, his reassuring manner.

“So much blood?” Barb raised her eyes in concern.

"Yes, well, they clamped it, sewed it right up, no more bleeding now. Might be bruising, but I'll tell you, if I had to put a hook through a man's arm—and I'm a surgeon—I couldn't have done it with any less damage. He's very lucky."

Dad regarded Barb, then Gayle, his smile putting them at ease. Both slumped back in relief.

"My guess is they'll send him home tomorrow or the next day. So you shouldn't worry. He'll be good as new in a week, two at the most. That arm, at least."

The Ditweiler women smiled and thanked my Dad, sighed at each other, holding hands.

"You can see him now if you want. He's awake. Room 204, down the hall." They started to stand. "But I have to tell you," he held his hand up, and they sat back. "He was drinking. Drunk. Blood tests confirmed it."

Barb examined her hands.

"Yes, Walker told us."

"Mrs. Ditweiler—" His formality commanded her to look at him. "I understand Norm's had a rough time of it lately, but you do realize the company gave him a warning last year. A final warning."

"Actually," she muttered, "I didn't know." Gayle sat up straight and covered her mouth with her hand.

"'Fraid so."

"What does that mean?" Gayle said. "He won't get fired, will he?"

They both locked eyes on my father, pleading. Several times, he started to speak, then stopped, at a loss.

Barb jumped in, as if sensing an opening. "Do you know how long he was out of work before AMC hired him, doctor? If not for that job, I don't know what we would have done. Or what we'll do if he loses it." She grabbed his hand in both of hers and whispered. "We're still waiting for the salon to turn a profit. If it doesn't—"

"I see."

"Isn't there anything you can do?"

The two stared at each other, the wheels spinning. Again, he gave me a look. I gave him the best poker face I could manage.

"The thing is—" Dad sighed, pulling away from her grasp, "Norm's hell bent on pressing charges. If he does, his drinking is bound to come out in court."

"Are you saying," Barb said, straightening, "if he doesn't press charges—" She searched his eyes, hope lifting her.

Maybe Manny would be okay. What I saw wouldn't matter. My Dad had saved the day. The way Gayle brightened, she sensed it, too.

"Well, it looks like the fight wasn't his fault, so let me talk to his foreman."

Maybe my not 'fessing up turned out to be a good thing. Everyone safe.

Barb grabbed my father's hand and stood up. "Thank you, Doctor."

"Well, don't thank me yet." We were all standing now. "You need to explain things to him first. Convince him to drop the charges."

Barb nodded an 'okay' and reached for her daughter. The two of them headed off down the hall, leaving me alone with my father.

"You can go, too," he said.

"Okay. Thanks for doing that."

"Well, he shouldn't be drinking, but it's not like this whole thing's his fault, now is it?"

"Yeah, right."

"Anyway, you okay? It's not every day you see something like that."

"Me, oh, I'm fine. A little wired, I guess." I gave him a weak smile.

"Look, son. I can tell this job isn't what you bargained for. To be frank with you, some pretty shady characters work in that plant, people you wouldn't ever imagine yourself having to associate with." Manny, he meant. Not Norm. "I'm still getting used to it myself. But, this may be the kind of life you're looking at if you don't improve in school."

As if they were all low-lifes, as if he was one, too. Stuck here. Dragged down.

"I've got catching up to do back at the plant," he said, pulling off his gown. "You headed home?"

"In a bit." I turned down the hall as Dad headed back to Surgery to dispose of his surgical gown.

When I got to Norm's room, he was sitting up, Barb on one side of the bed, Gayle on the other. From the way he glared up at his wife, betrayal souring his face, I could tell she had just presented my father's deal.

"But the guy put a goddamned meat hook through my arm," he said, echoing that irrefutable fact.

The ensuing argument made Norm sound like a toddler trying to knock away a spoon full of castor oil, which Barb patiently retrieved and refilled.

"They should fire him! Not me! Fucking spic."

"Do you want to keep your job or not?"

"I had one nip. One!"

"They'll fire you, Norman."

I could tell Gayle wanted to say something, the way she kept raising her hand, trying to get their attention. It was hard, holding my tongue. Norm would have sung a different tune if he saw me pull Manny's wallet out of my pocket.

Even if he was in pain, Norm was being such an asshole. I began to wish I had told the truth, and to hell with his job. In fact, the more I considered that whole fight scene, the more it occurred to me, my dad just wanted to know if I'd seen what happened. He wouldn't have asked where I was when I saw the fight, how I could have seen it. Nobody would have. Nobody needed to know I was on top of that boxcar. But I was so cowed by him, so afraid, I really did do something wrong—I lied to him. And if I tried to take it back, tell the truth, that would enrage him all the more.

Quietly, I made my escape to use the men's room, having had more than enough of Norm Ditweiler.

Afterwards, I headed back to Norm's room, but a heated argument was still going on behind the half-closed door, so I passed on by. I wandered around, thinking, turning down a different corridor, peeking into open doors. In one room, an old man slept, an oxygen mask over his mouth. In another, a young boy, his leg up in traction, read a comic book.

Through the next door, I spied Manny Camarasa, his bed surrounded by people. A family. I stopped outside and peered in. He had a family. Next to him stood a dark-haired woman holding a baby. Two little boys maybe five or six sat on his bed at his feet, staring up at him. Across from the woman, a Candy Striper clutched Manny's hand, her back to me.

Somehow, I had assumed Manny was a loner, a single guy in a tiny cabin across the river, or maybe sharing one with other men. I hadn't expected a family.

His face continued to twinge, jolted by pain, residual agonies reflected in every face in the room, making them all grimace, their eyebrows knit. But at least his eyes had focus. He was awake now, his head craning up. Everyone in the room followed his gaze out the door. At me.

"Can I help you?" the Candy Striper asked. A young girl, and pretty, too. Birth mark above and to the right of her eye—a mole. Stunning, tongue-tying beauty.

"I was just—" I managed, backing off.

"Wait," Manny said in a hoarse voice. His hand opened, and two fingers motioned, beckoning me forward. I hesitated, and he motioned again, so I shuffled into the room and stood at the end of his bed.

Now, he'd call me out, ask why I hadn't spoken up.

"Come closer," he whispered. "Come."

Still nailed to the spot, I couldn't find anywhere else to focus. Certainly not on the others around the bed. I was left with Manny. Despite a tingle in my spine urging me to run, his rheumy eyes drew me forward. As I passed in front of the pretty Candy Striper, her brows pinched together. She couldn't puzzle out who I was or what I had to do with anything.

"Come." He reeled me in, or perhaps it was only his bed, tilting him up to meet me. I was certain he would grab my shirt, scream in my face, tell me what a coward I was, even if he hadn't been lucid enough to hear me lie.

I bent forward, his hot breath on my cheek.

"It's okay." A puff on my face. He lifted his head off the pillow and gulped. "I won't tell."

I straightened, stunned. Said 'okay' or something, and backed away, avoiding eyes.

I won't tell, I thought, leaving the room. He was worried about me getting into trouble! After what I'd done? That was crazy.

Halfway down the hall again, I stopped, patting my pocket. The wallet! I made a half-turn, my hand feeling that bulge. But Manny's breathy promise continued to echo. *I won't tell.* Manny was obviously still delirious. If he'd been thinking straight, he would have asked what happened, did I see it, had I told anyone what I saw, that Norm started it. If I went back, I'd have to admit I didn't say anything. And everyone around that bed would want to know why.

And why *was* Norm after Manny's wallet? Another practical joke? Couldn't have been for his lunch money. Maybe something was in there I needed to see.

No, this needed more thought. I had to make sure I did the right thing. Right, by Manny. Right, by Norm. Right, by me.

Twenty-Four

Another interruption, someone coming in. I'd like to lock the damned door, so they'd leave Dad and me alone, but you can't do that in hospitals.

Christ, it's Piper. *But I'm not done yet!* Even as she drops a brown paper bag and takes off her coat, snow still clinging to her floppy hat and mittens, I can't close the laptop. I'm itching to tackle what happened next, dinner at home with pre-teen Piper causing trouble again. She pads over to the other side of the bed.

"Looks the same," she whispers, taking Dad's hand, squeezing it.

"At least, he's not worse."

"At his age, if he's not getting better, then he's probably getting worse," she says, turning, considering me, a frown forming. "What are you doing with that?"

"I told you. I'm writing."

"Have you even looked at him since I left?"

"Of course, I have."

She turns back to him, runs her fingers through his hair, cups the side of his face—intimacies that generate in me a frisson of, what? Jealousy? Revulsion? My shoulders jiggle.

"He's right here, Walker. Not in whatever it is you're writing. Here, in this room. Have you even touched him?"

I shut the laptop, chastened and angry both, as if I have no right to my own fucked up way of dealing with this. She turns to me.

"Have you?"

"No." I can't. That gap is too far to bridge.

She shakes her head at me, marches back across the room, picks up the brown paper bag and dumps it in my lap.

"Open it," she says, dragging off her knit cap, shaking her long hair, wavy as before but thinning. It flows red down her back without tumbling like it used to, a stream going dry. It's too red, some hair-dyed attempt at disguising her age, belied by crow's feet and puffy eyes. That fading scar I put on her lip, a tiny rice-kernel-shaped blister. She tiptoes back to the bed and stands over Dad. I reach into the bag.

"A pair of pajamas? For me?" I kid.

"Keep digging, smart-ass." She lets Dad go and sits down to peel off her wet Wellingtons. "I couldn't sleep last night, no thanks to you and that phone call, and I remembered finding this in Dad's dresser drawer while cleaning some months ago. We stopped by the house this morning to pick up those PJs for Dad, and I thought I'd bring that, too."

From the bottom of the bag, I extract a big, brown leather volume with uneven construction paper pages.

I'm thinking it's a photo album, some attempt to get me out of my funk by revisiting our family's happier days, but when I open it, instead of photos, it contains clippings. My clippings, neatly taped, top and bottom. Dozens of yellowed pieces I wrote for the wire service over the years, most likely snipped out of the *Belford Daily Telegram*. Clean-up efforts long after a tornado someone else got to write about. The incredibly depressing funeral for victims of a mass murder someone else reported. The United Nations. An economic summit in Geneva. A climate change conference in London. All the shitty stories editors in various bureaus shunted my way because, transferring as often as I do—I'm easily bored—I always have the least seniority. The price I pay to satisfy my wanderlust.

Under all the headlines I read "by Walker Maguire." Surprising. Usually, local papers grind up my pieces as flour for their own half-baked takes on my story—plagiarism allowed under the terms of the wire service's contract—or if they do use my story as is, they credit the agency, not me. Maybe that editor at the *BDT* knows I was a local boy, and that's why he preserved my byline. Probably not the same guy Dad sent letters criticizing his proofreading—who, when I was arrested, put my name in the police log.

"You think he didn't give a shit. Well, there's proof he did." She nods at the album.

"You sure Mom didn't put this together?" I say, noting how old some of these are, going back years and years.

"Look in the back. He's also got that whole series you did last year on Kerry's presidential campaign."

"Last time I was here," I say, leafing through those clippings, "Dad didn't want to talk about my work—especially on Kerry's campaign." My last major gig. For years I'd wanted to cover a campaign. All that traveling, the cringe-worthy debates, the dizzying pace. I thought it'd be exciting. It wasn't. Clipping after clipping reminded me how I'd spent most of a year going back and forth from Iowa to New Hampshire, then the hectic primary swing, state after state, listening to the same boilerplate stump speech day after day. I'd parse press releases for new tacks in strategy, watch candidates nibble corn dogs and ice creams, kiss drooling babies. Anything for a photo op. Between the many rounds I shared at hotel bars with the press pool, I climbed in and out of buses and airplanes, got herded hungover from high school auditoriums to town halls to state fairs to diners to tarmac rallies, only to report the same sound bites every other reporter heard.

"That's not news," editors complained. News only happened when candidates made egregious gaffes—Howard Dean laughing himself out of the race with his maniacal "Yee-Haw," John Kerry calling for 'regime change,' then apologizing for the unintended comparison of Bush to Saddam. Or news happened when candidates got nailed by some shady PAC, as Kerry did by those Swift boaters, questioning his war record. And *your* story only happened if you were lucky enough to corner the candidate between limousines, jockey to the front of the two dozen other reporters barnacling themselves to the man, microphones upthrust like more corn dogs. News rarely erupted unless you caught him or one of his staffers mumbling something marginally controversial that wasn't captured by TV cameras or radio mics, if you came up with a clever lede and filed your story before anyone else did theirs. That was news!

And now, thanks to my newfound 'political expertise,' I'm stuck in D.C., covering the House. Nothing but bickering, back-stabbing, and horse-trading. And they call that a promotion.

It stirs me to see this, though, story after story with my byline. Walker Maguire. Collected by my father. Here in the *Belford Daily Telegram*. Like they might actually respect me. Like he might. No, it's not as if they have a statue of me in front of the courthouse, but here I'm not anonymous, not a ghost-writer. I'm someone.

"Dad hated Kerry." I flip the album closed. It weighs heavily on my lap. So many stories. "I don't understand why he'd do this."

Piper grabs the album, flipping through it. "Did you see the feature you wrote about that *Angels in America* production Frazier worked on?" She holds it out to me. "A play about gay men dying of AIDs? He certainly didn't collect that because of what you wrote. Any of these, for that matter. It was because you wrote them."

She replaces it in the grocery bag. I'm still skeptical.

"If Dad's such a big fan, why did he give me the cold shoulder when I came home last Thanksgiving?"

"What do you mean, 'cold shoulder?' He was great the last time you came." She squints, driving the dig in. "Telling all those sailing and polo stories. Holding court. Pouring wine. Didn't touch a drop himself."

"Sure, but you were there. I hadn't been home in years, and he asked maybe two questions about what I'd been doing all that time."

"Yeah, I know." She nods, a concession.

"And when I got him alone, all he wanted to talk about were the Cubs or his antiques." I turn towards his bed. My father is so quiet I have to check his monitors for reassurance, green lines leaping, diving. "He wasn't the least bit curious about me and my life, like he could have cared less."

"He doesn't ask Frazier about his life either—and you know why." She points at the album she just put away, no doubt indicating the article Dad collected but was probably too squeamish to read.

"That's different, and you know that."

She pauses, thinking a long second. "I think," she begins, "I think you made him uncomfortable—in a different way. As a matter of fact, when we found out you weren't coming this year, he was almost relieved."

"Exactly my point."

"But that's not my point." She ponders this a second, an expression women often give me, like I never quite get it. "To tell the truth, Walker, I was relieved, too."

"You? Why?"

"You made *all of us* uncomfortable—even Frazier, I think."

"What? Why?"

"Because you spent the whole weekend brooding."

"Brooding?"

"Brooding and drinking. We were all trying to have a good time, and you were moody. Morose. I don't know what you're like out there. Frazier says you're better." She waves her hand, indicating some other world.

"You've talked about it?"

"Yes. And he agrees. Here, you're always miserable. You were the same way at Mom's funeral, even my wedding. Every time you've come. Here, some old horror movie is always playing behind that thick skull of yours that you can't turn off. I mean, look at you." She flips her hand at my laptop, dismissing it.

The only comeback for that are the sounds and lights of Dad's machines, looming like fireflies at dusk, ticking. While evening darkens the room, the green lines etch and the IV drip burbles.

Of course, she's right. If this is how I'll act, I shouldn't come back at all. But maybe I wouldn't be this way if I understood things better, if only I could talk to him.

"Would Dad be so interested in my newspaper career if he knew Kurt had asked me to come back to Belford and take over the *BDT*?"

"What are you talking about?" Her face contorts in concerned confusion.

"Kurt hasn't told you?" As I had suspected.

"No." Piper glances about the room, struggling to find a response amidst all the blinking lights and green screens. "Maybe he forgot."

Or maybe he knew you'd react this way.

"Are you thinking of taking it?" Piper asks, voice high, worried.

"You're not exactly jumping for joy."

"You're here so seldom, and you're so unhappy when you are here, I'm surprised you're even considering it. Your life has always been elsewhere. And you have nobody here." She says this without a hint of irony that might suggest she knows a certain maternity ward nurse. Didn't Piper have her kids in this hospital? Maybe Connie was Nurse Wheeler by the time Piper's kids were born, not the more memorable Camarasa. Of course, she only met Connie once, and only for a minute. No more reason she should remember Connie than Connie should remember me.

I see Connie's left hand again, her olive skin. Was that a tan line on that ring finger? Ridiculous to consider it.

Piper gets up and finds the sponge in the cup next to Dad's bed. She presses it to his chapped lips. They don't respond, but his eyelids twitch, his chin flinches.

"I have nobody back there, either," I say.

"Weren't you seeing some woman in New York?" She turns, quizzical. "What was her name?"

Elizabeth. One night last year, when I called her from New Hampshire at our usual time, she didn't answer her phone; and when I finally reached her the next morning, she said she'd been with someone, but refused to tell me who or what they were doing. Instead, she said that she'd been meaning to have a talk with me, that it wasn't working anymore.

"It didn't last, what with all my campaign travel."

"And you haven't met anybody in Washington?"

"I just moved there, Piper." But it wasn't that. What few flings I'd engaged in over the years usually began with flirtations over a cassette recorder, interviews that turned into something more. But my job always interested women more than I did. Me, the big-time reporter. The stories I could tell, the people I'd met, the places I'd been. Until, that is, women found out that, instead of reporting from the scenes of crimes and calamities, I lived on the phone and pounded a keyboard in an office. It didn't help, the many dinners and movies I missed to meet deadlines, the many questions I asked. How, while I worked, did they fill their hours? Who else warmed their beds, offered them real, and not reported, excitement?

Being my age and living in a strange city where I know no one makes it even harder. Nowadays, when I interview women, sparks don't fly, flings don't flare up. Making any more effort than that to meet women—blind dates, matchmakers, singles groups—always feels desperate and doomed, a pathetic cry for help that I'm too embarrassed for anyone to hear.

"I'm only saying that *if you did come back*," Piper put in, "it would be nice if you had something or someone to bring with you besides all that baggage you carry around." She nods at my laptop again. "What the hell are you writing about, anyway?"

I open my mouth, but she holds up her hand. "No. I don't want to know. It's ancient history."

"You think this doesn't involve you, what I'm writing here?"

"Me?" She shrinks away, voice softening. "Why would it involve me?"

"Because of how he treated us—has always treated us—differently."

"Stop right there. If he treats me any differently, it's because I've been here, Walker. I take care of him."

"I know. It's true. But he's *always* favored you, from the moment you were born, and now, when I do come home, you put a wall around him, shielding him from me."

"And this is why! I know how you can get, this grudge you're still holding after all these years."

"He beat me, Piper. Often. And you made him do it."

She stares at me, stunned, frozen. I stare back until, finally, she takes a breath, straightening, putting the sponge back, her hands on her hips.

"Is that what this is all about? Stupid kid stuff that happened—" She waves her hand in the air, counting, "Forty flipping years ago?"

"See? You won't admit it. Like it's nothing. And now, he's in no position to."

"He's dying, Walker. Or is that why you're really here? So you can watch him die. Would that make you happy?"

"No. Of course not." I can't explain. "That's not why I'm here."

"Well, you sure make it seem that way."

"Look, I have to finish this thing." I hold up the laptop. "Maybe I'm always such a shit when I come home because I've never really finished this. Do you understand?"

"Fine. But I don't want to hear about it anymore. And don't write that crap thinking he doesn't give a damn about you." She points at the brown bag. "Because he does."

It's been an hour since I left Piper alone with Dad. I'm in the reception area where Gayle and I sat those many years ago, waiting for her mom to arrive, for news from the surgeon on Norm's condition. I'm just waking up from nodding off, trying to psych myself up to dive back into my story.

I can't believe Piper wrote off all those times she tattled on me like it was child's play, accusing me of only being here for—what? Christ, I don't want to see him die. I don't. In fact, this thing I'm writing makes me feel closer to him than ever.

The sleep did me good. Calmed me down. I'm refreshed. Relaxed. Focused.

Funny how memory sharpens when you find yourself in the same setting where events occurred. I picked this waiting room because

I want to put an end to the brooding. That's why I have to write about it. And after talking to Piper, seeing Connie, the real Connie, my Consuelo, I feel like I'm close to it. Closer than ever. Maybe to what he would tell me if he could.

Twenty-Five

A half hour after I left Manny and Norm at the hospital, I sat down at our dinner table. Dad had just returned from the plant and was picking up the serving utensils—the big silver fork, the gleaming carving knife. He gazed around the table, puzzling at us.

"Is something wrong, dear?" Mom asked.

Steaming pork chops were layered across the platter. A dish of peas to Dad's left, mashed potatoes to his right. Condiments. Tableware. Mom, Piper, and I in our usual places. If only Dad's problem was as simple as missing napkins or unfilled water glasses.

"Walker didn't tell you what happened today?"

"What?" Mom perked up. "What happened?"

I straightened, unwilling to muster the drama Dad wanted. But I didn't want to make light, either, so I took a drink of water, my face burning. The fight was a big deal—just not something I wanted to talk about.

"Walker?" He cocked his head, waiting.

Dad *wanted* me to say some crazed Mexican attacked my girlfriend's father, more *bad* Mexicans like the ones stealing from our gardens.

"Gayle's dad was drunk at work and got into a fight," I mumbled.

"Got into a fight? It wasn't *his* fault," Dad harrumphed, flipping a pork chop onto a plate. "He was assaulted. Out of the blue. Maimed."

I shot him a look. That's not how he had put it to Barb and Gayle, his spiel so professional and unbiased.

"Struck Ditweiler with a meat hook, of all things."

"My goodness!" Mom said.

"Oh, he's all right. It went right through the arm. But one hair to the right or left, an artery gets severed, and he bleeds out in minutes."

Piper stares at him, open-mouthed.

"He's fine," he reassures her. "Lucky as hell—as is that greaseball who mugged him."

"Your language, Michael."

Indeed. *Greaseball?*

"And why is *he* 'lucky'?" Mom said.

"Ditweiler was drunk." Dad offered me a filled plate to pass along. "If he pressed charges, that'd come out, and we'd have to let him go. So this jerk will probably get off scot-free."

Dad loaded up a second plate. He made it sound as if Norm's impairment made him the victim, like a wheel-chair-bound cripple prevented from ascending some stairs.

I couldn't help pointing out, "You know that Norm was angry at Mr. Camarasa, right?"

"Yeah, Camarasa told me all about it. The promotion, the wallet."

"You talked to him?" This hadn't occurred to me.

"Right before speaking with Mrs. Ditweiler." He passed Piper her plate. "And if you ask me, he could've come up with a better story." He started on his own plate, scooping peas. "I mean, if it was the promotion Norm was mad about, why in God's name would he want Camarasa's wallet?"

"His wallet?" Mom asked.

"I know. It doesn't make any sense." He nodded at Piper. "Now does it?"

"Not at all," she said, puppy-like.

"Especially because Ditweiler didn't have the wallet. Security looked everywhere, but it seems to have conveniently vanished." He appraised each of us, his eyebrows raised, a mystery invoked.

"Wow," Piper said, fascinated.

The lost wallet was currently burning a hole in my jeans pocket. So, Manny had remembered what Norm tried to do.

"Walker—" Piper said. "The other night—you know, when we were *downstairs*—" She whispered the word, as if that could possibly make Dad less curious about her meaning. "You said Gayle's dad talked about this Manny being here illegally. Could that have something to do with it?"

Leave it to Piper to dredge up Norm's stupid conspiracy theory.

"I don't know how," I said, wanting to yell out, *It's none of your fucking business!*

"Norm said that?" Dad asked, quizzing me.

"That doesn't make it true."

"No, but if it is—" Dad considered.

"Yeah." Piper jumped in, "Maybe that's what they fought about."

"Better yet—" Dad pointed his fork at each of us in turn, a theory formulating. "Camarasa's wallet. If it's missing, his green card is probably missing, too."

"What are you saying?" I asked.

"I'm saying, if Ditweiler's right and Camarasa knows he's onto him, maybe Manny decides he has to do something before Norm can report him. So he hides the wallet and starts the fight but claims Norm did, that he stole the wallet. That takes the heat off of him and puts it on Norm, making him the bad guy. Meanwhile, the card is missing through no fault of his own, and if its a forgery, no one can examine it,"

"Hmm." I shuffled possible responses. If I hauled out the wallet, he'd be so angry, like I'd played him. *Look, I've had it all along.*

"You know what," Dad said, "I'll talk to HR tomorrow and see if they can confirm his status. Much as I suspect some of these new hires I examine, management keeps telling me there's no law against hiring illegals, and I shouldn't even discuss it with them. But that doesn't mean you can't deport one if he screws up." Dad took a bite, his inquiry having descended into inquisition. "So it may not matter if Norm can't press charges against this jerk. We might be able to get rid of him, anyway. And all," he dabbed his fork at Piper, "thanks to you."

She beamed, dancing in her seat.

"I can't believe how smart you are, sometimes."

Dad's astonished smile transformed into a frown when he turned toward me.

"Why didn't you think of that?" He shook his head at my stupidity, confirmed yet again.

The head shaking returned to nods and smiles at my sister—the natural order of things: Piper, brilliant; Walker, stupid. Norm, the hero; Manny, the villain.

Twenty-Six

Once my father saw that meat hook in Norm's arm, Manny became a 'bad Mexican.' Dad established a beachhead on the wrong side of the truth, aided by my little sister and that business about Manny's green card. I'd fallen into the trap of one of my father's worst—and sometimes, best—qualities. Once he got an idea into his head, it was impossible to change his mind.

Occasionally, this willfulness translated into unflagging loyalty. Later in life, my mother got sick and forgot our names. I remember the Christmas before she died, Frazier recounting his trip home that Thanksgiving. It was as if Mom could slip into her past as easily as if it had swallowed up the present, imagining Frazier and Piper costumed in the fashions of her youth, recast as long-lost friends. The den, the dining room, the kitchen—these became whatever favorite old haunt her imagination frequented. But according to Frazier, the remarkable thing was how my father played along, suffering the indignity of whichever part she assigned him: a Filipino houseboy to whom she complained about her husband's anger issues; a rich, former boyfriend who promised her the moon if she'd marry him. Dad even stood by her when she mistook Frazier for me, insisting for a time that I had finally come home, asking Dad, as Frazier sat there, "Aren't you happy to see Walker? Doesn't he look great?" Frazier said Dad was happy to see 'me,' agreed 'I' did look great—Frazier's not-so-subtle attempt to get me to come home. The thing was, she'd never called in all those years, so this wasn't the 'real' Mom talking. It seemed to me Dad was just playing along to keep Mom happy, another self-serving, cynical lie at my expense—and hers, too. Allowing her to believe I'd come home.

At least, that's what I thought at the time. After seeing those clippings he collected, I'm not so sure now.

My point is, Dad was stubborn to a fault, and sometimes it made him appear foolish. But even at the height of foolishness, he would continue to behave with such conviction that you couldn't help but admire him.

One time in church when I was much younger, Father Macklemore started his sermon by announcing a future steeple renovation project for which he wanted volunteers to help raise money. My dad rose in his battleship gray Sunday suit, climbed out of the pew, and in front of the entire congregation—a packed house in those days—marched up to the pulpit and stood next to the surprised priest. The man thanked him and said the sign up sheet would be in the vestibule after mass. Dad didn't catch the hint. Macklemore never intended anyone should come up then and there, and we all knew it, since no one else stepped forward. He didn't have the temerity to tell the prominent doctor and former Air Force colonel standing at attention to go back to his seat. So he stumbled through his sermon, and Dad remained by his side, as if he was the only one brave or charitable enough to volunteer. Torn between mortification and awe, I didn't know whether to crawl under my pew or jump up and cheer.

Like my mother in her last days, I'm playing out in my imagination what happened thirty years ago. My father wrote off those embarrassing moments with her as her sickly fantasies, no truth to them at all, and that diagnosis gave him license to stick to his version of things. Or so it seemed at the time.

I'd say I'm doing the same thing, supplying my version of events, but perhaps for the first time, and because I'm going into such exacting detail, I'm seeing Dad's version, too. Following the evidence as he must have seen it, the logic. And now, throwing in a new variable. If he cared enough to collect my clippings—if he really cared about me—I need to consider how that might have steered his thinking.

If Manny Camarasa was carrying forged documents, couldn't he want to cover that up by claiming Norm stole his wallet? Couldn't Dad have been right? Couldn't Manny have struck first?

Possibly. Except, he didn't. I saw it all, and that's not what happened.

The truth is not a suit or dress you can alter to fit your story, lengthening the hem, cinching in the waist. The story must fit the truth, even if it ends up an ill-fitting mess, torn sleeves and broken zippers. But I was only a kid that summer, not a trained journalist, and this truth was my own and too painful to discuss. It was so much easier to let a story emerge around which the truth could wrap and deform itself. That's my only justification for what happened next.

Twenty-Seven

Manny's wallet in my hip pocket was beginning to feel like a malignant tumor I needed to have removed before it metastasized and killed me. After dinner, I grabbed the phonebook, thinking I'd call Manny or, if he was still in the hospital, someone in his family. I'd tell them about the wallet, and maybe I could drop it off, get the damned thing off my hands; but there were no Camarasas listed, and when I called information, they confirmed there were no Camarasas in the phone book.

As soon as I got off the phone it rang, like maybe Manny knew I was trying to get hold of him, knew how I'd kept quiet, and wanted to wring my neck. But it wasn't him. It was Gayle calling, upset about the fight. Patty and Kurt were at her house. They all wanted to come over. I couldn't very well say no.

I waited in the basement, but they came to the side door upstairs. Piper led them down, the whole gang, the basement door swinging shut behind them. Gayle threw her arms around me, so I returned the hug, comforting her. The least I could do. She seated herself between me and Patty on the couch. Kurt plopped down in the easy chair, bright-eyed with excitement about the day's doings, and Piper, her ego still buoyant from Dad's flattery, perched on the piano bench, beaming.

"Gayle says the guy popped up out of nowhere and whacked her dad with a meat hook? Is that right?" Kurt tilted forward, eager to hear my eyewitness account. I ignored him, turning instead to my ex.

"Did your mom convince Norm to drop the charges?"

"No—"

"No?"

"I mean, yes, he dropped the charges, but only after *I* talked to him."

"*You*? What did you say?"

"Nothing my mom didn't say. But they've squabbled lately. He's still mad she started offering night time hours at the salon."

"He's mad your mom's stopped cooking supper for him, you mean," Patty threw in, nodding.

"Is that so bad?" Gayle looked at Patty, then me and Kurt. "He busts his ass all day and then has to come home to TV dinners?"

"It seems to me your mom busts her ass just as much," Patty mumbled. "If not more."

Gayle glared at her friend.

I let out a big breath. "Well, I'm glad he dropped the charges."

"Glad?" Gayle frowned at me. "That Manny guy should be in jail, stabbing him with a meat hook like that."

That bugged me, too, the way he'd let fly with that meat hook. Why the meat hook? Why not use his hand? Or did he mean to use it, laying in wait, seizing the chance to get back at Norm with all the weapons at his disposal? It was hard not to be swayed by the horror movie vividness of, "a meat hook through his arm," making Manny out to be a monster.

"We were talking at dinner," Piper threw in, trying to stir the pot, "And my Dad said this Camarasa guy told him your father tried to *steal his wallet.*"

"His wallet?" Gayle asked. "Why would he want his wallet?"

"Exactly! Nobody could even find the wallet, so what we think is—" Piper continued, leaning in conspiratorially, "Camarasa *hid* it so no one could check it for his green card—"

"He didn't hide the wallet!" I blurted, unable to take any more.

"How do you know?" Piper asked, indignantly. Everyone stared at me.

"Because I have it!" I grabbed it out of my pocket and tossed it on the coffee table where it flipped open on its back, a dead blackbird.

"Where did you get it?" Gayle asked, flummoxed.

"I saw the whole thing." I leaned back on the couch, scanned the hats on the opposite wall, as Kurt picked up the wallet and looked through it.

"You saw it?" Piper said, confused. "You saw it when?" As if my lies had so far removed me from the equation, I wasn't even present.

"I was right there on the loading dock. Manny works next to me. I saw it all."

"Saw what all?" Piper challenged. *Prove you saw it!*

I recomposed the picture from a different angle as if filmed from Kelly's office door. In the distance, from below, not from atop that stupid boxcar, defying the memorandum on his clipboard, not breaking the rules.

"What happened, Walker?" Gayle asked.

No, that was one detail I couldn't find words for. So I took myself out of the picture. I simply explained how Manny was sleeping on top of the pallets when Norm snuck up and tried to take his wallet. Manny reacted with the meat hook, the two of them tumbled, I found the wallet and didn't have time to give it to anyone.

"I don't understand," Gayle said, shifting to get a better look at me. "This afternoon, you said you didn't see anything."

"Yeah," Piper said, huffy now. "Why didn't you speak up at dinner?" Her chin lifted, as if provoked, the balloon of her grand theory having been popped.

I scanned the room. Mouths opened, expectant. What could I say? That I was scared of my father? Scared of what he'd think? Wouldn't Piper love that.

"I was afraid—" I took a breath and gnawed at my lip. Afraid my father might—what? Ask how I saw it? Force me to say I couldn't do the one thing he'd asked me to do. Do the job right. Follow the rules. Show some smarts. Be a man.

"Afraid?" Gayle said.

Afraid he'd hit me? Berate me. Not in front of all those men. Unless—I'd been *so* foolish, *so* immature. Such a child, a loser. Maybe he could have.

"Of what?"

Of that look on his face. How he'd slowly shake his head, unable to look at the other men. You couldn't respect a man with a son like that. A child at nineteen. An infant. An idiot. A giant stain on his white coat.

Gayle seemed to relax. She chuckled, some realization.

"What?" I said.

"You're protecting my father," she said.

"What??"

"Look, I know you don't like him, and it's hard for you to admit, but that's why you kept quiet, isn't it? You were afraid he'd get into trouble."

Protect her drunken fool of a father?

"That's so sweet of you," Gayle whispered, sighing. She rubbed her thumb appreciatively across the back of my hand. She bent close and kissed me on the cheek, her eyes wet with gratitude.

Next to her, Patty sat, open-mouthed, letting it sink in. Kurt chuckled, sitting back in his chair, setting his hands on the armrests, a smile widening on his face. Only Piper seemed doubtful. But then, she could imagine the scene easily enough. What I was *really* afraid of. My father in my face. She'd seen it all before.

For the others, a new puzzle had been opened, its pieces falling into place and painting a picture even prettier than before. I had saved Norm. What a hero I was. I'd even concealed the incriminating evidence—the wallet. All because I couldn't tell the real truth, the truth behind the truth.

"Does he have a green card?" Piper asked. "I mean, maybe Gayle's dad was right. Maybe that man is illegal and your father was looking for proof." She couldn't let go of her little success at dinner. At least, she wasn't focused on why I really lied. Or maybe she didn't want to go there, risk me confessing the whole, epic horror story going back years, and her role in it.

"Here it is," Kurt said, holding up the card. I reached over and snatched it.

He glared at me. They all waited. The proof. *Let's see what Norm was after!* I didn't want to look at it. Manny's fate hung on the authenticity of a card. Norm's, too. I'd be crushed it if was fake. If it was real. Either way. I studied it for a second. It sure looked real enough, picture, official text.

"Can I see it?" Kurt asked.

I shrugged and tossed it at him. He examined it, squinting, turning it over and back. Piper got up and looked over his shoulder, her hands hugging the back of his chair.

"If it's a fake," he said, "It's a pretty good one."

"It looks real to me," I said, taking the card.

"Well, here," he said, and reached for his own wallet. He pulled it out, found a card of his own and dealt it onto the table. I picked it up and examined it, wondering what his drivers license had to do with anything.

"What's your point?"

"Look closer," Kurt said. "The birth date."

"10/12/1953." He threw another card on the table.

"That's the real one," he said, smiling. "Got that fake off a guy in West Town a while back."

They both looked the same. The only difference was the year of birth: 1955 vs. 1953.

"How do you think I been getting my beer?" He smiled.

"Kurt Swanson," Patty sniped, swiping the two cards out of my hand, examining them.

"I'm only saying, it's not that hard to get a good fake if you know where to go."

"You're amazing." Patty shook her head.

"What?" he said. "Half the kids in town have these."

"Yeah, right." She tossed his cards back on the coffee table. They slid onto the floor. She snatched up the green card from where Piper had dropped it on the table.

"So, it *could* be fake," Piper said, perking up, hopeful.

"But if it's real," Gayle said, "It makes what Walker did that much sweeter. They might have fired my dad, had him arrested. I can't thank you enough."

She and Kurt nodded, agreeing, but not Piper, who was gauging my reaction. But what she saw, I couldn't make out. Maybe, what my father saw. A coward. A loser. A bum.

"You've got to tell," Patty blurted out, staring at me. "Tell them what you saw."

Gayle turned to her best friend.

"Why?" she asked. "Norm didn't bring charges. Nobody got arrested."

"This guy, Manny," Patty sat up. "He may not have been arrested, but everyone will think he started it, that he's getting away with murder, or attempted, anyway. And who cares about that stupid card? Maybe, he's just trying to hold down a job. Did you ever think of that? Like that guy you wash cars with—Fernando?"

Kurt rolled his eyes.

Gayle faced Patty. "Whose side are you on, anyway?" They glared at each other. "Look, if nobody saw it, it's still Manny's word against Norm's. What more do you want?"

"Right. And people in Belford will believe Manny from Mexico over Norm, the hometown boy?"

"I'm going outside," I said, getting up. I grabbed the wallet off the table and the green card out of Piper's hands.

Patty was right. 'Meat Hook' Manny would take on a whole new meaning—what I'd thought it meant the first time I heard it, the first time I saw him, that incessant smile of his, that bunny shirt, a crazy, maybe even violent man. He might never drive that forklift now. He'd be stuck unloading fuel tanks, and it wouldn't be just Norm treating him like shit. Everyone would.

After replacing the card in the wallet, I lurched out through the mud room to the basement door.

Outside, the world had gone dark red in the setting sun. I walked past the Adirondacks and the picnic table and along the top of the plateau to where the cherry trees no longer blocked my view of the river. But I didn't see the Foundry, the sunset or anything else. I was too angry to see anything.

A hand slipped into mine. Next to me, Gayle gave me a small smile.

Patty followed us out, talking at me. "This isn't right, Walker. If you saw something, you need to tell someone." I stared into the night. "You guys!" She tromped around us, facing us. My ex gave her a cold, quiet frown I'd never seen, like Patty was blocking the view.

"Gayle," Patty said "I know he's your dad, but—"

"You don't know!" she barked back. "That meat hook didn't kill him, but losing his job might."

"But it's not right. People need to know Manny didn't start it."

Right. And admit I lied to my father, lied to his face. Sure.

I pushed past the two girls down the hill, unable to stand still with that thought.

"You know what?" Patty called out. "I've had enough of you guys. I'm going home."

"Come on," Kurt said somewhere behind me. "You don't have a car."

"Well," she said, heading off, "you can give me a ride, or I can walk."

"Christ," he said. "Gayle! You coming?"

She clutched my hand. "You can't say anything, Walker. Yes, he's a jerk sometimes, but he's my dad and he needs this." Sure, somebody needed to take pity on the poor bastard. But did it have to be me?

"And you know—" Piper appeared on my other side, falling into formation, part of the team. "If Daddy finds out this Camarasa is illegal, it'll prove Gayle's dad was right about him all along, even if Norm did start the fight."

"Gayle!" Kurt called.

"I'm coming!" She squeezed my hand one more time, let go and ran after them.

I stared down the hill, wanting to jump in the river and get swept away.

Twenty-Eight

At work the next day, Kelly led me over to the fuel tank boxcar. He was making me take over for Manny. Of course. In my usual car, some older, stooped man with short, white hair was already making seat frame avalanches, slowly but methodically. In Norm's usual berth, a stocky, middle-aged woman in jeans and t-shirt was making quick work of hauling mufflers out of that railroad car. They made both jobs look easy, and it dawned on me, that maybe those jobs were easy, that they'd been going easy on Norm and me all along. Then I looked into the fuel tanks car.

"This is only until he comes back, right?" I stared at the tanks stacked in neat columns. At least, they weren't a tangled mess.

"Camarasa? If they let that son-of-a-bitch back in the door." Kelly shook his head. "It was hard enough for Norm with that hip of his. Then he loses the forklift, and now this?" Maybe Kelly'd had less say in who got that promotion than I had imagined.

"But he didn't press charges. They can't keep Manny from working, can they?"

The foreman chuckled. "That may be true, but how long do you think he'll last after what he did?"

"What do you mean?"

He cocked his head. "Do you want to work with that maniac?"

I shrugged, not sure what to say. Was he a maniac?

"Exactly," he nodded and peered inside the boxcar. "Now, these fuel tanks—"

"They can't just fire him, can they?"

"Maybe they won't need to."

"How's that?"

"You'll see," Kelly said, pulling a tank from the top of the pile. He wrapped both arms around the thing as he slid it down, settling it on the loading dock floor. "Now, after what happened yesterday, management said no more meat hooks, so you'll have to do this the old-fashioned way."

The gray, aluminum tank looked as if a large clamshell had been assembled from two of those hard plastic kiddie pools welded together.

"What's the old fashioned way?"

"Hug the bastard over to the train."

It didn't seem possible. The thing was so big and offered nothing to hold onto. I touched the little hole in its lip. What I'd have given for Manny's meat hook at that moment.

"Go on," Kelly said. "Give it a big old bear hug and haul ass. You'll get the hang of it."

Easy for him to say. I could only wrap my arms halfway around the damned thing. As he watched, I squeezed and took off, praying I could waddle the thing over to the tugger wagon before it slipped.

"Okay, then." Kelly said, slapping his hand against the side of the boxcar. "Good luck and happy loading."

After dumping the tank in the empty wagon, I knew why neither of those two other workers had been put on these tanks. No, put the strapping young college stud on those nasty old tanks. Me. I was learning the hard way that Manny had been stuck with the most difficult job on the dock—and he'd figured out how to make it easy. A meat hook—now forbidden to me.

Not ten minutes into the shift, I lost my grip on a fuel tank. The dock was a noisy place, but after that tank hit the ground, a thunk like a cracked church bell, all eyes were on me. It was a goner, one corner staved in. I took small comfort in Kelly not being there to see it. The breakage report would tattle on me.

Strike one. How many would I get before I struck out?

Although I managed not to drop another fuel tank, I struggled every trip from boxcar to tugger wagon, no matter what I tried. All day, I barely managed to keep up, warier than ever of that red button. Whenever an empty tugger train showed up, it juiced up my adrenaline, kicking me into high gear. As I drove home that afternoon, I was still coming down from it, a bad high. Pain pulsed from every muscle between my neck and my hips.

I knew Manny lived somewhere on River Street, the same one the Foundry was on, the last one before the bridge. Sitting at that stoplight, I considered turning, dropping off the wallet, but I didn't know Manny's address, and I wasn't at all sure what kind of greeting I'd get if I could find his place. Yes, in the hospital he'd said, "I won't tell," but he might have been in some kind of drug-induced stupor at the time. Maybe when he sobered up, he'd want to strangle me. If he knew I'd seen it. *I won't tell.* He knew I was up there, watching everything. How could I not have seen it?

I drove on, across the bridge. Better to hold onto the wallet until I had a better grasp of the situation.

While I was doing the dishes that night, Gayle phoned. She wanted to go for a walk. I hesitated, but she sounded upset on the phone, so I told her I'd be waiting for her in the back yard.

As soon as she got there, Gayle started in on Patty. As we walked down to the river, she explained how she and Patty had made up at work. They could never stay mad at each other for long, but halfway through the morning, Patty had gone home, saying she didn't feel well. Gayle had seen it coming, what with Barb and her customers buzzing about the fight at the plant. I could picture them, all those blue hairs, their heads covered in curlers or stuffed inside hair dryers, commiserating with Barb, baffled as to why Norm hadn't pressed charges. As Patty was leaving, she had told Gayle she'd scream if she heard one more woman say "poor Norm" while pointing out how bad the Mexican problem in town had become.

"At least you understand," Gayle said, patting my arm.

"What? That there's a 'Mexican problem'? If there's a problem, it's in the heads of those gossips getting those ugly Pat Nixon hairdo's."

"Those are my mother's customers, Walker. I'm not about to argue with them."

"They're small-minded bigots, looking for any excuse to persecute anyone in this town who doesn't look like them. And I only made things worse."

She pouted for half a second before smiling again. I couldn't tell if she agreed with those women or not.

"I meant you understand the situation," she said, squeezing my hand. She put an arm around my waist, pulling me close. "It's so sweet what you did for Daddy, for us, keeping quiet."

"Gayle—" I pulled away and grabbed her shoulders, turning her to face me. "I didn't do anything sweet, and I didn't do it for your father."

"Of course, you did. Why else would you do it?"

I held her at arm's length. Even if she didn't always understand, she did listen. I sat her on the stone bench.

"I know your father's had a hard time. But the reason I kept quiet—" But why? Because my father was bearing down on me? No, I wasn't going there, but I'd be damned if I'd let her think I was protecting Norm. So, I told her how I'd climbed atop the boxcar looking for a place to relax. "That's when I saw the fight. But going up there is forbidden. If I'd spoken up, they'd have found out I broke the rules."

"So you're saying you lied, not because my dad would get in trouble, but because *you would?*" Incredulity washed over her as if that was the last possible explanation she expected. I had to turn away, unable to face her, those eyes, damning me for my selfishness, making it all about me. But it wasn't all about me. It wasn't.

"No. Because of who asked."

"What do you mean, 'who asked'?"

"It was my father who asked me if I'd seen the fight. My *father*."

"Okay. So—this is somehow about your father?" She shook her head, more baffled than ever.

I'd only hinted at the troubles I had with him—how crazy he could get, his temper. She had no clue how far it went, what he really thought of me. How could she, the way he bantered with her whenever she showed up with a new hairdo, saying how clever she was? She'd scoffed whenever I'd made any off-hand remarks about run-ins with him. A fight with my father? That charmer?

"What happened with your father?"

How could I tell her he'd made me take this job to test me, wake me up, brand a message on my hide about *what*—responsibility? integrity? purpose? And in two days time, I'd already flunked the test, another F on my report card.

She sat there so patiently, squeezing my arm. She had me. Any confession would be a sign of trust, proving we were together again. Maybe it was time she knew that in all the time we'd been together, I'd *never* trusted her, not completely, not with the real truth.

"Walker?"

"He beat me, Gayle."

There. I said it. Squeamishness soured my gut as if I were the beater and not him.

She squinted with incomprehension and let out a scoff of disbelief.

"Beat you?" A smile. As if I was joking. Or maybe it was relief. Like, is that all?

"Yes, he beat me."

I had to explain, make her believe it. But I couldn't turn those pictures into words—punch, shake, squeeze—stupid as a Batman comic. Pow! Bang! Crunch! She was sure to laugh.

"When we first moved here," I added, as if distancing it made it more plausible.

"You're serious. He beat you."

"Yes," I said, but with uncertainty. Almost guilt. *He'd* beaten *me*. Not the other way around.

She tried to hide the smile, the amusement, putting on a straight face.

"That was, what, four, five years ago?" she said, as if time should have healed it.

"It doesn't go away, Gayle. When he gave me my physical the other day, touching me, you know, because he had to. Taking my temperature. Checking my pulse. It opened those old wounds again, brought them back, fresh as ever. I almost threw up."

She put her hand on my arm. "I had no idea. Your father?" She shook her head. "He seems like such a—"

"And then, when Manny and Norm were on the floor and my dad rushed in, he was in this state, guns blazing."

"Guns?"

"I mean, he was on a tear, all business, and here I'd pulled this stupid stunt, climbing on top of this boxcar. So when he asked if anybody had witnessed the fight—"

"But—" She squeezed. "He wouldn't have hit you, would he? In front of those men?"

"No. I don't think so. It's only that—" I slapped my leg, frustration mounting. Ridiculous notion, in front of those men. "I can't explain it." How it pinned me to the wall, wriggling.

"It's okay, Walker." She rubbed my arm, smiling.

"It's not okay!" I pushed her away.

"I'm only trying to say—" She reached a hand out. "You don't need to explain. I understand. I do. But why didn't you ever tell me?"

Because I knew you'd react this way! Pooh-poohing the spring shower I'd whipped up into a hurricane, making such a fuss over the kind of punishments all kids suffered. But it was my suffering. They were my beatings, and they were still with me, battering my insides every time he raised his voice.

Her hand alighting on my leg made me small again, a whiny little kid, needing a hug. I pushed it away.

"Why are you being this way?" Her voice cracked. Her eyes had gone wet, hurt, her hands in her lap. "I want to help. But you're like—I'm not the one who did this, Walker."

We sat that way for the longest time, the evening breeze playing over us.

"Well, I have to admit," she said, brightening. "I *was* a little surprised you'd lie for my dad." She patted my back, trying to see into my face. I shrugged assent. Yes, that much was true. "And it all works out in the end, right?"

"Works out?" I faced her. Had she heard a thing I'd said? "I lied to my father, Gayle. Now everyone thinks Manny Camarasa is some kind of monster. The women in your shop. My foreman, scheming to get him canned or make him quit. And it's my fault."

"Are you going to tell on my dad after all? Is that it?"

"I didn't say that. I need to figure out what to do."

"He could lose his job. And what if that man really is here illegally? Did you think of that? Maybe my dad was onto him, and that was the only way to prove it."

"Stealing his wallet?"

"He got stabbed with a meat hook. A meat hook, Walker. Who does that? Unless he has something to hide."

"Christ." I shook my head, standing up. The fact was, she could be right. I didn't know Manny at all.

She grabbed my hand again. "I know this is difficult. And I'm sorry about what your dad did to you. I am. I feel so bad for you. But can't you—forget about it? Why stir up more trouble?"

Because that was me: trouble, stirred up and roiling, on such shaky ground I didn't know where I was going or how to get there. For the past year, the earth had stood still while I'd been away at college. I'd stabilized, found landmarks, mapped a way out of this life, but now my world was quaking again, or I was. Clearly, I couldn't turn to Gayle. She only wanted me to keep quiet. She still didn't understand me, and she never would.

I couldn't answer her questions. All I could do was walk her back up the hill.

Twenty-Nine

We'd settled in at the dinner table the following night when Piper asked my dad if AMC had found out whether Manny was illegal or not. She couldn't leave it alone.

All day, I'd tried to focus on my work, the ball game, anything to forget my conversation with Gayle, this Manny-Norm crap, and now Piper was prying open the scab again.

Dad said the guy who runs HR explained that when Manny was hired, he showed them what appeared to be a valid green card. Immigration Services told them anyone who lost their green card had the right to apply for a replacement, which could take months. They could only fire him for being illegal if that replacement card was denied.

"Anyway, they aren't too worried about him at present since he hasn't come back to work."

"So, that wallet and the green card." Piper eyed me as she did that money thing with her thumb and index fingers, rubbing them together as if she had the wallet in her hand. "What if they showed up?"

For a heart-attack second, I was sure she'd blab.

"Well, if someone could get a better look at that card—" Dad cut his food, leaving the thought hanging. He was unaware of the staring contest that had begun between Piper and me. "But no one knows what Camarasa is up to, or if he's even still around."

Piper broke the stare first and resumed shoving food around her plate. We ate in silence.

More than a week had passed since the fight and since I'd last seen Manny. I kept hearing what he said in his hospital bed. *He* wouldn't tell on *me*. This guy, who was probably still in bed, hurt. Or gone.

Maybe he'd left town altogether.

Once Mom left us to the dishes, I flipped off the faucet, turned around to Piper and said, "Can't you give it a rest, Piper? This Manny stuff is none of your business."

She studied me for a long second.

"You know what? I don't think you lied to protect Gayle's dad at all. I think you lied to protect Manny," she said. "You know he's illegal, don't you!?"

"I don't!" *She thought this?* "Piper, you saw the same card I did. I don't know any more than you do."

"So why won't you hand it over to someone who can find out?"

"Because." Because I didn't trust our father or that company to do anything but railroad him out of his job, his home, his adopted country. "It's his right to do with it what he wants, not ours."

"Then what are *you* still doing with it then?

"I'm giving it back."

"Yeah? When?"

"I don't even know where he lives."

"Doesn't it say in his wallet somewhere?"

Of course, it would, *dolt!* I would have slapped my head for not thinking of it, but I didn't want to give Piper the satisfaction. And besides, that wasn't the real reason. The fact was, I still hadn't worked up the nerve to face him.

Before I could respond, Piper said, "You're protecting him." She dried a plate and put it away. "He attacked Gayle's father, you saw it, and you won't say anything because you're protecting him."

Thirty

Friday night, Patty worked late at the salon with Gayle, so Kurt called to ask if I wanted to shoot pool at Rambler Lanes. We weren't exactly pool sharks, but we had moved up from the coin-operated table to the good Brunswick nine-footers in the billiard room. On those tables, we learned sophisticated games like Nine-ball and Straight that not only required good eyes and steady hands but also strategy and planning. We even bought our own cue sticks, both with inlaid pearl above the wraps. Kurt and I hadn't done battle since the previous summer, and he had boasted how much he'd improved, hustling up games with anyone he could find in the pool room. Now, he was itching to do battle.

I made the mistake of trying to leave by the door in the den where my parents and sister were watching *The Rockford Files*. Dad asked where I was headed, so I hoisted the leather sleeve that held my cue stick.

"Can I go with you?" Piper jumped up from the couch. "Please? I haven't been to the bowling alley in ages."

I tried to tell her it was only Kurt and I shooting pool, but that only made her bouncier, repeating her pleas, promising she wouldn't be a bother.

"Can't you take her with you?" my dad said.

"Please?" she pleaded. She had her hand out, rubbing her thumb and index finger together again. Manny's wallet. The little creep had me trapped. I shook my head and said, "Sure. Why not?"

"I just have to get changed." She bolted upstairs.

Of course, I still hadn't taken back the wallet even though, yes, I'd found Manny's address inside. Riverside Cabins, 340 East River Street, Building # 4. I still hadn't worked up the nerve.

Ten long minutes later, she returned in a pair of blue jeans and a lime green knit pullover. At least, she looked her age for once, clothes fitted to contours I didn't know she had.

Once we were in the car, Piper apologized, saying she'd never tell on me. "I had to get out of that house is all."

I was too pissed to say anything. By impulsively showing her and the others Manny's wallet, I'd given my sister yet another tool with which to torment me.

The largest bowling alley in town, Rambler Lanes featured thirty-two lanes with a separate wing devoted to billiards. That night, cars packed the parking lot. A league night, no doubt. I parked the Datsun on a side street, grabbed my cue.

"You can play one game of Eight-ball, but then you'll have to sit down and watch, okay?"

"Okay. Sheesh," she said, wobbling her head.

Inside the bowling alley, wooden explosions of pins were followed by cheers. The heavy balls rumbled evenly on the hardwood, bounced into gutters and swooped up to ball returns, while pinsetters ticked and clanked, collected and dropped pins in perfect chevrons. The patrons, mostly men, chattered and laughed.

"It's noisy in here," Piper yelled in my ear, as if she'd never been in the place. We'd been here together before, hadn't we?

Juke box music was the mortar that bound all these sounds into a complete wall of noise as ear-pounding as the plant's assembly line at full speed.

"It's a league night," I yelled back, pointing out the team shirts. All the same style, these short-sleeved button downs sported big flat collars the same color as the sleeves, but all had white torsos with team names in big letters on back. The *Ho-Ho-Ho's*. Green Giant employees. *The Gremlins. The Ambassadors. Four on the Floor. Standard Shift.* AMC workers.

"What are we waiting for?" Piper said, looking around for the pool room. There were Bruce and Mort, sipping beers on lane five. I hadn't seen them together since the day the mutant car rolled off the line.

"I see some guys I work with." I pointed at them.

A few lanes over, Liam from the loading dock hunched over a ball return, his telltale mutton chops singling him out. I recognized two other guys with him whose names I didn't know. One unloaded bumpers. The other, fenders. *The Dock-ters.* Ironic.

"Are we going to stand here all night?" Piper asked.

Oddly, I felt left out, a party to which I hadn't been invited. I'd assumed these guys were as beat down after work as I was, but here they seemed happy, energized. Liam whipped his ball out, spinning it in a long arc. He battered down all but the ten pin. When he reached for his second ball, he saw me. I waved, but he only nodded, as if he didn't want others to witness his greeting.

"Who's that?"

"One of the guys. Let's go." Perhaps, it was uncool to fraternize with the doctor's son. I lowered my hand, self-conscious.

In the pool room, nine large tables were arranged in three rows of three. All but one of them was occupied by dark-haired men—Mexicans. Bent over the middle table was pale-skinned Kurt. With his long, blond hair dangling in his face, he stood out like the only *O* in a life-sized game of Tic-Tac-Toe, surrounded by *X*s. He straightened, a broad grin widening his face.

"Well, what do we have here?" he said, eyes wide at Piper.

"My dad made me bring her," I said, unsheathing my cue stick. *I was blackmailed,* I wanted to say.

"Have you played before?" he asked Piper.

"Not really," she said, swiveling uncertainly. "Can someone show me?" She glanced between us, her eyes spending more time on Kurt than on me.

"Happy to," Kurt said. He beckoned to me. "Lend her your cue."

I screwed the two halves together and handed it to him.

"This place has changed," I said. Over the past couple years, I had noticed the odd Mexican playing alongside us, but they had never filled the place like this.

"Tell me about it." It came out as grumbling, but his being here, the only white guy playing pool alongside these Mexicans, reminded me that he was still a big-hearted kid—a Camaro.

"Now," he began, looking at Piper. "Do you know how to make a bridge?"

"You mean, like, over water?" she asked, confused.

Kurt chuckled and got her set up on the table. With his index finger and thumb, he formed a donut shape through which he slid his cue, back and forth. She couldn't do it herself, so he turned to me.

"May I?" As if he needed my permission.

"Have at it," I said, looking away. A few of the other men watched, some with amusement, chuckling; others with unseemly interest, eyeing my little sister up and down as she leaned over the table, long, wavy, red hair draping her face, the only girl in the room, stretched out in form-hugging clothes, Kurt behind her, positioning her hands.

I caught the eye of one of these men, and he turned back to his game. That did the trick. I glanced about, catching eyes, dousing interest. Not the kind of problem I'd anticipated when I let her join us. In the far corner, one of the Mexicans looked familiar as he leaned on his stick.

"Isn't that Fernando?" I said, edging over to Kurt while he studied Piper's form as she attempted a shot. I'd only met him that day at the car wash, but he was wearing the same distinctive red bandana around his head to keep his black, shoulder-length hair out of his eyes.

"Yeah," Kurt grunted, watching Piper. She jerked her bridge hand off the table in the middle of the stroke, her stick glancing off the ball, which jumped, spinning.

"I can't do this," she said, reddening, trying to hand the cue back.

"Sure you can," Kurt said, pushing it back into her hands. "But you have to keep that bridge on the table."

"You didn't tell me he played," I said, watching Fernando sink another.

Piper followed my gaze. "Is he that wetback guy you work with?" she asked, as offhand as if that were his nationality, a Canadian or a German.

"Don't use that word," I snapped.

"It's what he is," Kurt said.

"If he's not supposed to be here," Piper said, glancing my way, then turning to Kurt, "why don't you tell someone?"

"Because my father likes the son-of-a-bitch, that's why. Now, you want to play pool or not?"

"Can you maybe show me again?" She scrunched up her face, as if she was afraid to impose. What a flirt.

"Sure." Kurt returned to the table and leaned over her from behind.

At this rate, I'd never get to play. So much for Piper not ruining the evening. I amused myself by watching Fernando. He was good.

Really good. He sank balls methodically and with great anticipation for the next shot, getting into a rhythm, chalking his cue between shots.

At the car wash the day I'd met him, Kurt and I had jawboned a good twenty minutes while Fernando worked on my Datsun, paying us no mind. He returned to the back seat of the car to vacuum it a second time, which made Kurt bellow and throw up his hands in frustration at how slow he was. Fernando played pool with the same attention to detail, checking out every angle.

"You two ever play?" I asked when Kurt backed away from Piper to let her try again.

"Fernando? He's too chicken-shit." Kurt said, monitoring my sister. "Good one, Pipes." She didn't put one in, but at least she hit the cue ball straight. Kurt continued his instruction: "Now imagine the angle that stripe has to take into the pocket—"

I tuned him out and turned to Fernando, again. He danced around his table, making one shot after another. After awhile, Kurt backed up next to me.

"Why won't he play you?" I asked. "He just sank five balls in a row. He could hold his own."

"And lose his whole paycheck?"

"His whole paycheck?"

"I don't do those pussy two-dollar games anymore."

Piper asked what ball she should shoot for next, so Kurt leaned in to direct her. I tuned back into Fernando's game. He glided about his table, in constant motion—smooth movements that drew the eye. He lined up the eight ball to win the game, but then straightened, looking my way. Must have spotted Kurt. I couldn't tell. His smile disappeared. He missed the shot, an easy two-footer into the corner. As his opponent took aim, Fernando continued to peek over at us, his face darkening,

"He sees us," I said, nudging Kurt. "Looks pissed. You guys have a run-in at work?"

Kurt shrugged, then pointed out another ball for Piper to aim at.

When his friend missed, Fernando bent over the table, another easy angle for the win, but he seemed distracted now, looking our way again. Without taking the shot, he slapped his cue down onto the table, disturbing the remaining balls, and stomped in our direction. His friend threw up a hand, shouting Fernando's name as he abandoned the game and weaved between the tables, patting guys to move, unconcerned about the wake of scowls behind him, shots he'd interrupted.

"He's coming over," I said. "And he's not happy." Some insult Kurt had hurled at work?

As Fernando approached our table, he raised a hand, pointing—pointing at me!

"You saw what happened to my friend Manny."

I stumbled, weak-kneed. Around us, play stopped, men straightening, turning.

"What—what are you saying?"

"He told me!" Fernando shouted now. Kurt moved toward him, stirred by Fernando's sharp tone, his insistent certainty. "He is sure you saw that *hijo de puta* try to steal his wallet, but you don't say nothing. And here you play games while he suffers." He waved a hand at the pool table. "Having a great time!"

All over the room, heads turned, eyes landing on me, waiting. The Mexicans whispered to each other, their faces wide with alarm or pinched with worry. Some guys peeked out the door, no doubt concerned about the *gringos* out there.

Kurt shoved his shoulder. "Back off, Fernando. It's none of your business."

Fernando went nose to nose with Kurt, lifting his finger and jabbing it at me.

"This *cobarde apestoso* won't talk, so now everyone thinks Manny's the bad guy."

Kurt shoved Fernando by the shoulders. He staggered and rushed back, raising a fist, rearing. Men grabbed him from behind and dragged him off. Alarmed, perhaps fearful, others glanced out the door, surrounding their compatriot, trying to calm him down. Fernando shook himself free, but the men hissed at him in their language, their hands up and out, corralling a wild mustang.

"Go back to your game," Kurt said, waving at the far table. "Unless you've finally grown a pair." He added. "Or are you still too chickenshit to play me?"

Fernando chuckled, waggling a finger in the air. "It is tempting. Very tempting, but your father, he won't like it if I take all your money."

"And he wouldn't like you fucking with my friend, either."

A threat that seemed to buckle Fernando's confidence, softening him. The men let him go. He stifled another comment, shaking with the effort to control himself, then turned and marched toward his table.

"Pussy!" Kurt called out. "You'd never take my money!"

Fernando put both hands up, and turned to face us, walking backwards. Again, he pointed at me, calmer this time, colder, almost a growl. "You gotta man up and do the right thing."

"Fuck off!" Kurt flipped him the finger.

But Fernando had circled back to his table, as the men around us glanced, back and forth, waiting to see if the disagreement was over.

"Asshole," Kurt grumbled. "I get enough of him at work, trying to tell me how to do my job."

Piper turned to me, open-mouthed, expectant. I took a breath, taking stock. My body was quivering, my heart battering my ribs, as if I'd just missed getting crushed by a semi. Men eyed me, whispering. Some pulled on their jackets to leave, wanting no part of this, while others stared, eyebrows pinched, sharing Fernando's anger, his blame.

"You ready for a game?" I heard Kurt say, but I was still stunned, scanning the room, gauging the reactions.

"Walker?" Piper said, trying to get my attention. I turned and reached for her cue stick. I unscrewed it, breaking it apart and reached for its leather sleeve.

"What are you doing?" Kurt said. "You aren't letting that guy get to you, are you?"

I grabbed Piper's arm. "Come on."

"Don't leave," Kurt said. "Let's shoot some pool."

"I don't want to go," Piper whined, trying to pull away.

"Well, I do!" I yanked at her and she staggered after me. Around me, men gaped at us, whispering at one another as we made our escapes.

"Come on, Walker," Kurt yelled after us. I didn't turn around.

Out in the parking lot, I fumbled with my keys to unlock the car as Piper stood there, her arms folded, sniffing out her frustration.

Kurt caught up, out of breath.

"How can you let that guy fuck up our evening?"

"Because," I said. "He knows. And you didn't make it any better by being such an asshole."

"Me? He's the asshole, telling you what to do. It's none of his goddamned business."

"Yeah, well, did you ever think that maybe he's right?"

"Oh, come on."

"I know, you're only trying to help, I do, but I fucked up. And all those guys in there," I pointed. "They know it."

"They're all scared rabbits. Say 'Boo,' and they scatter."

"Since when did you become such a jerk. You know the shit they have to put up with. I thought you were on their side."

He looked away, pulling a cigarette out of his shirt pocket. "Maybe I'm tired of it all. You show them a little bit of kindness, and what do they do? They move in, take over. Hell—" He waved his hand back at the bowling alley. "Next thing you know, we'll all be speaking Spanish and listening to mariachi instead of rock and roll."

Piper chuckled.

"That's not funny!" I barked at her. "You think this is a joke?"

She sobered, straightening, mouth shrinking to a pout.

"And you don't mean that." I pointed at Kurt. "You're just pissed at Fernando because your father likes him."

He rolled his eyes and lit up the cigarette.

"I don't see why you care about those guys if they're both illegal." Piper said. "Daddy's always saying—"

"Don't you ever think for yourself?" I barked, stepping towards her. She backed away.

"Okay, okay," Kurt raised his hands, pushing me away. "Give her a break, okay? She's just—"

"What?" Piper said, indignant. "I'm just what? A kid?"

"No." He looked at her. "Too smart for your own good."

Her expression curled into a frowning smile, not sure what to make of that. We all nodded at each other, agreeing to disagree. Kurt mashed out his cigarette and went off to his car.

Halfway home, Piper said, "I *do* think for myself. You'll see. Once I'm in high school, I'll think whatever I want."

Thirty-One

On a Thursday night, two weeks after Manny's meat hook found Norm's arm, I came home from another taxing day at work, hoping for a relaxing evening, only to have Gayle call me as I was getting into the shower.

"She can't stand to be there anymore. Keeps acting like it's all my fault, all that gossip about Norm and Manny."

"Wait a second." I said. "Are you talking about Patty?"

"Yes, of course. She quit today. Some excuse about her dad needing her help in his office, but I'm sure she was making it up. And now my mom's mad that she has to hire a new girl," Gayle said. "She *knows* something's going on between me and Patty I'm not telling her about."

"I'm sorry to hear that," I said, slumping down the wall onto the floor next to the phone.

"I get why she's mad at me," she said, "but I'm not convinced my Dad is the bad guy here."

"I know." Fact was, I wasn't convinced either.

I pulled my knees up to my chest and rested my head against them, waiting for her to continue. I was too tired to talk, but after what I'd confessed to her the other night, I was in thrall to her. She knew my secret and carried it too casually. *You're serious. He beat you.* A vial of nitroglycerin she was juggling. Not my heart, exactly. She didn't have that any more. More like my soul, if I had one. That's what I didn't trust her not to drop.

"Hey look," she said, "Can we do something tomorrow night? Maybe go to a movie at the Drive-In?"

"You mean, like a date?"

"Well, would that be so terrible?" She laughed. "I need a break from all this stuff. Don't you? I mean, what else are you going to do?"

The alternative was to watch the Cubs with my dad or listen to Kurt piss and moan about Fernando since shooting pool was no longer an option.

"All right," I said. "But not a real date. As friends, okay?"

"We're back to square one, are we?"

"We never left it, Gayle."

"Oh. Well. You gotta start somewhere, right?"

Saturday night, I pulled up to the curb in front of Gayle's house and honked the horn—a tacky move, but she knew I hated dealing with Norm. The sun had just set, but I could see how long the grass was, full of yellow dandelions wilting in the June heat. With his screwed-up arm, Norm couldn't mow now. Or was it his hip stopping him? But it wasn't only the lawn that needed work. The old porch pillar he'd replaced 'temporarily' with a couple of two-by-fours the previous summer still stood there, bowed under the weight of the tilting porch roof. Between the house's doors and windows, the white paint peeled and blistered, as if the whole place had a sickly eczema. I felt bad, like maybe I should volunteer to help out. If only he wasn't such a jerk.

The Ditweiler's station wagon clattered into the driveway. Barb climbed out and waved. She must have just closed up shop. I waved back. She creaked open the rusty tailgate, brown paper bags peeking out. She struggled to corral her arms around two of them. I rolled down the window.

"Need some help?"

"Oh, could you? That'd be so sweet of you, Walker."

I got out and grabbed the other two bags. I groaned at a case of Pabst Blue Ribbon Tall Boys that would require a second trip. And I thought I'd escaped heavy lifting for at least one day.

As soon as we were through the front door, Barb yelled "Gayle! Walker's here!"

A muffled "Be right down" came from upstairs as I followed Barb in. From this angle into the living room, only the TV was visible, the White Sox game on. Norm was probably holed up in there, somewhere. If I was lucky, maybe he wouldn't notice me.

In the kitchen, dishes were piled in the sink, the counter cluttered with uncapped jars, mayo and pickles, amidst bread crumbs, a splotch of yellow mustard. I shoved the mess back with the grocery bags.

"This kitchen is a disaster!" Barb called out.

"I'll take care of it." Yes, Norm was there, somewhere.

Barb thanked me and started emptying her bags.

"Can I help?" I wanted to avoid Norm.

"No, I got it, sweetie. But thanks for asking."

I crept back out, trying to sneak past the door, but there he was, sprawled on the couch, arm bandaged and in a blue sling. Enough beer cans for a small party on that coffee table. What little hair he had was uncombed. He clearly hadn't shaved since the fight, bristles scraggly on his neck and cheeks. Had he even showered?

Shit. He spotted me. All smiles, he sat up and mashed out his cigarette.

"Walker Maguire!" His bright voice belied his dark, tired bearing. He ran his good left hand over his scalp to flatten his hair. "How you doing, buddy?" He pushed himself up, lurched over and presented a hand to shake—the hand in the sling! I shook it gingerly. *Didn't that hurt?* So jolly for a guy who'd caused so much misery.

He craned his neck toward the kitchen, making sure Barb was out of earshot. Grabbing my wrist, he pulled me away, confiding.

"I owe you one," he whispered. "Keeping quiet and all." He disentangled that right arm out of its sling and put it around my shoulder. "You know, I just wanted to see if he had one of them green cards. I wasn't stealing nothing."

Gayle told him?

"Hey Barb," he shouted, head tilted up. "You get that beer?"

"In the car!"

He patted me on the back, backing away. I was frozen, fragile enough to crumble at those pats. *He knew what I saw?*

"By the way," he whispered. "Barb doesn't know. I'd just as soon keep it that way. Okay?"

"Um—" *Why would Gayle tell him?*

"Hi, Walker."

And there she was, the traitor, skipping down the stairs, wearing the leather skirt and skimpy, pink, spaghetti string top again, and yet another hairstyle, shorter than before.

"There's my girl!" Norm threw his arm around Gayle's shoulder. "Man, don't you look great. Doesn't she look great, Walker?" He grabbed me by the shoulder, too, shaking the both of us. *Which arm was damaged?*

"Uh, yeah. She does." I took a good look. In fact, it was disturbing, how young it made her appear, that new hairstyle. Like I'd been robbing the cradle all these years and hadn't known until now.

"What's that 'do called again?"

"The pixie. You know, like Twiggy wears."

"Oh, right." Norm nodded. "This girl and her mother, they can do anything with hair. Am I right, Barb?"

"What?" From the kitchen.

"But you keep cutting it, you won't have nothing left to work with."

"Oh, Daddy." She slapped his arm, beaming. She enjoyed the pedestal he stood her on.

"It's great to see you two together again," he said, shaking the two of us in unison. "Like old times. Warms my heart. Really does." Was it his daughter who stirred this sentimental streak or the beers he'd had?

Norm shouted out, "Those Tall Boys cold?"

"Always!"

He walked backwards, pointing at me with his left hand, his right back in its sling. "You want one?"

"No thanks."

He went out, door banging.

"Hey Mom?" Gayle yelled toward the kitchen as she grabbed her pocketbook off a table. "Can I have five bucks for the movie?"

Barb came out. "Dutch treat?" she asked, head cocked in confusion. Gayle gave me a look, too.

"Never mind," I said. "I got it."

"I should hope so," Barb said, retreating into the kitchen.

"Thank you," Gayle leaned in, giving me a whiff of that perfume again. My mother's.

"She does pay you, doesn't she?" I asked.

"Of course, she does," Gayle said, then mumbled. "When she can." She eyed me, straightening. "You ready?"

"You told him." I said, unable to wait.

"Told him? Told who?"

"You told your father I saw the fight."

She slumped a little, exhaling. "Walker—" The front door opened, and she straightened, going quiet.

Norm held the heavy case of beer in both hands. Around his neck, the sling hung useless, like a woman's scarf.

"Let me take that—" I offered, reaching.

"I got it," he said with a wink. He hefted the case, adjusting it without a wince, and pushed past me into the kitchen, one leg striding a shade faster than the other, but not the peg-legged limp I'd witnessed at work.

Norm hoisted the case onto the counter and yanked up a glued flap with that right hand again, now apparently quite healthy. He pulled out one of the giant cans, twenty-four ounces, and flipped the pull tab. He took a long swig, swallowing repeatedly and let out an "Ahh."

"Sure you don't want one?" he asked, as if that's why I'd been gawking at him.

"No thanks."

"We have to go, Daddy. The movie's starting soon."

"Okay." He limped back out, sneaking peeks back into the kitchen. "But I got to ask you"—he tilted the can towards me, toasting me, keeping his voice low—"I mean, first, I pegged you wrong, Walker, and I'm sorry for that."

"Uh, sure. I'm glad to see you're feeling better." I pointed at his hand, then down at his hip.

"Oh, the time off's done me a world a good. But I have to ask. You still got his wallet?"

Gayle told him about that, too? "Yes." I fumbled for words. "I just haven't been able to get it back to him." As if I'd really tried.

"But you still got it, huh." A sly grin crossed his face. "Does he have a green card?"

"Yes—"

"A real one?" He took the beer bottle in his good hand and returned the 'bad' one to the sling.

"I don't know. Look, we have to go," I said, turning.

"Because if it is a fake—" He let the question hang a second, then added: "Goodbye Manny, hello forklift, know what I mean?"

"The company's checking on that."

"Well, good then." He spread his hands. "That's all I ever wanted. Make sure the guy's on the level. Now we'll know." He brightened.

"Right."

"So, you two have a great evening. Back before eleven, right?" he said, raising the beer in a left-handed toast, patting his belly with the hand in the sling.

"Back before eleven, Daddy."

Once we were in my car, I inserted the key in the ignition, but I didn't turn it. I dropped my hand and sat, shaking my head. Gayle angled herself my way.

"He kept saying," she began, "how he'd get that Manny Camarasa, hunt him down like it was all that man's fault. I couldn't take it anymore. So I told him what you saw."

Even Gayle could only take so much of Norm's racist bullshit—unless she was bullshitting me, too.

"But now he thinks I'm lying for his sake," I said.

"Should I have told him the real reason you lied?"

"No." Norm would be delighted to discover how much more fucked up my family was than his. "But what's with his arm? And his hip, too?"

"What do you mean?" She faced forward again, looking out the window.

"Gayle. He carried a case of beer into the house like it was nothing."

She let out a big breath and rolled her head.

"He's always better after a few days off."

"Sure, but he's only staying home because of that arm, right? He doesn't even need that stupid sling."

"Look." She paused, taking a breath, seeming to shift gears. "No matter how many hours my mom and I work, we can't seem to pay off the start-up loan on the salon. We need Daddy's salary just to put food on the table. But if he doesn't get time off for that hip to get better, he won't last another month on that loading dock."

"And they won't give him sick pay for that hip."

"Exactly. But they might for that arm."

I turned to her. "If he makes it look worse than it is, you mean."

"Oh, don't give me that holier than thou shit. Daddy says people do stuff like this all the time," Gayle began. "Managers earn big bonuses for doing what? Cooking the books? Cutting corners with cheap parts, screwing people out of their sick pay—while the little guys like him who do the *real* work, bust their butts—they get the shaft. He's just found a way to even things out."

Maybe I'd spent too much time drinking my father's Kool-Aid or admiring how like clockwork the system ran at AMC, but this argument didn't sit well with me. Or maybe I couldn't stomach Norm's deceit on top of how he'd screwed Manny, another little guy.

"Your father's lying so he can get workers' comp."

"So what? It doesn't affect you."

"But it does *my* father."

She blinked a couple times.

"I thought you wouldn't care. You hate your father."

"I don't hate him." I knew that much, if only that.

"You sure make it sound that way."

"Well, I don't." I grabbed the steering wheel, squeezing. "I don't know how I feel about him, but I don't want to see him made a fool of, any more than you do Norm."

She turned to me again. "You're not telling him, are you? About Norm's arm?"

"So, if we stayed together—" I turned to her, "is this how you'd go about solving problems—the way Norm does?"

Her brows furrowed, hardening. "Is it any worse than how you're solving yours? Lying to your father? Letting him think Manny started that fight?"

"You know why I did that."

"You were afraid. We're afraid, too. Is it so different?"

We sat that way for a few minutes.

"I think it's too late for the movie now," I said, staring ahead.

"Too late for a lot of things, isn't it?"

I could feel her eyes on me, but I couldn't return the look.

She opened the door and got out, pausing only to lower her head for one final appeal. "Please, Walker. Don't tell your dad."

When I didn't respond, she closed the door and crossed her overgrown lawn to her house.

Thirty-Two

After that, Gayle stopped calling me. A leaky ship without the buoyancy of her problems to keep my mind afloat, I found myself sinking at AMC, all those hours filled with nothing but mind-numbing, muscle-straining work, regrets over Manny Camarasa, only the occasional White Sox broadcast helping me tread water through the long shift.

One of those endless afternoons, I drove home to find Kurt's Impala parked in the driveway, its rear fender staved in, the tail-light broken. Kurt and Piper were out on the flat, sitting backwards at the picnic table, side-by-side, looking down the hill toward the river. I walked over and asked what happened.

Kurt was bent over, elbows on knees, staring at the grass. He shrugged. Piper spoke up.

"Kurt went over to Fernando's house last night and soaped his car."

"What? Why?" *Fucking hot-head.*

"Because Pops finally let them wash their own cars, and when he compared them, he told Kurt he had to do all of his over, the way Fernando cleaned his."

"And for you," Kurt added. "Because he threatened you."

"He didn't threaten me." I sat next to Piper.

"Close enough. Besides...." He smiled and paused, a line coming he'd rehearsed. "I thought it'd be funny, soaping the car of the guy so fucking good at washing them."

"Only," Piper said, hesitating, "something happened and the cops came."

"Were you arrested again?"

"Hell no!"

He stood up and stepped over the lip of the plateau, starting down the slope.

"Fernando was," Piper said.

"What?" I shot to my feet. "How?" I followed him down the hill. "What did you do?"

He disappeared into the low-hanging branches of the cherry tree.

"What, Kurt?"

Piper caught up with us. From behind, she said, "He used the soap to write 'wetback' on his windshield."

"What the fuck, Kurt?"

He glanced at me, eyes wide and worried, as if I'd just now caught him in the act.

"Some neighbor must have called the cops," Piper continued, "and when they arrived, Fernando was out front, dragging Kurt out of his Impala, yelling at him over what he'd done to his car. When the cops saw how crazy he was acting and that word on the windshield, they asked to see Fernando's papers."

"I never meant it to go that far," Kurt said. "It was a joke. And then this morning, Pops throws *me* out of the car lot. Can you believe that? Puts up the bail for him, that—" He didn't say the word. "And he sends me home!" He turned on me. "I'm exiled, and that jerk's back at work, washing cars while he waits for his hearing."

"So you're mad about how *you* are being treated after what you did to Fernando?" I said.

"Kurt's your best friend, Walker," Piper said.

"And you—" I turned to my sister. "Do you have any idea what he's done? That poor guy may be deported because of this stupid stunt." I wheeled toward Kurt. "Pops likes Fernando, so you wanted him gone."

"He's not even supposed to be here," Piper said. "Why shouldn't he go?"

"He didn't do anything, Piper. He didn't hurt anyone. Didn't steal anything. Outside of not having a stupid green card, he didn't break any laws." I turned on my friend. "And Kurt knows that. Any other kid in town might have done that, but not you. And you sure as hell aren't doing me any favors."

Disgusted, I turned away from them. That's when I caught sight of Kurt's Impala, again.

"What the hell happened to your car?"

Kurt reached up into the cherry tree, bending down a whole branch rather than stretching for the ripe fruits higher up. With his free hand, he tore out a small cluster. He wasn't talking.

"Did you hit Fernando's car?"

"No," he said. "It was one of my father's new Chevys. I might have backed into one as I was leaving the lot."

"Might have? You didn't tell anybody?"

Kurt plucked a bright red cherry out of the bunch and stuffed it into his mouth. He offered Piper some. She took one. She gave him this pouty-lipped look of sympathy that made me throw my hands in the air and march back up the hill.

The next day, I'd come in the side door, home from work—fortunately, Manny was still out—to find Piper sitting in Dad's Barca-lounger. She levered it up, this weird expectant grin on her face, dying to tell me something. I hadn't spoken to her since I'd left her and Kurt on the hill, eating cherries.

"What?" I snapped at her.

She stiffened, offended. She cast her eyes to the TV, some old Tarzan movie, Johnny Weissmuller, swimming away from an alligator. "Nothing."

"What's going on, Piper?"

"Only that Kurt came over this afternoon and told me he'd broken up with Patty, that's all."

"He broke up with her?" Sure, they'd bickered over that Manny thing, but those two always bickered like an old, married couple.

"Well, maybe *she* broke up with *him*." Speaking matter-of-factly, her eyes on the screen, Piper explained how one of the salon's customers, a cop's wife, told Barb how her husband had arrested an illegal after Pops Swanson's son pointed him out, and everyone in the shop agreed it was about time they did something about all those Mexicans moving up here. When Patty heard that, she said it was the last straw.

"She doesn't want to see him any more." The corner of Piper's mouth twitched into fleeting smirks, barely concealing a newborn, infantile happiness.

"If I were her, I'd have done the same thing," I said.

"You would!" Piper snapped at me, whipping around. "And I suppose you don't want him to be your friend anymore, either?"

"My friend? I don't know who he is anymore. He acted like a complete jerk, and you're siding with him?"

She turned away, arms folded, chewing on this, her brow furrowed, so resistant to seeing her white knight knocked off his horse.

Of all people, why did she have to crush on Kurt?

Thirty-Three

That Friday, Manny was back. Sort of. Bent over, hands on his knees, right outside Kelly's office. Locks of his usually well-oiled and combed hair flared untidily over his unshaven cheeks, as if he'd endured round one of a ten-round fight. I hung back near the time clock. Once the shift horn sounded, I'd have to face him. I felt his wallet in my back pocket. I'd brought it to work every day, waiting for this chance, fearing it, too. I had no idea how he'd react when I handed it over.

From across the dock, I watched Kelly's door until the two of them came out. They were both jabbing their fingers in the air, Kelly toward the fuel tanks, Manny toward the forklift. I backed further along the wall towards the door. Kelly broke off and, looking around, caught sight of me. He waved me over. Was Manny scowling at me or at Kelly? Maybe with Kelly between us, Manny wouldn't punch me out.

"You'll be on mufflers today," Kelly told me. "Camarasa's back on fuel tanks."

"He isn't taking over the forklift?" *Stupid question.*

"Go." He pointed. "Mufflers."

Kelly brushed past us, making for the metal box of his office.

Manny had his head down, hands on his hips. Ready to spring at me? Maybe he was composing himself.

He looked up at me, chuckling. "Didn't I tell you they'd never give me that promotion?"

"Why not?"

"Because they think I started that fight. Me! When he was trying to steal my wallet. Kelly said the only reason he didn't fire me was because Norm didn't press charges." Manny huffed. "And now. Now, he wants to see my green card." He shook his head in disbelief. Any second, he'd point at me, say this was my fault for not speaking up. "He wants me gone." He turned to me. "And after what your buddy did to my neighbor, Fernando, I suppose you want me gone, too, right?"

"No, no," I said. "In fact, I'm on your side." I reached into my pocket.

"Bullshit."

"No, really." I fumbled the wallet out, "I've got it. Your wallet." I held it up, a burden lifting, even if only part way, a flag that would never get past half mast if he didn't buy my story. "I've been keeping it for you. I was afraid of what they'd do if I gave it to them."

The way he gaped, the wallet seemed quite impossible, a rabbit out of a hat. I had to place it in his hands before he'd take it. Gingerly, he opened the thing. His eyes widened at the cards and pictures, the smoke of his anger having wafted away. Drop-jawed, he said, "Where did you find it?"

"It was wedged between some crates." I pointed, vaguely, near where the fight occurred. I'd rehearsed this. "I found it just the other day, actually. Just dumb luck, happened to spy it there. I've been keeping it for you."

"*Gracias a dios*," he said, slipping out the green card. He kissed it, holding the flat plastic rectangle up like a talisman, a jewel. I half expected it to sparkle. "*Mi amigo*, that was smart, holding onto it. I don't know how to thank you." He turned. "Now, I'll show that *hijo de puta*!"

He took off, bent forward at a slow but sure clip, like hurrying through thick mud, a soldier in the trenches.

Manny was happy. Not mad at me at all, for the moment anyway. And clearly the card couldn't be a fake, not the way he prized it as he marched up to Kelly's door. He wasn't trying to hide it or anything.

The door closed behind him. I wound between towers of pallets and bins of auto parts, making my way to the muffler boxcar, sneaking peeks back at Kelly's door. They'd *have* to let Manny keep his job now.

Two empty tugger trains waited for me, and impatient as I was to find out what was happening in Kelly's office, I couldn't stand around, not with that red button waiting. I stepped inside the muffler car, neatly stacked with the metal contraptions, floor to ceiling. I pulled at one. It slid out easily, half the size and weight of a fuel tank. Ungainly thing, like an enormous, uncoiling steel Python that swallowed a briefcase, but it was a breeze to grip and lift. For me, that is. For Norm, with that hip?

I hadn't told my dad he was faking. As sore as I came home nights, I couldn't begrudge any of these guys a little extra sick pay, even a jerk like him.

Every time I crossed between my boxcar and the tugger train, I took a peek at Kelly's office until, finally, Manny came out. He stumbled toward the fuel tank car, his fury providing more propulsion than his back and legs could support. I shoved my mufflers into the tugger wagon and intercepted him.

"What's wrong? What'd he say?"

Breathing hard, he stopped and searched the floor as if the words he needed were down there, somewhere. He chuckled, shaking his head. "Kelly wants to show it to somebody in HR. Said they need to make sure the card is real." Manny raised his head and gazed at me, smiling.

"But when they confirm it," I said, "everything will be okay, right?"

"I didn't give it to him."

"What? Why not?"

"And let them fuck with it? Lose it again? I'm not letting this thing out of my sight."

"But you have to know how that looks."

"I showed it to them already." Anger crackled in his voice. "When I applied for the job, they asked for an ID, and that's what I gave them. I could have given them something else, but I didn't. I didn't hide it."

He looked at me.

"They trusted me then. Why the fuck can't they trust me now? Because that *jodido* redneck thinks I'm an illegal? Because I hit the thieving bastard with a meat hook instead of my fist? *¡Es una mierda!* Who is he to say who I am?"

"But you know what they'll think."

"What does it matter? They don't need my card to call the INS, muck around in my past. They can think what they want to think. I don't give a shit." He flapped his hand towards Kelly's office, nodding. "*¡He terminado con esta mierda!*"

"But Manny—"

"But nothing. If they want me working these fucking fuel tanks, then that's what I'll do. But I'll be damned if I'll let these bastards tell me who I am." Louder, now, he popped his chest with a fist. "*¡Yo soy Manuel Camarasa!*" He shuffled away, slapping a metal bin hard as he passed it, making everyone look.

He stared into the boxcar as if into a prison cell. Then he slumped, his shoulders dropping, and disappeared inside.

All morning long, Manny played catch-up, empty trains arriving while he struggled to load the trains before them. Toward lunchtime, he fell so far behind that three of his trains clogged the aisles. I was certain the line would run out of fuel tanks and I'd hear the shriek of that red button. I worked ahead on my mufflers, filling up my train before an empty arrived, and then ran over to help him. Bent and wobbling, he cursed and swatted at me to get away, a bothersome fly. He kept saying they wanted him gone, that I'd end up gone too if I didn't return to my own boxcar.

Even if he had struck Norm with that meat hook on purpose, I didn't care. He'd gotten a raw deal, whether he was here legally or not. And he hadn't blamed me when he easily could have. I unloaded a dozen fuel tanks for him, skipping around him each time, keeping him afloat until the lunch horn sounded.

Instead of lying down during lunch like he normally did, Manny disappeared, though when I looked, he hadn't punched out. Halfway through lunch, he limped back, banging around inside his boxcar, barking obscenities at the metal walls. I stashed my half-eaten lunch and peeked into his car.

"You okay?"

"I complained to the union steward," he said, bending backwards, hands on hips, stretching. He groaned. "Kelly warned the son-of-a-bitch I might be coming. The steward said they wouldn't let the company fire me if I can prove I'm here legally."

"So hand over the card, Manny."

"No way." He turned to me. "They've seen it once. They don't need to see it again. Anyway, that card proves nothing. Now get the fuck out of here."

Kelly's door was open. He was inside his office eating lunch, so I stuck my head in.

"How about I switch boxcars with Manny?" He looked up, so I stepped in. "He's hurting bad."

The foreman wiped his mouth and leaned back in his chair, his head, twisting in disdain. "What business is it of yours?"

I needed a different tack.

"Well, he's taking forever. Trains are backing up, blocking the aisle."

"If that's the case—" He pushed himself up. "Maybe I should go talk to him then."

"No." I motioned him back down. "That's not what I mean." I was making things worse, again. "I can do it faster, is all. Let me switch with him, okay?"

"You don't get it, do you? If the man can't do his job, he can't do his job."

"Come on," I said. "Give him a break."

He scrutinized me, scanning my face. "You know, security combed every inch of that area, and they couldn't find that wallet anywhere."

I should have expected this.

"I can show you where it was."

"I'll just bet you can. Why didn't you turn it in when you found it? Why hold onto it."

I considered a number of answers but settled on the simplest. "It's Manny's wallet. I wanted to give it to him."

He chuckled. "And maybe you've had it all along. What with all that talk about it being stolen, maybe you're the one who stole it."

"I didn't steal it!"

"For fuck's sake, Maguire. You saw what he did to your girl's father." He pointed out the door. "Why do you want to help him?"

"Because you're trying to get him fired."

"Not fired." He leaned back, his hands clasped on his belly, fingers interlaced. "I won't need to do that."

"Because you'll stick him with those fuel tanks, even though there's easier jobs he could be doing. Even though you promised him a promotion. Am I right?"

"Until we confirm his legal status—or until he quits, whichever comes first."

Thirty-Four

Whenever a shift ended, employees bolted out of the building, racing to beat two bottle-necks. One was at the lone gate out of the sprawling parking lot, the second a quarter of a mile down AMC Drive, at a long stoplight where a grassy island served as a turnaround for the Belford bus. That day as I inched my Datsun past the island towards the light, I saw someone laying on his back in the grass. Manny Camarasa. The other workers awaiting the bus milled around him as if he was a vagrant to be stepped over. I pulled up to the curb and stopped.

"Hey, Manny!" He got up on his elbows with a grunt, the bunny on his chest becoming visible. "You want a ride?"

"Nah, man," he said, voice hoarse. "I'm okay. I see you on Monday." He waved me away, lying back down, grimacing, one elbow at a time. Monday? He'd barely survived the afternoon. He couldn't keep this up.

"Hey look," I shouted. "You live along the Piscasaw, don't you?"

"Yes, but that's gotta be out of your way."

"No, it's not. My house is right across the river from you." As the crow flies, maybe, but ten times further by car. "Why don't you get in?"

He struggled up again, shaking his head, smiling. The workers standing nearby shared their disapproval in whispers and head shakes, as if I'd crossed a line, reaching out to the pariah.

"You sure you want to do this?" He eyed the hostile faces around us.

"Sure. Come on."

One hand on the ground, one on a knee, he pushed up. On his feet and stretching, he sighed, "It's your funeral, kid."

He folded himself into the car. Every time he bent too far, a twinge made him grimace and straighten, a jolt of electricity knocking the breath out of him. He'd pause a second, waiting for the pain to subside, before continuing.

"This thing go back at all?" he asked, trying to settle in.

"There's a lever down below."

He found it and sighed as the seat slid back and he stretched out.

"Thanks, man. It's a long walk from the bus stop to my place."

When the light changed, I pulled out onto the bypass for a couple of blocks, then turned down Main Street. A line of stoplights awaited us, plenty of time for uncomfortable silences.

"Why the fuck did you help me like that?" Manny asked, forcing the question. "You trying to get yourself fired?"

"It's not fair what they're doing to you."

"Why? I'm the maniac who put a *meat hook* through Ditweiler's arm." He laughed. "That fucking meat hook. If I don't hold onto it all the time, some asshole will take it and hide it. If I don't find it before the horn sounds, I have to work without it. Ten minutes. An hour. Might be all afternoon before it shows up again, hanging somewhere in my boxcar. Everyone gets a good laugh."

"You thought maybe someone was trying to take your meat hook, and you just reacted?"

"That's right." He looked at me, nodding. "These *pendejos* and their practical jokes, right? So funny."

"Yeah. Right." So there *was* a reason he was holding the meat hook.

Stopped at the first light, he said, "You saw it? The fight?" He eyed me, curious. Didn't he already think so?

"Your friend, Fernando, seems to think I did."

"You mean, the guy *your friend* is getting deported?"

I couldn't one-up him.

"'Nando told me he had a run-in with you two at the pool hall," Manny said. "Is that why your friend—what's his name? Kurt?—Is that why he did this to him? Because of that scuffle?"

"I don't know. I think it had more to do with work. You know they wash cars together, right?"

"Yes," Manny shook his head. "'Nando says your friend is a lazy slob who stands around half of the time while he washes cars for the both of them."

"Sounds like Kurt."

He stewed a second.

"I told 'Nando you *might* have seen it." He gave me this sheepish tilt of the head. "From where you were up there. Told him Norm's your girl's father. That's why 'Nando thinks you saw it, but won't say anything. Like you're protecting Norm."

The car ahead slowed to take a left.

"That's what 'Nando thinks," Manny went on. "But not what I think."

I pulled into the right lane and zipped past that car.

"What do you think?" I asked at the next light.

"I think if you *did* see it, and you're worried about anybody's father, it's your *own.*"

I gripped and regripped the wheel.

"What makes you say that?"

"What I know about him. The way he snapped at you that day."

"You heard that?"

"Just like my dad. Used to kick my ass." He sang the words, a memory in the song. "I couldn't do anything right."

The light turned green. I tightened my grip on the wheel, as if it might veer off on its own if I didn't.

"He wasn't all bad. Took care of us, anyway. Until he got sick, he always put food on the table. Every day, he drove the bus to Toluca so the villagers could get their goods to market. It kept a roof over our heads. But if I didn't do things his way?" The question hung until I gave him a glance. "Well, you know what happens."

As if such fathers were only rare here, not where he came from.

"So, 'Nando," Manny said, "I tried to tell him about fathers, but he didn't get it. His was always gone, in the States somewhere, trying to find work. He thought, if you *did* see the fight, you should talk. Now he's got bigger problems."

"I'm sorry about Fernando. What Kurt did—that was screwed up."

"No shit." Manny shifted in his seat as I sped through another light. "But I'm a father, too. And I need this job, you know?"

"I know."

The silence sucked at me to say something. Barb Ditweiler's salon, Dare to Have Hair, came up on my right. I caught a glimpse of Gayle, standing over some housewife in curlers. With her there and Manny here, it occured to me: Norm might get the forklift after all if they kept Manny on fuel tanks.

"Everyone thinks I'm some kind of slasher psycho now. Another crazy Mexican, like in the movies, two belts of bullets across my chest—" He draws an X on his chest, from one shoulder to the opposite hip, and then the other. "Big sombrero and bad teeth."

"Not everyone," I said. The light changed to green, and I sped towards the next one, only for it to turn red, forcing me to stop again.

"After lunch, today, I tried to get Kelly to let me switch jobs with you."

"What?" He turned, incredulous. "You're nuts, kid." He laughed, shaking his head. "That guy wants to stick me with them fucking fuel tanks until I fall apart. Same as what they're doing to Norm Ditweiler. Won't take long before both of us are gone."

"Those mufflers aren't that bad."

"Bad enough for a guy with a bum hip."

"You think they're trying to get rid of Norm?"

"Why else would they give a Mexican that promotion?"

"Don't you deserve it?"

"Maybe. But they passed me over three times. Why give it to me now? No, that racist drunk is screwed and so am I."

"Because of your green card?"

"Like I said, that card proves nothing."

His omnipresent smile had disappeared.

"So—it is a fake, then?"

He tried turning, but he couldn't, settling back. "Do I look like an illegal to you?"

I re-gripped the wheel, grinding my teeth. He faced forward, mumbling something in Spanish. He looked away, out the passenger side window. "If you only knew how I got that card."

"Sorry," I said, but I still wasn't convinced.

"Turn at the grocery store." He nodded at the IGA on the corner. I did as he said, and continued down River Street. We dipped down a hill and passed the Ironworks Foundry on the left, a more imposing structure this close up, six stories of corrugated steel with smoke belching out the two big smokestacks. An acrid metallic scent invaded the car, almost skunk-like in its strength, sticking with the car as we drove.

Past the Foundry, the road turned to gravel, and I drove under a sign that read, "Riverside Cabins." From across the river, I'd noticed how alike the buildings were, but I didn't know it was a campground. I'd never seen it up close, the small cabins with white clapboard siding, green roofs, built on posts. Most of the cars parked around the place could have come from Pops Swanson's used car liquidations. On the river side of the road, water glinted between the cabins, small docks here and there. I glimpsed my own dock across the water, our yellow motorboat tied up, our lush, green lawn behind it, rising up the hill, then the big brick house on top.

The summer we moved here, these rustic cabins were peopled by boisterous, boozy whites who, my dad was told, vacationed here every August, fishing off the docks or out in canoes or rowboats. The realtor assured him the buildings weren't made for cold weather and that the revelers would be gone by Labor Day. After Dad bought the house, most of the cabins did empty out—but not all. As the weeks wore on, smoke kept rising from the chimney of this one on the water. Occasionally, noise rolled across the river and up our lawn to the house, the sound of wood chopping. Or sometimes, partying. One time, music—mariachi. That really set Dad off. He asked around and learned a Mexican family, instead of returning to Mexico with the rest of the seasonal migrant workers, had stayed and rented the place for next to nothing, it being uninsulated and all. Dad predicted they wouldn't last past the first freeze. But they did, stayed the whole winter and through the summer. The next winter, three more Mexican families moved in. By our third winter in Belford, the entire camp was rented year-round to Mexicans toughing out the cold, chopping firewood and working odd jobs around town.

"Here." Manny pointed to a building on the river's edge, the only one with two stories. A small yard surrounded the place, neatly mown. I pulled up and parked. An orange Big Wheel tricycle sat out front, toppled on its side in the grass.

"Nice place," I said.

"Nicer than the dump we had across town last spring. We'll see how long it lasts."

"What do you mean?"

"Nothing." He shook his head. "You see that one there?" Manny pointed across the road to one of the small, one-story bungalows. "That's where 'Nando lives. For now."

The car sitting in the driveway, was that the one Kurt had soaped?

"Oh."

"What if I *was* illegal?" Manny faced me. "What if I *was* like 'Nando? Would you have me arrested, too?"

"No, I wouldn't."

"Then what do you care if my card is fake or real?"

"I don't want you to lose your job."

Manny stared at his friend's cabin, soon to be empty, it seemed.

"He's trying to earn a living, like me, take care of his family. He's got two little ones, a third on the way."

"Oh." *Fucking Kurt.*

"That's right. Wires a little money back to his parents every month, just like I do. He wanted a place he could live year-round so he wouldn't have to travel and pick, travel and pick—tobacco, oranges, blueberries. Where he could settle down and be someone. And he finally did. Got a steady job. His boss liked him."

"I know."

"My daughter saw your friend out the window, this white kid, long blond hair, fiddling with 'Nando's car. What's this white boy doing in our campground, right? We don't have a phone, so she went to the neighbor's and called the cops. And 'Nando is the one who ends up getting arrested. Like maybe this kid planned it that way. First time a cop asked about anyone's papers here. Really upset my girl, as if it was her fault."

"I'm sorry to hear that."

"It's not right what happened to him."

"I agree."

"And it's not right what's happening to me, either. We're good people. And my card is not a fake, okay?"

"Okay."

He sat there nodding, as if to convince himself of that truth.

"I'm sure they only want to look at it. They'll give it back."

"I keep telling you, the card is not the problem. It's how I got it, okay? That's more complicated."

"Manny. Are you legal or not?"

He turned to me. "*I* think I am." He rubbed his chin, worrying this thought before he opened the door. Methodically, he shifted himself out of the car, one appendage at a time. He slammed the car door and tried to stand, but he couldn't. He let out a groan and put his hands on his knees.

I waited a second, watching. He remained stooped, locked into his pain, a Tin Man rusted shut.

Switching off the car, I got out and rushed around to him.

"Here." I reached for him.

"I don't need your help." He yanked his arm away, waving me off. He tried to straighten, but he froze again, inhaling sharply, eyes squeezing closed, a tear coming down. As if against his will, he threw his hand out, and I grabbed it.

"Come on." I put my arm around his waist.

He rolled his eyes, but put his arm over my shoulder. After a few steps, he crumpled, so I hitched him up on my hip, taking his weight.

Thirty-Five

"Someone there?"

A girlish voice called out from inside. I peeked in the screen door. Bunnies were everywhere: a stuffed bunny in mid-tumble on pine stairs, childrens' crayoned drawings with big floppy ears pinned to a corkboard next to bills and phone numbers, pink ceramic bunnies in a wooden display case. They brightened up a decor darkened by cheap wood paneling. The screened windows and the floor, each pine plank of which shifted under my steps, reminded me this was a summer fishing cottage.

"*Si, soy yo,*" Manny said as we shuffled inside. Along the hallway sprawled a crumbling fort of Tinker Toys and Lincoln Logs, guarded by green plastic soldiers and little Matchbox cars. Still clinging to me, Manny took care to step around the scene, so I did the same. "That way." He pointed through a wide opening beyond which children chattered.

The two of us, attached at the hip, shuffled into the living room, the floor creaking at our every move. Sitting on an orange shag carpet with her back to us, a young woman held an infant to her shoulder. She rocked the baby, swaddled in a pink blanket, holding a bottle to its mouth. No, the woman wasn't simply young. A teenager. The mother? I could just see the side of her face, next to her eye, a birthmark. She'd been at the hospital—the Candy Striper who'd been by Manny's bedside. The beauty. But what was she doing here? Babysitting?

In front of her knelt the two plump, dark-haired little boys I'd seen on Manny's hospital bed. They leaned over a board game between them on the carpet.

"*Papá!*" one boy shouted, jumping up and running over, followed by the other. They both wrapped themselves around the legs of their father—something I could never do with mine.

"Now, now," he said, rubbing their heads. His face swirled from pain to pleasure and back again.

The girl shifted around, surprised at me, this strange young man in their house. She scrambled to her knees and, encumbered by the infant, awkwardly pushed herself up.

"Hello," she said, taken aback.

"Hi," I said. But then she caught sight of how I was holding Manny, and she took a step towards him, her surprise turned into concern.

"*Papá,* I told you it was too early to go back to work." Her lips pressed together, she tilted her head down in a small reproach. Manny's daughter?

He shrugged at her, his shoulders lifting and dropping.

"*Pobrecito,*" she murmured, coming over. She hoisted the baby higher on her shoulder, the ruddy-faced infant making tiny sucking sounds. The girl considered me again, this time with an embarrassed smile, testing and discarding speeches, until she said, "Can you get him over to the sofa?"

"Sure."

Across the room stood a big couch. Its flowery slipcover had pulled away from one overstuffed arm, revealing tattered upholstery underneath, stuffing puffed out. We maneuvered around an unvarnished, cable-spool coffee table, on which the stenciled words "RICHARD'S ELECTRIC" were still visible in black. In the middle of the table sat a few tattered kids picture books, on top of which a plastic plate teetered, holding one lonely cookie and a half-eaten strawberry. I helped Manny down on the couch. He gasped as he sank in. The two boys dropped to their knees by his side.

Under the window, the Candy Striper—Manny's daughter, whatever her name was—lowered the infant into a crib. She stood there, smiling down at the child, a glow on her face. The baby's body twisted for a moment, but the bottle she suckled anchored her head in place, her eyes closing in dreamy narcosis.

"You two go play upstairs," the girl said, turning to the boys. Together they shot up and rushed around the corner, pounding upwards on stairs that rattled in place.

Again, the girl gave me a quick embarrassed look, unwilling to let her eyes dwell on me. She turned to Manny as if looking for escape, then something caught her eyes. His boots. The girl got down on her knees and started to unlace Manny's boots.

"That's my daughter Julietta in the crib," Manny said. "And this one is Consuelo. I mentioned her in the car."

"Connie," she corrected. "And what did you say about me?"

"Nothing. Only how pretty you are."

"Don't talk like that." She bent toward the boot, as if trying to hide the blush blossoming on her neck, rising to her cheeks.

"Girls these days," Manny shook his head. "Can't say one nice thing without pissing them off."

"I'm Walker." I smiled, as if Manny's compliment permitted me to look at her. In truth, she was more than pretty. Big brown eyes, arched eyebrows; flawless olive-toned skin, shiny black hair tied in a ponytail. But no makeup. Nothing but the small mole above and to the right of her eye, a little ebony gem. Punctuating. Much more than pretty. That rarest kind of beauty—natural, unaffected and artless, any embellishment of which would only cheapen.

"Walker gave me a ride. He lives right across the river."

"Across the river?" She glanced out the window, eyes widening. "Where?"

"The one up the hill. With the fruit trees, right?" He looked at me.

"Right," I said, embarrassed.

"Oh," she said, nodding, unable to look at me—as if she was embarrassed, too. "That one."

That one. Why did it have to be so damned big?

"Walker has a summer job at AMC."

"Really." She seemed nervous, now. Maybe cowed by that stupid house.

"He works with me," Manny added.

"Something you have no business doing yet," she mumbled.

"Do I have a choice?" He winced as she lifted one of his legs and slipped off a scarred, steel-toed boot.

"Our family doctor told him he needed to rest." Connie said over her shoulder as she examined the knotted laces on the other boot. "He said my father's back would never heal if he returned to work too soon. But does he listen?"

"Will the food and rent pay for themselves—our hospital bills—while I'm laying there, doing nothing?"

"They would if you weren't always sending money back to Mexico," she grumbled.

"My cousins need it more than we do," Manny admonished. "You know that."

"Well, if you kill yourself working, nobody will get money and nothing will get paid for." She used her fingernail to pry loose the stubborn knot.

"Don't they give you paid sick days?" I asked.

He seemed surprised by the question.

"Sure," he said.

"Well, then—" At least, he wasn't dealing with some pre-existing condition like Norm was.

"The only problem is—" He nodded toward his daughter, trying to get her attention, but she was focused on the boot knot—"they're all used up." She didn't catch this.

"And vacation days?" I asked.

"Them, too. Poof. You hear me, Consuelo?"

"There," she said, getting the knot loose with a satisfied smile. Within seconds, she had the other boot unlaced and pulled off. "Better?"

"Yes, thank you, but listen—"

"And thank you for giving him a ride," Connie said "The bus is very hard on his back."

"No problem."

Manny seemed to regard me anew as if wondering why I was here.

"I just remembered—" He grimaced, twisting to reach his back pocket. "Look what Walker found." He pulled the wallet out and tossed it onto the coffee table.

"Huh." Connie picked it up, examining it. "You've had it all this time?"

"No, I discovered it yesterday." You couldn't bullshit this girl. I couldn't hold her eyes, certain she could see through me. "Wedged between crates."

"Huh." She nodded, dubious. "So—" She hefted the wallet. "Did you show it to anyone? Do they believe your story now?"

"I did. They don't."

"*Pendejos*," she mumbled. She tossed the wallet on the table.

"Language, little one," he admonished. "They wanted to see my green card, but I said no. I already showed it to them once."

"Hmm." She glanced at me, like if I weren't around, she might press him on this point.

"Maybe I should go—"

"No, no," Manny said. "It's okay. Sorry I snapped at you in the car. In fact, I should thank you, for the wallet, for being such a *loco* today, trying to help me, for the ride. Why you're not being like everyone else at the plant, I don't know."

"I just think—well, I agree. They are—*pendejos*?" I smiled at Connie, hoping I hadn't made the word unintelligible, but she smiled back. "But I was also wondering," I added, turning back to Manny, thinking about Norm, his arm in a sling, the paid time off he hoped to get. "Did you apply for workers' compensation?"

"I tried, but they won't give it to me."

"Why not?"

"Don't know. Probably some bullshit excuse." He glanced at me and shifted, perhaps remembering who my father was. "All I know is, AMC mailed me this notice that said they turned me down."

"AMC!" Connie said, spitting. "It was that *estúpido* plant doctor."

"You mean my—I mean—" I glanced at Manny, my stomach tightening. "Dr. Maguire?"

"Yes." He returned the look, keeping my confidence, yet again. "Dr. Maguire."

"Cold man," she said. "Military, right Papa?"

"That's right, but—" He gauged my response.

"Heartless, if you ask me," Connie jumped in. "He'd do anything to save that company a few bucks, no matter who it hurts."

"Did he say why?" I asked. "This doctor?"

I gave Manny another look. He smiled in return, nodding his consent to my secret.

"Nope," Connie said. "No explanation, which didn't surprise me. My father's back problems started long before the fight, and that man has never helped in all this time."

"Getting pulled off that pallet—" Manny sighed, "that was, how they say? The straw that broke the camel's back. Like, for real." He smiled, spreading his hands. "All I need is a couple of humps."

"The stupid quack never gave him a single day off."

"Okay, little one." He raised his hand. "There's nothing we can do about it now."

"There's something *I* could do," she hissed. "Get me in the same room with him."

"¡Basta ya!" He barked at her, another quick glance at me, then back at her, clearing his throat. "Tell me, tell me: Your mother? How is she?" He lifted his eyes to the right.

"Sleeping, I think." Connie gave me a self-conscious glance, another uncomfortable topic.

"So you were stuck with the three of them, again?"

"She took the baby for a while so I could take the boys out in the boat." She snuck a look at me, then scratched at her neck.

"That's good. And you found—you gave them lunch?"

She nodded.

"But wasn't this the day you volunteer at St. Francis?"

"It's not like I'm getting paid." Connie gave his hand a little shake.

"Still, you don't want them to think you're not dependable."

Connie shrugged, as if it was out of her hands.

Manny exhaled, but seemed too tired to take it further. "I guess it's up to us to make dinner again, huh?"

My cue to leave. I straightened.

"I can do it," she said. "But," she glanced around, searching. "Weren't you going to stop at the IGA?"

Manny grimaced.

"I was, but—"

"You should have said something," I put in. "We could have stopped. I can still run back—"

"It's not that," Manny said. "There wasn't a reason to stop."

"Sure there was, *Papá*. I gave you a list this morning. Hamburger, chicken, plantains, peppers, tortillas—"

"Yes, of course, but didn't you hear me?" Hesitating, baffled, he reddened.

"Hear what?"

"I said it would depend on my sick days? Vacation days? Whether I had any left? For them to pay me for?" She couldn't see whatever it was he was hinting at.

"Oh, no." She put her hand to her mouth. "They didn't give you a check?"

"No. But it's okay." An awkward glance my way. "I'm working again. We'll manage."

"This is 'working again'?" She held wide a hand, presenting the man on his back, unable to move.

"I have the whole weekend to rest."

"Hey," I said, reaching for my wallet. "I can lend you a few dollars—"

"No!" Manny barked.

"A couple bucks—" I said, making light.

"We take care of ourselves." His smile disappeared, his demeanor as flinty as my father's ever got.

I glanced at Connie. She shook her head, a warning.

"Okay." My hands up in surrender. "I only wanted to help."

Manny lifted his head to Connie, a suggestion coming. "That bag of rice isn't empty yet, is it? And we still have some beans."

"Rice and Beans? Again?"

"Go start dinner. We'll figure out something tomorrow, okay?"

"Okay." She sighed.

But it wasn't okay. Disappointment worked on their faces, and it went far deeper than rice and beans. She turned to me, then to her father.

"Should we invite Walker to join us?"

"No, no. I've got to run." They didn't need another mouth to feed.

"Oh." She seemed to wilt. "Well, it was nice to meet you." Connie stood, holding out her hand.

I took it, warm and soft, but her grip was strong. I shook it once, catching her eye again, a bashful smile.

"You know, I remember you now," she added. "You were at the hospital."

"That's right. And you were the candy striper."

"Yes, but—" A question on her mind.

"Connie starts their nursing program in September," Manny piped up, a hint of pride pressing through the veil of pain. She regarded him, uncertainly.

"Well, we'll have to see about that," she said, doubtfully.

"You're going," Manny said. I looked between them but said nothing—a family argument. Catching my eye, Manny explained, "She doesn't think we can afford it now, but the money's already been set aside and no one's touching it." He nodded at his daughter. "Understand?"

"We'll see," she mumbled, unconvinced. She turned back to me, that other thing on her mind, the way she cinched her eyebrows together, cocked her head up at me. "That day at the hospital, my father said, 'I won't tell.' What was that about?"

"Nothing," her father barked. "Go make dinner before we all starve."

"Some big secret, huh." She looked between us. "Well, okay. So—bye, then." She smiled, backing away, her eyes wide and curious.

"It was great to meet you," I said.

"You, too." She turned and headed out. Manny, eyebrows raised, had caught me watching her go.

"Look, Manny," I started, flushed. I couldn't leave like this, him laying there, his family going hungry, her future in doubt. "I'll try to talk to my dad. You know, about the workers' comp. Maybe I can find out what's going on."

"Are you sure? He's a tough cookie, as they say."

"I can try."

Thirty-Six

Back in the ICU, I find Piper sitting next to Dad's bed, doing a crossword puzzle, the same way Mom kept him company in the evenings as he watched baseball. She glances up, barely acknowledging me after the words we'd had earlier.

"Did you see the doctor?" I ask.

"Yes." She allows herself a moment's grimace at the memory, then looks at Dad. She purses her lips.

"Well?" I skirt the bed and sit in the chair on the other side, laptop on my knees.

She grabs Dad's hand, rubbing it, a lamp without a genie.

Her agitation yesterday had been painful to witness, her breathless recital of his medical condition. She'd been right there with the doctor in the cockpit, a co-pilot running down a checklist, requesting permission to change course. Permission denied. But this silence today is harder to take. Now, she's only along for the ride, in an aisle seat in the last row.

It's one thing for me to be resigned, but Piper? What's changed? Maybe nothing, and that's the point.

I open the computer to capture our little exchange, start typing, documenting everything.

"What exactly are you writing about?"

"I thought you didn't want to know," I mumble.

"Things I did when I was a lonely little kid?" I look up. "Stuck in that house with no friends, nothing to do, and no one to talk to? Is that what it's about? What an angry, nasty little monster I could be?"

That about covered it.

"Are you publishing this? Writing a play for Frazier to direct? A stupid tell-all about our dysfunctional family?"

"No. It's just for me."

"Well, thank God for small favors."

"And it's hardly about you at all."

"Then what else is it about?

I mention the summer I worked at AMC. Blank stare. The fight. Manny Camarasa. It takes a few hints before "the guy with the meat hook?" rings a bell.

"Oh, *that* fight." Everyone remembers the meat hook. "With the father of your girlfriend—Gayle, wasn't it?"

"Norm Ditweiler, yes."

"Ditweiler, right. She runs a hair salon, like, eight chairs, in that new mall on the edge of town. Her place and a dollar store are the only tenants, so far. It's always kind of empty."

"Dare to Have Hair's gone, isn't it?"

"Her mom's place? That's Delgado's Taqueria now. Best burritos in town. But what's this business got to do with Dad?"

"Dad handled Norm and Manny's workers' comp claims. Don't you remember?"

"No."

"The picnic? The big argument?"

"Vaguely."

"You do remember that was the summer you and Kurt started up, right?"

"Oh, *that* summer!" She brightens with disbelief, as if I'd been talking about some other planet until now. "I could never forget *that* summer. If Kurt didn't get into so much trouble, we never would have happened."

It figures all she remembers is Kurt. I turn back to my laptop. "Finish your puzzle."

"So, it's not only about me, then."

"No."

She sits back, picking up her crossword. I close my eyes, trying to visualize what happened next. The picnic I came home to after leaving Manny's.

"I was a little bitch." Piper's staring right at me. "And I'm sorry. I was mean. Petty. But I was alone. And—" She stops and swallows. "I never had anybody until Kurt. You know that, don't you? He was my first—not just boyfriend. My first *friend*."

Such pleading in her tone, it's clear she's been thinking about this, old wounds I've managed to poke. But she's not my target.

"I know that, Piper. He's been good for you. And you've been good for him. I've always thought that."

"Always?"

"Well, maybe not at first. After all, you were fourteen, and he was nineteen."

She leans forward in her chair.

"If I remember correctly, you wanted to kill him."

"'Kill' is a bit extreme. Beat the crap out of him, maybe." I gesture, invoking the scene, a satisfying punch.

She chuckles, gives me a questioning look. "Do you forgive me?"

"Yes, of course I do. That's all in the past." I glance at Dad, his face stubbly again, his breathing barely perceptible, reminded why we're both sitting here. "I didn't mean to make you feel bad about that on top of everything else."

"Okay then." She opens her crossword again, searching for clues, then adds, without looking up. "For what it's worth, that shitty little rag of a newspaper could use a good editor."

"So you wouldn't mind if I came back."

She peeks up at me.

"Not if you smiled once in a while."

Smile. A tall order.

Thirty-Seven

Driving toward the Ironworks Foundry after leaving Manny's house, I looked over and across the river. It was a three-mile drive back to Main Street, across the bridge, and back out Jackson to that house. From here, looking up that hill, I didn't recognize it any more, that brick building up there, more like a courthouse than a home.

The drive gave me a few minutes to wrap my head around what my dad had done to Manny, refusing him workers' comp. His family couldn't even put together a decent dinner. Their lives were so day-to-day, hand-to-mouth. Then there was that business about their hospital bills, the house, seeing how long they'd have it. It was worse than I ever imagined.

When I got home, Mom and Piper were setting the picnic table out back. As I crossed the grassy plateau towards them, the late afternoon sun behind the Foundry's smokestacks threw two oblong shadows over the river and up the hill. A loud clunk was followed by a hiss, sounds I'd heard a thousand times. Who knew what they were casting there now. Church bells? Backhoe buckets? Battleship anchors?

Piper breezed past me, turning her head away with a sweeping dismissal. Still angry at me for calling her and Kurt jerks the day before.

"It's about time you got home," Mom said "Here, make yourself useful." She handed me a stack of plates. I dealt them around the table as Piper set out the silverware, her mouth tight. Mom emptied a big bag of potato chips into a bowl.

She kept sneaking peeks down the hill toward the river, scanning upstream and down.

"What are you looking for?"

She shook her head, as if it was nothing, then thinking better of it, leaned close, and whispered, "I went down to the berry patch this afternoon. I promised your father a strawberry shortcake tonight, but the strawberries were all gone."

"More poachers?" I said, keeping my voice low.

She nodded. "I had to run out to the IGA to get some more before he got home. I sliced them up so he wouldn't see how small those store-bought ones are, but they don't taste the same."

"Walker!" Dad had fired up the grill.

"Do you think he'll notice?" she asked.

"I don't know. Do you have any other fruit you can mix them with? Disguise the taste."

"Good idea. I've got some blueberries and a couple bananas." As my mom rushed up the back steps, I reached into the blue cooler, grabbed a sweating, icy soda, and headed over to where the grill stood on a small wooden deck. Dad had just upended the charcoal chimney, the red hot coals spilling from the metal cylinder into the well of the spherical barbecue, sparks flying.

"Why are you late?" Dad said. "I told you last night the lawn needed mowing before it got out of hand."

"Sorry. I forgot." As I stepped up onto the deck, I wiped my wet hand on my jeans and popped the soda. When did he tell me about the lawn? At dinner? Bedtime? But quibbling over this was no way to start the conversation.

"I started on it myself," he said, "but the mower blade hit a root or rock or something, and it's jammed." He gave me an accusing look.

"Sorry." I perched my butt on the narrow deck rail and sipped my soda.

"Where were you, anyway?" He faced me.

"I had to give someone a ride home."

"Who?"

"A friend."

"A friend." He sniffed, snapping up the long-handled spatula. "Right." He smoothed the coals this way and that, replaced the round metal grate on top of the grill, then slapped on four fat burgers, grease sizzling in the flames.

What could I say about Manny, considering the shitty mood Dad was in?

"Can I ask you something?" I said, hands on my knees.

"Hmm?"

Fire licked at the red meat through the grate.

"You handle workers' compensation claims at the plant, don't you?"

"That's right." He nudged the burgers around.

"So, say a guy has a knee injury or a backache, he'll get paid if he can't work."

"Depends. If there's proof it started on the job, or he brings in X-rays, a doctor's letter, test results, then, yes, he'll be compensated."

Hm. Norm couldn't get comp for his hip because that didn't start at AMC, but Manny's problem certainly did. The thing was, I didn't know if Manny had talked to his doctor or had any X-rays taken.

"What if he can't prove it? What if he's just in pain."

"Are you trying to tell me—" He turned.

"No, no. I'm fine." I waved him off. "I'm only wondering what happens, you know, when a guy has no proof something's wrong."

"And that's the question, isn't it?" He pressed the spatula down on a burger, the grease oozing out, flaring up into snapping flames. "People come into my office, complaining about back aches or hip problems or knee pain or headaches, and, so often, there is no proof. No bumps, no bruises or swelling, nothing that shows up on an X-ray. Just pain. Or so they say."

"So what do you do?"

"Well, you have to decide based on the best available evidence."

"And if it's only them saying they're in pain?"

"Then you consider other things."

"Like what?"

"Like whether their pain appears real or they seem to be acting."

"And if you still can't tell?"

"Gut feelings, then. What you know about the person. Sometimes, it's a judgment call."

"Like with Norm Ditweiler?" I added.

"Norm Ditweiler?" His eyebrows pulled together, an unexpected turn. "His injury was quite evident, but—"

"So, you gave him workers' comp, then?"

"Actually, Walker—and I know he's your girlfriend's father, but I'm afraid I couldn't. Sorry."

"You couldn't?" I stood up.

"No." He considered, judging my reaction. "I tried to help Norm. He got to keep his job, and I know he's got that hip problem, but that happened before he started at AMC, and when I examined him—"

Dad put his hands on his hips, lowering his head.

"What?"

"He came in with this ridiculous sling, and when I took his arm out, he began caterwauling like a—" He gave me another shake of his head. "He had full range of motion, the wound was healed, so—" He sighed. "Look, don't take this as a reflection on your girl. She's a great kid, but her father? Let's just say he'll never win an Oscar, okay? Now I hope that doesn't cause problems for you with Gayle, but frankly, Norm—" He shook his head, dismissively.

Oddly, I felt bad for Norm, for Gayle, too. How this would add to their struggles.

"I understand," I said. The direction this was going! "But with that hip of his, he won't last on that job." I leaned back against the rail.

"I know. But he accepted that risk when he took the job."

"Still," I persisted. "They didn't have to put him on the loading dock, did they?"

"I've asked them to give him something easier to do, but it's not up to me."

"Okay."

"Good. I'm glad you see it my way. Sometimes I have to make tough calls. I can tell you, it's not easy."

"I know."

Mom reappeared with a fresh drink in her hand, which she handed to my father. She winked at me, nodding at the bowl on the table. Fruit salad. I nodded back and took a deep breath, turning to my father as he took a swig from his rum and coke. I folded my arms, tightening my grip on myself.

"It was really Manny Camarasa I was wondering about."

"Manny Camarasa?" He turned and gave me a squint of incomprehension, like he'd never heard the name.

"Yes." I straightened, standing. "He came back to work today. He was all bent over, in pain. He shouldn't have been there, but you didn't give him workers' comp."

"Manny Camarasa started a fight." He pointed the spatula at me, instructing. "When a worker gets injured starting a fight, he doesn't get workers' compensation. It's in the union contract."

The explanation couldn't be that simple, some kind of technicality. No, this went deeper. I stepped toward the grill. "But you know he is hurting, right? He shouldn't be working. Any more than Norm should."

"That's two different situations—"

"But you won't help Manny—why? Because instead of believing his version of events, you believe Norm's?"

He put the spatula down.

"I don't get you. Who gives a damn about Manny Camarasa. If it weren't for Norm Ditweiler not pressing charges, that sleaze ball would be in jail right now."

"He barely made it through the day. That's who I gave a ride home."

"That's your friend?" His disbelief straightened him.

"Come on, Michael," Mom said from outside the rail. Piper was right behind her, hand to mouth.

"He could hardly walk," I added. "I had to carry him into his house. I met his family. He's got four kids—a newborn baby, two little boys, a daughter my age. She said his doctor told Manny he shouldn't be working, but they can hardly afford to eat, and they may lose their home." I raised my eyes to meet my dad's. "They wouldn't be having these problems if you'd given him his workers' comp."

"So this is my fault now?" He leaned back against the rail, arms folded.

"You refused to believe him. You took the word of that drunken fool Norm Ditweiler instead. Why is that?" I'd floored it, going all in.

"Because Manny's story doesn't add up, that's why. That stolen wallet crap? Well, where is this stolen wallet, Walker? Did it disappear into thin air?"

I pivoted around, caught Piper's eye. She cocked her head, daring me. I glanced at my dad.

"What? You know something about it?"

I took a breath.

"I—I found it."

"You found it? What do you mean you found it?"

"The day of the fight, I found it as I was leaving to pick up Gayle. On the ground, near where it happened. I returned it to Manny this morning."

"You found it that day, and you never told anyone?"

"No—" I started, but I hadn't planned this many moves ahead. I was no more sure about Manny than he was himself.

Are you legal or not?

I think I am.

This conversation had veered onto this mountain road, dangerous twists and turns, drops on all sides. I had to slow this down, inch my way along. He straightened, taking a step towards me.

"Because why, Walker?"

I backed up.

"I was waiting to give it to him. I wanted him to have it, so he could decide what to do with it. It wouldn't have been fair if I gave it to you or Kelly without him having a say."

"The grill, Michael," Mom said.

"I know!" he barked at her, forcing her back a step. He grabbed the spatula and flipped a couple of burgers, thinking.

"I don't get where this is coming from, son. You're acting like he's the victim here."

"Well," I said. "Maybe he is."

"Oh, is that so?" He chortled, turning, arms folded. "Well, kindly explain yourself."

I took a breath, priming myself.

"I saw it."

"You saw it." Dad's shoulders shook, baffled. "You saw what?"

"The fight," I said. "I saw the whole thing."

"Oh, did you now?" He laughed.

"Yes." *Go slow, Walker.*

"And let me guess, it happened exactly the way Manny explained it to me." He pointed with the spatula, drawing it out in the air. "Norm tried to take this wallet which, as of today, you supposedly found, and Manny put a meat hook through his arm in self-defense. Do I have that right?"

"That's right," I said. "He was only holding the meat hook because guys are always taking it, playing jokes on him. And when Norm reached for his wallet, he reacted."

"He talked you into saying this, didn't he? This friend you drove home convinced you to lie for him."

"I'm not lying," I said. "I saw the fight."

"Then why did you wait until now, after having met Manny's lovely family—"

Mom stepped up onto the deck and put her hand on Dad's arm. "Come on, Michael."

"No," he shook her off and stepped towards me. "I want to know. That day, I asked if you saw anything and you said no. Isn't that right?"

"Yes." The rail was behind me, against my legs.

"So you lied then, is that what you're saying?"

"Yes, I lied."

"And *now* you're telling the truth. Or is this the lie. You took pity on this guy's family and decided to help him out by making up this story."

"It's not a story—" I scanned the house, the yard, hoping a reasonable explanation would jump out at me. Then I caught Piper's eye. She stood there, her mouth open, taking this all in.

"Ask Piper!" I scooted down off the deck, standing next to her, presenting her. "That evening, after the fight, I told her and all my friends I saw it, didn't I, Pipes?"

She backed up a step, hardening. She folded her arms, refusing to look at me.

"Piper," I said, advancing on her. "Tell him. Tell him what I told you guys." I grabbed her elbow.

"Why should I?" She shook me off, her mouth tight. "If I'm such a *jerk*."

"I'm sorry I said that, but you have to tell him—" I grabbed at her again.

"Leave her be," Dad said, coming down off the deck.

"But she knows I saw it." I released her, hands up in surrender.

"You know what? This picture—" Dad said, "is becoming very clear, son."

"I tell you, I saw the whole thing. I was up—" I took a big breath. "I was up on top of my boxcar—"

"On top of a boxcar. This is getting better and better." He leaned back against the deck rail, crossed his legs and arms, taking it all in, head cocked. The floor was mine.

"I wasn't supposed to be there, and that's where I saw it from. Manny was napping, had his wallet out next to him. Norm tried to take it, and Manny reacted." *That stupid meat hook!* "In self-defense.

Norm pulled him down, and that's how he got hurt. I knew I'd get suspended for being up there, so I didn't say anything."

"I'm not buying it." He stood, stepping toward the grill. "This guy, he's gotten into your head somehow."

"You have to believe me," I said, grabbing the rail. "Tell your company I saw it. Tell them where I was. I don't care if they suspend me. But don't take it out on Manny and his family."

"You mean the guy who, *in self-defense*, skewered Norm's arm." He grabs the spatula.

"It was a knee-jerk reaction. He even said so. He was half-asleep. And I saw it. That's how it looked."

He shoves the burgers around.

"Yeah, he told me the same cockamamie story, and it's no more believable coming from you than it was from him."

He turned around and faced me, his shoulders dropping, surrendering into disappointment. "I don't understand this. Why are you letting yourself be taken in by this guy?"

"I'm not being taken in." I step up onto the deck. "These people. Manny. Norm, too. They have bills to pay, families to take care of. Manny's got a sick wife—"

"Add a *sick wife* to the list," he scoffed, winking at my mom.

"Dad! You're supposed to help these people!"

He aimed the spatula at me, forcing me back a step, off the deck. His jaw worked, grinding.

"You think I enjoy doing this? I know what they're going through. I'm not blind. But I have a job, too. A house to pay for. Food bills. College tuition." He jabbed with the spatula, making points. "And there are rules. That's why I got you this job, so you'd understand that. We live by rules. Rules you have to learn in life. That's why you go to school, not to—fuck around, wasting my money." Mom and Piper jumped at the swear. "And when a guy hits another guy with a goddamned meat hook—and that happened, that's a fact—" He jabs. "And he still gets to keep his job, he sure as hell isn't getting any workers' comp, okay? You got that?"

He towers over me, hands on hips. That tone, bristling, hackles raised, the hot, bad breath—it took the air right out of me. My shoulders jiggled involuntarily, chilled, my stomach souring, cringing.

"If he doesn't like it," Dad continued, "he can get a goddamned lawyer and appeal the decision—if he doesn't get deported first!"

A very real possibility, it seemed to me. He climbed back onto the deck, glancing at the grill.

"And the fact that you would lie to me, lie to my face, to try and help these people—"

"Daddy." Piper grabbed the deck rail with both hands. "He did tell me about it before." A change of heart? Taking pity on me? "The night of the fight. After dinner. He told all of us about it."

"Don't you cover for him," Dad said.

"I'm not."

"Well, I'm not buying it. Walker's mad at me for making him work there, or not getting him an easier job, or something else, I don't know." He shook his head, breathing out heavily. "I don't know what to say. But I can't have this."

Piper turned to me, her hands wide with helpless surrender, as if that feeble attempt was enough to exonerate her.

"I'm not lying." It came out in a whisper, a balloon leaking its last gasp of air.

Piper and Mom both looked stricken, a hidden side of me revealed. I could barely breathe, let alone speak. Then, something occurred to me, a puzzle piece that fit nowhere in Dad's argument.

"What about the other facts?"

"What other facts?"

"Norm was drunk. That's a fact."

"What?" Dad stammered, a bit confused.

"They should have fired him, but you let him keep his job. Aren't you lying to your company, breaking the rules?"

"You want him to be fired?"

"I didn't say that. But if you're giving him a break, why can't you do the same for Manny?"

"It's not the same thing." He gave a dismissive wave of the spatula.

"How is it different?"

"It just is!" He whipped around at me, forcing me back. "Now, I've had enough of your meddling. We're done talking about this, until I figure out what to do with you, because this—" He pointed the tool at me, flipping it, once, twice. "This behavior—"

He stepped back to the grill and flipped the burgers over, then onto a plate, all of them too well done, using this work to blot out my presence, still standing there, stunned.

An arm corralled me, my mom turning me.

"Walker, honey," she whispered. "Could you go get the potato salad for me? It's in the fridge."

I was tempted to shake her off, stand my ground, but Dad was seething as much as I was. If I'd said another word, he might have exploded.

Thirty-Eight

Seated at the picnic table, we all settled into a silence interrupted only by an occasional chunk and hiss from across the river. Some fundamental shift had occurred, as if I'd been outed, some dark secret revealed. I'd lied big-time, and I'd admitted it. The days and weeks I'd waited to speak up were like flood waters building up from persistent rains, sinking the truth to where they couldn't see it anymore. They didn't buy my story, and I couldn't persuade them otherwise. Piper's half-assed effort only made it worse.

My stomach was a wrung washrag that refused to uncoil. The fat burger smelled delicious despite being overcooked, while across the river, a family of six dined on rice and beans, night after night. I couldn't touch it. I nibbled at a potato chip, sipped at my soda.

At one point, Dad took the bottle of juice off the pile of paper napkins to grab one, but a gust of wind caught them and whisked them all off the table. He snatched at them but missed, and they scattered down the hill, white squares tumbling, flitting amongst the fruit trees and beyond. The residual tension after the fight kept us chained to the table, unable to give chase. He sighed and turned to Piper.

"Can you get those after dinner?"

She nodded yes. An opening. I stood.

"May I be excused?"

"You haven't even touched that burger."

"I'm not hungry."

I headed toward the basement.

"Don't think that gets you out of the dishes," Dad called after me.

In the rec room, I plopped down on the couch, closed my eyes. Our argument replayed, over and over, nothing I could do to turn it off. *That you would lie to me. We live by rules.*

I used to think of my father as a hero, from the war stories we occasionally squeezed out of him. The day he defused an unexploded bomb in front of his portable hospital in New Guinea, unwilling to ask his men to take a risk he wouldn't take. The time he killed a man, a 'Jap' soldier—they were always 'Japs' in his tellings. The man had awakened my father in his tent, inches from bayonetting him, a sneak attack in the middle of the night. Dad had turned the bayonet around on the man.

When he told those stories, you only had to see the way he scanned the horizon, searching through walls and years, to know a vivid memory had captured all his attention. He'd been there and done those things.

Once we moved to Belford, he seemed to come unhinged from the world, distanced from the men for whom he was now responsible. Maybe when Dad started that job he thought these were his men, his troops, but unlike soldiers, these line workers weren't there to protect each other or follow his orders, nor did they feel any loyalty toward him. The company's top priority was to squeeze work out of its employees and profits out of its automobiles, so who could blame workers for making their top priority looking out for themselves, and to hell with the doctor who'd been hired to look out for them. Confronted with that, my father had decided that was his job, too—putting himself first.

After dinner, I helped my mother with the dishes while Dad cleaned the grill and Piper collected the paper napkins that had blown down to the river. When Mom asked me to wash, I was too worn out to fuss. She stood by my side, a white apron protecting her blue *muumuu*. She scraped food off plates into the trash and handed them to me.

"Maybe you can eat this later?" She said, holding up my burger, which she'd just wrapped in cellophane.

As she put the burger in the fridge, I said, "I wasn't lying. I saw what happened."

"Then why didn't you say anything?"

"I explained that. I thought I'd get fired."

She tapped her long nails on the counter. How could she not sense the real reason I'd shut up—how even the set of his jaw, a sharpening of his tone, made me sweat? I wasn't about to squirm in front of her, too, to make my point.

"Your father has a very difficult job," she said, "More difficult than you can imagine. And, if you're telling the truth, you've put him in a very difficult position."

"He's not in the Air Force any more. They can't shoot you for disobeying an order or whatever."

She passed me a plate. In the hot water, the bright yellow mustard and red catsup mixed, flowing off orange and greasy down the drain.

"Do you know how long your father was a full colonel?" she asked after a minute, watching me wash.

"No."

"Fifteen years. Since before you were born."

"Okay." Was this about to become another lecture?

"After running hospitals at all those bases, he was in line to move to the top, become a strategist, maybe even go to Andrews Air Force base near Washington where they plan the whole medical program. I remember him telling me once that one day soon they'd be taking that eagle off his chest and replacing it with a star on his lapel."

"General?" I glanced at her, putting a plate in the rack. She nodded, picking up the plate to dry it. "So why didn't he ever get it?"

"You know, I don't like to talk about your father behind his back, but you need to hear this. You need to understand something. Okay?"

"Okay."

"Now, I didn't hear the story from him. Just hints, at first, that something was wrong. We were in the Philippines—you won't remember; you were too young—but there was this Women's Auxiliary Group, a glorified garden club for the officers' wives. We'd meet for luncheons, card parties, that kind of thing. Then they stopped inviting me. A colonel's wife, and all of a sudden I was out. The chairwoman apologized. She said it was 'orders,' said she was so sorry, didn't know why. Of course, she did, but she wouldn't tell me.

"Then there was the Officer's Club. Your father took me there for dinner and drinks on Friday nights. But we stopped going. When I asked why, he mentioned a 'change in protocol,' whatever that meant. I shouldn't let it bother me. But the big thing happened when he got transfer orders eight months ahead of schedule. Not to Andrews, but to Chanute, yet another training base. Not up, but down. He said, 'there are no promises in the military.' And 'you go where they send you.'"

"So what was it?" I handed her a second plate. She paused, wiping it absent-mindedly.

"I didn't find out what happened until shortly before we were scheduled to leave, that time Frazier cut his foot on a Vienna Sausage can he left on the back steps, silly boy. I had to rush him to the Emergency Room. While I waited for him to be stitched up, I ran into one of your father's favorite nurses, a woman who'd stayed by my side when Piper was born. Margaret was her name. Held my hand through the whole delivery. She took me aside and told me how sorry she was to see Dr. Maguire go. Then, she said, 'If I were him, I'd have done the same thing, even if the man was a prisoner,' as if I knew what she was talking about."

"A prisoner?" I asked, leaning back against the counter.

"That opened my eyes, too. So I played along. I said, 'And how is the man doing now?' She said he had died. And then she said, and I'll never forget this, she said, 'If it weren't for your husband, it could have been so much worse.'"

"Worse? How could it be worse than dying?"

"That's what I wanted to know. I said your father hadn't given me any details. She hesitated when she realized he'd kept me in the dark, but after I begged her she finally gave in and told the whole story."

Mom peeked out the kitchen door. Dad was still down there, scraping away at the grill.

What an intrigue. My by-the-book, burger-burning, lawn-mower-breaking Dad plunked right into a spy novel. She continued, her voice low, confiding.

"She explained how one day an ambulance came from the air strip carrying a US Military Intelligence officer, a translator, a South Vietnamese officer—ARVN, they called them—and a badly injured Vietcong prisoner they had just flown in. The prisoner was near death, and the intensive care staff wanted to operate, but the MI officer said no. He wanted a private room right away for interrogation, and when the staff argued with him, the officer demanded to speak with the doctor in charge. So they called your father down. He and this nurse, Margaret, found this prisoner, near death, in a private room."

Mom snuck another peek behind her before continuing, her voice just above a whisper.

"He'd lost blood, was drifting in and out of consciousness, bandages all around his head and torso, in terrible pain. Your father said if they didn't operate, the man would die, but the MI only wanted Michael to keep the prisoner awake so he'd talk before it was too late. Michael asked, 'Too late for what?' but the MI wouldn't say. He refused to let your father administer pain medication for fear it would put the prisoner to sleep. The MI had the ARVN officer rough up the poor guy—he wasn't allowed to do it himself—slap the man to keep him alert, poke him in the side. Margaret said they had maps they wanted the prisoner to point to, asking him to locate troop movements, supply routes, tunnel networks. Apparently, the prisoner was a high-ranking officer himself. At one point, after the ARVN officer jabbed the man's wounds, making him scream, Michael tried to intervene, but the MI said, 'You have no clue what this man has done!' Your father pointed out that whatever he'd had done, he was suffering for it, and the MI said, "Suffering? This man is responsible for many deaths, and more innocent people—soldiers and civilians—will die if he doesn't talk. You want *that* on your conscience? Or his suffering?" Margaret couldn't bear to watch anymore, so she excused herself. Even down the hall, she heard it, getting louder and louder, all this screaming."

"They tortured him?"

"She said it sounded that way. This went on a while, until it grew quiet, and Michael and the other men came out. Michael and the MI argued. Your dad seemed shaken, his face white as his lab coat, I remember her saying. Apparently, Michael had given the prisoner an injection, and he'd died soon after. The MI and ARVN officer were furious."

I heard footsteps coming up the back stairs. My mom and I went quiet as Dad entered the back door, putting his greasy grilling utensils on the counter for me to wash. Without a word, he went back out the door and down the stairs. Mom snuck a peek out the back and then returned.

"He's out of earshot," she said.

"What happened with the prisoner?" I whispered, washing Dad's grilling tongs.

"Michael told them it was epinephrine he gave the man, a stimulant to rouse the prisoner, and the MI wanted to know why he died. Michael insisted his system couldn't take the stimulus, nothing else could be done, but the MI didn't buy it. He stomped out. The next thing they knew, someone from the base commander's office came over and demanded an autopsy be performed, but not by your father. So one of the other doctors did it. He found morphine in the man's system."

"Morphine?"

"That's my point. Your father disobeyed a direct order."

And he lied, too!

"Don't they court-martial you for something like that?"

"Indeed they do, but they wouldn't have, not with torture involved. They couldn't chance that detail being revealed even if, technically, the torture wasn't carried out by a US soldier."

"Did the intelligence officer ever get the information he needed?" I handed her the clean tongs, dripping water.

"I guess not." She wiped them.

"Did anybody die because of that?"

"I don't know."

"I remember Frazier saying he read somewhere that torture victims will say anything to make it stop, like it's not a very reliable way of getting useful information."

My mom almost smiled. "It's too bad he never talked to your father about it. That's one thing the two of them might have agreed on."

While I was cleaning Dad's spatula, a thought occurred to me. "If Dad didn't get his promotion, why didn't he just leave the Air Force?"

"Walker, honey, your father *loved* the military." She looked up at me, grabbing my elbow, willing me to understand. "He loved being in charge, being respected. To him, it was a noble calling, making life safe for us back here. But he also loved being a doctor, and a doctor's number one responsibility is to do no harm."

Do no harm. As a military doctor maybe. Not as a company doctor—or a father.

"And he never could reconcile the two. He sent me letters during the war, talked about patching men up on the beach one day only to send them back out to be killed the next, how absurd it was. That torture episode was especially hard on him. No matter what he did, someone would be harmed—either that prisoner or soldiers and civilians in the jungle somewhere.

"Personally," she continued, "I think he made the right decision, but I still don't know what he thinks, the way things turned out."

"You mean, ending up here?"

"Yes. Being forced out years before he was ready to go."

I ran my wet sponge over another plate. He'd been so matter-of-fact about it, taking his dismissal like it was just another assignment; I'd had no idea, or rather, only the faintest inkling.

"He hates it at AMC," Mom said. "You know that, don't you?"

Yes, that was clear. That cheap office. The paperwork. The red tape.

"The way they nickel and dime him, pressing him to cut costs, especially if it's some guy in pain who can't prove it, or like your girl's father with that bad hip they won't help him with. Every claim becomes a federal case. Some days he feels more like a lawyer than a doctor."

She nodded at me, awaiting my understanding.

"But Mom, he knows Manny's hurt," I said. "He could have believed his story, given him a break like he gave Norm, but he chose not to. It's as simple as that."

"Here's my point, Walker. He protected someone once, a man who maybe didn't deserve it, and this is what it got him. He won't make the same mistake twice."

"He protected Norm."

"Don't you see, it's too late. The decision's been made. How would it look on such a high profile case if he tried to change his ruling after all this time has passed?"

I rinsed a handful of silverware, thinking. I had to convince him, somehow. But I'd played all the cards I had. I didn't know what else to do.

"So, do we have a lawyer?" I asked.

"A lawyer?" She turned my way. "You don't mean for this Manny character, do you?"

"Dad said he could appeal."

"Yes, but you don't have to get involved." She placed a hand on the counter next to the sink.

"But do we know any lawyers?"

"We used to," she said, dismissively. "Ned St. John."

"Used to?"

"He and your father had a falling out. But he helped your dad find this job, handled the closing for the house, too. You met him. He's the one who gave us the tour."

"Oh, yeah. Funny guy. When the lights didn't work in the den, he said that was an energy-saving feature."

"That's right. And that hole in the roof." She smiled, remembering. "That was a natural source of air conditioning." She shook her head. "He had us all laughing. He and your father were great friends during the war."

"Then why the falling out?"

"Something happened." She sighed. "They don't talk anymore."

She turned away, like she didn't want to talk about it, either. Of course, Dad always pissed people off, but there was another story here—another intrigue, perhaps?

"Well, do you think he'll talk to me?"

"Walker—" she said, pivoting back, whispering fiercely. She took a guarded look out the door, then continued, speaking with urgency. "Your father needs this job. And this Manny thing could cause problems for him. So leave this alone, will you please? For me?"

The strain in her voice surprised me.

"I hear you."

"Don't just hear me," she said. "Listen to me. Do as I ask."

She waited for me to agree, but I stood my ground. I turned back to the sink, flipping the water back on, rinsing a glass.

"What do you think he'll do to me?" I said. "He thinks I'm lying. And we both know what he did to Frazier for lying."

"I'll try to talk to him, but frankly, Walker, I find your explanation hard to believe, too."

She patted my shoulder a couple of times, then backed away and walked out of the kitchen. She was right. I was a liar, and there was nothing I could do to change that.

Thirty-Nine

Piper has been sitting there for hours, holding Dad's hand. She stares into his gray face, willing him to wake up. Perhaps she's praying, something it baffles me to think she still does, churchgoer that she is.

Mom's story had explained so much about our lives in Belford, why my dad had become so hard-hearted and callous. All because he refused to participate in an act of evil. As if I know what that word means any more.

In the spring of last year, pictures emerged of the tortures American soldiers inflicted on prisoners of war at the Abu Ghraib prison, depriving them of sleep, shackling them in uncomfortable positions, making them stand for hours on end, playing loud music endlessly, subjecting them to barking dogs. My father had been involved in a one-time, isolated incident of torture, but this was nothing like that. This was around-the-clock and institutionalized, rife throughout the prison.

And yet, when I was in Iraq three years ago, I visited the same prison and reported on how, before the Americans took it over, it was used by the Iraqi dictator, Saddam Hussein, to imprison and torture his political opponents, many of whom were guilty of crimes no greater than speaking their minds, protesting his rule. And his tortures were so much worse than the Americans'. Sometimes simply for their own amusement, Hussein and his sons had people burned, electrocuted, disfigured, dismembered, raped, murdered, beheaded, disappeared. During Saddam's rule, Abu Ghraib housed ten times as many people as it could hold, small cells stuffed with so many people they had to take turns sleeping and standing, there was so little room. Those tortures were magnitudes worse than anything the Americans did—unimaginable, impossible to put into words.

My father was one man standing up to another man who, to save lives he claimed, had a third man tortured—and possibly killed. That act forever changed my father's life, and mine with it. I often wonder, who would care if such an incident came to light now. What I've witnessed as a reporter makes it so much more difficult to put my father's behavior into perspective, what he did to me, what he did to others. My sense of right and wrong, good and evil have been so distorted, those concepts barely resonate anymore. And yet, how can I—how can anyone ever hope to understand them if they don't grasp on some deeply personal, visceral level, how they, *themselves*, have been victims—or perhaps perpetrators.

Speaking of which, one thing about that summer and the way my father acted has always stuck with me, one act of kindness that didn't fit.

"Can I ask you something?" I say.

Piper rouses herself, blinking as she straightens.

"What?"

"There's one thing I've never understood. He was a stickler for rules, obeying the law. He wouldn't help Manny Camarasa because the rules said a man who started a fight couldn't get workers' comp."

"Okay."

"He even got pushed out of the military for refusing to do something illegal."

"That torture business."

"Yes." I leaned forward, agreeing. "But that's the thing. He was always by the book, right?"

"I guess."

"Except when it came to Norm Ditweiler."

"What do you mean?"

"Norm was drunk. AMC said they'd fire him if he got caught drinking again. But Dad bent the rules to save his job. That's not like him."

"He was your girlfriend's father, right?"

"Yeah, I know he liked Gayle, but for a guy so hell bent on following the rules to bend them for some girl whose father was a drunk and a fool."

"He didn't do it for them, Walker. He did it for you."

"What do you mean, for me?"

"For you! He didn't give a damn about her father. He bent the rules because she was your girlfriend. You liked her and he cared about you."

This takes some digesting. For me?

"It's like those clippings, Walker. It's not what you wrote, but that you wrote them."

I still find that hard to believe. Whether Dad helped Norm for me or not, it did prove one thing: He had a soft spot, a chink in his armor. In a moment of weakness, he bent the rules, maybe for Norm and Gayle, maybe for me, I don't know. But then I'd asked him to bend them the other way for a meathook-wielding psycho, a guy he felt sure was conning me. Maybe that's what happened that summer. He'd seen his son slipping away, being dragged under by this 'sociopath.' Seen himself being betrayed by that weakness again, that sympathy.

What happened not four days later revealed it again, at least one last time, that soft underbelly. He would cave in a way that made me think that I'd finally gotten through to him—only to discover, when the Camarasas disappeared, that he'd shut me out and covered it up for good.

Forty

I slept in that Saturday morning—a day when I didn't have to rise at dawn, psych myself for another shift on the loading dock. I only awoke when I heard clanging outside my window. I rose and parted the curtains. The John Deere lay on its side in the grass next to the driveway, the mower's blade facing up at me like a muddy propeller. My father, in grass-stained white shorts and an untucked polo shirt, banged away, trying to loosen it. He was taking something out on that blade, bashing it again and again, as if those blows were meant for me. I shivered. How long did I have before he decided I had to leave—go and live with his other failure of a son?

Something else caught my eye—Kurt's Impala parked behind my Datsun. Normally, Kurt worked Saturdays at Swanson Motors, sprucing up cars for the hordes that were sure to descend on the car lot on this, the busiest sales day of the week. Must have still been *persona non grata* at Swanson's Motors after what he did to Fernando. But why was he here? He never got up before noon if he didn't have to. Piper was not in her room, probably downstairs batting her eyes at my 'best friend.'

I went to the bureau at the top of the stairs and pulled the Yellow Pages out from under the phone. Sure enough, Ned St. John was listed under Legal Services. Glancing around first to make sure no one could hear, I dialed his number. Someone picked up on the first ring, responding with a quick, expectant, "Bob?"

"Ned St. John?"

"Yes?"

"Yeah, my name is Walker Maguire."

"You're not on my list."

"Your list?"

"Veterans. I've been leaving messages all morning."

"Oh."

"Who'd you say you were again?"

"Walker Maguire? Dr. Maguire's son."

"Doc's son! How you doing? What can I do for you?"

I explained how I had a legal problem I wanted to discuss if he had any time.

"Well, Walker, fact is, I had planned on spending the morning twisting arms before everyone's weekend gets busy. You'd be surprised how sheepish a guy gets about marching in the Fourth of July parade when his uniform doesn't fit anymore."

I had the lawn to do, anyway, if Dad could get the mower fixed. "How about this afternoon then?"

"Well, I was hoping to do some yard work around the house, but I do have some paperwork I have to get done. Maybe I can spare a few minutes before I head home from the office, say, mid-afternoon."

I found Kurt and Piper at the dining room table. Mom was serving French Toast, one of the few things Piper would eat.

"Thought we could hang out since it's your day off," Kurt said.

"I've got chores to do," I said, almost glad to have the lawn as an excuse to get him to leave. I didn't want to tell anyone about seeing Ned St. John and risk it getting back to my dad.

"I'll help." Right. In the past, whenever I had chores, the only thing Kurt volunteered to do was to come back once I'd finished.

Piper leaned over and whispered to him. "It'll be okay. You'll see." This new expression of concern puzzled me since the car soaping business had happened four days before.

"You need to eat something," my mom whispered in my ear as she placed a plate at my usual spot and pulled out a chair for me to sit. The three freckled and steaming egg-battered bread slices looked massive and heavy, enough to feed everyone. I sat and applied a pat of butter, poured syrup, took a small bite. My stomach felt full up with concrete.

Soon after, Dad came in from outside, sweat-soaked and huffing.

"Damned thing needs a new belt," he said, wiping his hands on a towel, as if the John Deere were a surgical patient and we were awaiting updates on its condition. "And I can't get the old one off."

"Why don't you take it into the shop?" Mom asked, filling a glass with lemonade.

"I can fix a lousy lawn mower." Dad glowered at her.

We all knew better. Mr. Fix-It here thought he only needed common sense to figure these things out. Sure, he did a lot of repairs around the house, but what about that upstairs shower stall he tiled with the wrong type of caulk? The tiles had slid off days after getting wet. Then there was that rusted-out Gremlin Dad got at Swanson's car lot for peanuts because it needed a paint job. He used leftover Latex to save money, but within weeks, the stuff had cracked like a 17th century Rembrandt. It was so embarrassing, he traded it in for the Datsun I was now driving.

"Well, maybe Walker can help you," Mom said.

"Walker's washing the cars this morning." He glared at me, then cast his glance over at Kurt then Piper, who nodded at Dad, expectantly. He returned the nod, his cue.

"You know, Kurt," he began, "over coffee this morning, I read that story in the police log, what happened with you and that Mexican the other day." Was Dad about to lecture him and send him on his way? "Piper was up, and I couldn't help mentioning it to her. She told me what your father did, throwing you out of the car lot." My sister lifted her hands, almost praying.

"This Mexican broke the law. He's here in the country illegally," Dad pronounced, "and Pops treating you that way for exposing the guy? It's not right."

"Do you understand what Kurt did?" I couldn't believe my ears.

"Piper told me." He seemed galled, as if the previous night I'd stripped myself of the right to speak. "I'm not saying I approve of how you exposed the man. If you were my son, I'd horse-whip you for pulling a stunt like that."

No shit.

"The fact remains, this Fernando is here illegally. And for Pops to treat his son that way after he harbored a criminal? That sticks in my craw. I wanted you to know that."

But of course. Dad hated those 'wetbacks,' stealing from our gardens, ruining the neighborhood across the river. Kurt darkened again, turning his eyes down to his plate, putting his hands in his lap.

"He threw me out of the house last night," he mumbled. "I—I slept in my car."

Piper's expression, a jubilant smile at Dad's support, turned prayerful and pleading.

"Well, you can stay here then," Dad said, nodding at each of us. "As long as it takes to straighten this out."

"Thank you." Kurt sat up, relief inflating him. Piper, her hands around Kurt's arm, bounced up and down in her seat, thrilled.

"But if you're going to eat us out of house and home, you can help Walker with those cars, okay?"

"Sure." He rolled his eyes after my dad turned away. Clearly, just what he wanted to do today—wash more cars.

"And that means the Cadillac, too."

I opened my mouth to object. That Caddy couldn't be dirty, having sat under a tarp for months. But I didn't want to press my luck.

While Kurt uncoiled the garden hose, I filled a bucket in the laundry room sink. The stiff yellow sponges and leather chamois cloths seemed to melt in the hot water. I was still in shock. Dad had actually offered Kurt sanctuary.

Once I got back outside, I found Kurt working a kink out of the rubber hose.

"Why'd your dad wait until last night to throw you out?" I asked, dropping the heavy bucket. "The thing with Fernando happened, like, four days ago."

"He saw the bashed-in bumper on my Impala. Connected the dots to that damaged Chevy in his lot."

Kurt was impulsive, but I had to admire his ability to let fly like that, consequences be damned.

I'd just plopped the soaked sponge on the hood of Dad's Ambassador when he came out of the house.

"Wash the Cadillac first. I'll move the other car," he said, rounding the big, boxy car and getting in. "Open the garage door, will you?"

I could have moved the Ambassador while he got the Caddy out, but he never let me drive either of them. This car-washing business seemed like some interim, holding-cell-type punishment while he figured out what to do with his liar of a son. I rolled up the garage door.

"Christ, that's a monster," Kurt said. The car under the gray canvas tarp was almost as big as another of my Grandfather's bequests, the boat tied up down at the dock, the runabout. The Caddy's tail fins, poking the tarp up to two fine points, nearly scraped the door.

We waited for Dad to park the Ambassador behind Mom's station wagon and return. He said, "Help me with this," grabbing one corner of the tarp. After we pulled off this skin, I folded it up while my father unlocked the car. The heavy driver's side door creaked, the complaint of an old man unexpectedly awakened. Dad disappeared inside, the door groaning shut. It took a couple of whinnying tries before he got it started, but once it warmed up, coughing and clearing its throat, the car rumbled, a lion's purr. He carefully backed it out of the dark garage and onto the sunlit driveway.

"That's one helluva car, Dr. Maguire." The swear triggered a glance from my dad, but Kurt didn't notice, too busy running his finger along a fin, admiring. "Pretty flashy."

I'd had no time to warn him what shaky terms I was on with Dad after the previous night. But Dad didn't react to Kurt's casual flippancy.

"My father-in-law left it to me." An unfamiliar waffling entered Dad's voice. Embarrassment. He joined Kurt, sliding his hand along the pristine finish, relishing my friend's admiration.

"It's a beaut," Kurt added. "Why don't you ever drive it?"

"My contract only allows me to drive American Motors products."

"Bummer."

It bugged me, the way the two of them ogled this hunk of metal while I had this weight crushing me—Manny's appeal to discuss with Mr. St. John. But then, my dad's relationship with that gaudy Cadillac DeVille had always been strange, so unseemly for the straight-arrow he'd always been. What with its plum purple paint job, two pairs of headlights, like bulging double eyes, that toothy metallic grill, its bumper a jutting silver jaw. All that chrome—the strips around the windows and along the fins—scattered so much sunlight, you couldn't help squinting.

"I'll bet Walker'd love to give this baby some exercise," Kurt crooned.

"Nobody drives this car but me," Dad said, squeezing one of the tail fins. No one drove that car at all.

"Your father-in-law must have been a real character," Kurt said.

"It was a practical joke, actually, him leaving me this."

That was news to me.

"He said I needed more fun in my life. Too many kids, too much responsibility. 'You're too tightly wound. You need to relax. Live a little,' he'd say." He chuckled, shaking his head, squinting at a discoloration. A bit of white spider webbing caught his attention. He scratched it away. "Of course, when he left it to me, I was a full colonel, running a military hospital." Wrapped up in the car, he seemed to have forgotten I was there. "And now I can't drive it at all," he said, chuckling again.

Yet, he admired it so, this guilty pleasure, like a kept mistress, a painted woman he'd never sleep with.

"You know, Doc, Pops would pay through the teeth for a classic like this."

"Not interested." Hands on hips, Dad allowed himself one final moment of admiration, his eyes sweeping along the car, front to back. "In five years, I'll retire, and I'll finally be free to drive it whenever and wherever I want."

He glanced up at Kurt and then straightened, sobering.

"Anyway, give her a good once over and then start on the others. While you're doing that, I'll trim the hedges out front. When you're done, I'll wax and polish her."

As we worked, I discovered why Pops Swanson favored Fernando's work ethic over Kurt's. Streaks on the windows. Crap in the seat cushion crevices. Every time he finished a task, I had to clean up after him.

And this was why he'd ruined a man's life. He was shitty at washing cars, and Fernando made him look bad in front of Pops. No way he soaped that car for my sake.

A door slammed and Piper skipped down the side steps in shorts and t-shirt, red hair gathered in a ponytail.

"Can I help?"

"Sure," Kurt said. "The more the merrier."

He reached into the bucket, dragged out the soaked sponge, big as a throw pillow, and with two hands lobbed it at her, a water balloon exploding as she caught it.

"Kurt!" she wailed, leaning over, shoulders arched, vampire-posed, water dripping from her chin and hands.

He laughed. "You said you wanted to help."

She pulled the soaked shirt away from her skin and turned away as she wrung it out, her training bra showing through. The tear in her eye, as she turned her head to regard us, made me wonder how she took Kurt's prank. After all, she'd only volunteered so she could hang around him. Piper never helped when I washed the cars alone.

"I'm sorry, Pipes," he said, shuffling over to her. He patted her on the shoulder. "I was only fooling around. I didn't mean to—" He shook his head, as if he really didn't know what he meant. "You know that."

She kept shooting him small, hurt looks, assessing intentions, bottom lip pushed out, before smiling uncertainly at his teasing, only in fun.

"That-a-girl," he said, giving her head a rub before moving back to the car.

Won over, she grinned, giving in.

"You can start on the white walls." I pointed at the tires.

"Okay," she said, her shirt wrung back to opacity. She bent over and inspected the front tire next to me. After we worked a while, it was time to enlighten Kurt—maybe Piper, too.

"Last night, I told my dad I saw the fight," I said.

"Oh, yeah?" Kurt perked up. "How'd that go?"

"He thinks I'm lying, waiting to tell him, like Manny conned me into it or something."

"Lying? But you told us about it that night. Does he know that?" He sought out Piper, her head popping up from the fender.

"He didn't believe me either," she said. "He thought I was trying to cover for him."

"Christ," Kurt said and added, "Well, you know, Norm might've gotten canned if he had believed you."

"I don't give a shit about Norm."

Kurt exhaled, slapping the windshield.

"Why'd you tell him, anyway?"

"Because Manny Camarasa came back to work yesterday." I lifted the Caddy's wiper blade on my side to wipe underneath.

"Huh. Bring his meat hook with him?" He mimed a sword fighter's parry and thrust.

"No, they won't let him use it. His back was so screwed up, it was painful just watching him work. I gave him a ride home. Met his daughter."

"The girl who called the cops on me?"

"Manny said she felt awful about that, like she was the reason Fernando got arrested." I shot him a look, but he only worked his sponge along the side of the car, refusing to take the bait.

I hadn't brought this up to dwell on Connie, but I couldn't help it. I kept seeing Connie's hands instead of mine as I worked, how she tackled that knot in Manny's boot, her long, tan fingers, the angle of her head as she patiently pried the laces apart, lifted his leg and slipped off the boot. Such tenderness. Such easy familiarity between father and daughter.

"She's incredible," I mumbled.

"Who?"

"Manny's daughter. Connie. *Consuelo.*" I couldn't help singing the name.

"Really," Kurt smirked. He slapped the chamois on the hood, then leaned on it with both hands, a smile widening on his face as he shared a wide-eyed look with Piper. "You and that hot tamale."

"Careful—" I pointed at him.

"Is that why we haven't seen Gayle lately?" Piper asked.

"No. I only met her yesterday. But—" I looked at Kurt. "You should know how things change. Look at you and Patty."

Piper perked up at this, peeking at Kurt curiously.

"That's been over for a while," Kurt said.

"Come on," I said. "Tell her you didn't mean it, what happened with Fernando. You got carried away."

"No, it's too far gone. Anyway, she doesn't get me anymore."

Piper couldn't hide a grin until she noticed the cautioning squint I gave her. She furrowed her brow, stuck out her lip, going all serious and back to her white wall.

"You actually like this girl?" Piper said, glancing sideways at me.

I speared her with a glare. She tried to shrug away her surprise.

"I got a glimpse of her standing on her porch, and she is pretty cute," Kurt explained.

"She's more than that," I corrected. "She's—tough. Doesn't take shit from anyone, you know?"

"But she's a—" Piper glanced between Kurt and me, seeking acknowledgement of some crucial, disqualifying fact.

"What?" I shot back at her. "She's a what?"

"Nothing," Piper said, shrugging, confused.

Kurt lifted his wiper blade and dragged his chamois underneath, missing half the spider webbing there. I stuck my rag in and dredged it out.

"You know," I said, "Manny told me Fernando's got two little kids, and his wife's expecting a third."

Piper glanced over the gleaming purple hood to gauge Kurt's reaction.

He stopped wiping. "So while I completely screwed up Fernando's life, you've made Manny's a fucking paradise, is that it?"

This stung, especially with Piper there. She ducked down, furiously scrubbing the white walls.

"My parents hate me," he grumbled. "My girlfriend's dumped me. I don't have a fucking job or a fucking home. And you of all people are ready to read me the riot act over what I did to Fernando—and for you, too." He slapped the chamois again.

"Don't you blame me for that."

"I'm fucked, and you get off scot-free."

"Yeah, right," I scoffed.

Piper peeked over the hood again, sad for Kurt, as if she wanted to hug the poor baby. So much for showing her he wasn't the crown prince she imagined him to be, not when I came off as the black knight in comparison.

"Pops is just punishing you," I said. "This will blow over, you'll get your job back and when he retires, that dealership will be yours."

"I wouldn't be so sure. He said I had to 'make amends,'" Kurt said, mockingly. "Or I couldn't come back."

I stood, squeezing the sponge, thinking, watching. "Maybe you can talk to him. Fernando."

"And say what? It's in the courts now. I can't do anything."

"Well," I wrung out my rag. "I know the feeling."

Forty-One

At lunch, I wracked my brain for a way to escape Kurt for the afternoon. After Dad left to finish the hedges, I said, "River's looking mighty inviting today. Good day for a swim."

"Can I come?" Piper asked, breathless. She'd assumed I was making plans with Kurt.

"Well, actually," I said. "I've got errands to run, so maybe you can take my place."

Her mouth popped open and she bounced, jolted with anticipation. She turned to Kurt, shrinking into timidity, same as when he'd exploded that wet sponge onto her chest. "If Kurt doesn't mind."

I half-expected Kurt to shoot me one of those withering looks, like why the hell was I running off and sticking him with my kid sister. Instead, he shrugged.

"Oh, why the hell not," he said, smiling at us in turn. "Good day to cool off, right?"

As I drove downtown, I rehearsed what I'd tell Ned. I knew the story so well now, my thoughts drifted to Ned's warm voice, his way of talking on the phone, as if we were the best of friends. It reminded me how he made us laugh that day he showed us this 120-year-old house, goofing at being a real estate agent. He'd pointed out the delicately cracked ceilings, the painted shut windows, remarking that they would provide great insulation. The house offered other "features"—the musical radiators, the slight incline in the front porch, as if it were designed to shed rain water and wasn't evidence of a failing foundation. Funny guy. I couldn't imagine why he and my father weren't friends anymore. But then, when I thought about it, Dad didn't have any friends.

My parents didn't invite people over or go to parties. I asked about it one New Year's Eve, why they had no plans. My mom said she'd had enough of parties in the Air Force, this women's function and that officers' ceremony. She declared she'd be happy if she never had to go to another party ever again. But it made me wonder.

Ned St. John's office was in the old Woolworths building, just down the street from Dare to Have Hair. It being a Saturday afternoon, Gayle was probably in hairdressers' heaven, washing and styling, soaking in the gossip. As I parked, I realized she hadn't called since the night of our aborted movie date. Did she know about Norm's workers' comp claim being denied? I wouldn't have blamed her for suspecting I had something to do with it. I certainly never expected Dad to turn Norm down on his own. After all, he'd let him keep his job even after he was caught drinking. Maybe I didn't give him enough credit. Maybe he judged it one thing to excuse a drunk for a problem over which he had no control, and something else entirely to reward the same man's bald attempt at deception—trying to hide that perfectly healthy arm in a sling.

As I made my way to the second floor of the musty building, hardwood floors creaking, I was reminded that Dad's ability to judge character only went so far. He'd be so pissed if he knew I was in this building, trying to help 'Meat-Hook' Manny the Mexican appeal his decision.

I found a door with frosted glass on which "Ned St. John, Attorney-At-Law" was painted in gold leaf. The door was unlocked. It creaked as I opened it. Inside was a tiny waiting room that smelled of cigarettes and stress. I knocked on the inner door.

"Come in," a hoarse voice yelled.

I entered. A small man in a white dress shirt sat behind a big wooden desk. His feet, shod in black cowboy boots with pointed toes, were up and crossed over the desk's corner. He cupped his hand over the mouthpiece of the phone and motioned me toward a leather couch. I moved a pile of manila file folders onto the floor so I could sit while he continued his conversation, saying "Uh-huh" and "Yep."

Bookshelves displayed large sets of identical legal volumes on divorce, bankruptcy, real estate, wills and criminal law—a jack of all trades, this guy. Framed diplomas from Northwestern and John Marshall Law School adorned one wall. On another was a black-and-white photo of Ned in the military, posed in a uniform and wearing a peaked cap.

"Ice cream, Bob," Ned said to the phone, then listened. "You can't work the grill. Dwayne Darby's working the grill."

Listening, he flexed his eyebrows at me, shook his head and sighed. I recognized him from when he showed us the house five years ago, but he was balder, his receding hairline defined by long, graying strands combed back over his head.

"Bob? Bob?" He waited, another eye roll. "I gotta go. Someone's in the office." Another listen. "Nope. Ice cream's all I got. Talk to you soon." He hung up.

"Shoot me if I ever volunteer for the Fourth committee again. Put a gun to my head and pull the trigger."

I smiled, not sure what to say. He squinted at me, trying to place me. He swung his legs down and sat forward in the chair, grasping a white coffee cup on the desk.

"You're Frazier's little brother, right?"

"That's right."

"And how is Frazier these days?"

Why did he want to know about Frazier?

"He lives in Chicago now."

"Any chance he and your father are back on speaking terms?"

"No," I said. "You know all about that draft business?"

"I do," Ned said, standing up. "Unfortunate situation, that one." Carrying the cup, he came around, grabbed the wooden chair in front of his desk, and straddled it backwards, like he'd mounted a horse. He cocked his head at me.

"So, I finally meet the unlucky fellow who got caught with a bottle of Boone's farm in his underaged possession."

He sure knew a lot for someone Dad wasn't friends with anymore.

"Yeah, that was me." I peered down at my hands.

He reached over and slapped my knee. "Don't be embarrassed. If you only knew how often the MPs threw me in the brig for drunk and disorderly when I was your age. In fact, that's how I ended up in your father's unit. My punishment. I got to empty piss pots and collect the bloody bandages he tossed out of those makeshift operating rooms. At least, that's what I did when we weren't taking the damned things down, dragging them even deeper into that mosquito-infested jungle, and putting them up again."

"You served under him?"

"That's right. Private First Class Edward St. John." Sitting up straight. I half expected him to salute, but he took a sip of coffee instead.

"How did you become friends?" I couldn't quite imagine it.

"Good question. Your father, he was kind of a jerk. Yelling, shoving people around—mostly getting us up off our asses and out of harm's way. He saved so many lives that way.

"We became friends because he was desperate. Not for friends, though. For books. I had them, and he didn't. I think it intrigued him to see this pimply faced private, who spent most of his time digging latrines and scouting camp for snakes and spiders, reading Voltaire and Balzac. All the other grunts read girlie magazines and comic books. As I recall, we'd received no mail for weeks, weren't getting much of anything, in fact. The Japanese had the beach at the time, and we'd holed up miles inland, our supply lines cut. Hellish few months. Rainy season. Camp was a quagmire. Anyway, a bunch of us sat around the fire, trying to dry our boots out, wolfing down our half-rations, and I was reading. You should have seen the way he stared at my book, like a dog at a bone. I threw it at him. I'd probably read it a dozen times already. He tried to give it back, but I insisted. It was a book of letters, from the home front to soldiers in World War One. I've got it here somewhere."

He waved vaguely at the bookshelf but didn't get up.

"My mother had sent it because I complained that I wasn't getting enough letters. When he finished it, we talked about it. It explained why we were fighting this war. Wives with car troubles, wondering how to discipline young boys who needed a father's touch, or how to pay the mortgage; mothers dutifully filling their sons in on the whereabouts of every sister, brother, aunt, uncle, and cousin. It was like they were addressed to us, and not to soldiers in the Argonne years before."

He held his cup in front of his mouth, remembering, seeing it all now.

"So," he said, "once we got the beach back and mail service resumed, we swapped other books, talked about them. Then I became his patient. Dysentery and malaria, though he got it, too. Everyone did. When things weren't crazy, we took turns reading to each other. Anyway, he soldiered on, and I didn't. They sent me home. But I thought about him a lot, all those months in that jungle. Figured he might appreciate a letter from home, like he did that book of letters. So I wrote. And he wrote back. The start of a beautiful relationship."

"Really?"

"Pen pals is all. We kept it up, even after the war. I think he liked my civilian perspective on things, needed to be reminded how lucky he was to get free housing, commissary food, a staff car. That was a sweet deal your Dad had."

"So you talked him into moving here?"

"'Talked him into'? No. I knew AMC was building this big new plant here and looking for a doctor. He was about to leave the Air Force and having trouble finding something he liked. I was only the messenger."

"My mom says you aren't friends anymore. Why not—if I can ask?"

"I still think of us as friends. When they arrested you, for instance, he had no problem requesting a consult, even though he hadn't spoken to me in months. And then, once it was all straightened out, he was quite angry with me when I refused to take payment. It's not as if I make that kind of phone call for all my clients."

"What phone call is that?"

"The one to the judge that made sure the only record of your arrest was the one that counted least and hurt the most."

I couldn't keep up with him.

"The newspaper?" he said. "I tried to keep it out of the police log, but the editor refused, even when I threatened to sue."

I nodded, getting it.

"Want some coffee?" he said, lifting the cup. "Soda maybe? Water?"

"I'm all right." This news about my arrest was totally unexpected. "So you are the one who got them to—*expunge* my record, is that the word? I thought my father—"

"Nope, that was me. That's what friends are for, I reminded your father of that, but he would have none of it. No matter how many times I mailed back his checks, another one would show up a few days later." He turned and pointed to his desk. "I still have one, uncashed, in my top drawer. Bet it still gnaws at him, seeing his checkbook going perpetually unbalanced."

I sat up. "But something happened?"

He sipped from the white cup. Must have been something, the way he sat there deciding how much to tell me. Like mom's torture story, maybe.

"It wasn't only one thing. Your father never should have moved here."

"Why's that?"

"Well, I remember this one time. Your father and I were sitting around a Sterno fire in camp, musing about what we were going to do after the war. Mind you, he wouldn't have told me this stuff if I hadn't passed muster first. I'd been accepted to law school before the war got in the way. Your father respected that. He talked about summers in some boating community where he'd been voted a Junior Commodore at the yacht club when he was in college. Of course, he wanted to return home to your mother, but he also wanted to join a country club and learn to play polo, not simply doctor the other players. Buy a house in Hyde Park on Lake Michigan and set up a practice.

"Instead, he spent, what, twenty-five years in the service, and what's his reward? AMC and Belford, the biggest small town in America. The first time I invited him to a VFW meeting, a couple of guys—enlisted men during the war, like me, now assembly-line workers—they started to rib him, good-naturedly, I thought. How is it, being a doctor at an auto plant? You enjoying life in the trenches with us average Joes? They wanted to knock the chip off his shoulder, you know? But he wasn't one of the guys. He was Colonel Maguire. Dr. Maguire. Not Mister, or Michael or Mike. He made some excuse and high-tailed it right out of there. Never came to another meeting. He thought I'd humiliated him, bringing him there."

Ned sipped his coffee, thinking.

"I don't even bother to phone him about marching in these parades, though being a Colonel, we'd put him right up front. That call I was on? Can you imagine your father getting his hands all sticky with ice cream, serving whiny kids in this heat? And behind him, grilling hot dogs, is Dwayne 'Dickhead' Darby, a guy I'm representing in a suit against AMC for wrongful termination. Plant security caught him having sex with a coworker in the back seat of his car during lunch. Can you see your dad in the Fourth of July parade next to some unemployed Korean War vet who brags how he uses his food stamps to fund his drug habit? Or some long-haired Vietnam vet who smells of marijuana and proudly shows off the peace signs tattooed on his biceps?"

He nodded.

"I admit, I generate half my business through the VFW, but they're not only my clients. They're my buddies, too. I may be a lawyer but I'm more like these vets than like your father."

"So he doesn't fit in? Is that why you aren't friends?"

"That's part of it." He drank from his coffee and peered over at me. "You look a lot like your brother. I almost thought you were him, paying me another visit."

"*Another?* You've seen him in this office?"

"He told me he was supposedly home from school for Christmas break, but he'd actually dropped out and hadn't told your parents. He'd lost his student deferment, had a low draft number, was sure he'd be drafted any day. He didn't know what to do, but he didn't want to go. I explained his legal options, how he could be a conscientious objector. Failing the physical, that was a solution Frazier came up with on his own. I stuck with the law. I don't think your dad would have minded the advice I gave him if I hadn't added my two cents about the war."

"Your two cents?"

"Not mine. My son's. William was in Vietnam. There—" He turned, pointing at the picture I'd seen earlier—his son, not him. "Khe Sanh during the height of the war. I photocopied some letters Will wrote me, and gave them to Frazier. They weren't anything like the letters your father and I wrote home from New Guinea. Sure, our war was awful, all wars are, but what Will witnessed of the way our soldiers misbehaved because they couldn't tell innocent civilians from enemy soldiers, it still turns my stomach, the people who were tortured and hurt."

More torture stories.

"I felt I owed it to Frazier to warn him how awful it might be. Apparently, after your dad found out how Frazier got his 4-F, your brother showed him those letters." This was all news to me. "Your father called me up, completely outraged. Thought I'd become a pacifist, advising Frazier not to go. He refused to believe those letters, that this war could be so different from ours. I never told your brother what to do. Those letters spoke much louder than I ever could have."

"And William?"

"He lost a leg. Below the knee. Friendly fire, it turned out."

"Sorry to hear that."

"He's okay. A little dark sometimes. Almost has the prosthesis mastered. Studying law at John Marshall in Chicago. Went there on the GI Bill like me. So—" He slapped his knees. "I doubt you came here to listen to old stories about my son or your dad. And I'm betting you weren't arrested again—"

I shook my head and smiled.

"I'm working at AMC this summer. It's about this guy who got into a fight."

I recounted the whole, long story just as I had practiced it in the car. I stressed that while I initially kept quiet because of the risk of suspension, I told my father the truth when I learned how Manny's family was struggling without that workers' comp money. Explaining why my father wouldn't believe me made me stumble. Maybe it was because I waited so long to tell him, or because of how cozy I'd become with this 'dangerous' man. I didn't know. I jumped ahead to the point of my visit.

"Anyway, he said if Manny didn't like his decision, he could always get a lawyer and appeal. That's why I'm here. Looking into how this appeal might work."

Ned sat there, processing it all.

"When you were arrested last summer, your father told me you said you were going camping."

What did that have to do with anything?

"We did go camping."

"Like I said, Walker, I raised a little hell at your age, too. Half-truths, deception—what self-respecting teenager can live without them? The problem is, you got caught, and now, when something like this happens, your dad doesn't know what to think. Make him believe you, and he could fix this whole thing with a swipe of a pen."

"It's not too late for that?"

"Trust me. If he's the one who signs off on these decisions, he's the one who can reverse them, too." He tapped on his cup. "Is there anyone who can testify you were up on this boxcar?"

"Manny, but nobody believes him, either. The night of the fight, I told my friends I saw it—"

"Yes, but that's hearsay. It wouldn't be admissible in a court of law."

We sat there. Me, quietly, perplexed. Him, chewing on the tip of his thumb. He slapped his hand on his thigh.

"Look, Walker. You seem like a good kid, standing up for your injured friend. Maybe a judge will believe your story. Manny could get his compensation. But appeals take time, lawyers cost money, and it might get messy, explaining why you lied to your dad, why you waited so long to talk. Do you want to stand across a courtroom from your father, airing this in public?"

That image, cleaving our already rocky relationship into that of legal disputants, all trust and hope of reconciliation gone and replaced by coats and ties and legalese—it weighed on me, a sinking sadness.

"No. I don't."

"Maybe if the three of us sat down together—"

"No!" I jolted. "I mean, he doesn't know I'm here. If he did, it would only make things worse."

"Well, he'd certainly find out you were here if you're involved in this appeal."

"I know."

"Find a way to get through to him. If you want to fix this, make him understand why you didn't speak up earlier."

"But what if I can't get through to him?"

"Then we'll talk. But before you involve me and the courts, try to work it out with your father. Maybe all you need is a good heart-to-heart."

When I left Ned's office, I used the phone in his reception area to call Frazier. After what went down with him showing Dad William's letters, I needed to talk to someone who could stand up to my father, even if Dad had thrown him out of the house. Once I got him on the phone—it being a Saturday, I caught him at his place—I went through my now word-perfect explanation of the fight, as well as Ned's advice. Maybe Frazier might have some insight into how I could explain things to our father.

"Why didn't you say right off what you saw?" he asked. "I mean, I wouldn't have given two craps if they suspended me."

"Dad would have been so pissed at me."

"Screw Dad."

"You haven't seen him lately. He's changed since you left."

"Maybe, but now you're up shit creek."

"I know. I think he might throw me out."

"You can always stay here. Could be a little tight," he added. "My girlfriend and her brother—he's a musician—they got evicted from their place over noise complaints, so I took them in. But, hey, bring a sleeping bag—and maybe some ear plugs. We'll squeeze you in."

Forty-Two

I couldn't stand it, writing away while he lay there next to me, immobile, a sleeping beauty waiting for a prince's kiss; so I packed up and left. I'm in Emergency now. I had to come down here sooner or later, the place where everything came to a head that summer.

Funny, how different the ER is from Maternity, with its expectant families and wailing mothers-to-be down the hall. With its Connie...Wheeler, I guess her name is now. How beautifully she's aged, getting better with time.

And how different the ER waiting room is from the one in Surgery where I sat with Gayle while Norm had that meat hook extracted.

I guess it shouldn't surprise me how much more distinctly I remember this waiting room than I do that other one. If, as that therapist explained, high emotions engrave indelible memories by plowing deep neurological trenches, then this one is my Grand Canyon, riven so deeply I remember everything. How late it was that summer night. How the chairs were set up—exactly like this. Who was in the room and where they sat. Over there, the dark-haired woman with her head on her knees. Over here, the couple with the fussy toddler between them. Against that wall, the gray-haired Chicano man in the brown suit. All watching me. But I'm getting ahead of myself.

Back then, there was no arctic chill in the air and no television. The sound is down but captions are on. 'Immigration Bill' scrolls across the bottom. The story I was assigned to cover before Piper's phone call yesterday morning, the same one Dad and I discussed on the phone the last time we talked.

What I knew at the time, and never told my dad, was that it was all for show, this proposed bill. Next week, Bush is visiting Mexico where he hopes to improve trade between the countries and cooperation on efforts to curb drug smuggling. His bill, an olive branch for the Mexican president, won't make it out of committee, let alone pass the House. But he had to make it look good, and that's why it was debated.

Laws are much stricter in 2005 than they were in 1974. Back then, it was, 'don't ask, don't tell,' just like in the military. Businesses didn't have to ask job applicants to see their papers, but if somebody outed an undocumented worker—the way a soldier might be outed as gay—then the powers-that-be were legally obliged to respond, and Norm knew that. Today, job applicants are required to produce their papers, so such a scenario is less likely to happen.

Of course, Norm's beef with Manny was never about his legal status. It was about pain, envy and anger. About frustration fueled by alcohol. Something I knew a little about—and still do, today.

Forty-Three

After I got back from Ned St. John's office, it started raining and continued all Saturday night until early Sunday after lunch. Once the sun came out, I jumped up from the table while the others were still engrossed in various sections of the Sunday *Chicago Tribune.* Plate in hand, I'd escaped into the kitchen and dumped the pancakes and bacon into the trash before anyone noticed they had gone virtually untouched.

Mom had left a few minutes before, her weekly summertime sojourn to Green Giant for sweet corn. Every Sunday afternoon, corn was sold right out of the back of the truck, picked the same morning, emerald bright and shedding silk. A brown man bagged them, and a white man handed them to her.

My father, Kurt and Piper migrated from the kitchen table to the den and were soon so entranced by *The Music Man* marching across the TV screen that they didn't seem to notice or care how the weather had changed for the better. Damned if I'd sit inside on a beautiful afternoon when I faced another dreary week of boxcar spelunking. I asked if anyone wanted to go fishing. They barely turned their heads to say 'no.' Maybe they'd had enough of the river the day before.

Just as well. I couldn't brainstorm how to change my father's mind with them around. What better place to think about it than out on the Piscasaw, meditating upon a treble-hooked Daredevil lure as it arcs into the water.

I changed into cut-offs and a t-shirt, collected my fishing rod and tackle box from the basement, and headed down to the river. The covered boat lolled at the end of the wooden dock. After a few popped fasteners, the canvas came off, revealing Grandpa Caspar's runabout. It was the first time I'd been out in it since last summer, and I ran my hand along the mahogany veins, gleaming gold-red in the sun. I untied and loaded in, wobbling a second before I caught my balance, then sank down onto the front bench with its blessedly comfortable white leather seat cushions. The runabout started up with a push of a button, a deep-throated gurgling—like my dad's old Caddy under water. The big Evinrude engine, built for Lake Michigan, possessed too much horse power for a small river like the Piscasaw, but at least I didn't have to sit on a wooden bench by a motor and turn a tiller like most everyone else boating on this river.

I guided her out, the water high and rushing from last night's rain. A number of good fishing holes upstream came to mind, inlets with downed trees where bass and trout and sometimes northern pike liked to congregate in the cool shade of the waterlogged branches. Truth was, there was little chance of catching anything with the current running this fast, but what the hell. Anything to get away for awhile.

On the opposite bank, the little fishing cottages neared. I singled out the only two-story house among them. On the dock before it, I could just make out a pony-tailed, teenage girl in the back of a dinghy, bent over the motor. It had to be Connie. I pointed the boat that way. She pulled repeatedly on a string, trying to start the little motor. It choked and chuttered but wouldn't catch. I cut back on the Evinrude and as my boat slowed, I watched her, the fast water pushing me downstream.

I wanted to talk to her, but I'd promised Manny I'd try to get my father to change his mind. If I tied up at their dock, he might come out. What would I tell him?

Pushing up on the throttle, I sputtered over to her dock, throttled back and drifted up alongside, my wake rocking her tiny skiff.

"Hi there." I grabbed her gunwale.

"Oh." Connie sat back on her haunches. "Hi." She wiped her brow, painting a streak of dark oil over that little mole. "Nice boat," she added, frowning at the runabout.

"Thanks. Need any help?"

"I don't know." She let out a breath. "I think it's a lost cause."

"You can join me, if you'd like."

"I'm going fishing," she said, an admonishment, as she held up a rod and reel.

"So am I."

"In that?" she smirked, panning her gaze over my boat.

"Why?" I chuckled.

"Aren't you afraid of getting it dirty?"

"Come on." I gunned the engine against the current to keep me there. "Where you headed?"

"Up river. Not far. Behind Green Giant?"

The canning factory? Nothing to catch there but flat water, sunshine, and corn from the back of a truck. But I wasn't about to dispute her. "I can do that," I said. "Get in."

She regarded me a long second and glanced back up to the house. Manny was behind the screen door, watching. My rumbling Evinrude must have drawn him. He waved her away, nodding his approval.

"Okay," she said. "But I don't plan on taking long."

"Fine by me."

Connie handed me her fishing gear and climbed in, then leaned over into her boat and brought over a small red cooler.

"Refreshments?" I asked.

"I wish."

Dumb question.

She pushed the cooler under the back bench and plopped down on the seat.

"The view is a lot nicer from up here," I said.

She took a second to decide.

"Come on." I patted the cushion beside me.

She climbed up front and sat down, hands on the dashboard to hold her steady. I guided the boat out into the middle, pointed it upstream and throttled up, the boat seeming to sink a bit as the engine dug in, drilling down into the water. The wind picked up, pushing against us, lifting her hair off her shoulders.

"Thank you." She spoke up to be heard over the motor. She kept pushing her hair back over her ear. Strands escaped from her pony tail and flipped in the breeze. "*Papá* can usually get that thing started, but he can barely move today."

"Sorry to hear that."

"Me, too." Her smile disappeared, replaced by a frank expression of concern.

I had to help them, somehow. *Talk to your dad*, Ned had said. *Make him believe you.* But how?

I pushed the throttle, speeding up.

"Not sure how good the fishing will be after all the rain we've had," I said.

"It's always good where we're going."

We bounced along for another half mile, pounding across the water's surface, spray splashing off the sides of the boat, the engine like it was sawing wood, *hunh, hunh, hunh*, making conversation impossible. Around a bend, the blue metal walls of the canning factory swung into view.

"There—" Connie shouted. "By that outlet."

I throttled back. She'd pointed at a large pipe that protruded out of the river bank, trickling rust-colored effluent into the river. As we got closer, a stink hit me.

"Here?" I shut off the engine. "Phew-ee." Where the sludge dripped into the water, a pool of brown swirled, then curled off downstream where it hit the current.

"Yeah, I know." She wrinkled her nose. "My neighbors work here. They say it's harmless vegetation waste. Attracts the fish, but doesn't smell very nice."

"I'll say." I nudged the throttle, moving the boat closer.

"This is perfect," she said. She climbed into the stern and grabbed her rod. I tossed my anchor into the water and pulled my rod up from where I'd clipped it to the wall of the boat. While I tied a red and white Daredevil on the end of my line, she was already flinging out her line, splashing. A bobber settled on the surface.

I reeled in mindlessly, the fishing a nuisance, interfering with what I really hoped to catch.

"Besides fishing, what else do you do for fun?"

"I don't know," she said, shrugging. "Not much."

It wasn't easy getting her to talk. I tossed out questions. Small talk. Did she read books? Listen to music? At first, I barely got nibbles—she didn't have much time for reading, she only listened to whatever music was on the radio—so I tried different tacks. Questions about her family, where they came from. Her schooling. Slowly, she opened up, answers made easier, perhaps, by not having to look at me, her focus on the bobber floating near the pipe.

She was born in southern California when Manny worked in a canning factory. When she was little, the family moved to Belford so he could work at Green Giant. After a few years, he found a better paying job at American Motors, the first of those workers to make that transition. That spring, she'd graduated from the Catholic school and had been accepted into the registered nursing program at St. Francis in the fall.

"But it doesn't make sense right now." She shrugged, looking off over the water. I remembered. The problem of tuition. "They also have a nurse's aide program, free training, on-the-job. It's not like being a real nurse, of course, emptying bed pans and such, but it's just till we get back on our feet."

"But I thought Manny set aside—"

"My father doesn't—" She shook her head. "My mom paid the bills until she got sick. Now, I do it."

"Oh. I see." I nodded. It killed me to think I was responsible for dashing her dreams, especially when she saw her future so much more clearly than I saw mine.

After this conversation stopper, I tried not to stare at her, but I couldn't help noting the careless expertise with which she reeled in, changed the sinker on her line, adjusted the bobber downward, cast out again. I maintained the pretense of fishing, reeling in the Daredevil, flipping it out again.

"What about you?" She turned to me, changing the subject. "You must be in school. What are you studying?"

Her question surprised me, her eyes searching mine. Was she really interested? How could she not see through me, know I was "that factory doctor's son"—that cold, "military man" she despised?

I babbled something about nearly flunking out that spring, how the only classes I attended were ones I wasn't enrolled in, trying to see what interested me.

"I hated all my classes, too," she said. "It wasn't until I volunteered at the hospital that I knew what I wanted to do."

I nodded.

"That's a nice place you live in up there." She nodded up the hill. "You must have a big family."

"There's just the four of us," I explained, a bit embarrassed. "Five, including my brother in Chicago." I wouldn't leave him out.

She asked about them, and I fudged a bit, not wanting to 'fess up about my father, so I told her my dad was an executive at AMC, a word-choice I winced at. At least, I didn't lie, but I didn't want to dwell on it. Instead, I talked about my brother being a draft dodger, a term that made her look over, wide-eyed, as if I'd sighted an exotic bird on the shoreline you hear about but never see.

"So, he's like a coward?" she asked, wrinkling her forehead in confusion and perhaps, disapproval.

"No, no, he's a conscientious objector, sort of."

"Sort of. So he does something else then, community service or something, to make up for not doing his part as a soldier?"

"Well, no, actually. He's against the war, you see—" I found myself floundering. "He's an activist. A protester. He doesn't believe in doing anything to support the corrupt war effort."

"Oh," she said, still confused. "So you believe anyone who serves in the military is corrupt, then?"

"No, I just mean—I don't know." Now I was as confused about Frazier as Connie was. "Maybe we should talk about something else."

"Maybe." She nodded. "What about your sister? What's she do?" Connie asked, thankfully changing the subject.

After the inadvertently ugly picture I'd painted of Frazier, I tried to be nice about Piper, saying how smart she was, how talented a musician, what a great girl scout and swimmer, all the while wanting to tell a different, darker story. Connie told me how her little brothers, Edson and Ramon, drove her nuts with their bunny obsession, always wanting to draw them, play imaginary games with their stuffed bunnies, watch *Bugs Bunny* on TV.

"Actually, Piper drives me nuts, too."

"Oh, yeah?" Connie brightened, as if I was about to launch into a charming tale of some sweet sisterly quirk.

"Yeah," I said, my enthusiasm for the subject draining as quickly as if we'd struck an iceberg, the boat promptly sinking. I went quiet. While we remained on our separate benches, the current pushed the boat in lazy circles, drifting the way our conversation did, keeping us in the same orbit—around what, I wasn't sure. We had little in common, but still, a certain shared curiosity drew us closer. Desperate not to let the conversation die, an observation occurred to me.

"Most girls I know don't like fishing. Putting worms on hooks, yanking them out of fishes' lips, all that slime." Gayle had always cringed at the idea.

"My father taught me way back before I could even bait a hook or cast out. He'd do all that for me, then hand me the pole and say 'Keep your eyes on the line.'" Connie had a treble hook at the end of her line onto which, as she talked, she skewered corn kernels from an open can. "The first time my bobber disappeared into the water, it was such a rush." Connie looks up at me, eyes wide at the memory, a smile broadening. "When the rod dips down, you know? That very first time? You remember?"

She nodded, looking for agreement.

"I do." I nodded back.

"I thought I'd caught a whale," she said. "Like it might swallow the whole boat."

"Yeah. Like…this monster, hiding in the water."

I couldn't remember my first time, but I wanted her to know how well I could relate. How in tune we were. She chuckled.

"Turned out to be this piddling little bluegill."

I smiled back, connecting. Hooked. Looking at her corn, it struck me, though. She could only be after one thing.

"Are you…Are you fishing for carp?"

"Uh-huh." She cast out and reeled in a bit to make the line taut, then hunkered down in her seat to wait. She whispered, "and we better quiet down if we want to catch anything."

"Right," I mouthed back, a hint of sound. But why carp? I tried to hide my incredulity by focusing on my line, which I slowly reeled in, jerking occasionally.

Carp were so gross, the way the fat fish floated up to the top sometimes, the wide coppery scales on their sides, big as pennies, peppered with rust and scum. Ten times bigger than any trout, bass or pike you might hook in this river, but not much sport in catching them. They'd fight a few seconds, then tucker out. About as much fun as hauling in a mud-filled boot.

All right, I thought. Whatever floats your boat, Consuelo Camarasa.

"What are you fishing for?" She kept her voice low.

"Northern pike."

"Oh. Fancy fish. This probably isn't the best spot for that."

"That's okay." I reeled in then cast out again, tugging on the rod as if I actually cared.

Connie's rod bowed.

"You got one!"

"I know." She brightened, pulling her line taut. "Took a little longer than usual."

I dropped my rod and grabbed the fishing net from under the bench. Connie's rod bent once, twice, the fish going under the boat and back out, but she kept the line taut and high, a practiced hand. The rod stabilized into a quivering arch, the tip almost touching the water. Had to be a heavy beast to do that, but it had already given up, its resistance easing. Slowly, she reeled it in. The fish's head popped to the surface, the hook embedded in its big fat lip. Ugly fuckers, those carp. I reached the fishing net into the water and scooped it up. It was huge, eight, ten pounds, foot and a half or so long. Took two hands to haul him up.

"Nice catch." It took a while to wrap my hands around the slimy, flopping fish, but I finally braced him, slipped two fingers under a gill, held him up and pried out the hook. So gross, that lip. I lofted the beast up so she could take a good look at her prize before I released it back into the water, but she reached for it first, grabbing it by the gill. She wanted to heft it herself—a big guy, even if it was an easy catch.

"Big son of a—gun," I said, censoring myself.

"Yes, it is." She hefted the thing a couple times. Nothing squeamish about this girl, the way she held it up one-handed. Strong girl, too. She admired it, but rather than dip it back into the river, Connie used her free hand to reach for the cooler, which she opened, revealing nothing but ice cubes. She curled the big fish in and covered it up with ice.

"Usually have to catch two or three," she explained, "but that one's big enough to feed the whole family."

"To feed the—" I spluttered.

Her smile dissolved, replaced by puzzlement.

"What?"

"You're not actually—" I couldn't help it. Nobody ate carp, did they?

She opened her mouth, some explanation coming, some defense; but instead, Connie went quiet, gazing out over the river. Those dark eyebrows hooded her eyes.

"I'm done," she said, her smile gone. "Can we go back?"

"Sure," I said, cursing myself. *Asshole! Blabbermouth!* I pulled up anchor and started up the engine with a puff of smoke and a roar. Glancing behind, I patted the seat next to me, but she was staring out over the water. Once I got the boat turned around, headed back downstream, I peeked back at her.

"I'm sorry," I said, only loud enough to make sure she heard.

"Why are you sorry?" she replied, but wouldn't look at me.

"I didn't know—"

"The ice helps," she said, defensive, miffed. "Cuts the muddy taste a bit. It's not as bad as you might think. And they're very easy to catch. Have lots of meat."

I glanced back again as we were nearing her dock. It wasn't the sun making her face go red. I steered near and grabbed the piling. She stood and unloaded her gear, grabbing the cooler last.

"That was—fun," I ventured, forcing a smile as she climbed out.

"Fun?" She darted a scowl at me and hoisted the cooler. "This is our dinner." Her glower dared me to say anything else. She swept her eyes along my boat, swiping her gaze over it, the red mahogany, the white leather seats, the big engine. She regarded me. "What are *you* having for dinner?" With one hand on the piling, she shoved my runabout with her foot. It did a slow spin outwards, the current grabbing it, pulling it downstream.

Forty-Four

Manny didn't show up for work on Monday, but Norm did. I was standing near Kelly's office door, waiting for the foreman to start his weekly pre-shift meeting, light-headed from not eating, when Norm came right up to me, his breath boozy. His face in mine, he jabbed fingers into my chest, forcing me backwards.

"You told your father, didn't you?" He jabbed again. "That's why I didn't get workers' comp. You told him."

You'd never know that arm had been skewered the way he kept jabbing at me with it.

"I didn't say anything." I shoved his hand away. Men watched us, curious about the ruckus, but Norm didn't care who heard.

"I thought you understood, but no. You had to get all righteous, break up with my daughter, say something to your dad so I wouldn't get it."

"It was my father's decision."

"Sure it was. You know, it's so easy for you," he hissed with see-sawing sarcasm, his breath making me back-pedal. "You'll do your time, finish out the summer, and then you'll take off to the good life in that school of yours, up in your cozy little dorm room, reading your stupid books, while the rest of the world busts its ass every day doing real work, making an honest living."

"An honest living?" I sidestepped the bins at my back, a boxer working his way off the ropes.

"You *did* say something, didn't you?!" He kept after me, his breath almost as bad as Dad's. "You couldn't be a regular guy, could you?"

"Honest? Regular?"

He grabbed my arm and pulled us face to face, hissing into my ear.

"You think I like having to pull that crap? Huh?" He hissed, these words meant just for me. "Lying to get paid time off? Limping to get that forklift job? You think it makes me feel good?"

He shoved me away, daring me to reply.

"It feels like crap, but that salon is gone if I don't keep this shitty job. And if that means showing my pain, instead of hiding it, well then fuck my pride. Because people won't do squat for you if you don't show them your pain. The squeaky wheel gets the grease. Haven't you figured that out yet?"

Limping bad as ever, he hobbled over to the other side of the circle of men. By now, everyone was there except for Manny Camarasa who was still absent—no doubt, still in real pain and getting no help.

Norm shook hands with his friend Liam, as well as Bumpers and Fenders from the bowling league, who welcomed him back with backslaps.

Kelly stepped out of his office, clipboard in hand, glasses on his nose, and began reading. He said breakage was down last week, though he added, looking at Norm over his bifocals, that management attributed the good numbers to recent changes in staffing—Norm's absence, no doubt.

Kelly worked his way down the clipboard. Today, management would inspect work areas for cleanliness ("so hide your ashtrays and your porn"). A memorandum from Dr. Maguire advised employees to drink plenty of water through this hot spell and said the foreman would make salt tablets available, which he suggested everyone take.

Someone barked out, "The hell with salt tablets! When are we getting those fans you promised us?"

Kelly reminded them that he'd put in a request, but didn't know when or if they'd be coming, which brought a few "when hell freezes over" nods of dismissal.

"So, last item," Kelly said, flipping through the sheets on his clipboard. "Now that Norm's back, he'll be taking over the forklift—*for the time being.*"

A smile widened on Norm's face, then a bounce of glee. "Fuck, yeah!"

"*For the time being,* Norm. While Camarasa is out and his situation is being reviewed."

"You mean, until they figure out he's a wetback and send his ass back to *Me-he-co*? No problem-o." He chuckled, then, scanning the circle, found me and flipped me the finger.

"Oh, yeah. Maguire—" Kelly turned to me, as if Norm had pointed me out. "You were so hot to do Camarasa's job for him the other day. Well, now you got it."

Asshole.

Forty-Five

Driving up South State after work, I slowed at Manny's street and turned. Work had been more like being stuck in a prison hot box than a boxcar. All day long, while slinging fuel tanks and swiping off sweat, woozy from not eating, I'd gone over angles for arguments I could make to my father. How to convince him I wasn't lying. I'd come up empty. Now, I was drained, but I couldn't go home yet. I had to see where things stood. Maybe Manny was up and about, playing a board game with his boys or bouncing that baby on his knee. He could be back tomorrow, slamming gas tanks onto tugger carts, and I'd never have to tell him what happened with my father, never need to have that heart-to-heart with my dad, get him to believe me. Maybe I could even say something to Connie. Apologize. But for what? I wasn't even sure.

She answered the door, straightening when she saw me.

"Walker." She wiped her hands on an apron and pushed a strand of dark hair out of her eyes. "What are you doing here?"

"I came by to see Manny."

"Oh." She nodded.

"That is—" I corrected. "I wanted to see how you were *all* doing. Manny didn't come in today, so I was wondering."

"He's no better. He tried to go this morning, but he couldn't even put on his work pants and boots. He asked for my help, but I refused. I said if you're in so much pain you can't even dress yourself, the last thing you should be doing is hauling fuel tanks. He's been pissed at me all day."

"I'm sorry to hear that."

"He's out on the back porch if you want to say hello. I'm making dinner, so—" She turned and pointed toward a screen door at the other end of the hall. I squeezed past her, our eyes connecting for a thrilling second. Maybe she didn't hate me after all. She followed me as I passed the living room. The two little boys were sitting cross-legged on the floor, watching cartoons on the black and white while the little electric fan waved at them, ineffectually.

Before I got to the porch, I turned back. As Connie pushed into the kitchen, she flipped her fingers at me, urging me out.

Trying not to make noise, I pushed open the screen door. Beyond the back porch, the river gurgled as it eddied amongst the pylons of the wooden dock. It had stormed again overnight, so the water ran high and fast, carrying spinning twigs and debris. The little skiff kept tugging downstream, a dog wanting off its leash.

Manny's eyes were closed. He lay sprawled in an aluminum chaise lounge. A concentration camp version of the overstuffed thing in my mom's bedroom, it was woven together with shredding bands of faded red and yellow plastic, one of which had frayed through. Manny's bare heel pushed through the hole, and the arch of his foot curved around the metal tube. He winced, and that foot twisted up and down, bracing against the pain.

"Manny?" I whispered.

He opened his eyes, the wince forcing itself into a smile.

"Walker." He grimaced, trying to push himself up. A bottle of Old Milwaukee was clutched in one hand. Every movement was a struggle, that foot pushing against the frame, confirming everything Connie had said about his pain.

"Don't get up." I held up my hand. "I thought I'd stop by, check in on you."

"Sure you did," he smiled, shaking his head, glancing up at the door. He sat back, relief flooding his face. He pointed me to a white wicker chair.

"Want a beer?" He hoisted his bottle. Then, before I could reply: "Consuelo! Can you bring us a couple beers?"

The wicker creaked as it settled under me.

"Fernando brought it over," he added, looking at the label. "Tastes like dog piss but you take what you can get, right?"

"Right," I nodded. "Missed you at work today. You coming back any time soon?"

"I'd have come back this morning but that daughter of mine...." He lifted his hand, his fingers flipping away the thought of her, causing him to wince again. He took a drink. His eyebrows twitched, doubtfully. "I'll try again tomorrow. If that doesn't work, the real test will be tomorrow night. Have to do this thing at the hospital. Have to see how it goes. I might want to stay and get a room." A joke. But it didn't sound like a joke.

The screen door opened, and Connie came out. She handed me a beer.

"Thanks."

"Where's mine?" Manny asked.

"You haven't finished that one."

Watching her, he downed the last third of the bottle, then tilted the empty at her. She sighed, snatched it away from him and as she retreated into the house, I couldn't help watching her go. I heard a soft chuckle, Manny watching me, watching her.

"I still haven't told her who your father is," Manny whispered.

"Oh, yeah," I replied, my face going red. "Thanks. I guess." I thought hard, wanting to change the subject. "Well, I hope it works out," I said, "The hospital."

"Me too." He nodded. "Me too."

I stared at the river, searching for words.

"You're so close to the water here," I said. "This is a great view. Much better than ours."

"I like watching," he said. "Especially when it's running fast. Some of the things that get swept away. Trees. Boats. Saw a dog the other day. Not sure if he made it out." He turned his head to me, a question molding his features.

"My daughter was kind of quiet after that little fishing trip of yours yesterday."

"Oh. Right." I regarded him cautiously. "I—I didn't know you could eat carp."

"Huh." Manny chuckled, then held his head up. "Consuelo! Where's that beer?" He settled back, eyes on the water. "Carp was all we could catch in the muddy river outside my *pueblecito* in Mexico. *Mi papá* showed me that if you put them on ice right away, they weren't bad."

"That's what she said." My stomach churned at the thought, a fat fish on my plate, eyes bulging, lips puckered.

"Lots of bones to work through. Needs a good sauce, too. Couldn't get ice very often. But we ate them anyway, bones and all, ice or no ice."

"Right."

"Ice for your carp," Manny said, stretching. "The American Dream."

I forced a chuckle, a nod.

"Ah, don't feel bad. You didn't know." He gazed out over the river, then as if it was an itch: "Connie!"

"In a minute!"

"That girl." He sighed, twisting in his seat. "She can be a real pain in the ass sometimes." He nodded at me, some kind of warning. But then a jolt of pain froze him, made him take big breaths for a while.

"You want mine?" I held out my bottle. "I can't go home smelling that way."

Without breaking a smile, he grabbed it, took a big swig and perched it on his stomach with two hands.

"Look, Manny—" I sat forward, elbows on my knees. "I don't know much about you and your family. What you're going through. I wanted to say I'm sorry, about this whole thing—"

"Let me guess. It didn't go well with your father."

"He turned you down because he believes you started the fight. And there's this rule—"

"I figured it was something like that. No money for troublemakers like me."

"I told him you didn't start it. I said I saw everything, and he still didn't believe me."

He turned to me. "So you *did* see it!"

"Yes. I did."

"You saw Norm trying to take my wallet?"

"That's right. That's what I told him. But—" The words came as if pulled from a toxic tar pit. "He thinks I'm lying."

Manny slumped back, chuckling.

"It's all my fault," I confessed, voice wobbling. "If I'd told him that day, none of this would be happening, but because I waited so long, he thinks I'm making it all up to help you."

His smiling face, shaking side to side, only made it worse, this burning sorrow. I sniffed, disarmed by how my betrayal had handcuffed him, stuck in that fucking chair. My stomach soured.

"Hey—" With a great effort, he pushed up, swinging his legs out, over and down. He put his free hand on my wrist, stopping it from that stupid gripping, re-gripping thing. I tried to yank it away, but he held it firm. "Walker, it's okay. I get it."

Something overwhelmed me, that hand over mine, holding it, refusing to let go. Whenever my father stopped my hand from doing that, he always let go, but not Manny. He held on, and that pierced some buried aquifer of emotion—a deep, deep sadness, overflowing. Finally, I yanked my hand away and turned, hiding my eyes, my shoulders convulsing. How anyone could be so patient with me after the way I'd screwed everything up. I felt his hand on my knee.

"Sorry," I said, wiping my face with the sides of my hands. "I fucked up. I want to fix it, but I don't know what else I can do."

"You don't have to do anything, Walker." He patted my knee. "It's okay. I understand."

He let go and lifted his feet back up into the chair, grimacing.

After a minute, he asked. "You ever heard of the *braceros*?"

"No." I shook my head.

He pushed his foot into that hole in the frame, resettled, and gazed at the river, his eyes caught up in the current, again and again.

"It was this grand government program they dreamed up during the war. 'He who works with his arms'—that was a *bracero*—*Mexicanos* who came here to work in the fields so American boys could fight the Germans and Japs. Great deal for us, right? Jobs in America, steady pay, food and housing, all taken care of and legal."

"You were in this program?"

"The Mexican revolution left most of us very poor, so the *braceros* was our big chance, so popular you had to bribe the mayor 1,000 pesos just to get on the interviewer's list. I got married in 1952, I guess it was, and we thought with that money we could buy a house, maybe start a business. My dad drove a bus for a living, his own bus, and I wanted to buy one of my own, do the same thing. So our wedding guests put up enough money to pay the bribe. I spent days waiting with thousands of others in Empalme for the interview, then many hours being examined and deloused. Then they packed us into boxcars and shipped us to California. I signed a six month contract to work for this farm association.

"It was backbreaking. Picking lettuce, sugar beets, celery, dawn to dusk, rain or shine, hot or cold. This foreman—much tougher than Kelly—he kept us in line. We had to pay for our own food, and we only got pennies for each crate we packed—twelve, fifteen dollars a week after blankets and board were taken out of our paychecks. Oh, and ten percent went to Mexico for our pensions—which the banks stole, by the way, but that's another story."

That last, like garbage he'd pulled out of the river of words. Otherwise, they flowed like driftwood and branches, things that belonged in the rushing current.

"After taking all those bites out of my paycheck, only crumbs were left to send to my wife. Then I got a telegram from home. The old bus my father drove to Toluca broke down, and without it, the villagers had no way to sell their goods in the city. Many people depended on that bus, not just my father. He needed 10,000 pesos to fix it, about $300. My farm association gave advances if you stayed on to work off the debt, so I signed up for another six months and wired home the money to fix the bus. My wife was not happy. She was lonely, and she wrote me that the job was not worth the few dollars I had sent her, but what could I do?

"I lived with forty other men, sleeping on cots in a Quonset hut, sweltering during the day, freezing at night. No running water. Outdoor toilets. Cooked meals of rice and beans outside in a fire pit. Ate out of cans when it rained. And I was lonely, too. After a year of this, my back was in agony. I stooped all day long in these furrows, hacking at the ground with this short hoe they gave us. It was torture. But if I didn't work, I'd never get home, and if I kept sending my wife money, I'd never pay the debt so I *could* go home."

Manny turned to make a point.

"I was never so ashamed of myself as I was living with that debt, month after month, slowly destroying my body, my life, my marriage. It was like a disease, eating away at me. Only after she left me and I stopped sending money home, could I pay them off."

"She left you?" I was confused. Wasn't that woman here in this house?

"Got an annulment from the village priest. Luisa? She's my third wife."

"Oh," I said. "I had no idea."

"I met my second at the camps." He shrugged, then lowered his voice. "Didn't work out." He seemed stuck on this, as if deciding whether to say more.

"What I'm saying is, don't feel like you owe me. I know why you couldn't tell your dad. You tried your best. Don't let it eat at you like that debt ate at me. You're a Catholic, right?"

"Raised that way, anyway."

"Well, like the priest says at the end of confession, *'Te absuelvo.'*

"I absolve you."

"Right. I absolve you. You don't owe me anything. I'm the one who hit Norm, not you, so forget about it." He sipped at his beer, nodding at me.

I got it. He may have thought he had freed me, but he hadn't. So many people had it so much worse than me, struggling to make it through each day. I didn't have those kinds of problems. How could I subject Manny and his family to that hell if there was a chance I could do something?

We stared at the moving water a long time before I wiped my eyes and got up.

"Thank you for understanding," I said.

"It's okay. We'll figure something out. We always do."

I nodded at him, then headed back through the house. I stopped at the kitchen door and knocked.

"Come in."

I pushed the swinging door. "Hi."

"Hello," Connie said. The indignation she'd displayed earlier was gone. Her mouth was small, her eyes wide, sympathetic. Had she heard?

"Thought I'd stop in before I took off." Thankfully, no carp were in sight. She was chopping green leaves and stems off strawberries on a cutting board in front of her.

"You gave him your beer, didn't you?" she said.

"Not a good idea?"

"No, it's not." She shook her head. She went back to cutting. "There's been too much of that lately."

"Sorry," I said. Great. I couldn't do anything right by this girl. "Those look good," I said, pointing to the strawberries. They did look good. Too good. "Much bigger than the ones the IGA sells."

"Oh. Really?" She straightened, as if surprised, then grabbed the bowl of berries, then put it back down, unsure what to do with it.

"Where'd you get them?"

She turned to me, eyes flashing. "Don't play dumb," she said, putting both hands on the counter. "You know where." She challenged me with a clenched jaw, those piercing eyes, daring me to speak. Did she have heirloom tomatoes, too?

"I…I'd never say anything, Consuelo."

She went back to work on the berries, cutting off a final few stems.

"Connie," she corrected, as she placed the bowl on the table. An uncomfortable silence settled between us.

"I don't care. Really, I don't."

She searched the room, looking for another task to occupy her, to avoid me. She opened a drawer and counted out forks, spoons.

"So, can I ask?" I said. "How is Manny *really* doing? Has he seen a doctor?"

"Yes. He said it might take months to heal and he shouldn't be working at all. I'm sure going back last Friday only made it worse."

"He says he has to go to the hospital tomorrow night. Are they doing more tests?"

"No, it's not for him. He's taking my mother. There's a group that meets every Tuesday night, husbands and wives."

"Oh." I nodded.

"It's not that kind of group," she said, reading my mind. "She had a very rough pregnancy, in and out of the hospital, and when she had the baby, she got depressed. Happens to a lot of women."

"Oh. Right. Postpartum depression."

"You've heard of it?"

"My mom had it with me. My father—" I hesitated, reminded Manny hadn't told her about him yet. "My mom once told me he wasn't very sympathetic, having to take over for her, all that work."

Both hands full of silverware, she straightened, looking out the window. She exhaled a few times. I had struck a nerve. She turned and held out the silverware to me.

"Do you mind?" She nodded at the table.

"Not at all." I took the silverware. "Four settings?"

"Five. She comes out to eat." Connie went back to her cutting board and pulled over a cluster of what appeared to be oddly shaped green bananas. She took up the knife and started peeling them. "They have treatments for it now. *Papá* doesn't want to go, even though it's free. He thinks group therapy is like trumpeting your family secrets from the rooftops. But I think it will be good for her to hear she's not all alone."

As I considered this, Connie sliced bananas into strips. She opened a bottle of oil and dribbled it into a pan. It sizzled. One by one, she placed banana slices into the pan. It smelled divine.

"You're cooking—bananas?" I finished placing the silverware.

"Plantains. Fernando brought them. A whole box of stuff, sweet man. Tried to tell us he was emptying the fridge of old stuff."

"That's nice of him," I said, glad to hear Manny let someone help him out, even if it wasn't me.

"Plantains are tougher than bananas," Connie said. "Not as sweet. You've never tasted fried plantains?"

Amused by this, she grinned as she moved the pale slices around the pan with a wooden spoon, the oil popping and fizzing.

"'Fraid not."

From a small bag next to the stove, she pulled out a big pinch of dark powder between her fingers and sprinkled it over the plantains. Brown sugar? Cinnamon?

"What's that?"

"Secret ingredient. My mother's recipe." Connie held up a dog-eared index card that was water stained and covered in handwriting. She slipped it back into a small box, closing the lid. "We don't have much, but we still have our secrets. Right?"

She gave me a questioning glance.

"Yes, you do," I confirmed, stealing one of my father's strawberries from the table. Delicious, of course. She opened her mouth to admonish me, then shook her head, thinking better of it. She dipped her finger into the pan to test a plantain, then licked off the brown sauce.

"Do you get out at all?" I asked.

"Not really. There's not much to do in town for girls like me."

While Fernando and his buddies had all but taken over the pool hall, *Mexicana* teens didn't have a hangout that I knew of.

"I enjoy taking out the boat," she said, "as you know." She jabbed the spoon into the pan and lifted a plantain slice. "Want to try one?"

She reached toward me. I leaned in and sipped, the morsel slipping off the spoon into my mouth as if I had licked her fingers. She watched me, a smile lurking. It was tougher than a banana but the powder—brown sugar mixed with something else—added the right touch, sweet and zesty and hot, too. Possibly the best thing I'd ever eaten.

"It's good," I said. "Is that chili powder?"

"I told you. Secret ingredient."

I realized I was ravenous, torn between the aroma of the plantain and the smile on Connie's face, different desires swirling, mixing. She seemed pleased to have pleased me. She had a large mouth, and it was a big, toothy smile. It lit up her face like Manny's smile took over his. That little beauty mark almost twinkled. I was hungry for more.

"I've looked at this house so many times." I turned from Connie to the window and back. Such beauty, so close and yet so far. "And here you were. Right across the river."

"Hmm." She nodded, smiling.

"If you see the lights on up there, bottom floor, that's usually me, hanging out, listening to music."

I imagined her coming over in her boat, hiking up the hill, but didn't like the thought of her running into my father. He'd be more likely to think he'd caught an intruder—the garden thief—than that I'd invited this *Chicana* over. An alternative occurred to me.

"Do you think I could call you sometime?"

"We don't have a phone."

"Oh, that's right." I slapped my head, forgetting.

"That's right?" She looked at me, taken aback. Like, why would I know that, unless I'd tried to call before, and why would I do that?

"I mean—" I let out a breath, turning red, my face hot.

"Nope, that's right. Why would any family that eats carp have a phone?"

"That's not what I meant."

"Then what?"

"I don't know. I'm sorry. I must come off like such a jerk—I just need to get to know you better, so I'll understand."

"What's to know?" She looked around the room. "What you see is what you get."

Which was fine with me. As I watched her cook, my blunder didn't prevent the thought of her visiting me in the basement from reviving, overwhelming any fears I might have.

"Maybe, one of these nights when you are out in your boat, and you tie up at my dock, you could walk *all the way* up to the house."

She gave me a look, grimacing at my dig, then went back to moving the plantains around in the pan. I'd gone too far, such a suggestion. The two of us, alone.

"You could meet my sister," I said, making it safer. "I told you about her. She's in high school now."

"The one who drives you nuts?"

"Well, yes. We can hang out, is all I'm saying. Talk."

She shrugged through a mix of uncertainties, her brow dipping, rising.

"So you'll think about it? Coming over?"

She looked uncomfortable. I didn't want to push it. She slid the spatula into the pan, lifted plantain slices into a serving bowl. When she was done, she turned around and faced me. She folded her arms.

"Tell me. What were you talking about with my father?"

"Oh. That." I looked out the window again, the river rushing by.

"These walls are thin. From the sound of things, that was a heavy talk you had out there."

I took a breath, searching for words.

"I know you're keeping something from me. Do you actually think I'd come over to your house with that going on?"

She had me cornered.

"We were talking about my father."

"Your father. He works at AMC. Some executive, you said."

If I really wanted to get to know her, she'd have to find out eventually.

"He's…the company doctor."

"*That's* your father!" She slapped her hands to her hips. "That SOB who won't give my dad any sick pay?"

I was startled by the flashing of her eyes, her voice. "I didn't know about that until you and Manny told me the other day. That's what we were talking about. I tried to change my father's mind."

"And he wouldn't, right? I'm not surprised." She backhanded a dismissive wave into the air.

I couldn't keep skating around this, not now that Manny knew. He'd tell her if I didn't.

"I thought I *could* fix things because it's all about who started the fight. Some stupid union rule. And I know who started it."

"We all know who started it."

"No, I mean, I saw who started it. I witnessed it."

"You saw it. Yourself?"

"Yes, but I waited until the other night to tell my father, so long that now he doesn't believe me."

"I don't understand." She came around by the table and gave me a quick shake of her head, hands spread. "Why did you wait? Why didn't you tell him when it happened?"

Somehow, my excuses about being on top of the boxcar, the suspension—those wouldn't fly here. Manny understood about certain kinds of fathers, but his daughter? I wasn't about to spill my guts to her like I had to Gayle, recounting that whole, pathetic sob story.

"I can't believe this." She nodded toward the back porch. "One word from you could have prevented all of this?"

"I'm sorry." Her insistence jarred me. Her hand gestures, whipping around, a flurry of birds, knocked me off center.

"And yet you come into my kitchen, chatting away like it's no big deal, a fly in the salsa."

"I didn't say that. It *is* a big deal."

"You're damned right it is. You see how he's suffering out there." She picked up the bowl of strawberries and slammed it back down, a couple of them toppling out. "How we all are!"

"I know."

"You know. And that's all you can do? Stand there and say you know??"

"Wait a second." This, after we'd been so close.

"Connie!" Manny yelled from the porch. "What's going on?"

"I'll fix it," I said. "I promise."

"What a hero you are!" she said. "The fight happened weeks ago, and you're going to fix it *now*?" Her words were smeared with contempt, gooey as the sauce on her plantains. "Go back to your fancy home on the hill with your—" She grabbed some strawberries slices from the bowl and threw them at me, hitting my face and chest. "Your stupid strawberries and your telephone."

"Stop this!" Manny stood in the doorway, bracing himself against the jamb. "This is his father we're talking about. You don't understand."

"Don't I? This is *mierda*, is what it is!" She untied her apron, tossed it on the floor and stomped past her father and out of the room.

"Don't mind her," Manny said.

"I know. It's okay."

"I don't want you fighting with your dad over me. This is my problem. I'll work it out."

I rubbed my wrist, fingers flexing uncontrollably. Inside me, relief and anxiety swirled together like branches in a river eddy, churning. I didn't have to do anything, and yet, I did.

"Go home," he said, leaning against the door, pain narrowing his eyes. "Forget about it."

"I can't."

"You can!" He hopped, straightening, eyes flashing open at some internal stab wound. "It's my problem."

I shook past him out the kitchen door into the hall. Connie was right there, her back pressed against the wall, arms folded as she listened. She refused to look at me as I passed by.

Forty-Six

"Hey there, bud." It's Kurt. "Finally found you."

I rise and give him a hug, so long since I've seen him last.

"I've been all over this—" he glances around before continuing, sitting in the chair across from me, his voice lowered— "this fucking hospital, looking for you. How you doing?"

"Surviving." I sit and close my laptop. "You coming from the dealership?"

My old friend is so slick in his double-breasted salesman's suit, his beige trench coat over his arm—too much like a high-class gangster for my money. He looks so much like Pops now, the way he combed his hair up high, the white kerchief sticking out of his breast pocket, the brass tie clip, the cuff links. Even his hair is thinning in the same way, his hairline receding like a low tide. "You want to sell luxury cars at fat margins, you have to look like you cost more than the car," Pops once told me.

"Yeah. We're usually open until 9, but I sent everyone home. Place was dead. No one's interested in test driving cars in this weather. Heard we're supposed to have six more inches tonight, so business should royally suck tomorrow, too." He stops and looks me up and down. "It's really great to see you again. I miss my old pool pal—my drinking buddy. It's been too fucking long."

"I know," I shrug. "It's great to see you again too. You're looking good—a bit too much like your Dad—"

Kurt laughs, his hands held wide. "Well, it wouldn't seem so weird if you came around more than once in a blue moon."

"You're right." He's succeeded in guilting me, and I'm tempted to chat, to chuck this laptop to the side and make up for lost time, but I can't. I tap its lid instead, drawing his attention. His smile turns into a frown.

"What the hell you doing down here?" he asks. "Place gives me the heebie-jeebies."

His shoulders shake, chilled.

"Me, too."

"*You?* You weren't the one getting worked over in those exam rooms all those years ago."

"No, but you don't know what happened out here." I nod around the room, at this chair and that.

"Out here? What happened out here?"

I raise my hand, putting him off. I'm not there yet. Still working up to it, making it real.

"Okay. Don't tell me then." He leans back. "Is that what you're writing about? That summer?" He nods at the laptop.

"Piper tell you what I'm doing?"

"Yeah. What's that all about?"

"I can't really talk about it until I'm done." Words only obfuscate. I need to see it first. Hear it, again. Everything in its time.

"Okay. Sure." He nods back. "So, um—" He leans forward and pats one of my knees. "I'm real sorry about your dad."

"Thanks."

"He was doing good for the most part, taking care of himself and everything. Forgetting a few things, but at ninety, who wouldn't? Shame about that fucking Caddy, too. *Christ.*"

"You always liked that car."

"That beautiful front end's completely stove in. I had it towed out back of the dealership if you want to see it."

"Why would I want to see it?"

"I don't know. From the looks of it, he wasn't even moving that fast. Thirty, forty, maybe. Driver's compartment's fine. Bumped his head, is all. No seat belt, of course, or air bag. None of that safety equipment in a '60 DeVille." Kurt puts a hand to his forehead. "Little different to bump your head when you're that age."

"Right." I nod.

"But it's not a total loss."

"He's dying, Kurt."

"I know. I mean, the car."

"The *car*?"

"Pablo, my head mechanic? He said it looks worse than it is. Engine's intact. Frame survived. Needs a new grill, hood, radiator, front axle, some body work. They'd be hard to find, expensive as all hell, too, but you can find anything on the internet these days. Fact is, I found a starter for her not too long ago—"

"Enough with the fucking car. Christ."

"Sorry," he says, looking down, penitent. "I just thought, it was such a sweet car—" He glances up, an appeal.

I stare him into silence.

"So—" He flips his hand at the laptop. "That summer, huh?"

"Yep. The same one you and Piper first got together."

"In a matter of speaking."

"Don't fuck with me, Kurt. That's when it started."

"Christ, Maguire." He sits back, throws an arm over the adjoining seatback. "That was so damned long ago."

"I know, and—" I put the laptop on the side table. "Maybe you can help me out because my memory's a little hazy."

"Help you out how?" He gives me a dubious tilt of his head.

"Talk to me. After you got Fernando arrested—"

"Really?" He throws his head back, wounded. "That's where you're going?"

"Now listen. Your dad threw you out of the house and you came to stay with us, right?"

"Yeah. Okay."

"And that's when you and Piper, you know...?" I nodded at him, prodding.

"Wow! What's that got to do with anything?"

"Look. Something happened when I found out about you and Piper. If it weren't for that—"

Here. In this ER. With those people watching.

"What?"

"Nothing. I'm only trying to remember what happened," I say. "That's all."

"Look, bud." He leans forward and plops that hand on my knee, again. "I know you're hurting. And you have every right. Hell—" He waves at the room, as if presenting it. "If you take the job at the paper, you'll have all the time in the world to poke around here and figure it out. But at the moment, there's more important things to think about."

I lean back, turning away from him. *I'm not ready yet!*

"Have you at least considered it? The job? Piper told me she gave you a thumbs up."

"I can't. Not until this is over."

"But you're not saying 'no.'" He points at me.

"I have to finish this." He slumps, a bit put off by my testiness, no doubt.

"Piper showed me those clippings of yours your father collected. I'd be willing to bet he'd think you should take the job."

"I'm not sure those clippings prove anything," I say, though I'm still not sure what to think about them. What did they prove? "Look, let me finish this. Then we'll talk."

"Okay. Finish it, then." He slaps his thighs and stands up, stretching, arching backwards. "But you need to get back upstairs."

"Why?" I give him a look. "Has anything changed."

"She wants you there."

"Just tell me, Kurt." I lean forward. "You and Piper. It started when you stayed with us, didn't it?"

"Look—" He lowers himself, sitting on the edge of the chair next to me, voice low. "I know it was screwed up, me falling for a kid her age. But nothing happened until we were older. We've been through this."

"Something happened, Kurt."

"Nothing…important."

"No??" I wave at the room.

He lets out a huge breath and straightens.

"Didn't we do this once…thirty years ago? You want to do this again, now, with your father—" He points at the floor above us.

"I think you and Piper are great together. You know that."

"Well, then forget it." He stands again, draping his trench coat over his arm. "Pack up your shit and let's get upstairs."

"Not until I'm done."

"Alright. But you'll get no help from me." He trudges off.

Yessiree. Something did happen.

Forty-Seven

"If the grass gets any higher," Dad said at the table that night, "I won't need a lawn mower. I'll need a hay baler."

He asked if anyone wanted to go for a drive after dinner. He had to pick up a belt the repair shop special ordered for him. The way he ate, you'd think he was already on the road, driving through Mom's lasagna.

I should have offered to go with him, even if he didn't want me to, but I was too focused on eating, wolfing down dinner. And what could I say? Wasn't it double jeopardy to argue a case twice? I had no new evidence to get Manny off. Dad was agitated enough, so worried about the damned lawn, as if the last two nights of pouring rain might make it sprout up into another jungle for him to battle through.

Finally, Mom said she'd go with him if he'd stop at that fancy seafood store she liked in the North End. She wanted lobster tails, a delicacy she'd gone without for months.

After they drove off and we started the dishes, Kurt asked, "Who wants to go to the Dairy Ripple after we're done here?" He winked at Piper and smiled at me again.

"I'll go," she said with a hop of excitement.

"Well, okay then," he said. "How about you, Walker?"

"No thanks," I said, turning to the sink and flipping the water back on. I hadn't been too keen on hanging out with Kurt since the Fernando thing. And besides, I'd told Connie I'd be hanging out in the basement if she wanted to come over, pointless as that now was.

"You know, Pipes," he began, "Dairy Ripple's where I had my first date ever. Bought a girl an ice cream after school. Sixth grade."

"You had a girlfriend in sixth grade?" I said, incredulous.

"This was back before I became a hated taco bender."

"A what?" Piper asked.

"Never mind. Long story. Anyway, this girl and I. We walked along the river's edge. So romantic. Then her family up and moved a week later. Like I scared her away. Broke my heart."

"Everyone goes there after school," Piper said. "Boys on one side of the parking lot. Girls on the other. Like a sock hop, except boys buy girls ice creams instead of asking them to dance."

"You must get boys buying you ice cream all the time, then."

I could barely hear her 'no' above the water splashing into the sink.

"Well, hell. You wait. Once you start high school this fall, you'll find hot fudge sundaes and root beer floats filled to bursting in your locker."

Piper blushed, a pleased smile on her downturned face. I gave Kurt an admonishing grimace, getting her hopes up like that.

"It's those juniors you have to worry about most," he said, elbowing me in the side. "Once they get their driver's licenses. Very tempting to freshman girls. Right, Walker?"

"Piper's nothing like Gayle and Patty were." I turned back to the sink, shaking my head.

"Why?" Piper shot back, indignant.

"Well, because they were a little more—" *Oh, Christ. What was I saying?* "You know—"

"What?" Piper grabbed my arm, pulling me around. "Go on, say it. I know what you're thinking."

"Forget it. I wasn't thinking anything." I couldn't look at her.

"Yes you were." She pushed me in the chest. "I know you were."

"Maybe," Kurt drawled, moving between us like a referee, "we should go get that ice cream before this gets ugly."

"Maybe we should!" Piper threw her dish towel in my face. "At least Kurt will buy me an ice cream—won't you?"

"Damn right I will," he said.

My sister stomped out of the kitchen.

"Look, bud." Kurt was up in my face now, making me back off a step. "You might not see the shit she's going through, but I do. I've been there. So, stop being such a prick, okay?"

His anger startled me, coming to her defense. But perhaps he was right. I might have had a hard time with my dad, but Piper and Kurt—they'd had hard times of their own.

Alone, I wiped down the kitchen counter while those three girls—Gayle, Patty, and Piper—spun like a roulette wheel in my mind. I wished I'd gone along to explain. But what would I say? I never thought twice about Gayle or Patty being fourteen when Kurt and I dated them. But Piper was, well, Piper. Opinionated. Smart. Bossy. High school wasn't a magic portal that would transform her into a social butterfly. And then there was Connie. Isolated, like Piper, but not of her own doing. Because of how she looked and where her parents came from. A world apart. So independent and grown up, the way she took care of Manny and her little brothers, volunteered at the hospital. She was a woman, and they were girls. Of course, Connie would never come over, now that she knew what a "hero" I was. Just as well. If Dad ever met her, he'd be so disappointed in me, "lowering" myself like that. It was a lost cause, but I skipped down the steps to the basement anyway. It was still light out, but I turned on the lamp anyway, flopped down on the couch, and wondered—would Connie notice it?

Voices invaded from beyond the basement door, waking me up. Kurt popped in, a half-eaten sundae in one hand, wiping at his t-shirt with the other. Spilled ice cream? He paused in the doorway, said "Hey," then bolted up the stairs. Piper came in right after, a drippy ice cream cup in her hand.

"Kurt!" she yelled, a pleading in her voice. Barely acknowledging me, a single glance, she bounded up the stairs after him.

Something had happened. I rubbed my eyes, trying to wake up, squinting at the window. Outside, the sun was setting, the yard going red. I rolled off the couch and stood, taking a step to follow Piper, when I heard a knock on the back door.

"Walker?"

Was that…?

Connie Camarasa poked her head in the door. I jumped back, straightening my shirt, running my hand through my hair. But she wasn't looking at me. She was out of breath as if she had run up the hill. Dark hair fell over her cheek. She looked different, dressed in nice jeans and a sleeveless top, wide straps over bare shoulders, shiny as chestnuts.

"Connie! Come in." I waved her into the rec room.

"I'm sorry to barge in like this. Is this a bad time?"

"No. Not at all. Come on in."

She took a few steps in, about to speak when her focus shifted. Her eyes darted about, catching on my dad's hat collection, the piano, caught up short, perhaps, by all our strange stuff. I motioned her in, but she didn't move.

"I only came by to apologize for what I said earlier. And to say—" She looked around the room, as if the words would come to her from the hats pinned to the wall, from the piano. "I know *Papá* told you not to talk to your father—" She glanced up the stairs. "But, the thing is, we really need this, and if you can do something, anything—"

"I'll talk to him, as soon as I can."

"As soon as you can."

"Yes. I promise. I will." *And say what?*

"Okay. Thank you." She smiled, briefly, then turned to leave, then back, her hands clasped together, wringing out some other anxiety, glancing up at me.

"Why don't you sit down?" I waved at the couch.

"No," she said, firmer now. "There's something else." A frown took over, concern buckling her brow. She took another brief peek at the stairwell.

"What? Tell me."

"Coming up the hill just now?"

"Yes?"

"I saw somebody."

She waited, blinking uncertainly at me, then away and back, as if I might know what she saw.

"Oh? That must have been my sister and—" And Kurt. Of course.

"So that was your sister. And was that her *boyfriend??*" She spat out the word, a rotten cherry.

"Boyfriend?? No, he's just—why do you say boyfriend?"

"Because they were kissing, like forever, all touchy-feely. Got pretty nasty about it when I caught them, too." Her face darkened, glowering at the memory.

"Kissing!" I couldn't even get the word out. "Excuse me," I said, pushing past her. "Don't leave. I'll be right back." I rushed up the stairs, two steps at a time. In the den, Piper stood at the side door, looking out. I joined her. Kurt's car revved. He peeled out of the driveway. Gravel spun out from the rear wheels.

"Where's he going?"

"I don't know." My sister was crestfallen, her shoulders slumping, her eyes going wet.

"Piper. Were you and Kurt—"

"What?" She jerked her head around, indignant, challenging, her lips pursed.

I grabbed her by the shoulders.

"What!?" She tried to pull away.

"Connie saw you."

Piper's eyes hardened.

"Connie? That was that girl you like? Where did she come from?"

"She saw you kissing Kurt."

"So what. It was a kiss."

"Piper—" I clutched her arm.

"I'm fourteen." She pulled away. "I can do what I want." Her defiance seemed composed of both resentment and resignation. She knew how this conversation had to go.

"You're too young for him."

"Gayle wasn't too young for you. Or Patty for him. Why can't I?"

"Because, he's nineteen!" It was different! Didn't she get that?

"I've never had anybody," she went on. "And now you want to take away the one boy who actually likes me?"

I was tempted to argue, but Connie was waiting.

"Connie's still downstairs. You stay right there. I want to talk to you." I pointed at the couch.

Connie was gone. I sprinted out the back door and down the dusky hill, or tried to, my sneakers catching in the long dark grass. Plowing past the cherry and apple trees, I steered around their fruit-laden branches, and by the time I clambered onto the dock, she was on her haunches, untying her boat in the near dark.

"Connie—" I grabbed her shoulder "Don't go."

"Don't touch me!" She whirled around, that earlier anger even more deeply engraved in her face. I backed away, my hands up, surrendering.

"I'm sorry."

She bent back to the pylon, untying the rope, her hands flying. "I only came here to ask about your Dad, not to get caught up in all this bullshit."

"I know. I'm sorry." I wanted to talk to her, to explain.

She stood, the freed rope in her hand.

"I can't believe your sister's involved with that boy, after what he did to Fernando."

"She's not. That's going to stop."

"And I can't believe what he called me. What have you been saying about me, anyway?" She straightened, lifting her chin. An accusation. A betrayal.

"What do you mean?"

"'It's that *hot tamale,*' he said." Her tone mocked. "'That girl Walker's *into.*'"

"I never said that."

"As if I'd ever be interested in you. With your *fancy* house and *screwed up* friends. Asshole father. You can all go to hell!"

"I can explain."

"No, you can't because I'm going home." She turned away and climbed into the little boat, which tipped dangerously amidst her angry stumblings to get back to the stern. She jerked on the starter cord, but nothing happened.

"Don't go."

She stopped and took a breath, trying to calm herself. "I need you to fix this with your father."

"I'll try."

"You'll try. That's the best you can do?"

She yanked again, and the engine caught, coughing up into an even sputter, a puff of white smoke, as she played with the throttle. The boat moved off over the water with the slow assurance of its low growl; then she turned the tiller, pointing the bow upstream.

Fucking Kurt. Why'd he have to say that? *Hot tamale*. Christ. So much for having my back. Blew any chance I had with her. And kissing Piper? Son of a bitch!

I marched up the hill, into the basement, up the stairs. But Piper had left the den. I listened. In her room above me, the radio played a cheery pop song. I took the steps two at a time. Her door was closed. I pounded on it and twisted the handle. Locked.

"Piper. Let me in."

"No! You'll just yell at me."

I took a deep breath, lowering my voice, taking a second. "I won't yell at you." I stood there, my head against the jamb, listening. "What happened out there?"

"It was only one kiss."

"What about with Connie? What did you guys say to her?"

Silence.

"Piper!" I banged on the door. Nothing. "Do you know what Dad will do if he finds out?"

"Daddy? He'd never do anything to me." Her words, thick with defiance, contained a quaver of doubt. "I was only—thinking for myself. Didn't you say that's what I needed to do? Think for myself?"

"That's not what I meant, and you know it."

The door moved, as if she was leaning against it.

"Kurt's nice to me," she sobbed. "And you asked me to go swimming with him."

"He's not nice! You saw how he treated Fernando."

The door opened. She glowered at me, tears brimming in her eyes.

"Fernando screwed things up with Kurt's father. Kurt told me. He talks to me like an adult."

"You are *not* an adult!" As if barking it out could stop her from becoming an adult.

"If you say anything—" She straightened, a defensive stance, a threat.

"You'll do what? Yell 'Daddy'? Huh?"

"I'll tell him. I'll tell him you lied about Manny because you like his daughter." She stared up at me, her jaw clenched, teeth gritted. "It's the truth, isn't it," she pointed at me. "I can tell."

Like the good old days. And here I'd thought that was behind us, but she had that ace in her back pocket, always available in a clinch. *I'll tell Daddy!*

A car pulled into the driveway, gravel grinding. Piper ran to her window, face pressed to the glass, searching frantically. From her drooping disappointment, I knew who it was.

"It's Dad," she said, turning, regarding me, waiting for my verdict. "Well? What are you going to do?"

"If this thing with Kurt doesn't stop, and right now, I will tell. And I don't give a damn what you say to him about me."

She glared at me and shoved on the door, but I held it firm. Her mouth tight and defiant, she stared until I removed my hand. The door slammed.

I couldn't go downstairs. One look at me and my parents would know something was up. I went into my room and plopped down on the bed, listening for Kurt's car to return. I lay back. Despite all the thoughts piling up in my head, they all came crashing down into sleep.

Forty-Eight

Piper wants to pull the plug.

"But he doesn't look any worse," I tell her, two minutes after returning to the ICU. What I want to say is, *We're not done. We haven't figured this out yet!*

"He won't get better," she insists. "He'll only get worse, and he may be suffering. We have to let him go. Now, I called Frazier. He's still stuck at LaGuardia, but he agrees."

While I was gone, the doctor had checked on him. He'd said Dad's pupils were fixed and dilated. He had no reflex actions, no response to external stimulus. It was time, and Piper agreed. No nutrition or hydration. Nothing but pain medication. Palliative care, she said. Fucking euphemisms.

"But he's still breathing on his own," I point out.

She'd asked about that, too. Breathing can go on even without cortex and brain stem function, she says. As if she knows what that means and isn't simply repeating the doctor's words. She points to a screen behind Dad's bed.

"EEG. Electroencephalograph," she says, as if all those syllables she sounds out contain the weight to convince me. "It measures brain activity, but it's flattened out, the doctor said. Yes, he's breathing, his heart's pumping, but he's more like this car, idling, empty, the driver gone."

"So, what? You want to let him—what? Run out of gas?"

"I know him, Walker. It's what he would have wanted. After what Mom went through? The mastectomies? The drugs? She was so much younger—in her seventies—he didn't want to let her go, not when she should have had so many years left. But the more things he tried, the more she suffered. And she didn't see what was happening, any more than he does now."

She grabs Dad's hand before going on, near tears.

"You weren't here. You didn't know what it was like to sit with him in a room like this while she was in a bed like this, hooked up to machines doing everything for her, intubated, a feeding tube, catheter. He said it was like doctoring on the battlefield. Fix a guy up only to send him back into combat. How could he do that to his own wife?"

"You always protect him."

"Protect him? Do you understand what I'm saying? I'm saying we can't protect him, not like this."

But I'm not ready yet.

"Look," she says, "We've only decided not to feed or hydrate him. It could still take days, maybe longer. And who knows what could happen in that time?"

I tell her I'll think about it and walk out.

Back at Maternity, a nurse tells me Connie's shift starts at eleven. I start to leave, then turn back.

"Is she married?"

The nurse frowns at me, like, 'Who is this creep?'

"I can't say." *Or you won't.*

"My dad's in intensive care, critical condition."

"Oh, I'm so sorry to hear that." Her voice inflates with emotion as she crosses her arm on the desk, leans forward and cocks her head, the practiced sounds and gestures of institutional sympathy.

"Has she got any kids?" I can't help asking.

She straightens, all business again.

"I can't talk about that."

"He's dying." I'm not making sense, but I'm so tired.

"You have to understand. I can't give out private information."

Why should she when there's this weirdo standing in front of her, looking like hell, where women are giving birth to babies right down the hall? But it's Connie I need to talk to, not Kurt or Piper—or even my dad. I need to know where she and Manny disappeared to, if he's even alive, whether she hates me or not. She has to tell me it didn't go completely to shit for them after that summer.

But again, I'm getting ahead of myself. It's what happened in the ER I need to focus on now, so I make my way back there, down the stairs and through the winding hallways, side-stepping patients on gurneys, in wheelchairs. I dodge carts laden with trays of saran-wrapped meals, carts with mops and buckets or inscrutable electronic equipment.

Back in Emergency, I find a seat in that waiting room. Across from me, a middle-school kid taps furiously on his Game Boy. An older girl, his sister probably, dangles a jean-clad leg over an armrest, kicking, watching tv. Judge Judy presides, the sound mercifully muted.

Oh, to be a bored teen again. Like Piper before that summer.

I reread the last stuff I wrote, the mine I'm digging in my memories. It's filled up with a deadly gas. The stink of my own bullshit as my world collapsed around me. I'm hoping this room will provide a spark, explosives detonating at the right angles, pressuring me from all sides to expose that seam of hard truth. I need to see it again. This room, the way it was all those years ago. The dark-haired woman, head on knees. That couple, their fussy toddler. That gray-haired Chicano, coughing, his white hanky in hand. All eyes on me.

Forty-Nine

The following morning, Kurt's bed was empty, his stuff still in Frazier's bedroom. I considered playing hooky from work so I could search for him, but Dad would find out. But wasn't that unslept-in bed proof Kurt knew he'd fucked up?

"I want you home at 3:30, right after work," Dad said as I downed corn flakes at the kitchen table. "It'll take the two of us to put that new belt on the John Deere, and I want you to start on the grass as soon as we get it fixed."

"Fine," I said. *After I swing past Kurt's house and kick his ass!*

Once again, Manny didn't make it to work, and all day long, I had nothing to occupy my thoughts but fuel tanks, boxcars, tugger trains, beating Kurt senseless, and any riotous babblings I could make to my father to change his mind and make Connie happy.

How far had Kurt gone with Piper, anyway? How could he be so stupid saying those things to Connie? By the time the horn sounded signaling shift's end, my heart beat almost as loud. Now I could get my hands on the stupid bastard.

I bounced my fists off the Datsun's steering wheel as I pulled out of the AMC lot. Why hadn't I seen it, Kurt and Piper? Sure, *she* was excited Dad let him stay with us, but Kurt!? So sly and put-upon when I'd asked him to take Piper swimming. *Oh, why not?* Why not, indeed! Piper in her little two-piece, and him, showing off his pecs, doing ironman poses. I could imagine the two of them, splash-fighting, water-wrestling, all that wet skin, those goose bumps. How stupid could I be? Enabling all their longing looks, their heart-to-hearts. And then there was that cutesy Dairy Ripple business. Kurt *knew* Piper would fall for that whole ice cream come on.

With all the post-shift rush-hour traffic, it took a while to get to the new subdivision where Kurt's father had recently built a sprawling two-story house. It was just like the other monstrosities around it, all owned by AMC execs, all twice the size of anything else around town except our house. Three-car garages, bark mulch aprons around tied-down saplings struggling to stay upright in winds that barreled across the empty fields. I looped around the end of the *cul-de-sac*, searching for the Impala. It wasn't there.

Next, I tried Swanson Motors, going upstream against the rush hour traffic. Amidst all the shiny new Chevys and the hodgepodge of vehicles in the employee's lot, nowhere was the telltale robin's egg blue of Kurt's Impala.

I pulled into our driveway forty-five minutes late. The Impala wasn't there, either. The mower was still tipped on its side, so long stuck in that position, it might as well be a lawn ornament. My father was nowhere to be seen, but his wrath awaited, as did a shaggy lawn, full of weeds.

One summer at Chanute Air Force Base, the yard around our house on Senior Officer's Row went without mowing for three weeks while we vacationed in northern Michigan on Mackinac Island. We hung out on the beach while our parents watched the boats finish the Chicago to Mackinac Yacht Club race. When we returned on a breezy afternoon, the yard was a flowing river of calf-high dandelions and seed heads, interrupted only by the house and trees. Cursing all the way into the house, Dad got on the phone and found out the kid he'd hired to mow the lawn had broken his arm and had no number in Michigan to let Dad know. It was late, everyone was tired from the six hour drive, but Dad said we had to cut the grass. Even at the mower's highest setting, the John Deere seized up and shut down every few minutes, the blade engulfed in wet, green concrete. Frazier and I took turns. One of us mowed while the other raked the fat snakes and mounds of cut grass the mower left behind. Meanwhile, my father hacked at the tufts around the trees and bushes. We worked well into the evening, but Dad refused to let us go in for dinner, as if at any minute the grass would shoot up beyond his control if we didn't cut it down to size.

I got out of the car and surveyed my dad's progress on the mower. At least, he had the blade off. The Caddy was still parked in the driveway. It wasn't like Dad to leave it out, but maybe he was still waxing it—or admiring it.

I took big breaths, closing my eyes, the stink of gasoline still leaking from the mower. He could be so ridiculous about the goddamned grass.

I climbed the side steps and slipped inside the door. The den was empty, the TV off, only the overhead fan spinning, ticking. Piper was probably hiding out in her room. Maybe Dad was down in the workshop. I found Mom in the kitchen, peeling potatoes and carrots into a large pot of water. When she saw me, she wiped her hands on her apron.

"Where have you been?" The words tumbled out, loud for her, like something accidentally dropped and broken. "Why didn't you come straight home like your father asked?"

"I know, I know, but I'm here now. Has Kurt been here?"

"Kurt?" My question confused her. She shook her head. "Walker, your father's waiting for you. Go!"

"Have you seen Kurt?"

"No, I haven't." She straightened, puzzled. "I'm not sure he even came in last night. Maybe he went home."

"He didn't. His car wasn't there."

"You went looking for him? Is that why you're late?"

"Yes."

"Why? Is something going on?"

She waited half a second for me to answer before shaking her head, changing direction, re-assessing priorities.

"Deal with it later. You need to get out there and help your father before he has a fit."

"Walker!?" Dad was outside, calling me. "Walker!" It came out in one syllable, he barked it so quickly. When I opened the den door, we almost butted heads.

"There you are." His hands were covered in grease, a smear of it across his forehead. "Where have you been?"

"I was coming out to help you."

"You should have been home an hour ago." He smelled like the John Deere, grass and gasoline, mixed.

"I'm here now, okay?" My voice raised, matching his.

He seemed taken aback by my tone, the challenge in it, perhaps. "If we don't get this fixed, we'll be mowing in the dark." He marched down the side steps. "Where the hell were you?"

"The car—" I needed a lie.

He bent over the mower, picking up the blade.

"It wouldn't start. I had to get a jump from one of the other guys in the lot."

"The car wouldn't start," he said, dubious. "It's never had that problem before." His voice was animated with insinuation, seeing right through me.

"I know. It was me. I left the overhead light on and the battery drained."

"*Sure* you did."

"It was stupid. Just me being stupid."

He twitched at this remark as if I exhibited a symptom he couldn't place.

"Okay, okay. Let's get to work. Hold this here, like that." He positioned the blade on the spindle and fiddled with the new belt.

Of course, he bought *this* lie. My stupidity was plain to see. But the truth?

Plying a screwdriver, Dad levered the new drive belt toward the spindle, but it had no give. It wouldn't stretch. He was Mr. Fix-It again, trying to figure it out on his own. Manuals were beneath him, especially any that told you how to work with your hands, an insult to his intelligence.

"Dad," I said. He didn't hear me. Each time the screwdriver slipped, an ember of anger flared up in my chest. "Dad!"

"What?" He spat out the word.

"Are you sure this is the best way?"

"Of course, I'm sure. Don't ask stupid questions." The screwdriver slid off again, tweaking his thumb. "Damn it!" The belt sprang away, whipping around my ankle, an infuriating burn.

"Like you never did anything stupid in your life," I said, rubbing at it. He pulled his bleeding thumb out of his mouth.

"What? What did you say?"

"Nothing." I straightened, reconsidering.

"If you have something to say, say it."

"You brought Kurt into the house, gave him the run of the place after what he did to that poor guy, getting him deported. He was only trying to earn a living. Like Manny Camarasa."

"Oh, so this is all about that *friend* of yours, is it?"

"Well, what if it is? What if I went to see Ned St. John?"

"Ned? Why?"

"To appeal Manny's case."

"Oh, for God's sake, Walker." He whirled his head around, winding up. "This is *none* of your *business*. Why did you go to him?"

"Because I told the truth, and you won't listen."

"That you saw everything." Mocking me, now.

"I did see everything! But I was afraid—" Dad glowered at me, a look of utter disbelief as I approached that same lame argument, boxcars and suspension. And he was right. It was another lie. I'd had enough lies. "Of *you*. I was afraid of you. I knew *you'd* be pissed. Your son, doing something stupid. Your son, the loser, the bum. The kid who got arrested, who almost flunked out." Oblivious to Kurt's fucking around with his naïve little sister. "I was afraid of *you*."

"Of me?"

The way he said it, as if I had pulled this out of thin air.

"Yes, you. You whaling on me again. You going nuts. But I'm done worrying about you. I don't care anymore. I'm telling you, Norm started the fight, not Manny, and it happened exactly the way Manny said, so you have to fix it. Do whatever you want to me. I deserve it. But Manny deserves that money, and you have to give it to him."

"I don't *have* to do anything. I'm the one who decides."

"That's right. You sit up there in that air-conditioned building with all your bigwig buddies *deciding*, while we do the work, while we break our backs. Norm's right about that much. All of you. Like you know everything, even when you don't. So goddamned smart, but you haven't got a fucking clue what's really going on."

He slapped me, knocking me back. *There. He finally did it again. And I didn't fall.* I staggered, dizzy, but I was still on my feet. I cupped my burning cheek and straightened, eye to eye with him. He lifted his hand, ready to backhand me, then dropped it.

"Go in the house!"

I didn't move, so he advanced on me, grabbing my shirt.

"Get in the goddamned house before I hit you again!"

He shook me around and pushed me stumbling toward the stairs. I took a few steps in that direction, but turned, detouring toward my car.

As I started it up, my tears streaming, I glanced out. Dad was hunched over the John Deere, staring at it. I sat there, hands on the steering wheel, gripping, re-gripping. He turned his head and caught my eye. He appeared shaken, drained, his face almost as white as his hair.

I shifted into reverse and backed out the drive.

Fifty

At Main Street, I turned left on the bridge, crossed the river and pulled into Dairy Ripple right on the other side. I backed into a parking slot and switched off the ignition, but I couldn't take my hands off the wheel. They gripped and re-gripped it, as if I needed to be somewhere. Only, I didn't know where.

A long line formed at the order window, a posse of pre-teen boys and girls. Two boys had squirt guns and chased two girls a foot taller than them in circles around the lot. Piper should have been here, playing with these kids, not mooning after a guy—a man, really—five years older than her. A stream of water arched across my windshield. I leaned on the horn. The boys backed away, holding up their weapons in surrender.

The order line shrank and lengthened as the shadows shifted. Cars pulled in, emptied of families, filled up on ice cream cones, sundaes and floats, and drove off. Never once had we come here as a family.

After an hour of sitting there, it occurred to me that River Street was just up at the corner. I was reminded of how Connie had reached that spoon over to me, allowing me to sip off that bit of plantain. Such warmth in that smile, wondering if—maybe even hoping—I liked it. I did. I liked it fine.

I pulled out of the lot, turned onto River and followed it past the Foundry, parking in front of Manny's house. On the porch of the house opposite, a pregnant woman sat in a rocking chair. Wearing a housedress and an open white cardigan, she absently cupped the globe of her abdomen with splayed fingers, observing me a second, then straining forwards to peer down the street. Fernando's wife. Two dark-haired children played at her feet, running little cars in circles on the wooden floor, making 'vrooming' noises. Behind the railing, a blanket covered a boxy pile of something. A suitcase handle peeked out. Fernando's car was gone. Maybe he and his family were planning an escape. Giving the Camarasas all their food? Yep. Definitely going somewhere. Fleeing before they could be deported. But where to? Florida? California? Picking fruits or vegetables? Living like *braceros*. Only worse.

This was what happened to people who lied to protect themselves. Though I couldn't compare. My problems paled next to these folks'.

The woman glowered at me, her mouth tightening, pointing out I didn't belong—a white boy like the one who got her husband arrested. I got out and, turning my back to her, stepped across the limestone slabs of the Camarasa's front walk, climbed the stairs, pulled opened the screen door, and knocked.

Connie answered, her eyes wide, mouth open.

From inside came squeals of laughter—the two little boys, playing at something. She stepped out onto the porch, shutting the doors behind her. She drew one hand up to the opposite shoulder, covering up, shielding. Those short shorts, that tube top, were meant for comfort in a sweltering house, not the eyes of uninvited boys. Her hair was in a pony-tail baring the curve of her neck. God, she looked good.

"I'm kind of busy making dinner. Why are you here?" Suspicion slowed the words.

"I—" Why *was* I there? "I wanted to apologize again. I never said those things about you, okay? Those were Kurt's words. I only said—" I glanced up at her. "I said I liked you. That's all."

Her arms folded, she shifted from one foot to the other, regarding me, a corner of her mouth twisting, reassessing.

"Okay," she said. "You've apologized. Is that all?"

"I—I also talked to my dad, again." Funny how I'd blotted it out until now. The yelling, the slap. Manny would understand. "Is your father home?"

"He just left for the hospital with my mother."

"Oh, right." I tapped my forehead.

"So?" She thrust her head forward, eyebrows up. It made me back off a step, consider my words carefully.

"'*No*,'" she said, jumping in. "He said 'no,' didn't he?"

"I—fucked it up." It coughed out, catching in my throat. "I'm sorry." That aquifer split open again, a damn bursting. But no, not in front of Connie. I wiped at my eyes, turning away. She remained quiet, so I chanced a look at her.

She bit her lip, concerned.

"So," she said, admonishing, as if she knew the answer already. "What happened?"

"He got mad. Then I got mad. I blew it. I'm so sorry." Welling up again, I turned and sat myself down on the top step, looking away from her. The step sagged as she sat beside me.

"I guess that's it then," she said, looking out at the street. "There's nothing more we can do."

"You can appeal. Hire a lawyer—" I peeked up at her.

"Pay a lawyer all the money we might have gotten from AMC? How does that make sense?"

"It wouldn't be like that—"

"Walker—" She shifted, whispering. "Please, stop. You've done enough, okay?"

A car went by and another. The pregnant woman watched us. Every so often, she leaned out, straining to see down the street, frowning. She turned her gaze in our direction, her face darkening even more.

"I'm sorry," I said, again. "I really am. About everything."

Connie folded her bare arms, rubbing them, as if she was cold.

That was it, then. I had reached the end of the line.

"I'm sorry, too," she said at last. She stood, so I did, too. "I have to finish dinner." She didn't move, but kept looking around at the yard. Finally, her gaze settled on me. "Was there something else?" she asked.

A million things. How had her day been? What was she cooking for dinner? What was she waiting for, standing there next to me? That odd look in her eyes, hurt but hopeful, the way she rubbed her arms with those hands, so cold on this warm day. But I couldn't come up with a thing. Or maybe I could.

"Only this. Stop going into people's gardens across the river."

She blanched, her head rearing.

"What?"

"Some people won't see a teenage girl taking a few tomatoes or strawberries. They'll see your skin color, your hair—"

She folded her arms again.

"But not the way I do," I blurted.

"The way you do?"

"I mean—" Were there any right words? "They'll only see what they want to see. Not who you are."

"I *know* what you're saying."

"No, you don't. I'm only saying, I don't want you hurt. Okay? I want you—" Where was the word?

"You want me?"

"Safe." I reddened. "I want you safe."

She considered me, then lowered her arms, hands at her side.

"Okay." A whisper. "I'll stop."

"Good. I'm glad."

"Okay, then." She grasped the door handle, turning it, but she didn't pull the door open. She turned the handle this way and that, then looked at me. One last time.

I stepped towards her, cupped her cheeks with my hands and kissed her, a long, fierce second, then backed off, letting her go. She blinked at me, stunned, staggered. Her hand went to her lips, but she kept her eyes on mine, burrowing in. They teared up, as if she was angry to be stirred up so. She turned and rushed into the house, the door slamming behind her.

As I headed back to my car, I tried to wrap my head around what had just happened, that unexpected kiss, the look on Connie's face, the warmth welling in my chest, but Fernando's wife had moved off the porch and was waddling out to the road, waving me over. Christ. I braced for a scolding.

"You don't belong here."

"I know. I was just leaving."

"My husband told me about you. You're friends with the boy who did that to our car, got 'Nando in trouble."

"I'm sorry. I had nothing to do with that. It was awful what he did."

"We were going away tonight. Before they could send us back. 'Nando went to say goodbye to some of his friends at the pool hall. He phoned me to say he'd be late. Your friend is there. Nando said he could make some money. Traveling money, he called it."

"They're shooting pool? Fernando and Kurt?"

Her expression changed, melting a bit. Her shoulders drooped, her hands clasped, wringing. "Please. I need him home," she pleaded. "I only want to leave. Can you—can you help me?"

Fifty-One

I hadn't been to Rambler Lanes since the night Fernando called me out. The lot was filling up, leagues about to start, but Kurt's Impala was parked in the spot closest to the front door. He'd probably been here since the place opened. I should have guessed.

The place roared with rolling balls, busting pins and jukebox tunes. The night was young, but already cigarette smoke hung in layers over the lanes. Through the archway into the Billiard Room, I saw a dozen or so men surrounding the center table, like a crowd watching a fist fight. I moved closer, and they gave way one by one, when they saw me—the *gringo,* the friend. I found a spot where Kurt might see me.

In constant motion, he stalked the table, circling this way and that, chalking his cue while he analyzed angles, leaned over and sighted down his stick. Nearby, Fernando stood, a statue, poker-faced. The spectators studied the table, all in jeans, cowboy hats or baseball caps. They mumbled to each other in Spanish, sipping from beer bottles as they leaned back against the surrounding tables.

Now that I'd found Kurt, I wanted to grab him and go, but a big pile of cash sat on the corner of the table. Not something you interrupted.

Eight Ball was the game, and from the way Kurt was aiming, he was a stripe away from taking on the black ball that would win it for him. He potted the stripe in the side, but the cue ball rebounded hard off the rail and returned to the middle of the table, leaving a tough angle for that last ball. The eight sat on the far rail. He'd have to clip it hard, a glancing blow, if he wanted to put it in the corner pocket.

Fernando held his cue like a walking staff, the butt end on the ground, both hands on the ferrule. From their intent expressions, it was clear everyone understood they weren't playing for money alone, but for revenge. Retaliation. Or possibly something quite the opposite, it occurred to me.

Kurt circled the table, eyeing the layout. He chalked his cue, circled again, taking forever, as usual. I edged even closer, making my way to the front of the crowd. Guys sat on the rails of the other tables, craning their necks to see. Snatches of Spanish passed between them, speculating, curious. Amidst the Lincolns and Hamiltons crumpled above a corner pocket, there was a handful or more of Jacksons. Big money.

"Kurt!" I called out. Everyone turned, glaring and roiled by my lack of poolroom etiquette. Kurt looked up, surprised. He glowered, a challenge forming itself in his eyes, daring me. I tilted my head, eyeing the money, glanced up at Fernando and back at Kurt, hoping to make a point. My old friend gave a big sigh and turned his back on me. I said his name again, but he resumed circling, studying angles, ignoring me.

Finally, he bent over the table and set up, positioning his bridge hand on the green felt, practicing his stroke. Then he stopped, as if rethinking. He straightened, grabbed the chalk one more time and applied it to the cue tip, giving me a sidelong glance. I returned him a grimace, my eyes wide, my arms folded. *Finish it, already!* He blew off the excess chalk, slammed the blue cube down on the rail and bent over the shot again, starting over—but positioned all wrong. His cue tip was high left on the cue ball when it should have been high right. He knew that. He'd taught me that. But he did it anyway! He poked the cue ball high left, nicking the eight, which rolled along the rail, hugging it, then dropped in the pocket. He smiled as if he'd executed the shot perfectly, but all eyes were on the white ball, which after rebounding, kept rolling, angling straight at the far corner. Seeing this, Kurt frowned and, at the last second, snatched up the ball before it could drop. He banged it down on the table, a big show. He had scratched. Fernando's game.

Kurt turned and eyed me, blame in his scorn. *Was I happy now?* As if unable to contain himself, he jerked around to face Fernando.

"Double or nothing," Kurt yelled. "Again, double or nothing."

"Enough!" I shouted. Was he for real?

All eyes turned towards me.

"You're done playing."

"He's right," Fernando said, snapping up the money. "I'm done." He counted the bills, flattening them.

"The hell you are!" Kurt grabbed at Fernando's arm with both hands. "You're done when I say so."

"I gave you your game. I'm done." Fernando barked, flinging Kurt away.

He tumbled backwards, falling, and disappeared downwards into a wall of men leaning on a table. His head hit the table, snapping forward, a solid thunk. I pushed guys to the side. They parted easily, dispersing. Kurt lay on the floor, rubbing the back of his skull with one hand, eyes squinting, unfocused, baffled. The *Mexicanos* hurried out, skittering past all the so-far oblivious white bowlers.

"Kurt!" I bent over him and grabbed his shoulders. His eyes fluttered, eyebrows furling, trying to sync.

"I'm okay," he slurred. "Where'd he go? It's double or nothing." Like a toddler talking. I pulled him to his feet, holding on.

"Sure it is." He faded in and out. His knees weakened, and I had to pull him up straight. The room had emptied. Out in the hall, Fernando stopped. He eyed me as he slid his cue stick into its leather sleeve. He waited, hesitating. I waved at him to go. He lifted his head, nodded, his lips pursed in ambivalence, then headed off.

I pulled Kurt up and made him lean against the table while I grabbed his cue and its leather sleeve. My arm around his waist, I led him out of the room. None of the bowlers seemed to notice, as if this was just another stumbling drunk, a common sight here. Once we were out the door, the June heat hit us, only a bit cooler, the sun still a ways from setting. I guided him to my Datsun, but he pushed away when he saw where we were headed.

"Where's my car? I can drive."

"You're coming with me." I shoved him toward my car, opening the passenger door. "We need to talk."

Fifty-Two

Rather than pull into the driveway where my dad might see us, I parked the Datsun on the street. I helped Kurt around the side of the house, hitching him to my hip like I had Manny. The way he stumbled along made me wonder if he'd been drinking, too, but I didn't smell it on him. All this from a bump on the head?

The John Deere was gone—back in the garage, I imagined, fixed or unfixed—and the Caddy had been moved down the driveway and parked in such a way it blocked the other two cars. Very unlike Dad. Had he taken it out—the car he wasn't supposed to drive?

I didn't want him to see Kurt in this condition, so I hauled him around back. Fortunately, the basement was quiet—no Piper pounding the piano. I could only imagine how she would have reacted, seeing Kurt hurt. The lights were off, so I snuck Kurt in and pushed him onto the couch in the rec room. He slouched, his head thrown back.

His eyes opened and closed, slow as butterfly wings. I glanced up the stairs. The door was shut, so I flicked on the light.

"Turn it off!" Kurt blinked, his hand up, blocking the glare. "It hurts."

I flipped it off and returned to his side. I pushed back the coffee table and sat on its lip so I could face Kurt.

"Why did you kiss Piper?"

"I didn't kiss—" He lifted his head, setting something off that kept him from continuing. He sat forward and put his head in his hands, cradling it. "Fuck!"

"Connie saw you!"

"She kissed me! Big difference. Got her fucking ice cream all over me, doing it, too."

"You're saying that was the first time?"

"The only time! She was mad at you, man." He exhaled. Exasperation or acting, I couldn't tell. "So I let her pick out whatever ice cream she wanted. She was so excited, someone actually being nice to her. And when we got home, I guess she wanted to thank me. And then that girl showed up. Where'd she come from, anyway? Always popping up out of nowhere, catching me in the act."

"She came in her boat to see me." I slid back on the table.

"So, it's true then. You and she—"

"She wants my help with her father."

"Sure she does," he smirked, the grin seeming to bring on more pain, his hand rubbing his head again. "Fuck, this hurts!"

"Don't change the subject! What Connie saw was a helluva lot more than a 'thank you' peck on the cheek."

"Okay." He rubbed at his head. "I like Piper. And everyone else ignores her. She and I, we know what that's like. Being ignored. Badmouthed. We talk about it. Patty won't. My parents. You. She—she makes it better. That's all I let her do. I let her like me. Shitty thing to do, huh?" He coughed again, running his hands through his hair, again and again.

"It is when you touch her, okay? She's only fourteen."

"Patty and Gayle were only—"

"It's not the same. We were kids. We're not anymore. So, you leave her alone."

He rubs the back of his head, squinting.

"And what the hell did you say to Connie?" I continue. "'That girl Walker's *into*'? 'That *hot tamale*'? Christ!"

"It was talk. That's all."

"*Talk*." I leaned back, regarding him. "Look, I don't know what that double or nothing business was about," I said, "but...I've seen you make that shot a hundred times. Making the eight ball is the hard part. The easy part is avoiding the scratch, a little topspin right. But you struck it high left. You knew where that cue ball would end up.

"Or I fucked it up," he mumbles.

"With all that money on the line?"

He put his head between his legs, his hands on his head, hiding from me.

"What you did to Fernando? And all your talk. Just *talk*, you say. About Connie, those *Mexicanos* at the pool hall. Wetbacks? That's bullshit, Kurt. Be mad at your dad. Believe me, I get it. But you are not *that* asshole. You *wanted* Fernando to win that money. And the way you were with Piper—at least until that kiss. The way you defend her. I see it. You're a good guy, and I'm telling you: You are *not* turning into another fucking Belford bigot, you understand?"

He mumbled something.

"Tell me you understand!"

"I'm telling you—" He faced me, his brow and cheeks sweaty, gone a curious shade of green. "I need a bucket."

"A bucket? Oh, Christ. Outside, quick!" I reached for his arm and dragged him up and out the back door as he put a hand over his mouth. He got down on all fours in the long grass, still ankle high. He retched. I backed off, turning away, the sour stench enveloping us. When the retching stopped, I turned back to him. He had collapsed, arms and legs crumpled at odd angles, his face in the puke.

"Kurt." I lifted his head away from the mess and rolled him over. He was out.

Fifty-Three

I hustled up the basement stairs and into the den. Dad had fallen asleep in his lounger, something he often did right after dinner. The Cubs game was just starting on TV, and a highball of Rum and Coke tipped in his hand on the armrest. Piper and Mom must have been upstairs, watching TV in my mother's room. I slipped the glass out, put it on the side table and shook his shoulder.

"Huh?" He squinted around and then at me, unfocused, groggy.

"Dad. Kurt's hurt. He needs your help."

He forced his eyes open, eyebrows lifting, trying to focus.

"What?"

"He's downstairs. He's hurt bad."

My father pushed himself up out of the chair, staggering a step. I grabbed his elbow, steadying him.

"Where is he?"

"Out back." He nodded and lurched towards the basement, teetering. In no better shape than Kurt, it seemed. He clomped down the steps, lumbering, his shoulders bumping the walls, left then right. How many had he had?

I followed him out the back door. Finding Kurt in the grass, he crouched, wobbling. He got down on his knees.

"He hit his head. In back, I think."

Dad turned Kurt's head left and right, raking his fingers through Kurt's long blond hair to feel around his scalp behind his ears.

"Helluva bump. What happened?"

I told him Kurt fell against a pool table at Rambler Lanes, and that he'd been awake a minute ago.

"Let's get him to the car."

Dad grabbed him under the arms and told me to take his legs. He shuffled backwards, looking behind him to navigate, stumbling, not enough to fall. He backed up the slope to the driveway.

"The Caddy's blocking the other cars," I said.

"Take it, then."

"The Caddy? You sure?"

"Yes! Just go! Saint Francis," Dad said, taking a breath. "You drive."

"Me?"

"I can't, Walker."

Why would he worry about AMC's stupid car restrictions in such an emergency? But then, I studied him. His heavy-lidded gaze, a momentary stagger. At least, he didn't make some macho pretense that he could drive.

While I held Kurt up, Dad opened the rear door and backed in, pulling him in as he scooted across the leather cushions. I went around and opened the driver's side door. That seat seemed as big as a cockpit, dazzling me with its busy chrome and wooden dashboard, all those strange buttons, knobs and levers, the steering wheel a hula hoop in my hands.

"Keys?" I coughed out, overwhelmed.

"In the ignition."

It started right away, that rumble, a jury of old men arguing. It took a second to figure out the transmission, the "PerNunDlerR," as Mom affectionately called it. There it was. I shifted into reverse.

When Grampa Caspar died and left Dad the car—back when he was still Colonel Maguire—he used to take us for Sunday drives. The corn carpeting the countryside around Chanute Air Base in southern Illinois was no more scenic than around Belford, but somehow riding in first class made those fields a Garden of Eden, a silky smooth cruise in cushy leather seats, all that leg room, those electric windows as magical as if they were raised and lowered by tiny fairies. The scenery didn't matter. We ruled the road.

But sitting in the driver's seat of Dad's Caddy, it was as if I'd forgotten how to drive—this yacht, this unwieldy power at my fingertips. I turned around and looked through the back window. That long, winding driveway. Dad's eyes were closed as he held Kurt's head in his lap. I relaxed. At least, there'd be no back seat driving.

Two huge elms abutted the driveway where it met the street. It was one thing to wiggle my little Datsun between them, but this was like steering the Titanic between two deadly icebergs. After shifting several times, going forward and back, turning and straightening, I squeaked out into the street. In the rear view, Dad still had his eyes closed.

Tentatively, I stepped on the gas, feeling like a five-year-old and not only because of the car. I could barely see over the steering wheel. I dropped my hand in front of the seat, searching for the adjuster.

"Two buttons," Dad said, from behind. "On the side."

Electric, of course. Like everything in this car. The seat whined, lifting me, an instant growth spurt. The length of the plum-colored hood came into view, the road in front.

"Thanks." Now that we were moving, I settled in and accelerated down the street. My question about the car resurfaced. "Did you take the Caddy out?"

"Huh?"

"The Caddy? Did you take it out?"

"Maybe."

Maybe? Dad wasn't one to be coy. Unless that was the booze.

"Needed a little air," he said, reviving. "A little scenery. To think things through."

Think what through? Our argument?

The stoplight ahead flashed from red to green. I steered left, a big turn, and straightened, heading down to the river.

"It's funny," he added, "driving this car when I'm not supposed to."

"Yeah?"

"Adds a little thrill, bumping over those country roads. Like John Dillinger in his getaway car."

I couldn't help chuckling. In the rear view, he grinned, replaying his little joyride, off in a land where Kurt's injury, our argument, work, broken lawn mowers—none of it mattered.

"Well, it is one sweet ride," I said, grinning in the mirror as I patted the steering wheel.

"That it is." He smiled back, a rare warmth filling his face. "One sweet ride."

Through the mirror, he continued grinning out the window, a desperate outlaw on the run. Catching my eye, he sobered, the smile gone.

"It's most likely a concussion," he said. "We'll have to see."

The car flattened out on the bridge as we passed the Dairy Ripple, then inclined as we headed up through the center of town. Stores were just now closing, lights blinking off, sidewalks emptying. For a while, the stoplights were green.

I pulled the car into a circular drive and up to an Emergency entrance, stopping behind an ambulance.

St. Francis. Manny was here with his wife. Their postpartum group.

It took a while to drag Kurt out, but once we did, Dad got his arm around him and hauled him up the walk and through the big double doors. I steered the Caddy around the ambulance, behind the building and parked her in the main lot, taking up two spots, away from any potential sideswipes or fender benders. Then I rushed back across the lot.

Fifty-Four

Once inside the Emergency entrance, I scanned the waiting area. Among three rows of chairs, a dark-haired woman rested her head on her knees. An anxious young couple sat with a listless toddler crumpled in the chair between them, their hands on his shoulder and head. A gray-haired Chicano in a brown suit watched me, a white hanky to his mouth, his necktie pulled loose, collar opened. He coughed into it, head jerking, his eye on me. Then I found my dad. Hawaiian shirt with pineapples, white linen pants. More the drunk than the doctor.

"How come you're out here?" I asked, rounding seats to where he sat against the wall.

"It's not an AMC situation." He leaned forward, elbows on his knees.

"Oh." I sat next to him.

"They don't like me very much here." He smiled at me. "I make the doctors nervous, looking over their shoulders."

Odd, he'd reveal this chink in his armor—the booze talking, unless he was too embarrassed about his breath and unsteady gait to be seen back there.

"So, how is he?"

"They're examining him now. The nurse said she'd give his father a call."

We sat there. With Kurt in good hands, the reason for our momentary truce was gone. A silence fell between us, heavy as poison gas, driving the good air out of the room, making it hard to breathe. I stood.

He grabbed my arm and pulled me back down into the seat. "Are you boys in some kind of trouble again?"

"No." But this was no time for lies. "Look. Kurt was shooting pool. He lost money. Wanted a rematch. The guy wouldn't do it. They tussled."

"Somebody did this to him?"

"Kurt tripped. That's all." I'd be damned if I'd implicate Fernando again.

"We'll see what the police say."

"It was an accident!"

Dad chewed on this for a few seconds.

"Is that why you were so upset this afternoon?"

"No—I was worried about Manny," I said. No way was I telling him about Piper and Kurt.

"You could have told me, you know," he began. "Sure, I might have gotten angry. Stupid stunt, being on top of a boxcar, but even more childish of you not to speak up."

I turned to him. *Stupid. Childish.* Yes, they hurt, but still—

"Are you saying you believe me now?"

"Out in the Caddy this afternoon," Dad said, "I started thinking. Maybe it was a mistake making you take this job. Hoping you could discipline yourself, prove I wasn't wasting my money on your schooling. If you could only see how uncivilized these people were, this life could be, you'd never want to end up in a place like this. You'd get your degree, learn a profession. But instead—" He gave me a glance, deciding how far to go. "It's like you've become one of them, breaking the rules. It mystifies me."

"But you believe me now. That Norm started the fight?"

"I couldn't help thinking about that time you two got arrested."

Where had this come from?

"Driving from the police station, you were shaking so much, I thought maybe the cops had done something to you. You remember?"

Sitting in that jail cell with Kurt, stripped of more than my shoe strings and belt. As if I'd ever forget that night. After being such a man only hours before, of legal age, bellying up to those Wisconsin bars, the idea of calling my father, telling him where I was and why—no wonder I was shaking.

"You cried," Dad said.

My skin prickled at the memory, going hot as if it would blister. My eyes riveted on a carpet stain as he took me back. That night I became all the awful things he'd ever said I was. A loser. A coward.

"I didn't get it," he went on, "why *you* were so shaken. And then, today, over that damned mower, you said you hadn't spoken up about witnessing the fight because you were afraid. Of me." He glanced at me, crushed disbelief settling over him like a heavy mantle, weighing him down. "That look you gave me that day on the loading dock, like the night you were arrested. I'd seen that look before. In New Guinea. During the war. When I turned that knife on that Japanese soldier. That look on his face? That's how you were, like I was about to—I'm your father, Walker. I'm not some—I don't know. Don't you see? It's my job to protect you. To take care of you. To prepare you for what you *should* be afraid of. You can't be afraid of me."

So this was my fault, being so childish and immature.

"Yes, I lose my temper." He shrugged.

"Lose your temper?" I burrowed my gaze at him. "Dad!" I shouted the word. The woman glanced at us as did the couple and the old Chicano. Even the sickly child lifted his head.

"What?" he whispered, lowering his head.

"You hit me," I hissed.

"That slap today? Come on." He chuckled, peering about the room, self-conscious—but not ashamed.

"Not only today. Many times. You even knocked me out once."

"Walker—" He squinted a warning.

"And the things you'd call me. They were just as bad."

He mulled this over, but distantly, as if these experiences were someone else's far away. The nurse who'd been watching us now focused on her desk again, writing. An orderly in blue swiveled back to the gurney he had been pushing.

"Okay, I get a little crazy when I drink—"

"Do you even remember?" I asked. For a moment, he waggled his head, his mouth open. "You don't, do you? And then, all that stuff with Piper."

"Now, with Piper—" he raised a finger.

"You always took her side."

"You hurt that girl."

"Once. By accident—" Tears formed, but I wiped them away. "I'm your child, too. Why does she mean so much more to you?"

"She doesn't."

"She does!"

"She's a girl. She's got no friends. You're always off, gallivanting around with Kurt and your girls, and she's stuck in that house all alone. And why? Because she's too good for the kids in this town. That's why. Too smart, too independent. She doesn't bow down to anybody, and because of that, she suffers."

"Like you."

He flinched, but didn't open his mouth.

"You can't see straight when it comes to her."

"It pains me to see her hurting." Dad examined his hands, running his right thumb along his left palm. He flipped his hand over, searching the other side.

"I get it. But that doesn't make it okay what you did to me."

"I'm sorry. Whatever I've done, I'm sorry."

"You're not sorry. You were so drunk half the time, you don't even remember what to be sorry for."

"What do you want me to say? I'm doing the best I can."

"I *want* you—" Wanted what? What was left worth wanting? "I want you to help Manny."

"Now *that*—" He shook his head and jabbed his index finger toward me. "Walker. We don't even know if he's legal or not."

"I'm telling you he is."

"You can't expect me to go back and tell them that, on top of all this immigration status crap, I got his workers' comp claim wrong because my son decides, days after the fact, to drop this little bombshell. Can you imagine how that will make me look? This is my job we're talking about."

"It's his job, too! He's got no income. Can't feed his family *right now.* He's taking handouts from the neighbors. He's laid up. Christ, Dad. What happened to that guy who was drummed out of the military because he wouldn't let a prisoner be tortured? Huh?"

His eyes shot to mine. "Your mother tell you that?"

"I know you'd still be in the Air Force if it weren't for that. Not in this shitty job. I know that's when you started drinking so much, started—" I couldn't say it anymore. *Biff! Pow! Whamo!* "And yet, you—what's that word you picked up in the war? Kowtow? You kowtow to them. If what they did to that Vietcong prisoner was wrong, then how can you let this happen to Manny? Why can't you be the man you were? Isn't that what you're always telling me? Be a man?!"

"Sometimes," he whispered, "it's not always clear how to be a man."

"Maybe," I said, giving him a second, a chance to breathe it in. "But at this moment, it couldn't be more clear."

He tilted his head sideways, gritting his teeth. Now he was making and unmaking his fist, the same way I did. But this was different. He wanted to launch this fist.

But I wasn't about to let this go, not when I had this chance.

"You know," I said, "Manny's here in the hospital tonight."

"Why?" He looked up at me. "Was he admitted?"

"No, though he probably should be, the shape he's in. He brought his wife in. I'm just saying, if you won't help, you should tell him. In fact—" I got up and crossed over to the reception desk, leaving Dad behind. The receptionist pushed up her glasses again as I approached and asked about the Postpartum group. I turned as the nurse explained. Dad stared my way, willing me to stop, but he didn't move. I crossed back to him.

"Room 212. They're almost done." I pointed down the hall.

"You will not shame me," he hissed, his eyes narrowing, resentment rumbling in his tone. He slapped his hands down on his thighs and pushed himself up, standing. I backed up a step.

"If you don't tell him, I will."

"Walker—" He straightened, his chest out. He glowered at me. Around the room, people were watching. Witnesses. Dad saw them, too, all the eyes on him, the old Chicano, the young couple, the child, the woman, the nurse. Then his gaze landed on someone else.

"Christ," he sighed, dropping his head.

Here was Manny now, the meeting over early. He limped past the front desk with his wife Luisa. She held his elbow with one arm and pressed the baby to her shoulder with the other.

"Go ahead," I said. "Tell him you can't do anything."

"It's not as simple as that." His jaw moved, his face distorting into a frown as he considered my ultimatum.

"Fine. I'll tell him myself."

I took a step in their direction but Dad's hand caught my arm. He pulled me down into a seat, slapping a hand hard on my shoulder.

Fifty-Five

I close my laptop. The ghosts—the dark-haired woman, the couple and their toddler, the coughing old Chicano—they're gone from this Emergency Room. The kid with the Game Boy lies curled between wooden armrests like a chick in its shell, still tapping away. His sister still sprawls over two chairs, her mouth agape.

Opening my laptop is like closing my eyes. I see the ghosts again, seeing me, watching me sit while my dad got up. As if they need to know how it ended as much as I do.

I can't do this alone. I need a fact-checker. I need Connie. It's 11:35. Her shift has started. She should be here. I get up and retrace my steps through the maze back to Maternity.

But it's a new nurse behind the reception desk, head down, scribbling. Not Connie.

"Can I help you?" She pushes up her bifocals. I lean against the counter, laptop under my arm.

"Connie Cam—What's her name? Wheeler? Isn't she supposed to be on duty?"

"Yes, actually," the woman sighs, a little put out. "But with this storm, I guess she couldn't make it in."

"She didn't call?"

"Some of the phone lines are down. She may have tried, but—" The nurse shrugs.

"I see. Thanks."

I push through the double doors into the long hall, a bank of windows down one side, the wind creaking them in their frames. Falling snow brightens the night, flakes ticking off the glass even as the streetlights dim into cotton ball blurs atop their poles.

A side door marked “Emergency Only” is ajar, a frigid breeze leaking in. Standing out on a metal fire escape, a young orderly in green scrubs lights a cigarette, the smoke swirling into the snow. I poke my head out, take a deep breath, the cold air as bracing as a Jim Beam on the rocks. I could use one.

It used to be beer, then it was wine for a while, then harder stuff—vodka, tequila, bourbon, but never rum. I cultivated my drinking. I knew it could get out of hand. Thanks to my father—Frazier, too. He’d probably still be married if it weren’t a problem for him. It was for me, too, what with all the deadlines, the unrelenting demand for copy, the personnel cutbacks increasing my workload. It took editors complaining about my work, dull stories, flat writing, before I straightened out, pruning the ever-present need down to its ineradicable roots, that craving always under the surface. I might not have been so hard on my drunken dad in that waiting room if I’d known the disease like he did, known then how much I’d give for one shot of JB now.

The orderly nods at me and takes a puff. It smells good.

Not much happening out there, only the white wind whooshing up over the top of the building. No cars move in the main lot. In a far corner, snow is piled high and wide enough to bury the Caddy I had parked right there that summer night.

The orderly drops his cigarette and twists his foot on it.

“Can I bum one?”

“Sure, bud.” He grabs the pack from a chest pocket and shakes one up. “Need a light?”

I nod and he lights it.

My first job out of college, cub reporter for the wire service, was the last time I lit up, going on thirty years ago. Spiraled up to two packs a day, but I quit after a bout of pneumonia. Cold turkey. Like Dad did when the Surgeon General’s report came out. Funny, how much harder it is to stop drinking than smoking, how that hunger lingers longer.

Strange, how scents bring stuff back: chicken and dumplings, my mother in the kitchen; gasoline, my dad over the old John Deere. And yes, this cigarette takes me back, too. The loading dock. The basement. Rambler Lanes. Cruising with Kurt.

Strawberries and cinnamon: Connie, always Connie.

I murmur a thanks to the orderly as he squeezes by. He nods back, leaving the door open, the fire escape all mine for the moment.

Fifty-Six

I never met Connie's mother. I only saw her those two times at the hospital, next to Manny's bed right after the fight, and that night talking to my dad in the ER. She gave me such a hooded glare from those dark, tired eyes. I remember how she cupped her hand over her infant daughter's head and hid the little one's face against her shoulder, as if my dad might do the baby as much harm as he had done her husband.

My father made me hang back across the waiting room so he could talk to them himself. The encounter was full of hushed whispers, less like he was offering help than that he was seeking it. *You have to understand!* He looked my way once, and Manny saw me. At the end of it, Manny took my father's hand in both of his, shaking it. Then, he gave me a grateful nod. Dad held him a moment longer as if warning him. *Don't thank me yet.*

Returning, Dad sat next to me and grumbled how appeals took time, he couldn't make any promises, there was a process, tests Manny had to take, his legal status to be confirmed, doctor's notes he had to gather. It had to be done by the book. He wouldn't look at me, pissed that I'd twisted his arm. Meanwhile, Manny and Luisa shuffled off down the hallway and out the door.

"But you agreed to help, right?"

"I'll do what I can."

On the way back home from the hospital, Dad drove, sober now. I asked what I'd have to do—testify? Talk to management? He said a written statement would do. It seemed too easy. Still, when we got home, I grabbed a piece of his stationary and sat down at the dinner table to write something out. Dad headed for the stairs.

"Don't you want to read it?" I asked.

"I'm tired, Walker. Can't it wait until tomorrow?"

"I'd like to do it now," I said. "What do I need to say?"

"Just write what happened." He went into the kitchen.

I documented everything I could remember from that afternoon, where I was, what I saw. Felt more like a confession. There wasn't much to tell. Dad came out, eating a banana. With one hand, he read my statement, holding the peeled fruit in the other hand.

"They're going to ask why you waited so long."

I took back the paper, and as he finished his fruit, I added a couple of sentences and handed it back.

Dad read it out loud: "'I'm sorry I waited to speak up, but I feared losing my job for being in an unauthorized area. Lately, I've come to realize that the truth, and defending this man's innocence, are more important than my job.'"

He read it over again.

"Okay," Dad said, folding it in half. "There's a personnel meeting tomorrow. I can present it then." He bent the sheet in half and creased it. "I'll let you know how it goes tomorrow night."

"Shouldn't you sign it?" I asked. "As a witness?"

He opened it again, scanning it. Finally, he took up the pen and wrote, 'Witnessed by Dr. Michael Maguire,' adding the date below.

"Great. Thanks, Dad."

"Hmm." He nodded at me, an exhausted droop in his shoulders. "I'm going to bed."

"I mean that. Thanks for believing me."

He shrugged, folding the sheet in quarters. "Yeah, well. We'll see how this goes," he said without enthusiasm as he headed down the hall towards the stairs. As if he'd signed away something he'd never get back.

Fifty-Seven

Having slept fitfully that night—I was so wired from the day's activities—I spent the following day sleepwalking a thousand or so fuel tanks fifty feet from a big train car to small ones. After work, it was all I could do to keep my eyes open waiting on the couch for my father to get home. Meanwhile, Piper paced around the den, wringing her hands in worry, tears welling in her eyes. I had just told her Kurt was in the hospital with a skull fracture.

"Don't let Mom or Dad see you acting like this," I said, peeking into the hall. Mom was banging around in the kitchen, preparing a pot roast. Piper insisted on hearing what happened, so I explained about the pool hall, how Kurt fell, leaving out the part about Fernando shoving him. If nothing else, the way she carried on—the worry in her voice, insisting this was her fault, kissing him like that, making him act crazy—confirmed she'd started it, just as Kurt claimed.

When Dad's car pulled into the driveway, I told her to go wash her face.

"One look at you and Dad will know something weird's going on."

She whimpered an "okay" and headed upstairs. I stood, waiting for him. When Dad came in, he held his hand out, pumping down the air between us, trying to quash my eagerness.

"Let me clean up. Then we can talk."

After he had his shower, he came down and mixed a drink at the liquor cabinet while I watched. He motioned for me to follow him into the kitchen. Mom was about to put dinner on the table when Dad told her he needed ten minutes to talk to me.

"What's so important it can't wait?" she said, the roast weighing her down, as if the platter had gained ten pounds.

Dad waved her off and headed down the back stairs. The grass on the plateau seemed wild and unruly now, dotted with yellow dandelion flowers and white seed balls. Dad didn't say a word about the overgrown lawn as he sat in one of the two Adirondack chairs. Instead, he gazed down the hill toward the river, across to the Foundry, the late afternoon sun still above its smokestacks, making him squint.

"So?" I said, leaning forward, elbows on my knees. "What happened?"

He took a long sip from his highball, ice cubes clunking against the glass, and leaned his head against the fan of the chair back. He scanned the vista below us, hazy in the humid air, looking for something.

"This personnel meeting I went to—always the same managers and union stewards, like teachers squabbling with parents over whether to expel their kids for bad behavior. They don't have the medical expertise to interfere in my worker's comp decisions, thank God, but this is different. This is about who started that fight and why, and whether Manny is here legally or not. The appeal will go to this committee. So—" He leaned back again, taking a big breath.

"What do you mean, it *will* go? I thought you were submitting it today."

"Manny's name came up before I had a chance."

"Came up how?"

"This VP from HR brought up a report from Manny's foreman, about his return to work last week, how his wallet magically reappeared—" He gave me a glance. "How he refused to surrender his green card. The VP said it only confirmed that, on top of the trouble Manny caused—"

I open my mouth to object.

"They think he caused," he corrected. "It pointed to Manny being an illegal. So this VP had asked our lawyers in Detroit to see what they could dig up about him, and they found something."

"Christ."

"It turns out he got his green card years ago by marrying a California woman he divorced soon after."

His second wife! The woman he met at the *braceros* camp.

"It's a common scam, Walker. Pay a US citizen to marry you, do the minimum to look happily hitched for a while, get your green card, get divorced. Happens all the time."

"That doesn't mean *his* marriage wasn't real."

"No, it doesn't. In fact, the INS already renewed his card once—'66, I think it was. But then, they don't have pockets deep enough to dig into these things. AMC does, and if they could prove he's illegal, they could fire him."

It's complicated, Manny had said.

"That started this debate, whether it's *cost effective*—" he rolled his eyes—"to hire an investigator, find this 'citizen' Manny was married to, etcetera, etcetera, just to get rid of one undocumented troublemaker—their words, not mine."

Citizen. Like helping people get green cards made her a monster.

"But he wasn't the troublemaker."

"I know. And the steward agrees with you. There seems to be an argument within the union as to whether he's being denied his promotion—and maybe even his job—unfairly. AMC doesn't want to cause trouble with the union, and an investigation would be costly, so as things stand now, they'll probably leave things as they are."

"But 'things as they are' suck!" He gave me a sharp look. "He deserves sick pay. My statement proves he's innocent, so he should get it."

"But does it?" His eyes bored into mine.

"What?"

"That wallet. Imagine the raised eyebrows in that room when the VP said *my son* told Kelly he'd found the wallet the day before, long after security had thoroughly searched the area. You told *me* you found the wallet right after the fight."

Fuck! Another lie!

"I did! But I couldn't tell Kelly that. It would have sounded weird, me holding onto it all that time. That's why I didn't mention it in my statement."

"So if they ask, you want me to lie, too?"

"You know why I lied!" I glared at him, before pushing back in my chair, gripping the arm rests. I felt his hand on mine, stopping that clenching thing I did. I jerked my hand away.

"Okay, okay." He held up his hand, placating. "But you also didn't trust Kelly to give him the wallet, and then you asked to switch jobs with Camarasa."

"Those fuel tanks were killing him."

"Yes, but, you have to know how that looks. And there I am—your father—about to make it look worse. It's weeks after the fight, and my son—who now seems to be Manny's good friend—is suddenly claiming he saw Norm start the fight, so we need to let Manny collect maybe thousands of AMC's dollars in worker's comp? They'll think he's conning you, and possibly me. They're sure to investigate him."

I imagined the Camarasas, scraping by, giving up their home.

"Maybe he has nothing to lose."

"But *I do!*" He stared at me, willing me to understand. "My job."

"Come on, Dad. This isn't about you."

"Isn't it!?" He glared at me, jaw set just so. I held his gaze. "It'll be the Air Force all over again," he grumbled. "You raise doubts about your loyalty, your commitment—" He turned to me. "AMC's already hounding me over all the worker's comp I approve. All that money I'm costing them. And it'll only get worse. There's already talk about hiring a consultant to 'help me out.' Right. Look over my shoulder. Question everything I do. I know how this works. They'll make my life so miserable—"

"That's what they are trying to do to Manny," I whispered.

He blinked at me, not comprehending, so I explained how Kelly told me they wouldn't have to fire Manny, how they'd make him quit. Instead of the forklift, they put him on fuel tanks without the help of his meat hook.

"That's why I tried to switch jobs. They're trying to break him. It's why I don't trust Kelly."

Dad sat back, stumped for the moment.

"That's how they work," he mumbled. "They ignore me when I advise them to move people to safer jobs—take Norm off the loading dock."

"They put him on the forklift."

"Well, thank God for small favors."

"Manny's forklift."

He exhaled, tossing up his hands, helpless.

"Look Dad, there's no proof Manny's an illegal. His green card's the real thing. And now his whole family's suffering because nobody knows what I saw. People need to be told."

Dad kept shaking his head.

"Well, if you're not going to do anything—" I started to get up. Manny had been so thankful, the way he shook my dad's hand in both of his, so hopeful. I straightened, looking out over the river. "I guess I need to tell him, then."

"Don't do that."

"Why?"

He stood, pulling his pants up, shoving his hands into his pockets.

"At this point, the best thing you can do for him—and me—is stay away. I'm supposed to be impartial when making these decisions, and right now I look anything but—"

"But you'll tell them? What I saw? Give them that testimony I wrote out?"

"I need to think it over. And you do, too. Consider the consequences. Is it worth it? For him? For me?"

"Dad. They're eating carp."

"Carp?"

"Out of this river." Maybe that made it sound worse than it was, but it would certainly sharpen the point. "Because they can't afford hamburger."

"Okay, okay. I get it." He nodded toward the house. "Speaking of food—" A bit sheepish, now. "We all have to eat."

He headed for the back steps. But I'd lost my appetite again.

Fifty-Eight

Dad was unusually quiet at dinner, as if he wanted me to sit there considering my position while I enjoyed the sumptuous meal of pot roast, mashed potatoes and green beans Mom had prepared. Instead, I did what Piper usually did, pushing the food around my plate, making it look as if I were eating.

What were my choices? If Dad said nothing, Manny wouldn't get investigated—and possibly deported—but he and his whole family would go on suffering. If Dad *did* tell my story? Told the truth? Then, they probably *would* investigate, and who knew what they'd find? Was Manny's second marriage legal or not? Was he legal or not? I wasn't so sure after hearing Manny's tepid "*I* think I am" when I asked him point blank. Maybe *he* believed it, but clearly he wasn't sure what other people might think.

It was also possible my father was bullshitting me, as if a Fortune 500 automobile company would pay to investigate one dock worker's marriage history, when the worst outcome for AMC was paying out a little worker's comp. Big deal. And keeping Manny around, of course. That bad influence.

But what if Dad was right? What if they went after him the same way they were going after Manny? All because of me. Fuck.

And what about Connie? Dad didn't even know about her, how I felt about her, how failing her would fuck me up.

Fuck, fuck, fuck.

That night, Piper held it together during our later-than-usual dinner, but afterwards, she followed me down into the basement so she could continue fretting over Kurt. Christ, she had it bad for that boy.

I kept promising her he'd be all right, we'd go see him in the hospital as soon as visitors were allowed, but she wouldn't stop whimpering, and I couldn't let her be around Dad in this upset state, so I put on some music and we listened for awhile until there was a knock on the back door.

"Why don't you go upstairs," I told Piper as I jumped up, my heart pounding.

"It's not that girl, is it?"

Another knock. If I didn't answer it, she might run off again. Piper watched from the rec room as I opened the door.

I hardly registered it was Connie before her arms were around my neck and we were cheek to cheek. She hugged me—some totally dazed and astonished version of me, anyway. Then she held me out.

"You did it!" she exclaimed, the biggest smile I'd ever seen on her lovely face. Another hug, tighter this time.

"Shhh." I whispered, thrilled. Her warm cheek on mine. Her arms encasing me.

"Your father's going to help," she whispered, breathily. "*Papá* told me what he said at the hospital. I can't believe it." She kissed me so hard, her body against mine, that my concerns about Piper's presence vanished. Her breath was spiced with, what was that? Plantains? Strawberries? Or was that the delicious smell of her hair, her skin? Everything, so much sweeter than I expected.

"Walker?" From the other room. Connie stiffened.

I held her out by the shoulders. "Would you like to meet my sister?"

"You sure she won't kill me?"

"Come on." I took her by the hand and led her into the rec room. I made the awkward introductions, Connie, her dark hair in a ponytail, a head taller than red-haired Piper. Both girls had trouble making eye contact, their discomfort with one another squeezing the air out of the room.

"Sorry if I caused trouble for you," Connie said.

Piper shrugged. "It's okay. You didn't know."

Didn't know *what*? I wanted to ask, but now wasn't the time.

"Could you maybe go upstairs?" I asked my sister.

"All right," she exhaled, exiled again.

"And Piper. You don't need to tell Dad or Mom who's here, okay?"

She considered me a second. "I'll keep your secret if you keep mine." She glanced at Connie and cocked her head at me, challenging.

Her and Kurt? Such a deal required negotiation, stipulations clearly spelled out, but there was no time for that.

"Fine." I cringed at what I was agreeing to. "Just go, please."

She nodded and disappeared up the back stairs.

"Your parents don't know about them?" Connie said.

"Oh, hell no. Piper and Kurt? If my dad found out...."

"And—" Connie turned and appraised me, uncertainly. "You don't want them to know about me."

I took a breath, but not for the reason Connie seemed to suspect, the frown forming on her face as I considered how to address this.

"Of course, I do," I said, at last. "But, you can guess what he's like. I need to go slow with them."

Slow? I could break this to them slow as a glacier migrates, and that might still be too much of a joy ride.

"Sure." She shrugged, sitting up straight. "It's no big deal. I mean, I only came over to thank you. In fact—" she turned towards the door— "they don't ever need to know."

"Come on, Connie." I said, shaking her hand. God, I was holding her hand! "Let's talk outside, okay?"

Why had I ever thought it was a good idea to have her come here, especially if Dad came prancing downstairs to tackle one of his furniture reclamation projects in his workshop?

"Sure," Connie said, suddenly tight again. "Right. Outside."

When we got to the plateau, she caught me looking up at the house, checking the dining room windows.

"Afraid he'll see?"

I pulled her down the hill, behind the cherry trees.

"Look. If anyone at AMC, my father included, knew that you and I were—whatever we are, they'd never help Manny."

"Why?"

"Because they'd think my dad was playing favorites, helping Manny for my sake. For your sake."

"Oh," she said, thoughtful.

"Now, listen. I have to ask you something."

"What?"

"Manny's second wife. AMC knows that's how he got his green card, marrying her. Was it a real marriage?"

Connie straightened, backing up a step, as if the air had been knocked out of her.

"Because they might investigate," I added. "Or, my dad might be fucking with me because he's paranoid about losing his job."

"What?"

"What I'm saying is if we appeal, and they investigate, will Manny be all right, do you think? Because he could be deported."

"I don't know. He never talks about her. What's a real marriage, anyway?"

"Beats me. How long were they together?"

"A year maybe? Is that real enough?"

I shrugged, raising my hands. "Well, should I have my dad appeal or not?"

She took a couple of big breaths, considering, looking this way and that before settling her eyes on me, again.

"If I went home right now and asked him if he was here legally, he'd say, '*¡Claro que sí! Cómo chingados puedes preguntar eso?*' " I shook my head, not understanding.

"'Yes, of course,' he'd say. 'How can you ask that?'" So, it has to be yes, even if they do investigate."

"I think so, too. That's the Manny I know." I shook her hand. "So we should go ahead then? Have my dad submit the appeal?"

"Walker. I just wangled a job scooping ice cream at the Dairy Ripple. Minimum wage. That's all the money we'll have coming in until my nurses' aide job starts in the fall or *Papá* can work again. Make the appeal. We need it."

"Okay, then."

"So, he'll do it?"

Connie's face filled with so much hope, it overflowed onto me. "I think so."

"Good." She closed her eyes and took my hand in both of hers, holding it to her chest. As if it was all over and not just beginning.

"But he can't know about you—about, you know, us," I added, squeezing her hand. I searched her face. She bit her lip.

"What's to know, anyway?" She gave me a grin that became a grimace. Was that a question? A test?

I answered, kissing her again, my hands on her cheeks. She turned as red as the few overripe cherries that still clung to the nearby tree, but she smiled, gladdened, then pulled me into a hug.

"Can I see you again?" I asked.

"I don't know when I'll have time. I'll be working weekday nights now, and candy striping on the weekends. In fact, I told *Papá* I was only going out for a quick boat ride. I need to get back."

"Would he mind? Me and you?"

"I don't think so. For some crazy reason, he seems to like you." She squeezed my hand again, smiling. "My first day off is a week from now. Maybe you can come over."

"I don't know if I should chance it, being seen there. Not while this appeal is going on. But we could meet here. Down on my dock."

"I guess. But it'll be different, after this is over, right?"

"Of course! We'll go places. Do things. I'll introduce you to my parents. And in the meantime, maybe we can still go out in the boat. Walk along the river." I looked around. I pointed. "Snack on those strawberries you seem to like so much."

She punched my arm.

We walked down to the river holding hands. I kissed her once more before putting her back in her boat. As her little boat putt-putted back across the river, she waved good night, and I marveled again to see that smile after I'd thought it was lost to me for good.

At the time, I lamented. The dock, the riverside, that's all we would have until the legal wrangling was finished. I didn't know that we'd just had all we'd ever have.

When I got back to the house, I caught my dad as he started up the stairs for bed. "I've been thinking," I said. "Manny believes he's here legally. He told me as much. And if appealing means they have to investigate, he'd say, 'go right ahead.' So, will you do it?"

He sighed, tapping the bannister again. "It may take a while. Depends on how deep they have to go. How much investigating they're willing to do."

Was that a "yes," or was he stalling?

"But you'll do whatever it takes, right?"

"It's not up to me, Walker," he admonished me, "but I'll do what I can." He turned and climbed the stairs.

The next day, Kurt was cleared to see visitors, so I told my parents Piper and I were going to visit him after dinner. On the drive over, I explained to my sister that, just because we had this pact to keep each other's relationships a secret, it didn't mean she could keep fooling around with Kurt.

"I've learned my lesson," she said. "We'll only be friends."

But "only friends" was not how they looked, the way she snuggled next to him on the bed, nesting between IV drip lines and EKG wires, so they could read a magazine together. He lifted the bandage so she could see where they operated on his head, drilling a hole to reduce the swelling, and he looked proud of it, as if he should get a purple heart or something. I didn't stick around to watch the two of them. Whatever I'd agreed to, I didn't want to see it panning out in front of me. Anyway, for me, visiting Kurt was a ruse to keep my dad in the dark. My real plan for the evening involved purchasing some sweet, sweet ice cream.

Fifty-Nine

I was uncomfortable standing in that long line. Up ahead, Connie took orders and rushed around the little stand, concocting elaborate sundaes and floats, holding sugar cones under the soft serve machine. Only now did I understand how other people saw her. Like the other two teenage girls on display in there, she was clearly hired for and dressed to emphasize her good looks, her ponytail revealing the nape of her neck, that tight, white "Dairy Ripple"-stamped t-shirt highlighting her figure. Despite fans blowing from every corner, it was hot in there. The small place was encased in glass on all four sides like a zoo exhibit, but Connie's perspiration didn't dampen her appeal. The light wash that had filmed on her chin, upper lip and forehead, glinted red and blue in the light of the drive-in's neon signs. If I was ogling her, I wasn't the only one. Maybe the other men and teenage boys in line were seeing and thinking the same thing. Maybe I was no better than them.

The first night she saw me, four customers up the line, she smiled until it was my turn at her window.

"Can I buy the server a treat?" I asked, leaning in.

"That's nice of you," she whispered, "but my boss said I'm here to take orders, not make conversation." She glanced behind at the old guy at the grill eyeing us. She spoke up again. "What can I help you with, sir?"

As the old guy slapped a hot dog into a bun, squinting at me with suspicion, Connie twisted soft-serve chocolate into a cup. When she returned with it, I leaned in and asked if I could give her a ride home when her shift was over.

"No, Walker," she hissed, taking my money. "You're the one who said we can't risk being seen together, right?"

I exhaled a frustrated "Yes, I know."

"I'll see you on my day off."

Even though she couldn't talk, I came every night. I'd stand in line to get my ice cream, give her my order, then sit in my car, all the while observing how, through those big windows, she busied herself behind that counter. Those moments might have tided me over until our date on the dock had it not been for how Connie's smile seemed to wane from one night to the next. By Friday night, she treated me like any other customer, barely acknowledging me when I got to the head of the line. I asked her what was wrong, but she shook me off, went to the machine and watched it twirl out my ice cream, avoiding my gaze. She exchanged it for my money and asked the guy behind me what he wanted, ignoring me for the few seconds I remained there, paralyzed by puzzlement. I wanted to bark out her name, make her acknowledge me, but I couldn't make a scene. We were pretending to be strangers, after all. No one could know about us. So I sat in my car, baffled. She went on serving customers, pinballing around the glassed-in building, the customer lines growing and shrinking. My ice cream, on the seat beside me, melted in its cup.

Were the demands of the job getting her down, all those hours on her feet, the insinuating stares from the boys and men? She had to be tired, all the work she was doing, here and at home. Unless the truth was we really were strangers. If only I could talk to her and find out what was going on. But Connie would be candy-striping at the hospital that entire weekend, and there was no way to reach her.

The night of our date, I showered, dressed in a clean, soft-collared golf shirt and waited by the dock in the early evening, looking out over the river at her house. As the top of the hour approached and passed, her dock remained empty. Nobody came out of the house. At work that day, I had thought of little else but her, the way she'd snubbed me at the ice cream counter. What had gone wrong? Those worries flowed back as, one by one, the Foundry's flood lights blinked on and the moon rose above the darkening willow trees. Across the water, I could just make out her tiny boat bobbing against its pylons.

Okay, she was late. But maybe it had nothing to do with those fading smiles. She wouldn't blow me off, not after how she'd thanked me the week before, that hug, those kisses. Maybe I'd misunderstood her. We were to meet on *her* dock—not mine. If only I could call her to clear this up.

I climbed into the runabout, started the Evinrude, too loud for this middling-sized river, especially at night. I steered upstream and across, the water lower and slower now that the incessant rains had stopped. The lights in Manny's house reflected on the water, undulating languidly in the calm currents. I tied up next to Connie's dinghy, surprised that my noisy Evinrude hadn't brought her out to greet me. I walked the creaking planks up to her back door and knocked.

She came to the door in a wrinkled t-shirt and jeans. Her arms were folded, her mouth twisted into a frown, her jaw working. No, she hadn't forgotten.

"What's wrong? I thought you were meeting me?"

"Someone from Immigration Services came to our house."

"Okay." That explained it. "So, they are investigating, then."

She nodded.

"Come outside. Let's talk about it."

She didn't open the door. She stood there, frowning at me, breathing heavily behind the screen. And then she spoke, haltingly at first.

"My father has this shoebox with that marriage certificate, some pictures. He kept saying, 'I don't know why they need to see this again. I'm legal. It's all here.' But they took his papers, saying they needed to authenticate them. He's been fuming ever since."

"But at least it means they're working on it."

"Does it? Or does it mean they're trying to get rid of us?"

Rather than look at me, she focused on the mesh of the screen, her troubled gaze burning a hole.

"We knew this wouldn't be easy. But we're good, aren't we? The truth will come out, and everything will be cool, right?"

She breathed hard, puffs of air hitting the screen.

"I'm sure it will all get fixed," I continued. "But it'll take time. And while were waiting, there's no reason you and I can't—"

"Yes, there is!"

"What?"

"Don't you see?" Her eyes found mine. "Nothing has changed. Nobody's ever going to believe my father. And I won't sneak around with you, acting as if everything's fine, like it'll all work out when it won't. We don't stand a chance, and it's crazy to pretend we do."

She turned and walked back up the hall. I called after her, but she disappeared into the living room. All I could hear was tinny, canned laughter coming from their little television.

Sixty

When I got home, my father was still up watching TV. I was so agitated by my talk with Connie—by her unwillingness to see me, like it was all my fault—I couldn't help telling him where I'd been, asking why the INS was visiting the Camerasas.

"I told you not to go over there!" he said, shaking his newspaper in half.

"I only wanted to see how they were doing."

"Well, now you know. Didn't I say they might investigate him? Nothing can happen with the appeal until that part's over. You just better pray you're right about Manny's second marriage."

"But you submitted my statement, right? Once the investigation is over, they'll consider his appeal."

"Yes, of course." He bristled, patience thinning. "You think they'd be going to all this trouble otherwise?"

But it made me wonder. Did Connie know better than I did? Maybe, AMC had sicced the INS on Manny just to get rid of him. Hell, knowing my dad's "fondness" for the Mexicans across the river, he could have tossed my statement in the trash and called the INS himself. I had no way of knowing.

At work the next day, fuel tanks and the White Sox game couldn't distract me from my worries over the delay, the wedge it had driven between Connie and me. I pondered it constantly, wondering what to do. I didn't know what my dad had told the company, so I concocted a plan to find out.

Careful not to be seen by my father in the administration wing, I snuck into the Personnel Office at lunchtime and was given a quickie appointment with one of the officers. He was a balding, thick-set, middle-aged man in a dark suit named Richmond who, despite the name I gave him, didn't seem to know who I was. In fact, he hardly acknowledged my presence, busy as he was shuffling papers on his desk, signing one and then another. I complained about being stuck in one job after I'd been told I'd have different jobs every two weeks, that I was a summer replacement and not in the union, so they couldn't help me.

"I work in receiving, unloading fuel tanks. Manny Camerasa's job?" I added.

He stopped shuffling and, clutching papers in both hands, gave me a look.

"You know what happened with him, right? The fight?"

I nodded again. He put down the papers and regarded me more closely.

"What did you say your name was?"

I told him.

"Doc's son."

Another nod. He considered me a second. Was he pondering what he knew about Manny's situation—about my statement—or my complaint?

With a sigh, he picked up his papers and, scanning them, started to explain how assignments change sometimes, how employees are expected to be flexible. He stopped and said, "You know, I can't send you somewhere else just because you're the doctor's kid."

"I'm not asking for that. I just wanted to know if Manny was coming back."

"I don't know." He flipped a paper, front then back, scanning it. "He's out on unpaid leave."

I seized on that word. "Unpaid? Isn't he getting worker's comp?"

Richmond put down the papers and glared at me. "That's between Camarasa and the company."

"I mean, I know he got hurt. I was just curious." I raised my shoulders, my hands, protesting his challenge.

"And what do they say about curiosity?"

"It's not a big deal," I said, backtracking, rising from my chair. "It's just that those fuel tanks are kinda hard on my back."

"Then maybe you should see your father about that," Richmond said. "And about Manny Camarasa, mind your own business."

"Yes. Of course." I backed out of the room. "Thanks for your help."

I cursed myself all the way back to the loading dock. That certainly hadn't gone as planned—and I knew no more now than I had before.

I dreaded what my father would say when he got home that night, certain he'd have heard all about my meeting with Richmond. He had.

"What the hell were you thinking?" he said, as soon as he got in the door. He stood over me while I shrank into the couch. "I expressly told you to distance yourself from this thing, and yet you go and act like a damned fool in front of that personnel officer. 'Why's your son so curious about this case?' I said you worked with the guy. That it was nothing. I'm still not sure he bought it." He points at me. "So I'm telling you, stop sticking your nose where it doesn't belong or your friend is screwed—and so am I."

"Okay. I'm sorry." I tried to apologize, and explained that I was just frustrated I knew so little about what was going on.

"They're investigating. That's all I know. Have a little patience, for Christ's sake."

Sixty-One

Norm operated the forklift for a month before he backed it into a twenty-foot tower of metal bins one day. The tower toppled over onto a tugger train, a tremendous crash that brought everyone running. He would have killed the driver, had there been one. As it was, the engine was crushed, as were two of its wagons. Nobody got hurt, but surrounding the wreckage, tens of thousands of small parts had spilled out of the bins and scattered as evenly over the concrete floor as grass around a pitcher's mound.

As Kelly barked orders, we gathered around the mess, uprighting bins, down on our hands and knees—Kelly, too—frantically sweeping screws, bolts, nuts and fasteners into piles. Some guys sorted and separated, item by item, which made Kelly furious. He told the idiots to dump them all in one bin and get the floor cleaned up so traffic could flow and we could get back to work. But it was taking forever. The dock was at a standstill, and tugger trains were backed up all the way out the door to the trim line.

That's when the horn blew, the red button, blasting, again and again, as if shutting down the lines might be as disastrous as the tornado its keening whine seemed to warn of. Everyone on the dock stopped and waited. The whole place hushed, siren echoes dissipating until the only discernible sound was the slurred voice of Norm Ditweiler as he wandered around in circles, appealing to anyone who might listen. "I didn't see it. I just didn't see it."

Soon enough, Norm's excuses were swallowed by an influx of idled line workers, hundreds of them joining the battle, grumbling at the interruption, laughing at the sight. Dumb-ass dockworkers. Kelly's face went crimson as an exasperated line supervisor dutifully bawled him out. While a small army of line workers converged upon the mangled Tugger train and manhandled it out of the way, others teamed up with those of us on our knees, sweeping up and dumping the small parts. Like a swarm of locusts in a field of corn, they rapidly swept the area clean. Soon, the assembly lines were up and running again, and Kelly had hauled Norm into his office and slammed the door. When you dam a river of money for even a few minutes, somebody has to pay.

Everyone stopped to watch how Kelly escorted Norm off the dock, walking ahead, waiting, impatient with the man's labored, limping progress. Later, Kelly confirmed what we already knew—alcohol was found on Norm's breath. This time he was not given a second chance.

I spent the better part of July and August in a corner of the loading dock, surrounded by metal bins, sorting out the muddle Norm had created—screws in this bin, bolts in a second, nuts in a third, fasteners in a fourth.

Sixty-Two

Despite Connie's despairing conviction about how things stood, I continued to stop at the Dairy Ripple right up until a few days before school started again. It only made her more impatient with me—and unresponsive, to the point where she didn't even ask for my order when I reached the front of the line. She'd see me, pour ice cream into a cup, put it on the counter and hold out her hand.

"It takes time," I'd say, paying her—a broken record, so broken I wasn't sure I believed it myself anymore. "It'll work out. You have to believe me."

"Seeing is believing," she said a few nights before I had to leave.

"Look, I have to go back to school in a few days." I passed her a slip of paper. "Here's my phone number at school." I pointed at the phone booth at the corner of the parking lot. "I want you to call me. Call me collect. I'll accept the charges."

"Why should I?"

Of course, I just wanted to hear from her, stay connected somehow, but I couldn't say that.

"I'll be talking with my dad. I'll know what's going on with the appeal. You'll want to know, won't you?"

She shrugged and took the paper. "I guess."

"Call me, say, every Sunday night. After work. I'll make sure I'm around, okay?"

She shrugged again. "You better go now or the boss'll get mad." She nodded at the old man, always eyeing us.

"Please, Connie. Be patient. It'll all work out. I promise."

She looked away. "Go. I have to work."

It was the last time I stopped in to see her. I couldn't continue to show up, night after night, my hand out, wanting, when she had nothing to give but ice cream.

As it turned out, it was the last time I would see her—until thirty years had passed.

Sixty-Three

One thing gave me a slim hope that my father might honor his promise to the Camarasas: he did honor our college tuition deal, paying his half when I paid mine. After I returned to school, I called my dad every week for updates, and every week he said the same thing. The investigation was stalled. The INS was still searching for Manny's second wife.

It was a tough start to the semester. I tried to focus on the sleep-inducing micro-bio and bio-chem classes I'd enrolled in, then distracted myself with lectures and movies, got high with Ed Granger, entered billiards tournaments at the Student Center. But my life revolved around another weekly phone call: Sunday night's when Connie called collect. I'd wonder for days beforehand what I could possibly say when my Dad was providing no new information about the appeal. I'd thrill at her voice, always so feverish with hope as soon as I answered.

"Walker? Have you heard anything?"

For days afterwards, I'd regret my empty promises, the small talk I'd made. Getting her to talk about the nurse's aide program she'd started didn't help, hearing the dismissiveness in her voice over the minimum-wage, menial tasks she was doing when she should have been taking classes, studying to be a nurse. As I blathered away, making excuses, her hope, always so keen at first—as if she really wanted to hear my voice, as if she cared about us—would fade away, like trees into darkness at dusk. She kept telling me she wasn't going to call anymore if I didn't have any news, and I'd always promise something was sure to happen soon. The weekly prospect of hearing her voice got me up in the morning, made me go to class and pretend I could keep up with my college charade.

Those first two months of school, I kept running into Capricia—in the cafeteria, at lectures, at readings. Or rather, she'd run into me, saying "Hi," bright-eyed, asking me how I was doing, how my classes were going. Sure, she was brilliant and captivating, but she wasn't Connie. One night, I bumped into Capricia at the campus theater, and she sat with me during the movie. Afterwards, she asked if I wanted to get a drink. I finally got it.

"I can't," I said. "I've got a girlfriend back home."

I saw Capricia many times after that. At bars, in lecture halls, across the room, but we never "bumped into" each other again.

Meanwhile, my father kept saying they were still investigating. The second Sunday in November, I waited by my phone as usual, dreading what I would say to Connie this time when she called. The phone always rang around nine, but that night the call never came. Nor did it come the following Sunday—or any other Sunday afterwards.

Over the years, I seldom came back to Belford because of what happened—or what I thought happened—the Thanksgiving after that summer job.

Ten minutes into my return home, my coat hung up in the closet, my duffel bag dumped in my room, I seated myself on the edge of the couch next to Dad's Barcalounger and asked him about Manny's appeal. He trained his eyes on the TV news and said, "It's all taken care of," like it was no big deal, a light bulb he'd changed, a doorknob fixed.

"Really?" Such a turnaround. "So they must have found Manny's ex-wife, then. Confirmed the marriage. Everything?"

He shrugged, still eyeing the TV. "I don't know about that, but I know he got his money." No big deal. All in a day's work. So nonchalant, I might have misheard him. "He's all set."

"Wow," I said, standing, a big breath. "So tell me what you do know. Was it a big tussle?"

Dad closed his eyes, gearing himself, finally looking at me. "Leave it alone, will you? It's taken care of. You can stop fretting over it."

Fretting? That stung. What he used to say about me when I was little, always fretting over things. Being a child. As bad as those other words he used to stab me with. *Loser. Bum. Stupid.*

I took a breath. Okay, now. It was only one word.

"I haven't heard from them," I said, taking a step toward the closet. "I'm just going to stop by their place for a few minutes to see how they're doing."

He turned in his chair. "Don't do that."

"Why not?"

"Forget about it, will you?"

"No, I won't," I said, grabbing my coat from the closet. "I want to make sure they're okay."

He gave me such a frown as I left the house. Of course, if he'd known my zeal had more to do with a lovely, feisty girl than with her grizzled, Mexican dad, he might have nodded his understanding.

Manny's house was empty, the door unlocked. This is how my father had taken care of them? This was them being okay? The place was cold and dark. It felt haunted as I walked through it, my steps echoing. I picked a crayon-drawn bunny off the floor. All that was left. Still, I could almost smell the plantains on the stove, hear the boys giggling over the TV, see Manny on the back porch, lying on that old aluminum chaise, studying the river; Connie, cooking dinner, cooing to her baby sister as she rocked her on her shoulder.

Fernando's family was gone, too, of course, replaced by a new man who closed his door in my face. None of the families living nearby spoke English, and everyone shook their heads when I knocked on their doors and spoke the Camarasa name, pointing to the empty house. They all shrugged. Nobody knew where they were.

When I returned home, Dad was still in his lounger, rocking his rum and coke back and forth, a slow metronome.

"They're gone. You said you'd taken care of them, but they're gone." I stood in the door, out of breath, out of anything to say.

He pushed back in his chair. "That doesn't surprise me."

"Why do you say that?"

"After getting a chunk of dough like that?"

"A chunk of—" I sputtered. "You think they ran off with the money."

"Maybe."

"You still believe he's a con man then, even though their investigation proved nothing."

He rocked his drink.

I rephrased the comment. "It *did* prove nothing, didn't it?"

The drink rocked.

"Where are they, Dad? Have they been deported? Is that what happened, and you didn't want to tell me?"

"Walker," he said, huffing, smiling at how ridiculous I was being. "They got their money. I cut the check, myself."

"Right." I had to laugh. "You cut it yourself." As if he moonlighted in AMC's accounting department. "Can you prove it?"

"Prove it?"

"There has to be paperwork? A stub? Something in his file. Notes from the personnel committee. A copy of the letter you sent Manny?"

"Walker—" He sighed, chuckling at my audacity.

"You've been blowing smoke up my ass this whole time. Taking my statement, doctors' letters from Manny, trying to talk me out of filing the appeal. But you never did file it, did you? Too worried about losing your own shitty job, you fucking coward."

He shot up out of the chair and grabbed my shirt. "You have no idea how much—" He shoved me away, sounding like Manny for a moment, what he went through to get that green card. He pointed a finger at my face. "You know what? I'm through proving myself to you. I tried to do your friend a favor and this is the thanks I get? No, I've had it. I don't care if you believe me."

He waved me away and walked out. So did I.

Sixty-Four

In the weeks and months that followed, I tried to investigate the Camarasas' disappearance, but I got nowhere. I called AMC's personnel department, but they told me they couldn't divulge private information about employees. The switchboard operator at St. Francis Hospital said she knew Connie, but that she had dropped out of the nurse's aide program at the beginning of November—the same week she'd stopped calling me at school—and left no forwarding address. The police told me they did not get involved in deportations, but they pointed me to the closest field office of the INS in Chicago. That office had no record of Manny or his family being detained, let alone deported, and refused to say one way or the other whether his status was being investigated.

Did the Camarasas take the money and run? How could they run if Manny could barely walk? Why run if they had money to pay rent and buy food while Manny healed? Manny loved that house, the river below it. Where would they run to, anyway? Was there any money to begin with?

My dad's story didn't add up, in particular, his unwillingness to show me proof Manny had gotten his money. They had no reason to disappear—unless they had actually received no money and had moved someplace else less expensive where they could better support themselves. Or unless AMC had continued investigating on its own. Maybe the company was getting so close to the truth that Manny and his family did what Fernando had done—moved away before they could be deported.

Meanwhile, I started spending my holidays with Frazier. That first Christmas break, I joined him and his girlfriend, Theresa, at their tiny north side Chicago apartment. For our holiday meal, we split a large, take-out cheese pizza, a salad and a bottle of Chianti. For gifts, we exchanged different strains of marijuana, sharing joints during a snowy, bone-chilling stroll through Lincoln Park while Theresa worked her shift at the Jewish deli on Clark street. I used the outing to tell him what had happened with Dad and to explain all my efforts to find the Camarasas. Frazier sympathized, though maybe he wasn't as convinced as I that Dad was to blame. He suggested alternative theories and made investigative suggestions. Nothing I hadn't considered or tried. He said he was proud I'd stuck up for myself, joining him in exile.

"It won't be easy," he said. "You're going to miss seeing Piper and Mom. I still dream about her chicken and dumplings, sometimes. Her pot roast."

"Do you ever hear from her?" I asked, knowing the answer already. "Does Mom ever call?"

"No," Frazier said. "I'm sure she's too cowed by him to chance getting caught."

I flashed on the image I used to have of her while Dad chased me around the house, desperate for help. She'd be up in her room on the bed, listening. She'd clutch the covers and cringe every time Dad yelled, a chair crashed or a door slammed.

"Not even when Dad's at work?"

"No," he said. "She's never called me. Not once." He looked up. "You?"

"No. Me neither."

He nodded.

At least, she hadn't shunned me any more than she had Frazier. Of course, I couldn't recall the last time Mom had called me at college before the fight, either.

I found a job at the university library over the holidays and, when I wasn't re-shelving books, I spent my time at the check-out desk reading. Weighed down by lies—my father's, the ones I'd lived with the previous summer—I was drawn to recent accounts of other lies. They were everywhere—an infestation, on the news, in our nation's capital. About Watergate and Nixon, the FBI's investigation of the civil rights movement, police abuse during the 1968 Democratic Convention in Chicago, especially about the Vietnam war.

On a whim, I cancelled my winter semester registration for a Chem lab and instead signed up for a journalism seminar. I didn't fancy myself a writer. I just happened to be browsing the reserved readings which various professors had set aside in the library for their students when I came across mimeographed copies of the Pentagon Papers, a secret government study of the war. The *New York Times* had managed to obtain and publish a copy of this–and journalism students would be reading it. How could I pass up such a class?

As the semester progressed, I learned from those papers and other publications how little chance the USA had of winning the war in Vietnam with the limited resources it had committed. Politicians and generals—men like my father—had spouted so many half-truths, claiming that, although they hadn't done what was publicly promised, their strategy served the greater good, protecting us from grimmer dangers. It was a contagion, this deceit, the few claiming to know what was best for the many, spreading across the world.

I called Frazier one night, told him what I'd been studying and said I just wanted him to know I'd decided he'd been right all along about the war. He was glad I'd stopped drinking Dad's Kool-Aid and asked if I'd read *All The President's Men* yet. I'd just finished it and he'd just started it, and Frazier warned me with a laugh not to spoil the ending for him. We marveled at the two journeyman reporters from the *Washington Post* who possessed the *grandísimo cojones* to expose the President of the United States for lying to the American public—and out of nowhere my brother remarked, "He's alive!"

When I asked, confused, "What do you mean?" he said he couldn't recall me ever being as excited about something as I was over these journalists and their writings. "You've been wondering what to do with your life, Walker. Well, I think you've found it."

When I hung up, I realized he was onto something. Maybe I couldn't write yet, but I could learn.

The first thing I wrote was a letter to my father, explaining how I'd decided on a major, and it wasn't biology or chemistry. I said I'd never had a sense of purpose until I discovered journalism. Now, if I could uncover truths like these reporters had, maybe I'd find a cure for what ailed me, a salve for my sadness since Thanksgiving. I said I'd understand if he cut me off, especially after what I'd found out about the government and his precious military. I explained that I would work part-time, take fewer classes, if that's what it took to pay for school until I graduated.

But he surprised me. He still sent checks in the mail, even when I didn't come home. Was it an acknowledgement of those truths I'd uncovered? Guilt over what had happened to the Camarasas? Over how he'd abused me? I don't know. Even decades later, he never discussed it.

When I look back over all the stories I've written, they were about other people, other events. The one front page story of *my* life was the mystery of what had happened to Connie Camarasa, Manny and their family. I was certain they had vanished because of my father and me. It was the one story I needed most to finish, but couldn't, though I never stopped trying.

The following summer I stayed in DeKalb to work in the university library, and one afternoon I took the hour-long drive home, not to our house, but back to Riverside Cabins. I was met with the same head shakes I'd received months before, not a soul recognizing the Camarasa name; so I took another tack, driving over to AMC to snoop around, getting into the employees' lot around shift change using my old ID. Once the horn sounded, I waited around until, amidst the mass of workers leaving the plant's southeast exit, I spotted a familiar face—Liam, Norm's friend with the mutton chops. I caught up with him as he was jumping into his truck and asked him if he knew what happened to Manny Camarasa—had anyone heard? Liam told me to fuck off, but when I persisted, my hand holding his door open, he said he didn't know. "If there's any justice, he'll be back in that shit-eating country he crawled out of."

Even if he wasn't deported, the idea of Manny running away didn't fit with what I knew about him. He believed he was legally documented, so I believed it, too. The older and more worldly I became, the less likely it seemed to me that a company like AMC would pay a private investigator to track down Manny's second wife. To a company that big, Manny Camarasa had to be a nobody, and not worth the hassle, especially if he was not around to cause trouble.

The Camarasas' disappearance just didn't make sense, especially if Dad's story was true. Eventually I came up with the theory that, after my lies had plagued him, he had decided to get back at me with lies of his own.

For the next few years, I spent my holidays with Frazier and his girlfriend, even moving in with them for a few weeks after I graduated before I found a job as a cub reporter for the wire service and a tiny apartment of my own. And then when Frazier and Theresa got engaged, he defected to the other side. She had convinced him they couldn't get married with the church pews reserved for Frazier's family empty except for me. She said it made no sense to continue this feud over a war that was ancient history. And so Frazier reached out to my father—and apologized for dodging the draft.

"I did some soul searching," I remember Frazier telling me, "and while I don't regret failing that physical and not going to 'Nam, I have to say, I learned a lot from the vets who came to my anti-war shows and debated their merits afterwards. The more I heard how difficult it was in 'Nam and how badly they'd been treated since coming back, the more I've regretted how my choices appeared to disrespect them—and anyone who chooses to serve, like Dad."

Apparently, that was good enough for my father, because he invited Frazier and Theresa for Thanksgiving—and asked them to invite me, too.

"Why couldn't he invite me himself if he really wants me to come?"

"Because he knows you're still angry, he thought I could talk some sense into you. Look, I know your issues with Dad are entirely different, and I'm not saying you should forget them, but I know what it's like holding a grudge. Nobody wins. If you don't come back, you're only hurting yourself—and Mom and Piper and now it'll be me and Theresa. And Dad, also. He misses you, too. Do you really want to spend the holidays alone?"

So I drove out with the idea that Dad might finally want to explain, to set things right. He was all smiles, shaking my hand when I came up the side steps, a bit stooped, white hair thinner than I remembered, paunch a bit more pronounced. Happy, no doubt, to be retired now, out of that fucking auto plant. Piper and Kurt were there to greet me, too. By this time, they were engaged, pieces from two different picture puzzles that somehow fit together to create a new image of perfect bliss. And it was great to see Mom, a bit rounder, hugging me so tight, like if she let me go I'd run away. It was great to see all of them. Too great, too nice, too lovely.

We all sat around watching football like we did in the old days, talked about our jobs, our lives in the city, our prospects—a day when Dad was so happy to have us home, he refrained from passing judgment on those things the way he had in the past and would going forward. I caught up with Kurt and Piper. They both had futures at Swanson Motors, him currently as a full-time car salesman; her, studying business at NIU with an eye toward developing a high-class marketing department for the company when she graduated. It was all fine. All good. And yet, I kept expecting—no, *waiting* for—Dad to pull me aside, sit me down alone somewhere. He'd begin, "About Manny Camarasa—"

But he didn't. In fact, no one mentioned the Camarasas, the fight, that summer, the reason why I'd been gone all these years. Instead, everyone was extraordinarily cheery, my brother and sister holding hands with their fiancés, Dad in his Barcalounger, Mom on her couch, clutching a crossword book she never opened once, so happy just to listen to her kids talk. I didn't want to be a downer, bringing up the subject myself. It was my issue, my hang-up. Just like Frazier, I needed to let it go. Except, Frazier had something to apologize for, a way to break the ice. I didn't.

For me, it was all up to Dad. The ball in his court. Every time I got up and left the room, I half-expected him to follow me out, take me aside. "About that summer and Manny Camarasa," he'd say. But he didn't.

By myself in the dining room, I sat on the bench under the bay window and looked down the snowy slope, past the cherry and apple trees to the river. The willows Dad had planted along the shoreline had grown so high and thick that only the top of the Foundry's twin smokestacks remained visible. The place was quiet now, closed, Dad had said, up for sale. Unless you trudged down the slope to the river's edge, as I did in my mind, and looked between the willow trunks and across the icy water, you'd never know there was a campground of white, clapboard cabins on the other side.

I turned and scanned the dining room table, set with my mom's finest white lace tablecloth, her best china. Silver gleamed everywhere—flatware for each of the seven place settings, serving dishes at the head of the table, gravy boats, butter dishes, salt and paper shakers, wine goblets. Two giant brass candlesticks Dad had brought back from the Philippines graced the middle of the table, the crystal chandelier hanging down between candles big and tall as baseball bats, never lit because they were irreplaceable. How could this be the same table my dad used to chase me around, pulling out chairs to detour me into the kitchen or the living room so he could corner me? How was it I always thought about *that* when I came home?

That Thanksgiving, the only reference Dad made to any of his differences with us boys was a toast he offered at the dinner table before carving the turkey, so glad to have us home, our family back together again, as if that was splint enough for all the broken bones of our relationships.

I barely touched the turkey, consumed with mounting anger at how easy everyone was, how light the chatter, how cozy the gathering, how heedless they were of the past. And then dessert came.

"Walker's favorite," my mom said, "to celebrate his homecoming."

She placed it in front of me, a large cake, the circumference lined with whipped cream and dotted with large strawberries. In the center, she had placed the three fattest, shaped in a heart.

"I froze some from the garden," Mom added, "in hopes you might come back this year. And you did." She leaned in and kissed my cheek.

I looked around the table at Piper and Kurt, Frazier, Theresa, everyone expectant, hopeful, my dad awaiting a speech, a thank you, willing me to lighten up and smile. I looked down at the cake.

All day, if I'd thought of the Camarasas, it was of Manny, of the fight, waiting for Dad to mention his name. I'd tried not to think of Connie. Thoughts of her only brought pangs of regret, jabs of sorrow that made my hands clench, my eyes squeeze shut, blocking her out. I'd tried to forget, knowing she'd been snatched away from me and nothing my father could say would bring her back. But here she was, biting into red flesh, juice dribbling, eyes shining. Here she was—and wasn't. Still gone. Gone, but not forgotten.

"I'm sorry," I said, getting up. "I can't do this." I gave my baffled mother a long tearful hug. As I fled the room, my father barked out my name, but I ignored him.

After I grabbed my coat and bag, my mother stopped me at the side door and, instead of saying, "Don't go," like I expected, said, "I'm sorry, too."

"What do *you* have to be sorry for?"

"Everything. I'm sorry for everything." She rubbed my arm and gave me a hug. "Promise me you won't be a stranger."

"I wish I could, Mom, but it's too hard."

Unlike Frazier, for me, there was no salvation, no other girl who might bring me back home, except the one those berries had resurrected. The girl who—until I bumped into her in that maternity ward—I wouldn't see for thirty years. The one I thought had disappeared.

I'd had ideas, of course. I pictured Connie and her brothers, like Fernando's family, working produce fields in California or picking oranges in Florida, living in Quonset huts or out of the trunk of an old car while Manny snoozed in the back seat, unable to walk. Or maybe they were back in Mexico, Manny driving his father's old bus to Toluca. Were they eating carp caught in the dirty river outside their little village? Wherever they were, it wasn't the American dream.

That's why I didn't remind Connie who I was, there in the ward when I saw her earlier, why I was glad she didn't recognize me. I dreaded finding out what kind of hell her family had endured—or worse, that it wasn't her American dream that was lost, but mine, that all those years she has been perfectly contented, happier than I have ever been. I spoke earlier of rebuilding my relationship with my father like it was an edifice, its completion missing only the answer to what happened to the Camarasas. Now, after seeing Connie, reading those clippings my father kept, and revisiting my painful past one more time, I'm wondering whether, perhaps, it hadn't been a place of love I'd been building, but a wall of anger, using the mystery of the Camarasas to fortify it and to keep my family at bay.

Sixty-Five

Back in the room, Piper and Kurt sit on either side of Dad's bed. It's close to midnight, but they are both still wide awake, watching him—until they see me.

"Take mine," Kurt says, jumping up. "I'll find another."

"Where were you?" my sister asks, straightening, full of concern. She is so pale, she could have vanished in this blizzard, the bags under her eyes, tiny snow drifts. Kurt shimmies past me out the door.

"Around. What's this?" A tube is strapped to Dad's mouth and leads to a machine.

"A ventilator. He was having trouble breathing."

I sit on the edge of the abandoned chair, surveying his gray face. She watches me watching him as if she needs me to take this in. *But it's only oxygen, isn't it? And isn't that stubble?* Hair growing. Cells dividing. Aren't these good signs?

"Here's the thing," Piper says. She grasps the rails of the bed as though girding herself for a roller coaster. Slowly at first, the ride rising, she explains that while I was away, Dad started gasping. Alarms went off on his monitors, and the medical staff came running. *But if he was gasping, didn't that mean he was fighting?* They gave him oxygen, sedation, but he continued to have trouble so they called in the Attending.

"He said they could put him on a ventilator or let it play out. I obviously couldn't make that decision myself, so here we are."

"Okay." So? So they put him on a ventilator.

"I talked to Frazier," she continues.

She explains how our brother is still at least eight hours away, waiting for United to de-ice his plane at LaGuardia.

"He didn't want to make it worse," Piper says. "So he gave me his blessing. Us, that is. To do whatever we thought best."

"Okay." *To remove the feeding tube? But that still leaves days or weeks, even.*

"He was so easy about it, I thought I hadn't made myself clear, so I explained. 'Dad's on a ventilator, can't breathe on his own anymore, and once we turn it off—'" She chokes in a breath, wringing the bedrail.

"What? You mean—"

"Yes." Her whispers are an appeal, a prayer. "I thought you understood."

"But it still takes a while, right?"

She shakes her head, hands tightening on the rail.

He's barely hanging on? And she wants to peel away his fingers, let him plummet. I search him for signs. His chest rises and falls. He's still alive.

"So—we take him off that machine, and he suffocates?"

Piper clucks her tongue. "They do it gradually. With morphine and tranquilizers to reduce any sense of, you know—"

"Suffocation?!"

"You think I *want* to do this?" So loud, a passing nurse pokes her head in the door. Piper waves her away.

"Sorry." I nod.

She sits back in her chair, arms aligned with the rests, hands gripping the ends. Why do I keep blaming her? She didn't put him here.

"So, now that Frazier has agreed, that leaves you."

She wipes away the tears and stares at me, toughening, stubborn. Her bangs magnify the furrowing of her brow, defiant. Looking at Dad doesn't help. That stupid ventilator. He was fine before they clamped that on, and now she's telling me it's the only thing keeping him alive.

Kurt returns with a chair, its legs screeching on the floor.

"Sorry," he says, sitting. Oddly, I welcome those shoulder-jangling goosebumps—anything not to answer my sister.

"Walker!" Piper says, but I don't take my eyes off my friend.

Kurt perks up as if I'm waiting for him to speak. "So, Pipes," he says, "Maybe you should tell your brother what Dad wants to do."

"Wants to do?" I ask, happy to change course. I bounce glances between them.

She says, "Now's not the time, Kurt—"

"What? Tell me."

"It's not important," she says.

"Let me be the judge. What's he want to do?"

Piper sighs, squinting Kurt down for bringing it up. He sinks into his seat, shrinking. She swings around to Dad, observing, as if he still might have a poker tell, a twitch of the eye, telling her what to do.

"Okay," she says, heaving another preparatory sigh. "You know Dad has a will, right?"

"I never thought about it, but he must have. A man his age."

"But you don't know what's in it."

"And you do?"

"For the big stuff, yes. He sat me down and explained it a while back."

"He made her the exec-u-tor," Kurt pronounces, nodding.

Piper rolls her eyes at him.

"What? When were you planning on telling me?"

"I'm telling you now."

Dad *would* choose Piper. Even if she is the youngest kid, the least experienced. It was so obvious. I take a few breaths. We're done fighting. We've made nice. I don't want to ruin it.

"You okay with that?" she asks, a testing tone.

"I guess that makes sense." The words are forced out. "Your being here and all."

"Thank you. But also," she takes another breath, steeling herself. "He wants to leave me the house."

"The house? You mean, the whole house?"

"No. The kitchen. Of course, the whole house. I told him I don't need it, but he insisted. Because I stayed in Belford, and Kurt and I looked after him. He said it was only fair. And, he hated the idea of us kids selling the place."

"Can you imagine?" Kurt says. "The riffraff in this town, living in that house?"

It's not the money, what we'd get for it, that unleashes that old pang of envy. It's her, once again, Daddy's Little Girl. Why wouldn't he give her the whole fucking house?

"But—" Kurt smiles at his wife. "I've been thinking, Pipes. We're pretty happy in Pops' old place, aren't we? I mean, sure, Dad's has the river and the lawn and all, but our pool is a lot cleaner. We got that central air, heated floors, that southern exposure. Dad's place needs a ton of work."

Piper glares at him, uncomprehending.

"We talked about this," she says. "Living on that lovely river, having as our own and for our grandkids the yard our boys played on growing up."

"Yeah, but it'd be such a hassle to move all our stuff. And Dad's lawn is a bitch to take care of. And I happen to know the perfect person for the job."

He grins at me; then, seeing his wife, her head cocked, that determined frown, he pushes back in his chair and scratches an ear.

"We'll discuss it later," she says.

He considers her, puts his hands on his knees and hoists himself up. He thrusts his hands out, one for each of us, a sales pitch coming.

"You were so pissed I didn't tell you about offering Walker the job," he says, turning to me, then her. "Well, this is why. You two are ridiculous. If I had any family of my own—and you are all the family I have any more—and an opportunity like this came up??"

"I know you mean well, Kurt, honey, but please. Can we discuss this later?"

He throws up his hands and sinks back into the chair, shaking his head.

"So," I'm backtracking here, turning to Kurt, "'what Dad wants to do,' really means what *you* want me to do, right? Take that job. I mean, I appreciate the thought, but the fact is—" I pose this one to Piper—"When Dad wrote his will, he didn't even think about me, did he?"

"That's not true," she says, shaking her head; but instead of continuing, she just eyes me, thinking, deciding.

"He *did* leave you something," Kurt puts in, tentatively.

Piper shoots him a look.

"Something *special*," Kurt adds, defying his wife. He sits back down but keeps an eye on her, the fire lit, waiting for it to catch.

"Oh, this'll be good. His hat collection? His pickle castors? Or how about the John Deere? I can mow the shag rug in my apartment."

"No," she says. "Not that it's worth anything anymore."

"His American Motors' shares! Of course! Just what I needed—worthless stock in a defunct auto company. I can frame it and put it on the wall."

"No. The Cadillac," she whispers and looks again at Dad, a pained expression. "Damned car."

"The Cadillac?"

"Yes. The Cadillac."

"Poor old gal," Kurt mumbles.

"But why me? Why not Frazier? Or Kurt!" I flap my hand his way. "He always loved that car."

"Tell me about it," he mutters.

"You knew." I address him. "That's why you were going on and on about it this afternoon."

Kurt and Piper share a glare again. "I didn't think it was my place to tell you," he says.

"All I know is," she starts, "he kept that stupid car under a tarp in the garage for the last thirty—no, forty years. And every six months, like clockwork, he'd dust if off, drive it up to Kurt's for his mechanics to give it a once-over, run it through the wash, give it a spin around town, and plunk it back in that garage to be forgotten for another six months."

"It was in great shape, too," Kurt says, sliding forward. "Last time he looked at it, Pablo put on new tires, brake linings, sparks and plugs. That starter I mentioned? Wasn't easy tracking one down. 1960 DeVille? But like I said, you can find anything on the Internet. Anything."

He nods at me, a bobble-head.

"So how'd he decide who'd get it?" I turn to Piper. "Flip a coin?"

"Not at all. He wanted *you* to have it. I tried to tell him that Kurt might appreciate it more—I mean, even you agree with that, right?"

"Yeah, I guess." Though I'm now intrigued by the notion. The Caddy, all mine, babied all those years for me. No, it's got to be some kind of joke—like Grandpa Casper's giving him the car to begin with.

"It was because I don't have a car, right? He wants me driving to work in a forty-five-year-old, air-polluting, gas-guzzling Cadillac that takes up two parking spots."

"Don't be ridiculous. You know it was more than a car to him." She pushes forward in her chair, reaches over and grabs Dad's hand, running her thumb over the age-spotted skin. For the first time, I hear the ventilator breathing for him, a mechanical sound, ballooning his chest. "He said he wanted you to have it—I remember how he put it—he said, 'Because Walker needs a good getaway car.'"

"A getaway car?" I hadn't made that up?

"I asked him what he meant, and he was like, 'Never mind. Just make sure Walker gets the Caddy.' Does that mean anything to you? Getaway car?"

A dozen thoughts flash by. Why has that stuck with me? Because that time, driving the Caddy to the hospital, he seemed so trapped, shackled. Like he needed to get away?

"Well—" she sits back, "if he hadn't taken the damned thing out again the other day, you could have asked him yourself what the hell he meant."

She glares at me, her jaw moving. She closes her eyes and drops her head, exhaling.

"Sorry," she says. "It's not your fault. Only, I keep thinking—we took away the keys to the other cars ages ago, but we completely forgot about that goddamned Cadillac."

I sit up, trying to understand this. "Where *was* he going?"

"He'd made an appointment with my Service Department," Kurt says, "but none of those dunderheads thought to tell me. Heads are gonna roll. As soon as I have a second—"

"We get it Kurt," Piper motions him down and turns to me. "If I'd known, I'd have been over to the house so fast, scooped up those keys—" The wobble in Piper's voice makes me turn, note the tears brimming.

"I remember it eating at him, this need to drive the Caddy," I say. "But he couldn't because of his contract. I figured, once he retired—"

"He kept promising the boys," Kurt says. "He'd get them in that car and drive them to a Cubs game or up to Mackinac Island to see the Yacht Club races."

Mackinac. Mom and Dad, both in summer white, lounging in Adirondack chairs on the lawn in front of the Grand Hotel. They'd watch the sailboats tilting into the waves, while down at the beach Frazier, Piper and I splashed each other in Lake Michigan.

"But he never did. After your mother died, and he was kind of down, it seemed like a good sign when he brought the car into the shop, like he was finally planning on taking it somewhere. So I tried to encourage him. 'Now's your chance,' I told him. And you know what he said? He said, 'I used to think about driving the car someplace I'd rather be, but these days, I can't think of any.'"

"Hello?"

Someone in a turquoise parka and snow-covered stocking cap pokes their head in the door, a flowering plant in one hand. I'm about to tell them we're in the middle of something, when the light catches just right. A mole above her eye.

"I'm so sorry to intrude." She pulls her cap off. Long brown hair spills out. Snow melts on the shoulders of her puffy parka, the red striped winter scarf dangling around her neck. Water puddles under her red rubber boots. I stand.

"Piper, Kurt," I say, motioning. "This is Connie Camarasa—or Wheeler now, is it?" I glance at her, questioning.

"Divorced," she offers quickly and unprompted, as if correcting me, setting the record straight. She reddens, mumbling, "I never changed it back." So—not married! Relief floods me, like something from one of those IVs, warm and relaxing. She quickly adds, "Then, you *do* know me?"

"Yes. I recognized you right away." I turn to Kurt and Piper. "Connie works in the maternity ward. I ran into her there." I swing back to her. "I thought *you* didn't recognize *me*."

"What's going on?" Piper asks, looking between us, lost.

Connie steps inside, another puddle. "I saw Walker—" She nods at me, asking for confirmation.

"That's right. Walker." Not sure about my name?

"He looked familiar, but he didn't say anything," she continued. "So I figured I had to be wrong. Then I remembered he said his dad was in the ICU, so I called down and found out a Michael Maguire had been admitted. It was all such a shock, that name, confirming who you were, hearing how sick he is. I wanted to pay my respects. I hope that's okay."

Pay her respects? To a man she must hate?

Connie does a double-take at my sister, then peers at Kurt, the gears tumbling, reviewing, stopping on a single frame towards the beginning of a long movie. A kiss, maybe.

"I'm sorry. This is my sister, Piper," I say, adding, "and her husband, Kurt Swanson."

"Husband?" Connie flashes me a questioning look. Does she remember? "Swanson Motors, right?"

"That's right," he says.

"Well. Congratulations." She looks between them as if they've only recently gotten hitched.

Kurt and Piper mirror each other's confusion.

A bit flustered, as if she doesn't know what to do with herself, Connie zeroes in on the window. "I couldn't get flowers, but I had this plant on my desk. Can I put it on this sill?"

"Yes. Absolutely." I wave her over.

She crosses the room, leaving little puddles, and positions the small plant, bright green leaves and little red flowers, against the black glass. She turns to the bed and stands by it. She reaches out and touches my father's hand, stroking it with two fingers, looking into his face, then glances at us, embarrassed at her moment with him. My mouth is open, speechless.

"Sorry," she says, glancing back at us, her eyes unmistakably moist. "I'm late for my shift, but I wanted to stop by."

"Thank you," Piper says, standing now. Kurt stands, too, nodding.

Connie gives them a parting nod and, as if against her will, gives me a smile before she turns and heads out the door. I start to follow her, mouth open to say her name, ask her what that was all about.

"Walker!" Piper calls.

I pull up. "I need to talk to her a second."

"That can wait."

"But she knows—"

"Knows what?" She gives her head a quick shake. "What can she possibly say that will change what's going on here?"

I'm about to explain, but then I turn to my dad, his pale face, the tube keeping him alive. I'm breathing like I've come in last in a long race.

"You can't run off again," Piper adds. "We have to deal with this. Now."

Connie's at the end of the hall, turning the corner. She disappears. Piper's right. Nothing Connie knows can change the course of the next few hours, nor can anything I've recounted in my laptop.

So now I sit here. I've written down as much as I know. I've given Piper my consent. There's nothing left but to wait for the doctor and his team to come.

And to wonder. Why would Connie pay her respects to a man who had driven her family out of their home? Sent them God knows where—Mexico, California? Did she come up here out of common decency?

And what did it mean—a *getaway* car?

My father's getaway, it seems, was to stay put. Sure, he had Piper, Kurt, his grandchildren. So he had finally embraced this town, his house on the hill above the river.

But what about my getaway?

Did he think I needed to escape the scene of the crime? If so, whose crime? His? His abuses? Or my own? Making such a criminal case about what he did to me? What Piper did? What I did, letting things with Manny and my father and that stupid car company get so out of hand?

Or was he saying, finally, "Let this go. Get past it. Stop giving it so much say in your life. Isn't that a crime, too?"

Piper holds his hand.

"Are you sure Pablo can fix it?" I say, turning to Kurt.

Piper purses her lips at me and him. She refrains from giving voice to her exasperation and goes back to watching Dad. She clutches his fingers and ignores us.

"Yeah, I think so," he says, grinning. "But it may take a while to find all the parts. Maybe by this summer?"

I nod.

"I don't know what it's like in D.C.," he adds, "but you can't get to work in Belford without some kind of car."

Hearing this, Piper turns and regards me with curiosity, waiting. She stands, holding Dad's right hand with her left. She reaches across the narrow bed, palm up, beckoning me. I stand, grab her hand.

"C'mon," she says, nodding at his other hand. "Take it."

I'm frozen. A statue, gaze aimed at him.

She whispers. "He's your father, Walker."

I reach down. No shock this time, except to discover warmth, plasticity in the skin, giving way to my fingers, compressing, his hand conforming, fitting. And something else, reaching inside of me, into my guts, my chest, buckling me.

"It's okay," Piper says, squeezing. "It's okay."

Sixty-Six

Belford Daily Telegram
Editorial, June, 2005

Many of you may wonder why the owners of this newspaper hired an outsider as its new editor. It's true, I haven't lived in Belford for many years, but I did go to high school here. My father was the first company doctor at the American Motors plant before Chrysler took it over. That was back when Ramblers and Pacers rolled off the line, when so much of the work of building cars was still done by hand, with air-driven screw guns and hand-held welders, not by robots and computers. I even spent a summer working at the plant, unloading seat frames and fuel tanks from boxcars.

Of course, it's different now. Back then, there were more jobs with less automation, so it was more dangerous and repetitive. It wasn't an easy life, not even for my dad, who helped workers deal with those health and safety issues.

Today, Belford's problems are different, too: unemployment, soaring housing prices as more and more tech workers from Chicago move here, a growing Latino community feeling that pinch, especially those recent immigrants seeking to establish a toehold in their adopted country.

But perhaps the folks most affected by this growth are our long-time residents, who never sought change but are being priced out of their own housing market, who are finding good jobs harder to come by, seeing their schools become overcrowded, crime and drug use on the upswing, all while budget impasses trim the government services they once took for granted.

Yes, Belford has its problems, but this city is more than the sum of its problems. At AMC, I learned that we have a diverse population of hard-working men and women from all walks of life, who have the toughest kinds of jobs, yet for the most part, good lives. I never forgot that. But at the age of twenty, I wanted to see the world, so I left town.

I worked as a reporter covering a wide range of stories throughout the United States, Europe and the Middle East, and most recently in Washington, D.C. Some of my articles have appeared in this newspaper.

Now, I'm proud to return home as the editor of this paper. This place has its own stories that need to be told, too, and I'm glad I can help tell them.

The BDT will continue to cover the local scene, providing coverage of breaking news, school sports teams, community cultural activities, and business development; but I also want the BDT to tell your stories, so that we can learn from each other about the different challenges and rewards of living here.

No one would mistake Belford for a wealthy town. We don't have fancy restaurants, gated communities, or posh private schools. But the people who live here have a wealth of experience and knowledge, a richness in their diversity. I want to help spread that wealth.

I'd like this newspaper to broaden the lines of communications between us, to build understanding and trust amongst us so that, in the future, as much as possible, the news we print will be good news.

Sixty-Seven

A couple of days after I publish that editorial, I work up the nerve to call the St. Francis maternity ward. Connie Wheeler's not on duty the first time I try, which makes it easier when I do reach her, working a night shift. By this time, I'm well-rehearsed.

As someone passes her the handset, I hear phones ring, machines beep, voices over a loudspeaker, telling some doctor to report to the ICU.

"Connie Wheeler," she says. *Divorced,* I remind myself. She just never changed it back, she'd said.

"Hi. This is Walker Maguire."

The loudspeaker repeats its request. Connie is breathing hard.

"I'm calling about your father. Manny. I never got to ask. Is he—"

"He's fine. He lives with me now. Me and my two kids."

"Oh. Glad to hear it. I mean, that he's okay." That's a relief, anyway. And only two kids. "Do you think I can see him?"

She says nothing. She's still there. I hear her breathing—and more beeping, more from the intercom, directing Dr. So-and-So to go who knows where. Maybe she didn't hear me with all that noise.

"Connie, I said—"

"I heard you. You want to see my father." she says. Maybe that's why she hesitated, disappointed it's not *her* I said I wanted to see.

"Well, you, too, of course." I have questions for both of them, sure, but she's the one I want to see, just these few words from her already raising hopes.

After another moment's hesitation, she says she only gets Sundays off, and she always has a family dinner that day.

"It's really the only time of the week we can all be together."

"I have no problem with that," I say, though I'm pretty sure she's saying alone together, without some near-stranger intruding. "I mean, I'd like to meet them, too, if that's okay."

Another pause, a phone ringing in the background.

"Well, I suppose—" she starts.

"Great then," I jump in. "What's your address?"

Another long hesitation. Reminds me of talking to my editor over a satellite link, the words taking long seconds to fly thousands of miles. But this is something else, this reticence. Are we really that far apart, she and I?

She blurts out an address and a time, all in one breath, like an admission of something, or perhaps, an accusation. Nonetheless, I chisel it into memory,

"I'll be there."

Another big breath from her side despite all the noise.

"Sunday, then," I add, jumping in, bridging the gap, not giving her a chance to back out. "It'll be great to see you all again."

I hang up, and stand over the phone, waiting for it to ring, for her to protest that she has no interest in dining with me. But the phone doesn't ring.

When I arrive the following Sunday, I find a noisy, brick walk-up in a housing unit a few blocks from the hospital. I climb four flights, a hike carrying flowers in one hand, ice cream in the other. On one floor, people fight. On the next, kids laugh. Different worlds: Hot dogs. Curry. Kimchi. On the top floor, something spicy and appetizing. My mouth waters.

I shuffle my gifts into one arm and knock. As soon as the door opens, I recognize the smiling man, bent slightly forward, a permanent semi-bow. He's wiping his hands on the apron he's wearing. His hair is gray, the wrinkles that make up that smile triple in number at his apparent pleasure, seeing me again. He embraces me, his warm, rough hands shaking my free hand. Like he's congratulating me, a prize-winner. I can't believe it, his delight. I peer over his shoulder but don't see Connie.

"Welcome to my home, Mr. Newspaper Editor."

Awkwardly, I hold up the bouquet, the bag with the three pints of ice cream—Coffee, Rocky Road, French Vanilla, trying to cover all the bases.

"For me?" he says. "How nice of you."

Clutching the flowers, he hobbles forward into a single space with everything—kitchen area, a square table with four chairs, a couch and TV, a formal family portrait on a counter, flowery throws, red and green, on the furniture, a framed illustration of Jesus on a wall. The room, all the color, gives the illusion of space, but only the illusion.

Two steps over to the living area, Manny introduces me to his grandson, Mateo, a short, skinny teen with shaggy black hair in a t-shirt, shorts and flip-flops. He is sprawled on the couch watching the White Sox on a boxy old TV, an antenna on top. He has Connie's eyes. The boy concedes a brief, skeptical handshake before kicking back to watch his game, resolutely ignoring us.

Manny waves me back toward the kitchen—a corner of the room with a sink on one side, a stove on the other, cabinets above. He searches for something to put the flowers in, tries to reach the cabinet over the fridge; but, unable to straighten, he quickly bypasses it, opening other doors, closing them. He's not in pain, or so I hope. Steam vents from a covered skillet. Smells so good, it reminds me I have eaten nothing all day in my worrying about tonight. As he pokes around, he explains that his granddaughter, Lydia, is talking on the phone with her boyfriend, down the hall in a room she shares with her mother.

"She has ten more minutes," Manny says, closing another cabinet, opening one more. "I'm timing her."

I crane my neck, tilting to see. The narrow hall is flanked by two doors—bedrooms, I assume—and ends in a bathroom, a toilet peeking out the open door. I can't imagine where Connie is, assuming the other room is where Manny and the boy sleep. Or, maybe, after my pushy phone call, this is how she's decided I'll see her father—alone.

Slamming a lower cabinet door, Manny finally throws both hands wide with an annoyed exhalation, eyes the counter, and finds an old campfire-style coffee pot next to the sink. He fills it with water, shoving the flowers in. Then he goes to the fridge and pulls out two Coronas, holding one out. Without thinking, I reach, but then stop, backing away.

"No, thanks. I'm trying to cut back."

I don't want *that* to fuck this up. Manny regards me a long second, and I wonder if he hasn't sensed the iceberg beneath this tiny tip. He puts his beer back, too, and offers soda and water, both of which I politely decline.

"That's ice cream." I point to the bag on the counter. "You should probably put it away before it melts."

"Ice cream—" he grimaces. "Connie won't have it in the apartment, ever since—" He points at me—"that summer, as a matter of fact. Working at that ice cream place."

"Oh, sorry."

"It's okay. You didn't know." Without taking the pints out, he shoves the bag into the freezer. "The kids and I will be happy to take care of it."

"But speaking of that summer—" I say, an early opening.

"Now, now, now. We can talk about that later. I wanted to congratulate you on taking over the paper. Maybe I can finally stomach the damned thing. Might even get a subscription."

I chuckle. "I hope you do."

"Hope, yes. That article you wrote. You have a lot of hope. I'm not sure how many of your readers feel about this town the way you do."

If only he could see some of the letters to the editor, telling me what a "fucking hypocrite" I am, talking about "sharing the wealth" when I am the son of a "rich-assed doctor," a "management tool," living in a "silver-plated mansion on the river." Or the one saying I should take my "liberal, main-stream media ass" back to that "Times Square faggot ghetto" I came from.

"I got some bad reviews, but some good ones, too," I say. Yes, some welcomed me home and appreciated my message without reservation; but too many of those "good ones" were like the programmer, mother of two, who commutes to a western Chicago suburb and was relieved the paper had hired somebody who could give these "bumpkins" something better than the "chaw of tobacco" the newspaper used to be.

"Connie took an extra shift, today. Should be home any moment now," Manny says.

"Great." I try to hide my relief.

He pulls the heavy iron lid off the skillet, sticking a spoon into the mixture, then into his mouth. He smiles. Emotions swirl in me like the scent rising from Manny's concoction, sweet but peppery, sour but salty, the spices of origin hard to pinpoint.

The question bubbles to the surface, what I need to ask him, when Manny jumps in again, explaining how Sunday is the only day of the week the family gets together for dinner. He talks so quickly, I have to lean in to catch every word. Mateo has a summer job at Green Giant as a corn detasseler, marching up and down rows, dawn until dusk, wearing a rain coat against the dew and sharp leaves, snipping tassels off the stalks so the plants won't self-pollinate and reduce the seed quality. Sounds to me like the kind of work the migrant workers were once bussed up here to do, but I don't go there.

Manny says that when Mateo's not working, he plays goalie for a club soccer team—a sport that barely existed in this country when I was a kid, let alone had organized leagues all over the country. Then he talks about Lydia, his granddaughter.

Like Connie did, the girl volunteers at the hospital when she isn't off with her friends, "doing God only knows what," he adds, shaking his head. But I know all too well. Cruising through town, drinking, smoking. I was a teen here, too.

He oils a second skillet to heat the tortillas he's unwrapped. He's stopped talking, at long last.

"I wanted to ask about that summer."

"That summer? Yes. That summer." He nods.

"Actually, about what happened to you guys. I remember dropping by your house that Thanksgiving. It was empty, and I couldn't find you."

"Too bad about that place. I loved it there." With two fingers, he places a tortilla into the spitting grease. "But the rent was more than we could handle. It was cold in that house, too. No insulation. We had to move."

"Move—" Not leave? "Where?"

"West side. An apartment. Something we could afford."

West side. Those low-income developments. Rough neighborhoods. But still Belford.

"So, you never left the country? I mean, you've been here, all along?"

"That's right."

"And you managed, even though you couldn't work."

"Yes." He shrugs. "Well, I was in bad shape, but we, yes, we managed."

"Did AMC ever come through for you?"

"Yes, after a while—"

"They did?" My mouth is open, jaw dropped.

"There was a lot of paperwork. Doctor's visits. Test reports. And then there was that investigation."

"Right." I have to take a breath, take in all this unexpected news. "You once told me it was complicated how you got your green card."

"I did?"

"But you never explained."

"I got it by marrying an American citizen—my second wife."

I knew that much, but let him go on.

"You know," he scans the ceiling, smiling, "it sounds crazy now, but at the time, I didn't want a green card."

"No?"

"I never wanted to stay in the US. I just wanted to make enough money to pay off my debts and go back to Mexico, maybe start a little business like my father's, buy an old bus and drive the villagers to the city like he did. But then I met Angela, the woman I married."

"She changed your mind, then."

"Well, no. And that was the problem. Angela was from Minnesota, just out of high school, got this summer job working for a church organization that took care of *braceros'* kids while we were out in the field. She wanted to improve her Spanish, so she used to hang out with us around the campfire at nights, listening to our stories. Lovely girl. And after my first wife had our marriage annulled, I was tired of being alone, so—"

He shrugs at me.

"You got to know her."

"And asked her to marry me before she could run away back home. I knew she loved me, but still, it surprised the hell out of me when she agreed."

"And how long were you together?"

He chuckles. "'How long were you married, Mr. Camarasa? And what kind of marriage was it?' I got that question a lot after that fight at AMC. As if there's more than one kind of marriage."

"I'm sorry. It's none of my business."

"No, I know how it looked. A couple of the men in camp even got women in town to marry them for money so they could get their green cards. I told Angela, as soon as I paid off my debt to the farm association and saved a little money, I was going back to Mexico to start my business. She said 'fine,' she'd go with me. We got married. The farmer let us rent this old, one room cabin on the property and hired her to work in his house as a domestic. We lived together, a real marriage. We both put our money into the same account. She could have taken it at any time if that was all she wanted."

"But she didn't."

"Some of the men around camp didn't help much, whispering in her ear how crazy I was to want to return to Mexico. This one *cabrón estúpido* from my village made it sound awful. Like all the officials were corrupt. Like there was no electricity or plumbing, like we all washed our clothes in the river. Sure, some lived like that. And yes, there were only dirt roads in my village, but it wasn't that bad, I kept telling her. Just the same, she changed her mind, asked me to get the green card so we could stay in America. I said I didn't want to, but she threatened to leave me, so—"

He pinches out a tortilla and puts another one in the pan, sizzling.

"So, you got the card."

"I lied. I said I'd stay and find work in the canning factories. I thought I could change her mind while we waited for the card to come through. I couldn't. When I finally got it, the other workers threw a big going away party for us. Food, music and dancing. Everyone celebrated our new American life outside the camps; but I was still hoping she would come to Mexico with me. And after the celebration that night, that's what I told her—I still wanted to go back. I'd be someone there, respected, a man with his own business, not just this pair of hands—of *brazos*— this bent back. We had a big fight, back and forth. *But you promised, Manny*, and on and on. The next morning, she was gone. Days later, I went to the bank. She had taken her half of our savings. Much more than that. She'd made that much more than me. Now I didn't have enough to pay my debt and leave the camp, so everyone thought I'd given her all my savings to help me get my green card. But it wasn't true. She'd only taken her money."

He dabs his spatula into his pan.

"Sorry to hear that."

Manny smiles up at me.

"The funny thing was, she got her wish. There was no money for a bus, so I stayed here after all. I've worked in factories ever since."

"And AMC's investigation? They couldn't prove anything?"

"You know what? I don't think they really tried. Spend all that money to investigate one Mexican dock worker? No, I think it was cheaper to keep stalling and hope I'd go away, take another job. But I didn't go away because I couldn't work. Your father—he's the one who kept pushing them. It took a couple years but that company finally came through, thanks to him."

A couple years? My dad had said they'd gotten their money at Thanksgiving, just months after the fight. And if it was two years, how did they survive? I'm about to pursue this, when a jingling comes from the front door, keys engaging the lock, turning.

"There's Connie now," Manny says.

Connie breezes in, dropping her purse and keys on a table by the door. She's in her blue hospital scrubs, hair wound into a ponytail. She staggers when she sees me. The fluttering in my gut turns to flapping. There's that little mole, that jewel in such a beautiful setting. Her hand goes to her mouth. I'm almost nineteen again, and Connie, that candy striper again, leaning over Manny's bed. Were we ever that young?

"I told you he'd come," Manny says, nodding at her.

She collects herself and focuses on him. "I didn't say—" She stops, an eyebrow raised, the one with the little mole. She turns to me. "I wasn't sure—what *time* you'd come." The searching emphasis gives away the lie.

"Walker. It's nice to see you again." Official now, she extends a hand, keeping her distance. I shake it. "Let me change, and I'll be right back."

I nod. The heat of her fingers lingers as she pushes past me. She stops behind the couch, leaning over the cushions. "Don't you think your grandfather could use some help?" Mateo sluggishly sits up, scratching his head.

"Oh, give your son a break," Manny says. "He works hard all week."

She shakes her head and disappears up the hall. She opens a door, and I hear, "Are you on the phone with that boy again?" before she goes in and the door closes. Mateo resumes sprawling.

"She kept saying you'd never come," Manny chuckles. I smile back, not sure whether she was worried I wouldn't show up or wishing it.

"Can I ask how you lived for two years if it took that long for AMC to come through?"

He glances up, surprised by the question. He shrugs.

"You know. We got by."

A cheer rises from the TV. Snowy reception. An antenna! A guy circles the bases.

"Still in first place," Manny points. "Can you believe it?" Manny tosses White Sox players' names at me. Konerko. Dye. Finally, some power hitters. The improved pitching. I stand there, my mouth open, waiting for him to get back to my questions. But he doesn't. Maybe it's too painful to talk about, and I shouldn't push him.

Sixty-Eight

Connie returns, changed into a lacy, white summer blouse over blue jeans. Her thick, brown hair is combed out onto her shoulders.

"I thought we agreed to limit Lydia's phone time," she says, sticking a finger into Manny's ribs.

"Ten more minutes," he says, flinching, tickled. It's been at least twenty. "I made her promise."

Connie sighs and sniffs at the pots and pans on the stove as if I'm not even there.

"What are these?" she says, pointing at the bouquet.

"Walker brought them. Nice, huh?"

"Well, they don't belong in a coffee pot, *por el amor de Dios*." She reaches up and opens the cabinet over the refrigerator, pulls out a vase, fills it with water, takes the wrap off the flowers and inserts them. She turns, looks around, then seeing me, asks, "Would you put these on the table?" Like I'm an errand boy. Or is she simply nervous?

"But they are nice, aren't they?" I hear Manny say as I place the vase. "The flowers? Pretty?" He's tipping his head toward me as I return.

"Oh, yes." She grins at me, a nurse's smile, being cordial. "Very nice. Thank you." I smile back. Awkward. She turns away. I get it. She doesn't want me here, doesn't want to remember those years of scraping by. Years!

"Smells good in here," she says, and starts darting around, helping her father.

"Don't you look pretty," Manny says. The lipstick and eye shadow are new, her brown eyes deeper than before, lips fuller. Not her usual routine? She slaps his arm, glancing at me for only the second time.

"Did you offer Walker something to drink?"

"I did." He focuses on the hot skillet, stirring.

"I'm good," I say.

"Why don't you two sit down," Manny says. "I can handle this."

Her mouth works. Flustered, swiveling around, wanting something to do, she doesn't want to sit down. She can see the question I asked Manny, too. She knows why I'm here. The thing is, they're the ones who should demand answers, not me.

"Well, I'm starving," she says. She makes a beeline for a cabinet. "Let's put dinner on the table."

Connie grabs a stack of plates and passes it under my nose.

"Sit." She points at the table, adding, "Anywhere you like." A polite afterthought. So direct. Always liked that.

I sit, watching her distribute the plates. She calls the kids for dinner. Mateo brings in another chair from his bedroom. Manny carries in a steaming serving dish. Chicken Fajitas. Another with refried beans. A bowl of rice. Another of red beans. A salad from the fridge. Everyone takes their places, five people at a square table meant for four. Connie takes Manny's and Lydia's hands, and bows her head, eyes closed, telling the girl it's her turn. The teens gape at her, a bit helpless, mouths open.

When nothing happens, Connie opens her eyes and says, looking between the boy and girl, "He won't bite. Take his hands." They do, tentatively.

Lydia recites in Spanish, speaking rapidly. Not until she speeds to the end, "*...que este alimento nos ayude a servirte de todo corazón te lo pedimos por Jesucristo nuestro Señor amén,*" does my high-school Spanish kick in, and I recognize a prayer similar to what my family said at holiday dinners. I wonder how big a part that Jesus on the wall plays in their lives. But before I can dwell on it, serving dishes are passed around, everyone filling their plates.

Connie asks her children how their weeks went, apparently a Sunday dinner ritual as integral as saying grace. Or is she sending me a message? *Whatever you're here for, we don't want to talk about it. Let's get through this so you can leave, and we can get back to our lives.*

Again, the two kids appeal to Manny and Connie, mouths open.

"Walker's an old friend," their grandfather says. *Old friend?* "So speak up. Tell us about work, Mateo."

Haltingly, the boy starts, the cracking tones of a teen whose voice is still evolving. After some prompting and prodding, he reveals that he has ongoing tussles with the man who runs his detasseling crew. The man treats them all like children, insists everyone speak English, even to their friends during breaks.

"I know hardly any Spanish, and it still pisses me off," the boy complains.

"Mateo—" Connie warns, head cocked.

"Sorry."

I learn he is an excellent soccer goalie, having skunked his club team's opponent the day before. Maybe now the high school coach will see he should start on the varsity squad in the fall, he remarks.

"Isn't his son the goalie?" Manny asks, giving him a warning nod.

Mateo nods back, then shakes his head, stabbing at his chicken, going quiet.

Lydia—a pretty, plumper but lighter-skinned and freckled version of the Connie I remember as a teen—shoves food around on her plate and only says, "Okay," in response to questions about her week, her volunteer work, her girlfriends. When her mother asks about Franklin, her boyfriend, the girl grumbles about him expecting her to go to his place and never wanting to come here, uncomfortable in the largely Latino neighborhood. It's a roller coaster of an argument she's reliving from her phone call moments before.

"I don't know what you see in that boy," Connie says, and I can't help wondering what a boy named Franklin looks like, what I would see, how I would feel about that.

"I can't break up with him now." Swooping the last word. "He just got his driver's license."

"You're not serious," Connie starts, leaning forward; but Manny speaks his daughter's name, shaking his head. She takes a breath and leans back. A conversation for later.

After a minute, this week's review over with, Connie comments on the editorial in the paper, saying she thought it was "very refreshing."

"Refreshing? She loved it. She read it out loud to all of us," Manny says. He seeks the kids' agreement. Both roll their eyes, nodding. *She loved it?*

"I simply liked the idea of people sharing their stories, getting the real truth out instead of some reporter's idea of it," Connie says. Can

I tell her I couldn't get her face out of my mind as I wrote that, hoping for just such a reaction?

"As long," she continues, "as that's what you meant and weren't feeding us a line to get more readers." She picks at her food a second, the gauntlet politely thrown, her distrust revealed.

"Connie—" Manny starts.

"No." I raise my hand. "You're right to be skeptical. I know they're only words, but that's all I have to work with, and to rebuild readers' trust in the paper, I have to start somewhere with my words, don't I?"

She shrugs an assent, then perks up, changing the subject. She asks where I'm living. I'm tempted to lie—to say I have a studio apartment somewhere, but I tell the truth. I'm back in my father's house. I explain about the renovations I'm doing, the new kitchen I'm putting in, the new roof. She continues to pick, nodding. I don't need to mention the woman who cleans it every week, the guy who mows my lawn, all the takeout I eat—Delgado's Taqueria, best burritos in town. She gets the picture. My story can't compare with what this family has been through, with how they live now.

Shifting back to her kids, Connie asks Mateo if he has looked at that college catalog that came in the mail.

"All my friends want to work at Chrysler," her son mumbles. "And I'll never be able to play goalie on a college squad."

"Chrysler." She wipes her mouth with her linen napkin and looks at her father. "You tell him. Tell him what it was like back when it was AMC."

Manny shrugs. "There are worse jobs."

"Did you go back to AMC?" I ask.

"After some time. Drove that forklift for twenty years. Not a bad job at all."

"Big help you are," Connie says. "You need to see the world, Mateo. Like Mr. Maguire did." Mister. Maybe she's making fun of me, mocking me for the life I've lived. "The world offers so many opportunities for boys like you. Isn't that right, Walker? So many things he could do if he has a good education."

She waits for me to answer, but I can't tell if she's serious or not. What does she want me to say? "Yes, Mateo. Leave your family. Go live your own life. You are the only person you need to worry about." Does she want to hear me say I'm still the same selfish bastard, or am

I reading way too much into this? That's what happens when you spend thirty years imagining a moment, worrying how easily you could ruin it.

"Well," I begin, "while I would definitely encourage you to go to college—" Connie gives me a thankful smile and nod, but I continue—"I have to say, one reason I came back is because I think a lot can be done here. I mean, look at your mom, working at that hospital all these years. This town needs people like her and your grandfather."

She exhales, slumping a bit. Is she disappointed because she wants her son to aspire to a better life elsewhere, or because I came back? We eat in silence, and I mull this over until, just like that, she's up, clearing the table. Mateo is still cleaning his plate, but her hand is out, fingers beckoning him to hand it over. Manny sits back, mouth open, watching his daughter hustle dishes to the sink. I'm tempted to mention the ice cream, but Manny doesn't—Connie's aversion, perhaps?—and the kids are already up and returning to their lairs, Mateo's couch and Lydia's bedroom, leaving dessert in the dust.

"It was nice to see you again, Walker," Connie says, wiping her hands, "but I've had a long day." She edges toward the door.

"Consuelo—" Manny begins, getting up, pushing his chair in. I do the same.

"I didn't mean to upset you," I say. "Either of you."

"Upset? We're not upset," Manny says.

"Can I say something before I go?" I glance between them, my gaze settling on Connie, whose twisting body language urges me out. I wait. I'm going to say this whether she likes it or not. She turns and steps toward the table, grabbing the back of her chair, conceding one last moment of her time.

"What would you like to say?"

"Before you got home, Manny and I talked about that summer. He told me how slow AMC was in helping you. You had to leave that nice house on the river. He doesn't want me to know how bad it got. I just wanted to say I feel responsible for that."

"Well, you shouldn't," he says. "You saved us."

"No, if I'd spoken up sooner, they would have given Manny his workers' comp right away. But for it to take years—" I shook my head, trying to imagine.

"It wasn't like that." Connie peers over at Manny, as if for permission. He sighs and shrugs. She turns to me. "Your father never told you I talked to him, did he?" Connie asks. "I could tell, that day at the hospital. You didn't know."

"You talked to him? When?"

She looks at me, then casts her glance across the room. She asks her son to go to his room so the adults can talk. The boy rolls his eyes, turns off the TV and disappears up the hall. She sits down again, pushing in close to the table, motioning for me to do the same. I sit. She scrapes a smidge of dried food off a placemat as she gathers her thoughts.

"That fall. We had just moved." She looks again at Manny, waiting. He heads into the kitchen, turning the water on, rolling up his sleeves.

"It had been months since he agreed to help us and, well, we *were* in bad shape," she begins. "Even though we got a cheaper place, we still couldn't make ends meet, and no one at AMC would tell us anything. It made me mad. So, one night, I came by your father's house, knocked on the side door. I needed to talk to him, face to face. I wanted to see what was in his heart, whether he really cared or not. He recognized me from the hospital, but he didn't know I was Manny's daughter until I told him. Even so, he didn't invite me in.

"So there I am, on his stoop, explaining why I was there, how difficult it was for us. He said there was nothing he could do until they finished their investigation of my father's documentation. That set me off. I exploded, saying this had been going on for months, how we were scraping by, living on handouts and food stamps, how I'd become a nurse's aide because I couldn't afford the nursing program I was supposed to be in, how little I was paid and that's all the income we had for a family of six—how none of this would have happened if it weren't for—well, I was upset. So I guess I blamed you."

"It's okay," I say.

"But you know what?" She leans over and puts her hand on my wrist. "He stopped me right there and said it wasn't your fault. It was his fault. He was to blame for you not speaking up earlier. And I said, 'Great, take the blame, but—'"

"Wait a second," I interrupt, my hand flat on the table. "He said it was his fault?"

"Yes, but—" She stopped, maybe seeing how stunned I was, sinking back into my seat. "Are you okay?"

"Yes. Sorry, please go on." *His fault, not mine?*

"Anyway, I didn't care whose fault it was. We needed help. And then he asked me a question that totally threw me."

"What was that?"

"He asked if I was involved with you."

"Involved?" *Piper!*

"That brought me up short. I hadn't expected that. I mumbled something about barely knowing you. I had to think about my family. I was confused and started blubbering. He said, 'Okay, okay. I'll fix it.' He went inside, was gone a long time, and finally, I decided he was calling the cops, *esta chica loca* having a meltdown on his porch. I was halfway down the sidewalk when he came back out and told me to stop. He was holding a checkbook."

"A checkbook. He—*cut you a check?*"

"Not at first. That made me mad. A loan, he said. I didn't want *his* money. *Papá* taught me how borrowing money can destroy you. *AMC* owed us, not him. And besides, we needed so much. We had nothing for food, next month's rent, my mother's medical bills, *Papá's*—" She waves at her father who shakes his head. "Your father asked how much, but I wouldn't tell him. I'd had enough of people treating us like we couldn't take care of ourselves." She appeals to her father, leaning toward the kitchen. "It was the last thing *Papá* wanted. After the way he lost his first wife."

Her father stares down at the floor.

"But your father started writing the check out. I tried to stop him. 'Five hundred,' he said. 'No,' I said. 'A thousand?' 'We don't want your money,' I said. He ripped it out, handed it to me. He'd doubled it. I reached to tear it up." She looks at her father. "I did! But your father, Walker, he says, 'Don't. You need that. It's only until AMC comes through; then you can pay me back.'"

"So you took it."

"Yes." She peeks at her father's back. "I didn't tell *Papá* until I'd cashed it and paid some bills. I said the check came from American Motors, that I'd signed it myself because he was sick, but he wanted to see the letter, so I had to confess. He was so mad, but I'd spent too much. We couldn't give it back."

"Your father was being kind," Manny says, turning off the water. "But it was like being stuck in the *braceros* again, only worse. There was only Connie's tiny paycheck coming in to pay off my debt, and no work I could do."

"Yes, but it was a godsend, too. We could breathe again—at least, I could. And my mother." She nods up at Manny. "You remember how it brought Mom out of her funk? She started cooking again, taking care of Julietta and the boys, joining in." Connie turned back to me. "She said prayers for your father, lit candles for him in church."

"My father lent you money," I said, as if repeating it might make it seem possible. But that was the only way he could ever express his feelings. Checks. Cars. Houses.

"He apologized for the delay, that stupid investigation, said he hadn't realized how bad off we were."

"He told me he'd cut a check," I say, "But he never said it was his own." Of *course*, Manny's personnel file would have no proof he'd been paid, no evidence my dad could give me.

"Well, that's what he did." She stands, pushes the chair back in. She runs her hands down her blue-jeaned thighs. "So now you know. That's how we got by. A loan. From your father. And that's why I came to his room at the hospital. I had to. He saved us."

But I didn't move from my chair. Something wasn't right.

"But why couldn't he tell me? Why couldn't *you*? Why did you disappear?"

I search her face, then Manny's. Both have their mouths open, looking for words.

"My dad and I, we had this huge fight. He let me leave home over that. It doesn't make sense. And you—" I find Connie's eyes again. "I looked for you, Connie. When I found your house empty, I talked to your neighbors, called AMC, St. Francis, even the INS, and I got nowhere. I was certain you had left town, that he'd done that, somehow, sent you away. But he hadn't, had he? You were still, always, in Belford."

She squeezes the back of the chair, looking at her hands. "That was Cecilia."

"What was?"

"The woman you talked to at the hospital. She answered the phones. I warned her you might call. I told her what to say."

"To say you weren't there, you mean?"

Connie nods.

"Did he *pay* you not to see me?"

"Walker, no." She shakes her head, sitting down again, grabbing my hand a second before letting go.

"Why does it sound that way?"

"Look," she begins, her body tensed, as if bracing herself. "When I tried to give the check back, he said something else. He warned me. 'Whether you take this check or not, Manny will lose this appeal if anyone finds out about you and my son.' He said it was bad enough what the company knew about your unusual interest in our case without me coming to his house, being involved with you. He said he could lose his job if they found out. He said—" She looks away now, her face flushing. "'I can tell you have feelings for my son, but if your family comes first, you risk everything by seeing him.' He said he was sorry, but that's just how it was."

I can't look at her now.

"I had to choose, Walker. And I kept thinking how you came by the Dairy Ripple every single night, how persistent you were. And then, how you were on the phone when I called you those Sunday nights at school, how you tried to persuade me everything would be all right. I worried that if I even talked to you again, to tell you we couldn't be together, you'd find me, make a scene, ruin everything for my family—and for your father, too. Even now, listening to how hard you tried to find me—I was right, wasn't I?"

Was I *that* crazy? Would I have ruined it for them?

"He was going out on such a limb for us," she adds. "It wasn't fair to him, either, if it came out he was loaning us money. It seemed safer for everyone if we simply disappeared—at least, from your life."

I lean back in my chair, taking this all in. Dad helping them, protecting them—and from me!

"So, you've been here all along. Manny at the plant. You at the hospital. You both probably even saw him around."

Manny nods.

"I did," Connie says, "And whenever he saw me, he asked me how we were doing. When I said not so good, he promised to send us some more money. And he did. He sent a check in the mail."

She was right here the whole time. The words I'd whispered to my comatose father after I first saw Connie Wheeler in the maternity ward—I hope he smiled inside to hear that.

"And all the while," she continues, "you were off in school, then later, becoming the world traveler—" She flips her hand. "New York, the Middle East, DC. Every time I saw your byline in the Belford paper, I felt this little pain right here—" she taps her chest "—for what I'd done to you. I'm sorry if I hurt you."

My byline. All those clippings Dad had saved. 'Not because of *what* you wrote,' Piper had said. 'But because *you* wrote them.'

She gets up again, finally ready for me to go.

"But I'm back now," I say, standing. "For good."

"I know. Editor at the paper. I'm very happy for you. And for Belford, to have your generous view of things."

"What I'm saying is, I want another chance." I take a step around the table. She doesn't back away. I'm next to her now, but I speak up, no longer whispering. "Maybe you deserve one, too."

"I don't know, Walker." She takes a step back, distancing herself. "It's been so long."

"At least, let me return this favor, have you and Manny and the kids over for dinner at my house sometime." I look over her shoulder at Manny. "Next Sunday, maybe?"

Connie shakes her head. "Sundays are for—" Catching my eye, she stops.

"Family?" Manny says. "Sunday's fine for us."

She turns to him, and they glare at each other.

"He only wants a chance," Manny adds.

I'm forcing her again, like I did when I invited myself here. Like I would have if I'd known where they were in Belford all those years ago, risking and possibly ruining everything.

"No, Manny. She's right. It's her decision." I take a step towards her. I want to put my hands on her shoulders. "Connie—" I lean, whispering. "When you showed up in my dad's hospital room with that little plant in your hand, I couldn't believe you were there to see him. After what he did—what I *thought* he did—it didn't make sense." I straighten, hands out, a surrender. "Now it does. He helped you. Took a huge risk doing it, too. And, to tell the truth, hearing that means more than you could possibly imagine. But—" And now I do touch her arm, an elbow, making her look up. "I guess I don't want to believe he was the only person you came to see."

She blinks a couple times, but her expression doesn't budge, so I back off a step, bumping into a chair. I shove it under the table where it belongs.

"But that seems to be the truth. And speaking of truth, I'm a terrible cook. So, if you want to forget dinner, I understand. I'll just say good night, and thank you for the lovely dinner."

She looks up at me, considering for a long second, her lips pursed, brows tensed, that mole flexing. I turn to leave, but she grabs my elbow, stopping me. She holds up that hand, telling me to wait. She steps past me, around the table and into the kitchen, reaching into a cabinet above the stove as Manny watches, perplexed. She pulls out a small plastic box with a hinged lid, opens it and ruffles through some index cards, pulling one out. It's dog-eared, stained and covered in handwriting. A recipe? She returns to me and, with her palm, she presses the card to my chest, backing me up a step. The warmth of her hand spreads deliciously.

"You run a newspaper. You can read, can't you?"

It's hard to make out the words, but I don't say anything. It could be in some lost, prehistoric language, and I'd find a way to decipher it.

Sixty-Nine

Manny and Connie have taken over my new kitchen. Plantains simmer on the stove, and the counter is littered with tomatoes, limes, onion, cilantro, garlic, scallions and peppers—red, green, big and small, hot and sweet—ingredients for a salsa and a marinade for something special Manny will grill for us on this Fourth of July.

When Piper arrives carrying a big salad, she is cordial enough, though somewhat disconcerted to find the Camarasas commanding every square inch of available counter space. Or maybe it's Connie wearing Mom's old apron. I can't tell. It's the first time I've seen my sister since my initial dinner with Connie's family last month. After waved greetings—the Camarasa hands are too busy cutting and peeling for handshakes—I tell Piper I could use her help setting the picnic table. She puts the salad in the fridge, and we go down the back steps into the bright afternoon. I bring a stack of plates topped by a pile of napkins. She carries plastic cups, a store-bought paper tablecloth and Scotch tape.

"When you said they were cooking, I had no idea," she says, freeing the tablecloth from its packaging as I set my load on the bench. "I feel kind of useless." She unfolds the tablecloth, positions it over the table, and presents me with a corner to hold so she can tape it in place. A hot wind is whipping up the slope today, and she doesn't want anything to blow away.

After the Foundry went out of business, a developer purchased the property, as well as the Riverside Cabins campground next door. He razed the buildings, all those clapboard cabins, and replaced them with high-priced, five-story condos, a whole fleet of which now hug the river's edge like misplaced Carnival-line cruise ships placed in dry dock. They're at full occupancy, housing that new wave of migrants, the young tech workers who commute into the Chicago suburbs. Not that I have to see much of them, fortunately. In the thirty-five years since my dad planted the willows along the river's edge, they've grown so high, they hide everything. I prefer it this way, the curtain of trees. Sure, they block the view, but it's a green screen against which it's easy to imagine the little fishing cabins, the tiny boats coming and going from their docks, the Foundry's massive smokestacks, its clunk and hiss, comforting in its regularity, its mystery.

Kurt is watching the ballgame in Dad's Barcalounger. My nephews, home to work summer jobs at the Swanson car lots they will inherit one day, are motoring the runabout up the Piscasaw to our old swimming hole, and I can't blame them. It's a gorgeous day to be on the water, hot and bright.

I had asked the Wheeler teens to join us, but Manny whispered that they were spending a rare weekend with their father. Connie never mentions the man.

The occasion for all these visitors? An inaugural drive in the rebuilt Cadillac and an opportunity for the Swansons to get to know the Camarasas. For months now, I have refrained from mentioning them to my sister. It didn't feel right, bringing them up while we were still in mourning, and without finding out what had happened to them. Now that I know, and Piper knows that Connie is back in my life, the time is right for this chat, especially with Connie's revelations raising new questions which only Piper can answer.

"Connie told me something interesting," I begin. Watching Piper fuss with the Scotch tape, I explain about Dad giving the Camarasas the loan. She seems baffled, even after I remind her of the circumstances—the fight, Manny trying to get workers' comp, AMC dragging its feet, Connie coming to the house and arguing with Dad. After Piper applies a piece of tape, she pauses, thinking through what I've just said.

"I do remember that night." She rests both hands on the table, learning in. "What a blowup it was. Dad talked to her outside so Mom and I couldn't hear, but they were loud enough that we caught a few words here and there."

"He asked Connie if she and I were romantically involved."

"Really?" Piper straightens, gawking at me. She seems to consider this, inhaling, something coming to her that makes her turn away, unwilling to look at me.

"You were the only one who knew, Piper."

She bends and slides onto the fixed bench, sitting, wiping wrinkles out of the table cloth as she thinks.

"After you went back to school," she begins, "you called every single week, just to find out about the Camarasa's appeal. You never called like that your first year of college, and he remarked on it at the dinner table, how you were driving him nuts." She looks up at me. "He couldn't understand why this man and his family were so important to you."

"So, you told him."

"No." She shakes her head, but her vehemence flags, her eyes leaving mine, fixing on something. "Not exactly."

"What did you say, Piper?"

"Nothing he didn't already know—"

"What?"

Her shoulders lift, then stop, mid-shrug. "All I did was remind him that Manny had a daughter."

"For God's sake, Piper."

"It was dumb." She reaches across and grabs my arm, words tumbling out. "I knew it as soon as I said it, but he didn't say anything, so I figured it wasn't a big deal."

"We had a pact, Piper. I'd say nothing about you and Kurt if you said nothing about Connie."

"I know." I try to pull away, but she keeps hold of my arm, squeezing it. "That's not me anymore, Walker. You know that, don't you?"

I do know that. Not just in how she cared for Dad all these years or how she produced two wonderful boys, both of whom grew up happy and well-liked, but in how she loves Kurt and helps him grow his business. They've sponsored charitable and fund-raising programs around town that produced a lot more goodwill and customers than Pops' cheesy late night car-lot commercials ever did. The years and this marriage have knocked that nasty chip off her shoulder, and nudged her heart into a good, giving place. I nod, conceding her point. She lets go.

"After she left that night," Piper continues, "he looked relieved." She looks up at me, as if it's all coming back. "I remember now. He explained what she was worried about and said that he'd talk to the company and fix it. But he didn't say anything about a loan. He just said—" She hesitates.

"What?"

"He said, for their sake, Mom and I should never mention to anyone that she came to the house—especially to you."

"Me? Why me?"

"He said you might make a fuss and ruin it for her family—and for him, too, like he could lose his job. And then, when you came home that Thanksgiving and ran off after you learned they'd disappeared, Dad said it just proved how consumed you were by them, how it was just as well you were not around to cause trouble for everyone." Distractedly, she smooths down more tape, another corner affixed. She peers up at me. "I don't think he imagined you wouldn't come back."

Rather than respond to this, I fold the tablecloth around the last corner. As she fixes it in place, she tentatively asks. "You don't think I was the reason you and Connie never got together, do you?"

I consider this, briefly, so tempted to lash out, lay the blame anywhere but where it belonged. But I can't.

"I don't know. Maybe he was right. The way I felt about her. Some of the stupid things I did that summer. I might have ruined everything."

"I'm sorry if I did anything to screw things up for you." She pats my hand. "And I'm glad things may be working out for you this time."

We finish with the tablecloth; Piper deals out the plates, arranges the napkins. As I watch her, I can't help mulling it over. I haven't said all I need to say, not after how I misjudged him all these years.

"I thought he got them sent away," I say, barely audible.

She straightens, blinking at me.

"All those years ago. I thought he did something truly awful."

She rounds the table and places her hand on my back, hugging me from the side as I continue.

"I thought that justified all my anger at him, for everything he did to me. It just proved he was the bad guy I always thought he was, and I was right to hate him." I glance at her, gauging.

"And now you know—"

"I know he helped them, yes. He did, while I did everything in my power to fuck it up. But he didn't want me with her. I know that, too."

"He was protecting them—"

"Maybe, but he could have told me. After they got their money, when it didn't matter anymore. He could have explained what he'd done and why."

"Did you ever discuss it?"

"No. I mean, I meant to. I tried the last time I was here. But I could have done more, come home more." The words come out weakly—like the attempts. "It was too hard." I look up at her. "He helped them, yes, but the secrecy—it wasn't *all* about protecting *them*."

"Maybe he thought he was protecting you, too."

"From what?"

I look up the stairs towards the kitchen. Connie is standing in the doorway, watching us. Having removed Mom's apron, she's lovely in her sleeveless summer dress, a white knee-length thing with blue flowers, her dark arms and hair, her bare shoulders shining in the sunlight.

"My father's ready to start grilling," she says, tentative. Maybe she heard us.

"It's fine," I say, waving her to come.

She disappears and reappears, carrying a large pan full of meats and vegetables. She starts down, and Manny follows her, one step at a time, holding Piper's salad to his chest with one hand and the rail with the other. Both of them eye me and my sister.

"Have I got a treat for you!" Manny says, pride rippling across his well-lined face. Beaming, he puts the wooden bowl on the table, takes the pan from Connie and heads towards the grill.

Connie remarks on the beautiful salad Piper created. Piper thanks her and goes back to arranging things on the table, our conversation ended. Connie helps Piper finish, the two of them glancing over at me occasionally as they work and chat, checking in.

With each of our encounters, Connie and I are more in tune. The first Sunday I had her over, I conquered her mother's chicken *tostadas*—yes, I deciphered her recipe—and slapped her with my mother's chicken and dumplings, which the following Sunday she cooked to perfection.

Manny and her kids are always nearby, buffering. That's all right, for now. Family gives her something to focus on besides her own feelings, her ambivalence about me for so many reasons, her caution about men, in general. Who can blame her, having married an unreliable line-worker who left her while she was still pregnant with her second child? I'd like to think I'd have done better, but then, I'm hobbled by my own issues.

One time, when I had her alone in the kitchen, I tried to tell her again how hard I'd searched for her back then, worried she might have wondered why, if I really loved her, I couldn't find her here in Belford.

"You know it's better you didn't find me, don't you? The problems you might have caused?"

"I know, but I just want you to know, even while I was off, around the world, I never forgot about you."

"It's okay, Walker," she told me, patting my chest. I realized then that, over the years, she hadn't thought about me nearly as much as I had her—that, in fact, she might well have forgotten me.

Maybe it's human nature to dwell on the bad and forget the good, to brood on the past rather than to celebrate it. The bad stuff's why I never forgot. I just hope the good is why she did.

The next time she looks over, I smile. She smiles back, melting the grip those depressing thoughts have on me. My regrets ebb as I listen to the two women, a promising warmth to their pleasantries, a sweet willingness to connect, which heartens me.

I join Manny at the grill.

Seventy

Connie's riding shotgun, as Frazier and I used to say. Piper and Kurt sit in the back. Kurt can't stop jabbering about his restorations, all the internet sleuthing he did to dig up the old Caddy parts, as if he personally had stalked those websites and worked under the hood, and not his secretary and Pablo. He says Pops would have loved this car, would have given it the place of honor on the showroom's turnstile, spinning for everyone to see.

The windy ride makes it too hard to talk, which is fine with me. For Piper and me, at least, this is more than a ride in the country. Connie senses something, too. I'm connected to my father through her family now, even if he was never straight with me about a lot of things. Maybe, that's why he gave me this Caddy. An apology, of sorts.

We head down Jackson Street toward the edge of town. Kurt finally quiets down, and all of us take in the smooth ride, the cloud-layered midwestern sky opening up over the approaching cornfields, blue above with white wisps and billows, green rows below flipping by like book pages.

I'm reminded of the day my dad came home from Grampa Caspar's farm with this magnificent, plum-colored boat of a car. How my mom and we kids fawned over it, running our fingers over its fins and big chrome bumpers as my father stood next to it, rubbing his chin, not sure what to make of the giant, outlandish gift. Our first excursion came on a Sunday, still in our church clothes, Dad and Mom up front, Frazier, Piper and me in back.

The silence in the car now attests to how bittersweet this journey is, full of memories of long ago. And yet, I'm breathless, too, bright-eyed and grinning, like the day of my first ride. The existence of such a car is ridiculous. King of the Road, or perhaps the king's jester, majestic and loud, commanding, a joke, obsolete, useless, magnificent. An incredible, indecent waste of money. An embarrassment you can't help showing off. My hands grip and re-grip the wheel, that thing I do, holding me in check so I don't burst.

After a few miles of this, I flash on something Dad did during that first ride, and, on impulse, I pull off the blacktop onto a narrow dirt road amidst the corn rows. My passengers gasp at the shock as we drop off the pavement. Connie grabs at the armrest, at my elbow, the dust rising. I fight the wheel, fishtailing through ruts, until it steadies. The floppy dog-ears of corn leaves slap the sides of the car. Connie's hand holds on, clutching tight. My mom's hand on my dad's arm, shocked. So unlike him to let loose. We hit washboard, stuttering along, then dip into a huge mud puddle. Water splashes outward, slowing us to a near stop, before I gun the Caddy up the other side. Everyone laughs.

It's a miracle, the flowing ride of the rebuilt car, our smiles after months of grieving, the feeling I have, giddy and possessed, that we are being chased, a siren wailing in the distance.

Author's Note and Acknowledgements

Like my main character, Walker, I wrote this story in an attempt to better understand my father who was mustered out of the military early and unexpectedly ended up in a town and a job both of which disappointed him. I did work for two summers at the Chrysler Assembly plant in Belvidere, Illinois, where my father worked; but none of the events in my novel's assembly plant happened, and all of those characters are fictional, as are Walker's friends. My depiction of the Maguire parents is loosely based on memories of my parents, though I've distorted some of the stories for dramatic effect. Otherwise, except for an occasional anecdotal similarity between my real siblings and the Maguire children, any resemblance between my characters and actual persons is purely coincidental. I wrote this book not to depict the truth about my father and my childhood, but to portray how I experienced them. That's the only truth I know.

While a Latino community has been growing in my hometown for many years, I only remember the Foundry and a baseball field across the river from my house—all of which my father successfully hid from view with his willow trees.

This book started with a certain 'kazoo' scene, a true story which I wrote for a Grub Street class in Boston taught by Becky Tuch some seven years ago. Early drafts evolved through a number of classes I took at Grub, and for everyone who taught those classes and provided feedback, I am grateful. I received invaluable help on my early drafts from a group of readers from all over the world — in Singapore,

New York, Texas, the U.K. — whom I met on the writer's website, Scribophile in the Uber Group. Subsequent drafts were aided substantially by developmental editor, Stephen Beeber and by my writers' group, which I joined some five years ago. This extraordinarily bright, talented and generous monthly gathering includes Deborah Good, Rich Marcello, Christine Giraud, Marc Foster, Rebecca Givens Rolland and Rob Wilstein. Special thanks, also, to group member Jerry Whalen for help with my Spanish. Thanks to all of you!

I would never have developed the skills or discipline needed to complete this novel without the year I spent in Michelle Hoover's Novel Incubator program at Grub Street, learning so much from her as well as from classmates Louise Miller, Susan Bernard, Lissa Franz, Michele Ferrari, Kelly Robertson, Cynthia Johnson, Anjali Mathur, Margaret Zamos-Monteith and Patricia Sollner. Thanks also to fellow Incubees Belle Brett, Emily Ross, Kelly Ford, E.B. Moore, Stephanie Gayle, Pam Loring, Sharissa Jones, Leslie Teel, Cara Wood, Milo Todd, Lisa Birk, Carol Gray, Bob Fernandes, Jen Johnson, Mandy Syers, Michael Nolan, Rachel Barenbaum, Bonnie Waltch and all the rest of you for your ongoing support of our writing and publishing efforts.

I'd also like to acknowledge my long-time friend and fellow novelist, Michael Antman, without whose feedback and advice I probably never would have found my publisher and editor, Betsy Delmonico, who has supported and encouraged me beyond all expectation, as has her husband, Neal Delmonico, and their intern, Lexie Biggs. Thanks also to Jason Anscomb, who designed my beautiful book cover, to Jason Shaw whose lovely guitar music I used in my audiobook, and to Sarah Miniaci, Emma Boyer, and Smith Publicity for helping me promote my book.

I also want to acknowledge my patient and ever-encouraging wife, Carol Israel, my son, Jonah, and daughter, Emily. A psychologist, Carol helps me keep my characters real and believable, and the three of them—good writers, all—have nurtured my desire to make up stories and write them down, even while suffering through rambling bedtime/car-ride stories and readings, and various drafts of my work, bad and good. (Listen for Emily's stories on KPCC public radio in Los Angeles.) I love you all!

Finally, I want to acknowledge my sister D'Arcy who provided feedback and family history for my book; my brother, poet Christopher Guerin, who has encouraged my writing ever since our college days together; and my younger sister, Laura, who for years looked after my dad after the rest of us moved away. Laura *was* my father's favorite, but she was always my buddy and ally growing up in our father's house—where she now lives. I'd also like to thank them, as well as brothers Jay, Michael and Charlie, for encouraging me to finish when I told them I was writing a book based on our father. We all have our own stories about our father. Thank you for letting me tell mine.